ADEPTUS ASTARTES

'They shall be my finest warriors, these men who give themselves to me. Like clay I shall mould them and in the furnace of war I shall forge them. They will be of iron will and steely muscle. In great armour shall I clad them and with the mightiest guns shall they be armed. They will be untouched by plague or disease, no sickness will blight them. They will have tactics, strategies and machines such that no foe can best them in battle. They are my bulwark against the Terror. They are the Defenders of Humanity. They are my Space Marines… and they shall know no fear.'

- The Emperor of Mankind

CONTENTS

PRODUCED BY THE WARHAMMER STUDIO

With thanks to the Mournival and the Infinity Circuit for their additional playtesting services

Codex: Space Marines © Copyright Games Workshop Limited 2020. Codex: Space Marines, GW, Games Workshop, Space Marine, 40K, Warhammer, Warhammer 40,000, the 'Aquila' Double-headed Eagle logo, and all associated logos, illustrations, images, names, creatures, races, vehicles, locations, weapons, characters, and the distinctive likenesses thereof, are either ® or TM, and/or © Games Workshop Limited, variably registered around the world. All Rights Reserved.

No part of this publication may be reproduced, stored in a retrieval system, or transmitted in any form or by any means, electronic, mechanical, photocopying, recording or otherwise, without the prior permission of the publishers.

This is a work of fiction. All the characters and events portrayed in this book are fictional, and any resemblance to real people or incidents is purely coincidental. British Cataloguing-in-Publication Data. A catalogue record for this book is available from the British Library. Pictures used for illustrative purposes only.

Certain Citadel products may be dangerous if used incorrectly and Games Workshop does not recommend them for use by children under the age of 16 without adult supervision. Whatever your age, be careful when using glues, bladed equipment and sprays and make sure that you read and follow the instructions on the packaging.

Games Workshop Ltd, Willow Rd, Lenton, Nottingham, NG7 2WS
games-workshop.com

INTRODUCTION

Welcome, brother, to *Codex: Space Marines*, a tome dedicated to collecting, painting and gaming with Space Marines Citadel miniatures. Packed full of information regarding the warriors, vehicles and leaders of the Adeptus Astartes, as well detailing their organisation, heraldry and peerless skill at arms, it contains vital lore for Space Marines collectors.

Few factions in Warhammer 40,000 have such an extensive range of Citadel miniatures as the Space Marines. Whether you are a hobby veteran with numerous service studs to your name, or a neophyte brand new to the Warhammer hobby, you will find something in the Space Marines range that fires your imagination and fills you with inspiration.

The Space Marines are a highly flexible fighting force, with tough, reliable infantry, a plethora of powerful battle tanks and combat walkers, and a whole host of light, fast-moving vehicles and bikes. You can field an entire army mounted in rugged armoured transports, or a strike force purely made up of rapid reconnaissance experts and assassins. Dominate the skies with a range of aircraft armed with a vast suite of devastating weapons, or deploy your strike force from orbit using Drop Pods and hard-hitting jump pack-equipped warriors.

Each Space Marine belongs to a Chapter, an independent fighting force. Over a thousand Chapters exist, all with unique heraldry and visually strong colour schemes. There are few more impressive sights on the tabletop than a fully painted Space Marine army arrayed for war. For any hobbyist, this is an incredible opportunity to make their army their own, experimenting with their favourite colours and delving into their imagination to invent epic origin stories and tales of victories for their warriors. For those who find the pull of narrative play impossible to resist, this Codex includes bespoke additions to the Crusade Forces rules found in the Warhammer 40,000 Core Book, tailored to the Space Marines.

This book is replete with stunning artwork and glorious photography, showcasing the Space Marines in all their grim might and terrifying splendour. Each has a story to tell about the Adeptus Astartes, whether it be of their bravery, sacrifice, traditions, organisation or how they wage war. Each is but a glimpse into the lives and ways of the defenders of Humanity, and a source of inspiration.

In this book you'll find all the rules you need to field a mighty army of Space Marines, including datasheets for every model in the range, and a collection of Warlord Traits, Psychic disciplines, Stratagems and Relics. With such invaluable intelligence, you'll soon be able to transform your collection of Space Marines Citadel miniatures into a truly formidable fighting force, one both worthy of the title Adeptus Astartes and able to strike terror into the hearts of your foes.

The Space Marines are the Emperor's will made manifest. They are his Angels of Death, descending to the battlefield from mighty warships to cleanse the foes of Mankind from the face of the galaxy. For ten thousand years the Space Marine Chapters have been Humanity's shield and sword in the face of the horrors that beset it.

Genetically enhanced super-soldiers, they are among the greatest warriors to have ever existed. They are stronger, faster and more resilient than the Humans they are sworn to protect. They are psycho-indoctrinated from youth, rendering them immune to fear and staunchly loyal. On the battlefield they are relentless, determined warriors who will stop at nothing to achieve victories nigh on impossible for unaugmented soldiery to achieve.

In the Era Indomitus, the Imperium is assailed as never before from both within and without. The Space Marines hold firm, meeting the onslaught head-on with unbreakable faith in their hearts and oaths on their lips. They are the champions of Humanity, and they know no fear. Defeat is only for the enemy, and while one Space Marine stands, hope remains for the Imperium.

CREATION OF A SPACE MARINE

Every Space Marine is a mighty warrior, a champion almost beyond compare. These post-humans are heavily augmented, the products of years of arduous training, agonising surgery and psycho-indoctrination. It is a process of arcane and horrific science, one which not all inductees will survive. Such are the sacrifices Mankind must make to weather the storms that batter it so ceaselessly.

It is only thanks to the Emperor's skills and knowledge that the Space Marines exist. Only he knew the subtle arts and infinitely complex nuances of gene-craft. It was his vision that led to the creation of the Primarchs and the gene-sons that followed from them, and the arcane alchemies he developed have since allowed generation after generation of Space Marines to serve the Imperium.

For all their phenomenal physical prowess, the incessant and intense warfare that Space Marines fearlessly endure sees even these mighty warriors suffer casualties. To avoid extinction, every Chapter must constantly recruit fresh warriors. How these individuals are selected varies enormously, each Chapter having unique and sometimes clandestine methods by which it conducts its recruitment. All aspirants are youths, for if selected at too mature an age their bodies will reject the implants, derived from a material called gene-seed, they need to become Space Marines. All have to pass immensely tough trials, whether it be crossing vast distances of extremely inhospitable country with few supplies, hunting local megafauna with naught but a sharpened stick or any of a hundred other tests of physical or mental fortitude. Many fail, the lucky killed in their efforts and those less fortunate lobotomised and turned to mindless servitors.

For those who have been accepted to commence training, their journey to becoming Space Marines has only just begun. To be a Space Marine is to be subject to hardships and horror that ordinary Humans cannot begin to comprehend, and the chosen must be prepared physically, mentally and spiritually. Over a period of years, aspirants are put through an extremely harsh process. They are trained rigorously in diverse styles of combat, how to wield the Space Marines' weapons and operate a number of their vehicles. Relentless martial training is interspersed with periods of hypnotic suggestion, prolonged meditation, psychological and spiritual testing and gradual initiations into the Chapter's rites, history and traditions. In addition to this, they receive their implants.

The gene-seed implants are specially grown organ grafts. Some serve to give the Space Marine unique abilities, such as the Betcher's Gland, which allows them to spit poison. Others enhance existing abilities, such as the Sinew Coils, which dramatically increase strength and durability. Implantation of these organs must occur in a precise order. Why, exactly, is unknown to even the most adept Apothecaries. Gene-seed is a finite resource, impossible to manufacture without the implants known as progenoid glands that have matured within the body of another Space Marine, and the recovery of these should a battle-brother be slain is of the utmost importance.

Despite every effort to maintain the purity of gene-seed, quality levels vary between the Space Marine Chapters. The Ultramarines' is highly regarded, a source of pride to the great number of Adeptus Astartes Chapters that can trace their lineage to Roboute Guilliman. In contrast, the Imperial Fists' gene-seed is missing the genetic information to create certain specialised organs.

PRIMARIS SPACE MARINES

In addition to the nineteen specialised organs that almost all Space Marines have been implanted with since the First Founding, the Primaris Space Marines possess a further three. These organs enhance their physiology to an even greater degree, making them yet stronger and tougher. It was only thanks to the Sangprimus Portum – a device that held potent genetic material harvested from the Primarchs themselves – that Archmagos Belisarius Cawl was able to create these biotechnical miracles. In the Ultima Founding, many tens of thousands of Primaris Space Marines reinforced depleted Chapters or formed new ones. Since then, many Chapters have used these technologies to develop their recruits into Primaris Space Marines.

The biggest breakthroughs of all, however, were the surgeries that allowed Space Marines not matured with the three Primaris organs to be implanted with them. Arguably first braved by Marneus Calgar, Chapter Master of the Ultramarines, this extremely dangerous set of procedures lasts for days. Many others have since risked their lives in such a way after witnessing the undeniable battlefield capabilities of the Primaris Space Marines in action.

We make day into night and light into dark, for we are the bringers of doom! We are the Space Marines!

A THOUSAND CHAPTERS

It is believed that over a thousand Space Marine Chapters – independent, autonomous armies – fight the Emperor's wars. Nine are named for the Legions that remained loyal to the Emperor during the Horus Heresy, others are Successor Chapters, brotherhoods who can claim genetic descent from the nine loyal Primarchs.

Over the millennia, the number of Space Marine Chapters has waxed and waned. Some have been destroyed, wiped out in cataclysmic battles with the fiercest of enemies, but their existence has been deemed so vital to Humanity's defences that there have been a number of Foundings throughout the millennia. The decision to initiate a Founding is one of such magnitude that only the High Lords can authorise it, and only twenty seven such events are believed to have occurred.

The very first Founding was the creation of the original twenty Space Marine Legions by the Emperor himself. In the aftermath of the Horus Heresy, Roboute Guilliman's Codex Astartes decreed that the Legions be broken down into smaller brotherhoods called Chapters, with one keeping the name of the Legion from which it came. These flexible fighting forces were to number little more than a thousand warriors across ten companies, and many dozens were formed. This was known as the Second Founding.

There are no defined intervals between Foundings; they are launched as and when the High Lords – and thus, the Emperor – decree, and there are no rules in place limiting how many Chapters can be created. There may be no Foundings for a millennia, and three Foundings in the space of a decade. One Founding may be of but a handful of Chapters, while another might be made up of dozens.

Records of the Foundings are frustratingly incomplete. Some lie buried in massive archives beneath stacks of documents miles high. Some have rotted to nothing, their vellum and parchment pages falling to entropy long before scripto-savants can copy them. Others have been destroyed deliberately, most notably in the Reign of Blood, when ream after ream was burned. Prying Inquisitors scouring Adeptus Mechanicus records in secret have discovered ominous gaps in the data trail that reek of tampering and falsification.

Some Foundings are particularly noteworthy or notorious, and demonstrate the fragmentary nature of Imperial records. The Thirteenth Founding came to be known as the 'Dark' Founding; the Adeptus Terra has no knowledge of many of the Chapters created as part of it, nor which gene-seed was used to create those it knows of. Some believe that the Exorcists were founded at this time, though a minor Inquisitorial war failed to settle the issue. The Twenty-first Founding – later known as the 'Cursed' Founding – was intended to perfect gene-seed and resolve deficiencies, but instead had the opposite effect for many of the Chapters created for it, such as the Black Dragons.

Those not affected by serious mutations have instead been beset by misfortune after misfortune, as the Lamenters can attest. The Twenty-third – or 'Sentinel' Founding – was initiated to ensure vulnerable areas of the galaxy were secured. The Iron Lords, Star Phantoms and Marines Errant are among those that can trace their origins to this event. The Ultima Founding was the most recent. Consisting entirely of Primaris Space Marines, it was created at Roboute Guilliman's direct order shortly after his resurrection. It is arguably the largest and most significant Founding to date. Chapters known to have come into existence with this Founding include the Void Tridents, Rift Stalkers, Rift Cobras, Knights of the Chalice and Umbral Knights.

Even if every Space Marine Chapter operated at full strength – nigh on impossible due to battle attrition – the number of Space Marines in total would likely not exceed one per Imperial world. Thus the Space Marines have to decide where they will fight and where they will not. Some fight for personal honour or to uphold ancient vows, whilst others make war only where the Emperor's Tarot dictates or according to strict pragmatism. Regardless, wherever they fight, the Space Marines butcher their foes and crush them beneath their ceramite boots.

THE PRIMARCHS

The Primarchs' origins lie in the Imperial Palace's deepest vaults, utterly secret places where the Emperor embarked upon his great work of gene-craft. Using his own genetic material, unfathomable technologies and his awe-inspiring intellect, the Emperor crafted twenty beings, known later as the Primarchs. They were to be his generals and paragons of his ideals for Humanity's future. At the time of their creation, Terra was cut off from the galaxy by ferocious warp storms, and Mankind was scattered across the galaxy. The Primarchs were intended to unite the Human race under the Emperor's banner, but this great endeavour was stalled. By means utterly unknown, the Primarchs were scattered across the galaxy in the early stages of their development. Yet the Emperor still held their genetic records, and from these he created the Space Marine Legions. Bereft of their gene-sires they were launched into the stars to bring Humanity together. During this Great Crusade, the Primarchs were recovered and took command of their Legions. The Great Crusade ultimately failed, however. All records of two Legions have been expunged and none truly know what happened to them. Nine more turned against the Emperor, though this too is a secret kept from the Imperium at large.

The Space Marine Chapters fighting for the Emperor today are all descended from the nine Primarchs who remained loyal, the gene-seed of the others sealed away, lost or destroyed. Some Chapters no longer know their genetic ancestry, whilst others revere their believed heritage. Many echo the unique genetic traits of their forebears or zealously duplicate the ways of their parent Legion. Others exhibit few signs of their descent, with their own culture and traditions dominant instead.

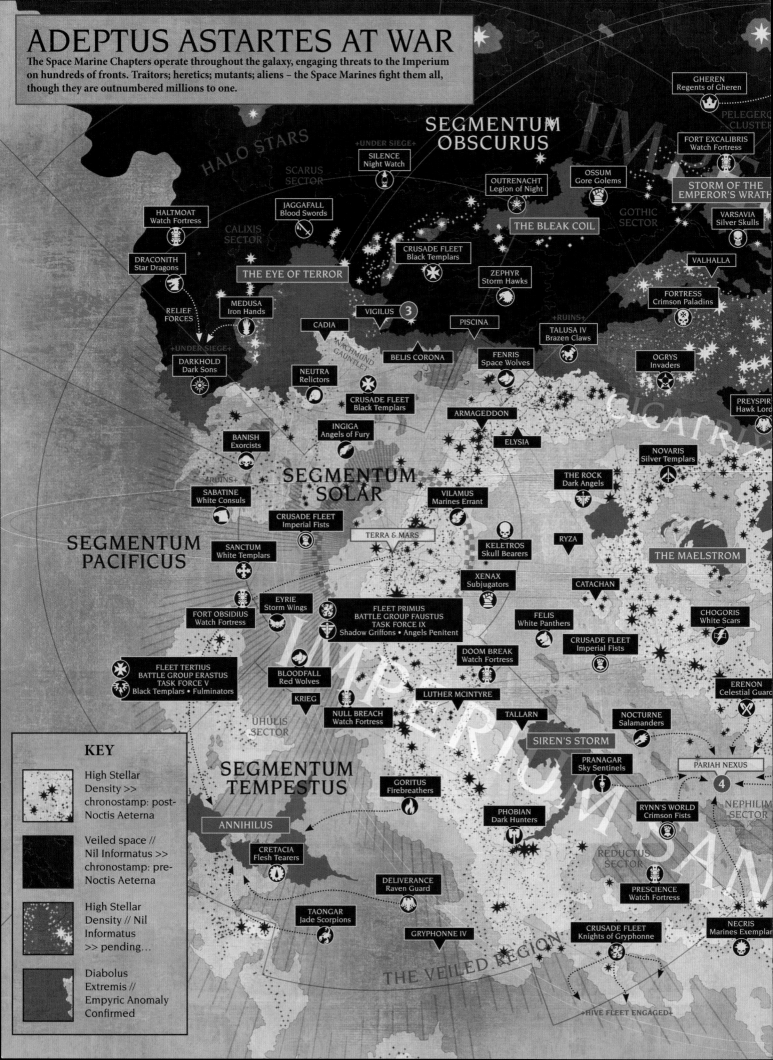

ADEPTUS ASTARTES AT WAR

The Space Marine Chapters operate throughout the galaxy, engaging threats to the Imperium on hundreds of fronts. Traitors; heretics; mutants; aliens – the Space Marines fight them all, though they are outnumbered millions to one.

HALO STARS

SEGMENTUM OBSCURUS

SCARUS SECTOR

+UNDER SIEGE+
SILENCE
Night Watch

GHEREN
Regents of Gheren

FORT EXCALIBRIS
Watch Fortress

OUTRENACHT
Legion of Night

OSSUM
Gore Golems

STORM OF THE EMPEROR'S WRATH

GOTHIC SECTOR

PELEGERO CLUSTER

HALTMOAT
Watch Fortress

JAGGAFALL
Blood Swords

THE BLEAK COIL

VARSAVIA
Silver Skulls

CALIXIS SECTOR

DRACONITH
Star Dragons

CRUSADE FLEET
Black Templars

VALHALLA

THE EYE OF TERROR

ZEPHYR
Storm Hawks

FORTRESS
Crimson Paladins

RELIEF FORCES

MEDUSA
Iron Hands

VIGILIS 3

PISCINA

TALUSA IV
Brazen Claws

OGRYS
Invaders

+UNDER SIEGE+

CADIA

WACHMUND GAUNTLET

FENRIS
Space Wolves

+RUINS+

DARKHOLD
Dark Sons

NEUTRA
Relictors

BELIS CORONA

PREYSPIR
Hawk Lord

CRUSADE FLEET
Black Templars

ARMAGEDDON

NOVARIS
Silver Templars

BANISH
Exorcists

INGIGA
Angels of Fury

ELYSIA

SEGMENTUM SOLAR

THE ROCK
Dark Angels

+RUINS+

SABATINE
White Consuls

VILAMUS
Marines Errant

RYZA

THE MAELSTROM

SEGMENTUM PACIFICUS

CRUSADE FLEET
Imperial Fists

TERRA & MARS

KELETROS
Skull Bearers

SANCTUM
White Templars

XENAX
Subjugators

CATACHAN

CHOGORIS
White Scars

EYRIE
Storm Wings

FELIS
White Panthers

FORT OBSIDIUS
Watch Fortress

FLEET PRIMUS
BATTLE GROUP FAUSTUS
TASK FORCE IX
Shadow Griffons • Angels Penitent

CRUSADE FLEET
Imperial Fists

DOOM BREAK
Watch Fortress

ERENON
Celestial Guard

FLEET TERTIUS
BATTLE GROUP ERASTUS
TASK FORCE V
Black Templars • Fulminators

BLOODFALL
Red Wolves

LUTHER MCINTYRE

KRIEG

TALLARN

NOCTURNE
Salamanders

UHULIS SECTOR

NULL BREACH
Watch Fortress

SIREN'S STORM

PRANAGAR
Sky Sentinels

PARIAH NEXUS

4

NEPHILIM SECTOR

KEY

High Stellar Density >> chronostamp: post-Noctis Aeterna

Veiled space // Nil Informatus >> chronostamp: pre-Noctis Aeterna

High Stellar Density // Nil Informatus >> pending…

Diabolus Extremis // Empyric Anomaly Confirmed

SEGMENTUM TEMPESTUS

GORITUS
Firebreathers

RYNN'S WORLD
Crimson Fists

ANNIHILUS

PHOBIAN
Dark Hunters

REDUCTUS SECTOR

CRETACIA
Flesh Tearers

DELIVERANCE
Raven Guard

PRESCIENCE
Watch Fortress

TAONGAR
Jade Scorpions

GRYPHONNE IV

CRUSADE FLEET
Knights of Gryphonne

NECRIS
Marines Exemplar

THE VEILED REGION

+HIVE FLEET ENGAGED+

① WAR ZONE BAAL

In the aftermath of Baal's salvation from the ravages of Tyranid Hive Fleet Leviathan, and the naming of Commander Dante of the Blood Angels as regent of the Imperium Nihilus by Roboute Guilliman himself, war still rages in the Red Scar region. Many worlds are infested with Tyranid bioforms, and the Blood Angels and their successors work to cleanse them all of the foul xenos. Particular effort has been made to secure planets of strategic importance, such as bastion worlds, forge worlds, industrial worlds and supply worlds – all of which will be vital to Dante's planned expansion into the wider Imperium Nihilus. Under his watch will Imperial rule return to those worlds lost.

② WAR ZONE ULTRAMAR

Fierce debate rages among historitors as to when the events collectively known as the Plague Wars began. Some contest it started even before the emergence of the Great Rift, others maintain it was some time later. Regardless, Ultramar and its neighbouring regions have been under attack from the foul forces of Nurgle and Mortarion, Daemon Primarch of the Death Guard Traitor Legion, for years. Worlds have been devastated by the Plague That Walks, Eyerot, the Oozing Pox and countless other maladies. The War of Flies saw Iax, Talassar, Circe and Laphis all beset by attritional war. As the Creeping Death Offensive continues, Ultramar's worlds are tested anew.

③ WAR ZONE VIGILUS

Few worlds in the galaxy have the strategic importance to the Imperium as Vigilus. Always a bulwark against the forces of Chaos, since the Cicatrix Maledictum's galaxy-splitting appearance, it has found itself at the mouth of the Nachmund Gauntlet – one of the few known routes through the Great Rift that is relatively stable. Faced with Genestealer Cult uprisings from within and Ork invasions from without, the defenders were already overstretched when Abaddon the Despoiler and his vast hosts attacked the world. Only by Marneus Calgar's leadership has Vigilus remained in Imperial hands. Calgar knows this is something Abaddon will not tolerate.

④ WAR ZONE PARIAH

Numerous Adeptus Astartes Chapters are striking into the region recognised as the Pariah Nexus. Created by the Necrons using the energies of a caged star and a complex network of void-scraping blackstone pylons, within this territory a supernatural barrier separates the warp from realspace. Many worlds within are considered lost, their populations having had their souls snuffed out by the Nexus' power. With the Necrons hell-bent on expanding the Nexus' reach further and further, the Imperium is determined to see it destroyed. For all this, the Necrons' numbers are increasing and Humanity has few reliable defences against the nefarious effects of the Necrons' fell technology.

CHAPTER PLANETS

Most Space Marine Chapters operate from a home world, where they carry out much of their training, recruitment and rearming. It is their sovereign domain over which they have total authority, the Chapter Master lord of all. Only Terra will be of greater importance to a Space Marine Chapter, and only to the Emperor do the populace owe greater loyalty.

The origin stories of a Chapter's dominion over their home world are as diverse as the Chapters themselves. For most of the First Founding Chapters, their home world is that which was their Primarch's. For those of later Foundings, some now rule worlds their Primarch seized in the Great Crusade. Others liberated their planets from tyranny, or captured them from heretics or xenos. Others still received them as gifts of gratitude or reward for heroic deeds. A great many Chapters cannot account for how their Chapter planet came to be, all records lost, forgotten, destroyed or even hidden. All they know is that their home world, and the mighty fortress monastery built there, is their realm and bastion, and they will defend it unto death.

Many Chapters maintain feral and death worlds possessed of tenacious and hardy populations, people who endure bitter struggles for survival on a daily basis. On these worlds, life itself is a near impossible test that only the toughest survive, and the Space Marines seek in their aspirants the qualities required to succeed in these conditions. Whether they are forced to by high casualties or gene-depletion on their home world, or simply choose to, many Chapters recruit from more than one world. Some demand aspirants from a world they have saved from invasion. Others have ancient ties with neighbouring worlds which provide aspirants on a regular basis. Though some might call this a dilution of their recruitment pool, many Chapters that do this heavily indoctrinate their 'outsider' recruits so that soon they are virtually indistinguishable – culturally and in outlook – from a locally recruited aspirant.

The culture of many Chapters is thoroughly intertwined with their home world. The Salamanders embrace the way of the smith and the forge, just as their people mine and work the rich metals extracted from their planet's rock. The Space Wolves' feasting and drinking halls mirror those of the tribes they are recruited from, and their warriors bear hunting trophies just as do the tribal chieftains and heroes of Fenrisian myth.

Most Chapters have a sphere of influence that reaches beyond their home world, even if it is just to the boundaries of their home system, but a significant number have seen this increase. In these dark times, many areas of space have been given over to direct Space Marine control for security and stability. In the Imperium Nihilus especially, a growing number of worlds cede some or even all of their authority to Space Marine Chapters based nearby, or offer resources, aspirants and serfs to them in exchange for protection. A great many Chapter home worlds have been inundated with refugees as war drives many of the Imperium's teeming trillions to flight. In the case of some Chapters, such as the Ultramarines, their realms have the resources and means to absorb these great throngs to some degree. Others, who oversee inhospitable fiefs, have no means of accommodating these masses, often demanding they serve the Chapter directly in exchange for sanctuary, or leaving them to fight for themselves on their deadly worlds. For these unfortunate souls, life scarcely improves at all.

FLEET-BASED CHAPTERS

A number of Space Marine Chapters have no home world. These nomadic warrior-orders traverse the stars aboard an armada of battle barges, strike cruisers and blade-like escort craft with the power to lay sectors to waste and conquer countless worlds.

For fleet-based Chapters, their vessels serve the roles of a fortress monastery. Ships will house the Armoury, Librarius, Reclusiam and Apothecarion as well as barracks, training cages, practice ranges and strategiums. Some may keep these vital functions aboard a mighty flagship; others spread them across a number of vessels to reduce risk of catastrophic and irreplaceable loss.

There are many reasons as to why a Chapter might be fleet-based. Some are orphaned, their home world lost in cataclysmic battle, such as the mysterious Dark Angels. Others have never had a home world, such as the Black Templars, who have been on the hunt for the enemy since their very inception. Some Chapters have temporarily forfeited the right to a home world in penance, such as the Mantis Warriors, who sided with the traitorous Astral Claws Chapter in the murderous Badab War.

Every fleet-based Chapter recruits in different ways, depending on circumstance. The Imperial Fists maintain a number of recruiting worlds to which they periodically return to claim fresh aspirants. Others appear to have no regimen of any description, simply taking recruits wherever they find them; they are unheeding of all but the most vigorous of protests, and often only if these are made by fellow Space Marine Chapters.

We are the Space Marines, the champions of Humanity. The Emperor's chosen warriors. For every one of us that falls in battle, one hundred enemies will die.

Every fortress monastery is unique. Every element of its design shaped by the Chapter's traditions, preferred methods of warfare and the topography of its home world, which itself shapes the Chapter's culture and values. All, too, are indomitable bastions with countless hangars, void shield generators, impregnable walls and thousands of fearsome defensive weapons.

CHAPTER ORGANISATION

The organisation of many Space Marine Chapters owes itself to the Codex Astartes, a masterwork of the Ultramarines Primarch Roboute Guilliman. First composed ten thousand years ago in some of the Imperium's darkest days, it is considered a holy book and is revered by many Chapters for its age, provenance and authorship.

The Horus Heresy devastated the Imperium. The damage wrought by the Traitor Legions was so severe that the Emperor's realm never fully recovered. The terrifying power of the Space Marines was shown more clearly than ever before, their fallibility tragically revealed. It was clear to Roboute Guilliman that the Primarchs held too much power, that the awesome might of the Legions was simply too dangerous to place under the control of so few individuals. Thus he composed the Codex Astartes. Into it he poured every iota of his deep military and logistical knowledge. He transcribed strategies and tactics for every conceivable battlefield situation in utterly precise detail. No element of Space Marine warfare and organisation went without thorough examination and analysis, down to the exact wording of command protocols, squad size and the hue of myriad uniform markings. Finally, it included comprehensive detail of all wargear and technical equipment in the Space Marines' exhaustive and formidable armouries.

No detail in all of the Codex's many thousands of pages was more significant than the decree that the awesome fighting forces of the Legiones Astartes – which at their height included many tens, or even hundreds of thousands of warriors – be broken down into much smaller brotherhoods called Chapters. Each of these fighting forces would be independent, with complete autonomy over their actions and recruitment, and have their own heraldry and colours. With the power of the Space Marines fragmented in such a way, never could treachery spread with the fury of a raging forest fire in the way it did when Horus turned against the Emperor and corrupted fully half of the Imperium with him.

Not all welcomed these ideas. Rogal Dorn of the Imperial Fists and Vulkan of the Salamanders argued the most vigorously against them, but all of the remaining loyal Primarchs eventually acquiesced. Thus the loyal Legions that had conquered the galaxy in the Emperor's name were no more.

THE AGE OF THE IMPERIUM

Since the Codex's original composition, the great majority of Space Marine Chapters have attempted to follow it, though none but the most reverent have done so successfully. Over the millennia it has been amended and erroneous copies have circulated, meaning some Chapters may all swear to be Codex-compliant, yet have noticeably different combat doctrines and even organisational structures. Some Chapters, such as the Space Wolves, openly spurn significant parts of the Codex, adhering instead to their own traditions – though they still regard it as an important source of knowledge and wisdom.

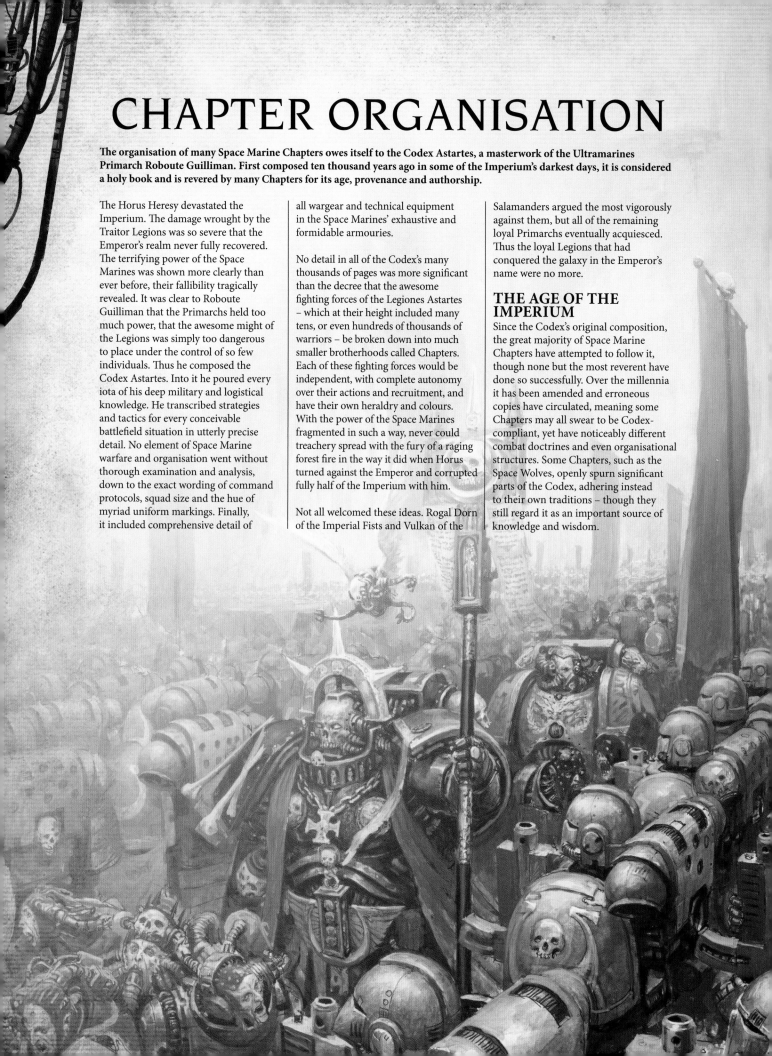

At the core of the Codex Astartes is the organisation of the Chapter. A Codex-compliant Chapter comprises ten companies, each consisting nominally of a hundred Space Marines.

ARMOURY
Master of the Forge
Techmarines
Serfs and Servitors
Battle Tanks
Land Raiders
Warsuits
Light Attack Vehicles
Transport Vehicles
Gunships

CHAPTER COMMAND
Chapter Master
Honour Guard
Chapter Equerries, Serfs and Servitors

LIBRARIUS
Chief Librarian
Epistolaries
Codiciers
Lexicaniums
Acolytum
Serfs and Servitors

RECLUSIAM
Master of Sanctity
Reclusiarch
Chaplains

APOTHECARION
Chief Apothecary
Apothecaries
Serfs and Servitors

VETERANS

1ST COMPANY
Veterans
Honour Guard
(at Chapter Master's discretion)
Dreadnoughts

BATTLE COMPANIES

2ND-5TH COMPANIES
Battleline Squads
Close Support Squads
Fire Support Squads
Dreadnoughts

RESERVE COMPANIES

6TH-7TH COMPANIES
Battleline Squads
Dreadnoughts

8TH COMPANY
Close Support Squads
Dreadnoughts

9TH COMPANY
Fire Support Squads
Dreadnoughts

SCOUT COMPANY

10TH COMPANY
Vanguard Squads
Scouts

Command
Captains
Lieutenants
Company Veterans
Company Champions
Company Ancients

Veteran
Terminator Assault Squads
Bladeguard Veterans
Sternguard Veterans
Terminator Squads
Vanguard Veterans
Veteran Assault
Intercessor Squads
Veteran Intercessor Squads

Battleline
Tactical Squads
Intercessor Squads
Infiltrator Squads
Heavy Intercessor Squads

Close Support
Assault Intercessor Squads
Assault Squads
Attack Bike Squads
Attack Bikes
Bike Squads
Centurion Assault Squads
Inceptor Squads
Incursor Squads
Invader ATVs
Land Speeders
Outrider Squads
Reiver Squads
Storm Speeders

Fire Support
Aggressor Squads
Centurion
Devastator Squads
Devastator Squads
Eliminator Squads
Eradicator Squads
Hellblaster Squads
Suppressor Squads

Just as every Chapter is a highly flexible fighting force, so each company within it is strategically viable in its own right. Each have their own command elements – including Captain, Chaplain and command squad – as well as a pool of bikes and armoured transports. Additionally, Chapters may differ in organisation. The Salamanders have three Masters of the Forge and the Iron Hands have no central Armoury, their vehicles instead held by their companies. Other Chapters adapt the Codex to suit their needs in countless ways.

CHAPTER COMMAND

A Space Marine Chapter is a highly sophisticated and efficient fighting machine. The impossible demands that each has to face – gruelling attrition and numberless foes – make being this way nothing less than essential. To succeed, Chapters need impeccable leaders who breathe the arts of war and logistics.

CHAPTER MASTERS

Chapter Masters command entire Chapters and are exemplary warriors. For centuries have they slain the foes of the Imperium, and countless campaign badges adorn their personal standards. They are some of Mankind's greatest heroes. They appraise entire war zones with the merest glance, understanding every threat and opportunity that presents itself. The arrival of a Chapter Master to a planet afire with battle can turn an imminent, crushing defeat into a resounding, glorious victory.

Few in the Imperium have as much personal authority as a Chapter Master. At full strength their Chapter and its fleet can lay waste to entire systems. Their home world, wittingly or otherwise, is theirs to command, and many enjoy the loyalty of planets and systems further afield.

Chapter Masters answer to almost no one. They are petitioned for aid, rather than ordered to provide it, and of the many thousands of supplications a Chapter receives, it is the Chapter Master who decides which his warriors shall respond to. In this, he holds the power of life and death over entire systems. Even in a war zone where multiple Chapters are fighting, it is only by choice that those involved follow the leadership of another Chapter.

Chapter Masters have access to some of the very finest wargear in the Imperium; many don armour and bear weapons millennia old. These ancient relics are sources of immense pride to the Chapter to which they belong, and such is the honour in even touching them, only Chapter Masters are permitted to use them in battle.

While most Chapters are led by a single individual serving as a Chapter Master – and many may refer to him by a different title – not all Chapters operate in this way. The Sons of Medusa are led by a triumvirate of Iron Thanes. Conversely, the Iron Hands' Iron Council is its ultimate authority, with Kardan Stronos serving as Chapter Master only for as long as the Iron Council deem him fit for the honoured duty of being the voice of the Chapter. The Raven Guard have a clear Chapter Master figure in Kayvaan Shrike, but the Shadow Captains of the Chapter's companies have considerably more free rein to select which campaigns they fight, and how they do so, than their equivalents in many other Chapters.

A Chapter Master's role is supplemented by other officers whose roles exist outside of the formal company structure. These vary from Chapter to Chapter, but include such positions as the Lord of the Household, Chapter Master's Secretarius, Securitas Primus and countless others.

HONOUR GUARD

Most Chapters have an honour guard, an elite cadre of warriors who answer to no one but the Chapter Master himself and have a multitude of functions. They

are the Chapter Master's protectors, responsible for his security at all times, whether in council on their home world or in the raging inferno of war. They also serve as advisors, drawing upon their combat experience and wisdom to provide their liege with informed guidance. In this capacity they may also serve as naysayers, their task to challenge the decisions of the Chapter Master to prevent the rot of arrogance and complacency from taking the slightest toehold. An honour guard might include a Chapter Champion – a superlative warrior and living embodiment of all his Chapter's ideals. Very often the honour guard are responsible for the Chapter's standards and banners. This task is a sacred one, borne with great gravitas.

How an honour guard is formed varies from Chapter to Chapter. For some it is a standing institution, its membership only changing as its members fall in battle or volunteer to resign their duties to return to the companies. Such self-demotion is a rare occurrence, but does happen in the event that a company suffers such severe casualties that it lacks experienced members. Some of these honour guard have felt compelled to join the Chaplaincy, or to serve as an officer in the Scout Company where they can pass their experience on to the next generation. These honour guards provide a formal link between Chapter Masters new and old, ensuring a continuity in the Chapter leadership. In other Chapters the Chapter Master will select his own honour guard. These may be warriors he has fought alongside in battle after battle, or mentors whose knowledge and wisdom he greatly values. Some Chapters may have a combination of both, to best secure the advantages of each. Others will draw their honour guard from the 1st Company.

Thanks to their esteemed position, the honour guard have rare access to their Chapter Armoury, and will often bear formidable relic weapons and wear magnificent ornate armour. Such artefacts have been borne into battle by hundreds of Chapter heroes, and with their choice of weapons each warrior is perfectly equipped to deal death to all but the most dangerous of foes.

SYMBOLS OF AUTHORITY

Many Space Marines across virtually all Chapters adorn their armour with heraldic symbols, laurels, trophies and iconography denoting their names, ancestry and battles they have fought. They also honour fallen heroes or celebrate the champions and leaders they follow into war. Such practices vary enormously, not just from Chapter to Chapter, company to company and squad to squad, but also among individuals. Some Space Marines use identical symbols in different ways, and many Chapters particularly favour practices inherited from their home world.

The banners that Space Marines boast are each masterworks crafted by the hands of the most skilled artisans – or even the Space Marines themselves – and blessed in long, sombre rituals. Some are made to commemorate legendary battles, or celebrate the heroics of the Chapter's battle-brothers. Others represent the Chapter as a whole, the companies, or certain bodies such as the Apothecarion or Armoury. They are richly decorated, and each symbol, icon, word, name and embellishment represents something of deep significance to the Chapter and its warriors.

The crux is regarded as a symbol of veterancy throughout many Space Marine Chapters and is sported by their finest warriors as a badge of honour.

It is not uncommon for Space Marines to honour dead brethren or favoured serfs by adorning their wargear and insignia with the bones of those who once served.

Many Space Marines carry sanctified reliquaries onto the battlefield, storing the bones of fallen brothers, slain enemies or honoured personal serfs.

Our standards inspire courage in our warriors and fear in our foes. Our ancient weapons spill our enemies' blood as the sight of them stirs our hearts. Our reliquaries teach us the meaning of sacrifice, brotherhood and steadfastness – and these characteristics are the deadliest weapons in our arsenal.

1ST COMPANY

A Space Marine Chapter's 1st Company is its most elite fighting force. A warrior is only appointed to it after decades of war in the Scout, Reserve and Battle Companies and after having performed legendary deeds of bravery. To be one of this number is to be an exemplar of the Chapter, and a superb example of what it means to be a Space Marine in the highest sense.

There are no ways of war that the warriors of the 1st Company have failed to master, and any battlefield role is second nature to them. Whether it is holding ground against endless hordes of scuttling Tyranid horrors, storming the formidable leg bastions of an enemy Titan, meeting the towering wraith constructs of the Aeldari, or engaging in ferocious duels with lithe Drukhari blade-masters, 1st Company Veterans are equal to the task.

Most frequently 1st Company squads are attached to other Space Marine strike forces, rather than the entire formation fighting as one. Primarily they serve as devastatingly powerful warriors adept at any role required of them. When working with other forces they serve as peerless mentors, sharing with their brothers their hard-won experience and wisdom. To the rest of the Chapter they are heroes, and their mere presence strengthens their brothers' resolve and compels them to fight all the harder.

Veteran squads take their pick from the Chapter's armouries. Thus, each warrior wages war with his preferred weaponry for the task at hand. Space Marine Captains know that Veteran squads are best utilised when given a wide remit to prosecute the battle in whichever way they deem best, their experience such that they can swiftly identify where they are most needed and what tactics to apply to bring victory. As such, Veteran squads are much less rigid in their doctrine than the battle-brothers of other companies.

STERNGUARD AND VANGUARD VETERAN SQUADS

Sternguard Veterans are masters of ranged warfare with all manner of Space Marine guns. They exemplify the power that can be brought to bear by the union of mighty Space Marine and sacred boltgun, and they bring to war a range of specialised ammunition types, all suited to different foes. Some possess unstable flux cores which make them the bane of heavily armoured foes. Others replace the core and tip of the standard bolt round with thousands of needles that tear into the target and pump in mutagenic poison which eats organic enemies from the inside out. Some bolts allow the Space Marine to engage targets at even further range thanks to additional propellant. Particularly sophisticated bolts release gouts of superheated gas that reach and slay foes embedded deeply in cover.

Vanguard Veteran Squads are ever on the move, using their jump packs to blast from foe to foe. Wielding all manner of heirloom power weapons, relic blades, thunder hammers and lightning claws, they make a mockery of the thickest enemy armour and toughest alien chitin

with their strikes, made all the more devastating thanks to the incredible skill with which the Vanguard wield them. Each kill they make is a celebrated act, one that honours their weapons' machine spirits as well as the battle-brothers who bore them into battle in the past.

Rivalries often develop between the Sternguard and Vanguard Veterans, each determined to kill more foes, win more battles and secure the most dangerous duties. Nevertheless, all are battle-brothers, and when the situation calls will gladly lay down their lives for each other.

BLADEGUARD VETERAN SQUADS

The Bladeguard go to war covered in purity seals, clad in finely crafted armour and bedecked with icons of victory and heraldic devices. Their towering storm shields are the work of many generations of toiling Chapter serfs, and the powerful force field generators they contain are said to protect the bearer's soul as much as his flesh. This wargear is brought out from the Chapter's reliquaries in times of war, and when seen in battle reminds all brothers of the legacy they have sworn to uphold since their induction to the Chapter.

TERMINATOR ARMOUR

More formally known as Tactical Dreadnought armour, Terminator armour is the most impervious plate ever conceived by the Imperium. The ancient technologies required to maintain its bonded ceramite plating and fully electromotivated exoskeleton are highly mysterious and restricted; only a handful of forge worlds have access to the means to build new suits, and

scant few Chapters have the knowledge to fully repair those damaged in the extremely hazardous theatres of battle they are deployed in. Terminator armour is precious for another reason. One shoulder pad on each suit bears the Crux Terminatus, a sacred cross-shaped icon sculpted in relief. It is said that within it is a fragment of the Emperor's own armour.

The most fortunate Chapters have access to Terminator armour more revered and ancient yet than the Indomitus pattern most commonly seen on the battlefields of the 41st Millennium. Cataphractii and Tartaros are foremost amongst these rare patterns. Each relic Terminator suit is a marvel in its own right, a working symbol of the Imperium's technological might. Only in the direst circumstances are these artefacts deployed by those Chapters they belong to, and they have turned the tide of countless battles thought lost.

Regardless of which pattern of Terminator armour a Space Marine is clad in, to be trusted with such a treasured relic is a great honour, and is the truest statement of the warrior's skill, courage, honour, discipline and fortitude.

STORM SHIELDS

Grasped by the wielder's hand, the storm shield is an advanced personal protection device carried to war most frequently by Space Marine commanders, Veterans and squad sergeants. Storm shields are commonly shaped in a similar manner to the Crux Terminatus, though other variants exist, such as the tower shields borne by the Deathwatch. Many warriors of different Chapters adorn their shields with purity seals and etch on personal or Chapter sigils. Some Blood Angels depict angelic wings or droplets of blood. The Salamanders often drape their storm shields with scales taken from great reptilian beasts they have slain on their home world. The Guardians of the Covenant affix parchments inscribed with Chapter lore to their shields. Powered by generators built in to the user's armour, storm shields crackle with lightning and are sheathed in a blue energy when activated. This defensive field is so effective it has been known to protect its bearer from even super-heavy weaponry.

BATTLE COMPANIES

Whether it is infiltrating a heretic stronghold and bringing it crashing down from within, plunging from space into the heart of a ferocious siege or scouring worlds clean of foes riding in squadrons of armoured transports, Space Marines excel in all manner of war. It is the foremost duty of the Battle Companies to be at the forefront of their Chapter's campaigns.

Bringers of Doom: Avenging Angels of Death; they are the Space Marines.

The Codex Astartes decrees that the 2nd through 5th Companies of a Space Marine Chapter are the Battle Companies. It is to these mighty and flexible formations that the principle combat duties of a Space Marine Chapter are assigned. At the head of each of these formations is an array of warriors, leaders and veterans who are true exemplars of their Chapter. Battle Companies are led by Captains, with two supporting Lieutenants. A Chaplain joins them, who is responsible for the company's spiritual welfare. The Company Champion is one of the formation's finest warriors, a fierce bladesman who guards the Captain and the company's honour with his life. To the Company Ancient falls the most honoured task: to bear the company standard to war. Alongside these individuals stand the Company Veterans, outstanding warriors raised from the company's squads. In times of war a Battle Company might also be accompanied by one or more Librarians. These fearsome battle-psykers lend their considerable powers to the strike force, as well as provide invaluable guidance and wisdom.

In addition to his company command duties, each Captain of the Battle Companies has a number of titles and duties, traditionally tied to the company he leads. At times they can be purely ceremonial, and at the discretion of the Chapter Master can be altered according to the needs of the day. Nominally, however, the Codex states that the 2nd Company Captain is the Master of the Watch, the 3rd Company Captain is Master of the Arsenal, the 4th Company Captain is Master of the Fleet and the 5th Company Captain is Master of the Marches. To these individuals the Chapter Master entrusts many vital tasks, whether it be overseeing the deployment and disposition of the Chapter's fighting strength, the home world's defences, managing the Chapter's vast inventory of munitions and wargear, commanding the Chapter's mighty fleet in battle or

assessing the most desperate pleas for aid. Not all Chapters follow these doctrines precisely, over time developing their own specific titles and duties for their officers.

Each Battle Company principally has ten squads, six of the battleline role, two of close support and two of fire support, each with ten Space Marines. The Codex, however, makes provision for there to be twenty squads, for when squads from the Reserve Companies are attached. Additionally, a company's squads can be split in two, forming combat squads.

Such an organisational structure makes the Battle Companies highly flexible. They are frequently split into two demi-companies, each under the direct command of a Lieutenant. A Battle Company will go to war with a vast arsenal of wargear and specialist equipment, far too much for it to use at any single time. Including Phobos armour, Gravis armour, Centurion and Invictor Warsuits, Land Speeders, bikes and rack after rack of weaponry, no squad will be lacking for the equipment it needs to fight its war. An entire company can fight a campaign of stealth, every one of its number donning Phobos armour that enhances their agility and speed, and bearing sophisticated equipment that scrambles communications.

Even the squads themselves can be broken down to fight in a variety of roles should their Captain require it. Should three brothers be detached from their fire support squad to form an Eliminator Squad, the remaining seven can form a Hellblaster Squad, pilot Invictor Warsuits, or fulfil a number of other roles for their squad designation, including operating the company's Rhino and Impulsor transports.

Should the awesome fighting power of a Battle Company be deemed insufficient for a campaign, it is supplemented by

reinforcements from one of the Reserve Companies. If the Captain expects that he will need more fast-moving forces to rapidly secure ground or counter agile enemies, he will request one or more close support squads. In the event that he expects his forces to fight atop mighty fortress battlements, defending against endless hordes of xenos foes, additional fire support squads will be immensely valuable to lay down the punishing fire needed to destroy the enemy.

Each Battle Company maintains its own pool of Rhino, Razorback and Impulsor vehicles so that its entire strength can be moved rapidly across the battlefield, but there are times when even Space Marines need armoured and air support. For these resources the commander issues the Armoury with his requirements to acquire the swift gunships, thundering siege tanks and powerful anti-air assets he needs to ensure victory.

THE SACRED BOLTER

Bolt weapons have been synonymous with the Space Marines since before even the Great Crusade. Billions of the Emperor's foes have been laid low by their explosive, mass-reactive rounds, known as bolts.

The standard bolt is a high calibre, partly self-propelling round with a dense metallic core and diamantine tip. Detonating after penetrating a target, they kill the foe in an eruption of splattered gore, shattered bone and armour shards.

Bolt weapon technology has been applied across a number of different weapon types, including the compact bolt pistol and the punishing heavy bolter. A whole suite of specialised bolt weapons are utilised by the Space Marines, each suited to a squad's dedicated role. The auto bolt rifle wielded by some Intercessors is a highly aggressive weapon that allows its user to rake his enemy with relentless fire, whereas the stalker bolt rifle has the range and accuracy to enable its wielder to pick the foe off from afar.

A Space Marine's personal weapons must be constructed by hand. Sometimes this is carried out by the Space Marine himself in the Chapter's own forges and armoury. Others are fashioned on Adeptus Mechanicus forge worlds, many of which have developed their own unique designs – though all are redolent of the same martial legacy.

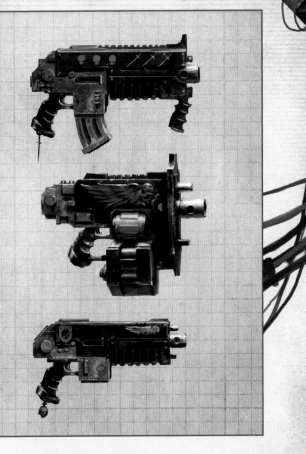

WAR ZONE: ABERRUS

A tendril of Tyranid Hive Fleet Kraken slithered into the Aberrus System like a venomous serpent. Countless millions of scuttling horrors flooded the system's worlds, and monstrous bio-titans shook the ground with each thundering step. Four Adeptus Astartes Chapters responded to the threat.

When the Iron Lords ancillary scry-station Hédhan warned that Aberrus had come under attack, the Chapter responded immediately, pulling together a strike force under the command of 2nd Company Captain Nikeras. If Aberrus fell, nothing would lie between the Tyranids and the Grendl Stars. They could not allow the Great Devourer to consume the genetic material of the hyper-violent Barghesi. Knowing the magnitude of the threat that opposed them, the Iron Lords called for allies. The only Adeptus Astartes response came from an unexpected quarter: the Lamenters Chapter. Having been ravaged by these Tyranids in the past and now reinforced with Primaris brethren, they were eager for revenge, though they remained aloof from the Iron Lords, communicating only when necessary.

When the distant allies reached Aberrus, it was already drowning in bestial bioforms. Saint Vaux's Hope had fallen.

Luann and Glacemaw were deluged with millions of xenos creatures. To the Space Marines' surprise, two other Chapters were already in-system. The Knights of the Raven continued their hit-and-run war of penance against Hive Fleet Kraken, and an all-Primaris Battle Company of newly assigned Scythes of the Emperor desired nothing more than to spill xenos ichor.

Their goals aligned, the Chapters set to cleanse the system of its all-consuming invaders. They first had to make safe Luann and Glacemaw, with the Iron Lords and Lamenters deploying to the former, and the Knights of the Raven and Scythes of the Emperor racing for the latter.

On Luann, the Lamenters swiftly broke through to the Four Towers – a string of fortresses originally constructed to hold back local carnivorous fauna – which were each under siege. The Iron Lords made for the Hurac Mountains,

observing that they could cause a colossal landslide that would sweep aside hordes of bio-constructs with well-placed and well-timed charges.

On Glacemaw, the Knights of the Raven moved rapidly over the planet's sweeping tundras. Infantry scoured them for vanguard organisms while armoured forces rushed to relieve the Lashsanos Bluffs. There the Vostroyan 103rd were fighting alongside the 21st, 34th and 76th Glacemaw Ridgeguards, the 12th Truskan Snowhounds and several detachments of Anvarsian Ice Rangers against dozens of bio-titans.

The arrival of the Space Marines brought a new momentum to the campaign to defend Aberrus, and Imperial forces throughout the system rallied. Though the outcome was far from certain, victory was not out of sight.

SPACE MARINES OF WAR ZONE ABERRUS

The Chapters that sent warriors to the Aberrus System all had a deep history of conflict with the bio-monstrosities of Hive Fleet Kraken. All had suffered greatly at its claws, and were eager to rip the tendril that coiled around Aberrus from Kraken's main body.

IRON LORDS

2ND COMPANY
'Asmund' ....battleline (Intercessor) squad
'Brecoa' ....battleline (Tactical) squad
'Fyrenos' ....close support (Assault) squad
'Hama' ....fire support (Devastator) squad
'Cunnan' ....close support (Incursor) squad

8TH COMPANY
'Grettix' ....fire support (Devastator) squad
'Thunor' ....fire support (Hellblaster) squad

10TH COMPANY
'Syrcan' ....battleline (Infiltrator) squad
'Moerdan' ....Scout squad
'Lothar' ....Scout squad

LAMENTERS

STRIKE FORCE 'LETANZAR'
'Goriel' ....Veteran (Sternguard) squad
'Vitrian' ....fire support (Suppressor) squad
'Gallani' ....close support (Outrider) squad
'Tyborel' ....close support (Inceptor) squad
'Arteino' ....battleline (Tactical) squad
'Bardella' ....battleline (Tactical) squad

KNIGHTS OF THE RAVEN

VANGUARD STRIKE FORCE 'TRISTYAN'
'Adhemar' ....battleline (Infiltrator) squad
'Bardus' ....battleline (Infiltrator) squad
'Doran' ....close support (Reiver) squad

ARMOURED TASK FORCE 'CORARIKUS'
Destriers of the Raven.....................Predator squadron
Purgers of the Field ....Whirlwind squadron
Might of Coralax.........................Repulsor Executioner

SCYTHES OF THE EMPEROR

3RD COMPANY
'Kamiol' ....battleline (Intercessor) squad
'Holokios' ....battleline (Intercessor) squad
'Lukaen' ....battleline (Intercessor) squad
'Furica' ....battleline (Infiltrator) squad
'Nesoi' ....battleline (Heavy Intercessor) squad
'Lantos' ....battleline (Heavy Intercessor) squad
'Enkalados'...........close support (Invader ATV) squad
The Reapers.... close support (Storm Speeder) squadron
'Macrinas'...................... fire support (Aggressor) squad
'Gordian' .... fire support (Eliminator) squad
'Herennian' .... fire support (Hellblaster) squad

++ Information 88.93% accurate as of the principle battles on Luann and Glacemaw. Note that multiple units apparently bearing the same squad identification markings were identified. Cross-reference with File 389£//Codex/Astartes//27 indicates Adeptus Astartes' propensity to alter wargear allocated to squad-size elements depending on battlefield conditions and available equipment. Further study indicates that squad monikers are frequently taken from the squad leader's name. Force dispositions provided do not refer to command elements, ancillary vehicles, transports and other machina. ++

++ All attempts to catalogue Tyranid forces present resulted in catastrophic cogitation and bio-density calculation failure. Accumulated accounts from varied local sources suggest numbers in the hundreds of millions. Visual analysis of pict feeds indicates presence of forty-seven known bioforms, with thirteen unknown others unidentified. ++

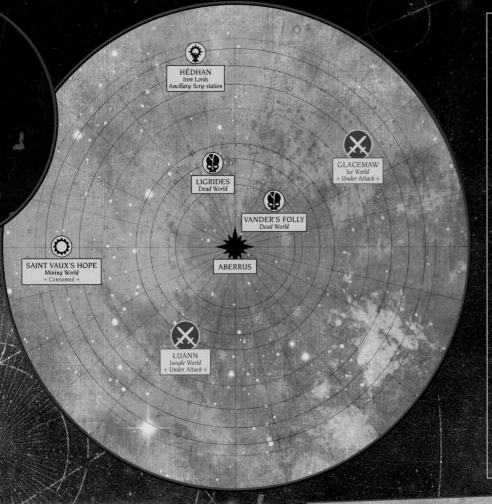

HÉDHAN
Iron Lords
Ancillary Scry-station

LIGRIDES
Dead World

GLACEMAW
Ice World
+ Under Attack +

VANDER'S FOLLY
Dead World

SAINT VAUX'S HOPE
Mining World
+ Consumed +

ABERRUS

LUANN
Jungle World
+ Under Attack +

GRENDL STARS

Formerly known as the Wings of Sanguinius, and called the Fourteen by some, the Grendl Stars are home to the hyper-violent Barghesi race. The xenos have been confined to this region by the Iron Lords for three thousand years, held within the Chapter's 'Iron Grip', pending the massing of Imperial forces with strength enough to exterminate the Barghesi forever. No such crusade has been forthcoming, and with the emergence of the Great Rift, seems all but impossible.

The Grendl Stars are located on the Eastern Fringe of the Imperium Nihilus. Surrounding beacons warn travellers to 'avoid at all costs', though this has not prevented pirates and fugitives from delving into the Fourteen's depths in search of sanctuary. Most are dead within months, often slain by xenos. The others are identified and destroyed by one of the Iron Lords' fourteen fortresses, known as the Holdfasts, that are responsible for monitoring each star.

Stylised sigil of the Iron Lords set before the Grendl Stars constellation. The gauntleted left fist holds a spiked halo. This most obviously represents the Iron Grip – a sign of strength, tenacity and implacability.

Urgent Request: Maxima Interdictio - Epsilon Clearance

Watch Captain — I'm sure you are as aware as I of the escalating conflict in the Aberrus System. My acolytes are deployed throughout the system. They inform me of the collapse of the Luann Lineholders' 81st and 935th on the Hinnoq Delta Tri-bridge and the toppling of the Permaberg Citadel on Glacemaw. The Tredi Forest, viewed as impenetrable for millennia, is all but consumed — only by the efforts of the Catachan 55th, supported by the Knights of Houses Curtana and Borgius and Sisters of the Order of the Crimson Chalice, have the outer reaches been held. The Sanctuary of Saint Vilutia will surely fall if the forest is lost. The ice fields of Kutris crawl with Tyranid bioforms rampaging towards Glation City — my servants estimate the habitation will be destroyed within three local days of a concerted attack. These events alone, I am more than aware, would not warrant the involvement of Indomitus Point watch fortress, but they serve to indicate pre-existing vulnerabilities ahead of the threat I contact you to discuss. Another tendril approaches Aberrus. Three of my void-watchers have already been destroyed by it; the fourth only survived after suffering terrible injuries. This tendril is twice the size of that which ravages Aberrus as we speak. If it arrives intact, it will devastate the system and sweep on into the Grendl Stars. This cannot, I repeat cannot, be countenanced. I fear the fate of the Eastern Fringe hangs in the balance.

— Inquisitor Shalisha Talaris, Ordo Xenos

RESERVE COMPANIES

The Companies of Reserve are a vital element of a Chapter's organisation. For all their adaptability, fury and valour, the Battle Companies nevertheless sustain losses in the savage war zones in which they fight, or are not number enough for the hordes of enemies they face. The 6th through 9th Companies are therefore designated Reserve Companies, one of their primary tasks being to reinforce the Battle Companies.

The tenets of the Codex Astartes dictate that the Reserve Companies serve the Chapter by maintaining the Battle Companies' next generation of warriors. It is a task of great import, for in their time in these formations Space Marines will further develop their skills and gain vital experience. When a Battle Company suffers losses in the tumult of war, it is from the Reserve Companies that replacements will be drawn.

Rather than formations of mixed squad types, the Reserve Companies contain squads of the same strategic designation. The 6th and 7th Companies each maintain ten battleline squads, and the 8th and 9th Companies are made up purely of close support and fire support squads respectively.

The Reserve Companies have the responsibility to embed additional specialties to provide the Chapter with the resources it needs to fight its bloody campaigns. The 6th and 7th Companies undergo extensive training in all manner of transports, Land Speeders, battle tanks and even gunships. With these swift assault vehicles Space Marines of these companies serve to provide highly mobile firepower, launch devastating flank attacks and smash apart enemy lines. The close support squads of the 8th Company storm defences, exploiting weaknesses to make a victory-winning breakthrough. Their well-timed assaults have earned the admiration of their Battle Company brothers on numerous battlefields. Armed with a plethora of heavy weapons, the squads of the 9th Company excel at providing devastating salvoes of covering fire, knocking out enemy strongpoints and blowing apart their armoured columns.

Typically, squads from the Reserve companies will serve alongside the Battle Companies, though on some occasions – particularly if much of the Chapter is fighting in one war zone – a Reserve Company might fight as a whole. Such is the genius of the Codex Astartes that, should it be necessary, ad hoc task forces in demi or even Battle Company strength are created entirely from the squads of the Reserve Companies. A Lieutenant or Captain from the Companies of Reserve will be nominated to take command of such a force and has the power to request armoured support as necessary.

The leadership of each Reserve Company follows that of the Battle Companies, with a Captain, Chaplain, Lieutenants, Apothecary, Ancient and Veterans. Each Captain has additional roles and duties, in line with his counterparts in the Battle Companies. Depending on the Chapter or even Chapter Master, some of these will be ceremonial, though others will be essential tasks the Chapter cannot function without. Again, the Codex has stipulations as to what these should be, but allows for flexibility and individual Chapter traditions. The Captain of the 6th Company of a Chapter strictly following the Codex will be Master of the Rites, and the 7th Company Captain Chief Victualler. The Captain of the 8th Company is Lord Executioner and the 9th Company Captain is Master of Relics. Among the essential functions delegated to these officers are the maintenance and codification of the Chapter's customs and conventions, the logistics of non-martial resources, the management of the Chapter's serfs, the enforcement of the Chapter's strictest punishments and the satisfaction of its grievances, and the oversight and security of the Chapter's irreplaceable artefacts. Every Space Marine takes pride in their Captain's duties, and willingly aids him in carrying them out whenever called upon to do so.

It is through these companies that a Space Marine progresses after they have left the 10th Company. In the 9th Company they hone their understanding of wider battlefield strategy in the application of heavy firepower against the most vital targets. The 8th Company teaches them the value of the rapid assault, the importance of constant movement and the precision required to carry out the perfect feint. In the 6th and 7th Companies they prove to their battle-brothers and commanders that they have assimilated every teaching of the Reserve Companies and have forged them into an unbreakable weapon of experience, skill and duty. They must be masters of all manner of combat, as adept in every battlefield situation as they are familiar with every verse of the Codex Astartes and other tomes of lore that the Chapter holds in high esteem. Only once they have demonstrated their worth are they welcomed into the ranks of the Battle Companies, who can trust in their courage, determination and expertise from the off.

Explosions ripped up the ground, sending chunks of rubble tearing through the air. The heretics had intensified their shelling as soon as the Blood Krakens attacked, even firing on their own troops to stall the Space Marines' advance.

Brother Mordaresh's power armour was scarred, much of its granite and heliotrope colour worn away by shrapnel.

His Land Speeder shot over the broken terrain, completely passing over the shattered trunks of destroyed trees. Brother Naram manned the skimmer's multi-melta, his armour as damaged as Mordaresh's. They were through the worst of it for now.

Mordaresh looked to his left. A Land Speeder Typhoon sped alongside them. 'Joried and Agarath made it through,' he said.

'Banicus and Caros too,' said Naram. Mordaresh could see their Land Speeder Tornado to his right, its assault cannon whirring in anticipation of the slaughter to come. All three Land Speeders bore the indignium markings of the 7th Company, though much had been worn away.

'Leave none alive,' Lieutenant Klegor said over the vox. 'Too many of the Fourth Company have died to those cowards today. Make them pay.'

'Aye, sir,' said Mordaresh. Vox clicks indicated the other pilots affirmed as he did. He could already see the outlines of the traitor Basilisks ahead. He saw figures rush out of the artillery tanks' hatches and jump to the ground. In moments the lightning-fast Land Speeders were upon their foes. Krak missiles whooshed towards their targets. Basilisks exploded in massive fireballs as their fuel tanks and ammunition stores detonated. The relentless thrum of assault cannon fire filled the air next. Fleeing crew were reduced to puffs of pink mist in the fusillade. The roar of Naram's multi-melta added to the cacophony, each focused beam of intense heat reducing a Basilisk to a bubbling pool of molten metal. The enemy was broken, their armour destroyed. The Blood Krakens had won.

Death and Duty are all we must give.

SCOUT COMPANY

In a galaxy home to horrors and threats unnumbered, even the mighty Space Marine Chapters suffer losses in the ceaseless grind of wars they fight. It is the vital duty of the Scout Company to take the rawest aspirants and metamorphose them into fully fledged Space Marines, so that the ranks may ever be full.

The Codex Astartes states that a Chapter's 10th Company is the Scout Company. Every Space Marine in a Chapter that follows the Codex has passed through it, including the mightiest of heroes. Marneus Calgar of the Ultramarines, Dante of the Blood Angels, and Kayvaan Shrike of the Raven Guard all remember their formative years as a part of this body, and the missions they completed which taught them so much.

There are no regulations dictated by the Codex as to the number of neophytes a Chapter may have. The recruitment rate is not fixed and methods differ between Chapters. The Ultramarines' stellar dominion is replete with academies where youths train and compete to join the Adeptus Astartes, meaning there are always plentiful neophytes aspiring to join Guilliman's gene-sons. The Salamanders, on the other hand, recruit almost exclusively from their home

world of Nocturne, and their particularly meticulous methods result in a relatively low number of Scouts serving in their 7th Company.

The Scout Company is arguably the most important, such are its responsibilities. A novitiate must prove himself worthy as a Scout before being awarded the honour of donning the Black Carapace, the final implant that allows a Space Marine to operate their power armour effectively. Chaplains, Librarians, Apothecaries and officers all closely observe the aspirants as they progress in their training. Only those who perform admirably on the battlefield, demonstrate the Chapter's most valued characteristics and show complete learning of the Codex Astartes and their Primarch's teachings will progress to become full Space Marines.

Scouts learn the way of the sacred boltgun and the blade, the sniper rifle,

the shotgun and the heavy bolter. They learn how to handle the fearsome power of Space Marine bikes and the dizzying velocities of Land Speeders. They also learn how and when to best strike against the foe, when the optimum moment to tactically withdraw arrives and how to identify, isolate and exploit enemy weak points. Their manner of war is that of stealth, reconnaissance, sabotage, raiding and disruption. They gather vital battlefield intelligence, pick off sentries that might betray a Space Marine assault, mercilessly cut down enemy patrols that disrupt their Chapter's plans and destroy ammunition and fuel dumps to leave their foes woefully under-equipped. All of these hazardous missions put the Scouts under immense pressure – all the better to test the widest array of skills, measure their strength of will and commitment and ascertain who truly has the adaptability required of a Space Marine.

With unwavering devotion, we commit. With fire in our hearts we refuse the foe all quarter. With the will of the Emperor and the Primarch guiding our hands, we will never fail in their service.

'I am the guardian of my Chapter's future. By my orders are our neophytes trained in the fine arts of conflict, in the dealing of death, the mastery of terrain, the thrust of the attack, the iron bulwark of the defence and the flow of the controlled withdrawal. On my shoulders rests the burden of ensuring my brothers are reinforced by warriors of the highest quality, worthy of the weapons they wield, the armour in which they are clad, the colours they wear and the symbols they bear.

I am my Chapter's eyes and ears, and the dagger in its fist. At my behest do the Vanguard deploy. By their careful data gathering and close attention to the smallest details are the most minute chinks in our foes' armour discovered. By a thousand of their knife strokes and a thousand of their bolt rounds are our enemies reduced to terrified, disorganised rabbles. With rapid thrusts do they pierce the heart of the foe, striking from the shadows and leaving naught but blood, terror and devastation behind. How many times have my warriors turned the tide of battles thought lost? How many times have they crippled enemy armies outnumbering them thousands to one? You will soon learn the answers, and you will dream of one day being part of that martial legacy.'

- Brother-Captain Taelos,
Master of Recruits and Master of Reconnaissance,
Ultramarines 10th Company,
addressing new recruits

Much like the venerated warriors of the 1st Company and the stalwart brothers of the Reserve Companies, Scouts are often attached to different Space Marine forces and are rarely deployed in a singular formation. They fight alongside the warriors they hope to one day call battle-brother with great vigour, determined to prove their worth. The fully inducted battle-brothers expect nothing less, and look upon the warriors of the 10th with pride – they have all served their time in the company, and know the rigours the novitiates and newly initiated face.

Since his return, Roboute Guilliman has revised the Codex Astartes to allow for the inclusion of Primaris Space Marines, and the myriad ways in which they wage war, in Chapter structure. One of the most sweeping of these additions is the creation of a standing force of ten Vanguard squads in the Scout Company. Fighting as Infiltrators, Incursors, Suppressors, Eliminators and Reivers, and piloting the rugged Invictor Tactical Warsuits, these expert infiltration warriors are masters of shadow warfare tactics. Their objectives are nothing less than full-spectrum superiority over the enemy. They destroy supply convoys, assassinate leaders, break communications, sabotage transport links and shatter morale. Whether fighting in support of other task forces or operating independently, they are trusted to perform these missions.

To aid them in this, Vanguard squads are equipped with highly sophisticated specialist wargear and given advanced training. There are the grapnel launchers and shock grenades of the Reivers, the smoke grenades of the Infiltrators and the jump packs and grav-chutes of the Suppressors.

The occulus bolt carbines and Divinator-class auspexes of the Incursors feed directly into their transpectral combat visors. Combined, there is no battlefield data this highly advanced system cannot gather and analyse thanks to an enslaved machine spirit that cogitates vast quantities of variables in seconds. It presents its conclusions to the Incursor, giving him timely front line intelligence he could never have acquired otherwise.

Suppressor Squads are clad in unique Omnis-pattern armour, formed by gelling elements of both Gravis and Phobos patterns. With inbuilt shock-absorbing servo-plates, they can handle the immense recoil of their rapid-firing cannons, which launch salvoes of foot-long, armour-piercing rounds.

The Eliminators' bolt sniper rifles possess customisable scopes perfect for any battlefield situation, and can fire numerous types of deadly ammunition. Hyperfrag rounds explode in a hail of lacerating shards that shred infantry. Executioner rounds are miniature, self-guiding missiles that seek out and destroy targets embedded in cover, and are even capable of changing direction. Mortis rounds cause the complete collapse of the target's biological systems thanks to the mutagenic toxins contained within them.

RECLUSIAM

A Chapter's Reclusiam is a hallowed place. Reverent silence is punctuated only by Chaplains chanting liturgies and administering rites, and the gentle footfalls of robe-wearing serfs. Shrines line its alcove walls, dedicated to fallen heroes, the Chapter's Primarch and holy relics from the brotherhood's glorious history.

The Reclusiam is a place of immense cultural and spiritual significance to a Space Marine Chapter. This central shrine is the primary place where prayer and worship is conducted, though most Chapter fleet vessels have their own cathedrums and chapels for those Space Marines on campaign. In the Reclusiam the Chapter's Chaplains, led by the Master of Sanctity and Reclusiarch, preserve ancient traditions, conduct meditations and perform ceremonies of indoctrination, vindication and inauguration. To Space Marines, these are no less vital to their purpose as warriors than their skill at arms, the maintenance of their battle gear and their honour roll.

Almost all of a Chapter's most precious relics are secured in the Reclusiam. Company and Chapter battle standards hang from the cold walls in shimmering suspensor fields. Fragments of armour worn by the Chapter's legendary heroes are presented side by side with ornately crafted blades and hammers and the bleached skulls of vaunted champions. Other artefacts include the quills used by enlightened warriors who scribed majestic works of battle wisdom, or bolter shell casings collected from battlefields where the greatest glories were won. Many hundreds of serfs work to preserve a Chapter's relics, each a master of metallurgy, gilding and other crafts. Multiple generations spend their entire lives polishing a single relic blade, have the sole task of picking broken chainsword teeth from sundered battlefields or keeping the Reclusiam's many thousands of ceremonial candles lit – with the tallow of their own bodies removed from them upon their demise

to produce more. Even in death they still serve.

Keeping these wondrous artefacts safe is a great honour and solemn duty for the Chaplains and those training to join their austere ranks, and they work closely with the Chapter's Master of Relics – if such an officer exists within their Chapter's structure – to do this. The Master of Relics selects an honour guard for the Reclusiam made up of warriors from his company or the Chapter at large.

It is not unheard of for some Chapters to have scores, perhaps hundreds of investigatus analyticor helots poring over ancient lore, forgotten texts and fading after-action reports, searching for the slightest hint of knowledge as to where more relics might be discovered. They will pass on this information to teams of recovery acolytes – or even Space Marines – dispersed around the galaxy in the hunt for artefacts that tell of the Chapter's historic deeds.

In stark contrast to the deep care they take of their own Chapter's relics, Chaplains make it their task to topple xenos idols, cast down false prophets, purge heretical shrines and destroy heathen artefacts and lore. This they do with iron-hard conviction, exhorting their brothers to do the same.

The Chaplains themselves are the Chapter's spiritual authorities and wrathful warrior-priests. They are regarded with awed respect by their battle-brothers for their incredible strength of will and selfless dedication to the Chapter, as well as for their faultless knowledge of the Chapter's rites, catechisms and liturgies. They are notoriously fiery and strict, quickly roused to anger by the hated enemy and closely observant of every brother of the Chapter for lapses in devotion. For all their grim demeanour, Chaplains care deeply for the spiritual well-being of their brothers. Their booming oratory of the Chapter's tenets and dogmas is intended to armour their brothers from heresy and instil in them the humility, integrity and honour worthy of the Emperor's finest warriors and servants.

From the moment of his induction to the day of his death, a Space Marine will interact with a Chaplain on a daily basis. As an aspirant and neophyte, his spiritual and cultural training will be conducted by the Chaplaincy. As a fully fledged battle-brother, he will be led in prayer by and fight alongside his company's Chaplain, a most respected warrior, advisor and officer who accompanies his charges into the hell of battle again and again with inspiring, zealous fury.

Chaplains are as grim in appearance as they are in character. They wear skull-faced death masks and are clad in archaic, ornate armour the shade of blackest night, adorned with purity seals, devotional pendants and holy tokens of battle. Many wear thick chains, cloaks and heavy robes that billow with each purposeful step. Arguably the most distinctive of a Chaplain's badges of office is his crozius arcanum. A devastating type of power mace, it crackles with an intense disruption field. Combined with the Chaplain's great strength, it is a deadly weapon with which its wielder crushes skulls, shatters knees and caves in armour.

There are multiple ways by which a Space Marine can become a Chaplain, and these vary from Chapter to Chapter. Many Space Marines who have felt the calling to join the Chaplaincy follow the path of the Judiciar. They are given a mighty executioner relic blade and mysterious tempormortis – an archeotech relic incorporating esoteric stasis technology and filled with all manner of material spiritually important to the Chapter, such as sand from their home world. The Judiciar can use the tempormortis to direct stasis energy at his foes, seriously hampering their ability to fight. This device symbolises the Judiciar's need for patience as well as representing the need for them to earn their role. Judiciars are sworn to silence. It is their duty to embody their Chapter's values, forbidden to speak until they can live them, for any can simply recite litany and verse.

For all the deep reverence in which the Chapter's Reclusiam, mighty ship-based cathedrums and other places of sanctity are held, the battlefield is seen as no less of a place to honour Chapter and Primarch. Chaplains lead from the front, smashing aside foes as they recite litanies of death, invocations of slaughter and credenda of blood. Around them their brothers are inspired to righteous fury, roaring oaths of their own as they hack down enemies with chainswords and power axes, or blast them apart with bolt and plasma fire. To a great many Chaplains and Space Marines, there is no more devout offering to their spiritual lieges and no greater symbol of their dedication than mountainous piles of enemy dead.

THE ECCLESIARCHY AND THE ROSARIUS

Many of the Space Marines' traditions evolved long before the Adeptus Ministorum and the Imperial Creed. Though there are many theological differences between the Space Marines and the Ministorum, and the number and severity of these will vary depending on the Chapter, the primary disagreement revolves around the divinity of the Emperor. Space Marines revere him as a brilliant, inspired man. To the Adeptus Ministorum, the Emperor is a god. Many Chapters therefore disdain what they see as the fanatical ravings of the Ecclesiarchy in favour of their own ancient ways. Scant few Chapters, such as the Black Templars, have ever adopted the Ecclesiarchy's teachings on this matter.

Many in the Ministorum regard the Space Marines as dangerous heathens, but none can deny the Space Marines' dedication to the Emperor, their immense tally of mighty victories and that to some extent they share parts of their genetic heritage with the Emperor himself. Thus is there an uneasy truce between the two, only occasionally fractured by conflict. As a symbolic gesture of this peace, the Ecclesiarchy gifts Chaplains with the Rosarius. This amulet, taking many forms, emits a powerful force field that is sometimes referred to as 'soul armour'.

APOTHECARION

The Apothecarion is a Space Marine Chapter's most vital facility. On its metal medicae slabs neophytes are implanted with the organs that transform them into Space Marines, and those grievously wounded in battle receive life-saving treatment. Deeper within the Apothecarion the Chapter's gene-seed is held, and to the Apothecaries falls the honour of its safekeeping.

A Chapter's Apothecarion never sleeps, whether it be on the home world in its magnificent fortress monastery, or aboard its galaxy-traversing flagship. The aroma of antiseptics and disinfectants hangs thickly in the air, dispersed by lobotomised servo-meds or part-Human, part-machine cherubim swinging unwieldy censers. Dozens, if not hundreds of iron medicae-slabs are in use by Space Marine, aspirant and serf alike. Around them loom Apothecaries assisted by medicae serfs administering balms or carrying out detailed operations – aided by pneumatic servo-arms equipped with savage-looking surgical tools and operated by slaved machine spirits. Whether in the middle of a complex procedure, performing administrative duties or cleaning the blood from a surgical slab, med-helots intone endless chants of purity, healing and sterility. These gentle tones are frequently drowned out by the screeching of chirurgical drills, the screams of the wounded and the cracking of bones being re-set.

Adeptus Astartes Chapters are ever at war, the stream of wounded Space Marines and serfs in need of life-saving treatment never ending. A Chapter's constant recruitment methods ensure that there are always neophytes in need of organ implantation or surgery following the terrible injuries many suffer in their arduous training. Most Space Marines undergo periodic treatments, surgeries or therapies for their entire lives to maintain a stable metabolism, and for this they must go to the Apothecarion. Simply by their fragile Human nature, the tens of thousands of serfs that spend their lives working for a Chapter will become sick or injured in the course of carrying out their duties.

A Chapter's Apothecarion is where the bio-vaults containing the bulk of its gene-seed are stored, though many vessels will have the means to transport gene-seed safely and securely. This makes the Apothecarion one of the most vital locations in a fortress monastery, and often they are maintained at their very centre, constructed with additional armour and blast-absorbing walls. Should gene-seed reserves be in any way threatened by an enemy, all Space Marines in a Chapter will fight to the death in their defence – few with more vigour than the Apothecaries. During the Badab War, the Salamanders battle barge

NARTHECIUM

Apothecaries bear specialist wargear into the field to carry out their duties. Their primary tool is the narthecium, which is either built into a bulky gauntlet module or incorporated on articulated armatures that protrude from the wielder's backpack. Containing anti-venoms, healing agents and stimm packs – as well as having built-in surgical equipment and chainblades – this device can be used by the Apothecary to crack open armour, carry out transfusions, repair torn ligaments, plug holes in organs and close terrible wounds.

The narthecium also includes a pistol-like tool to give those too wounded to fight the Emperor's Peace. The Apothecary places this device at the Space Marine's temple and pulls the trigger. This drives a metal piston through the skull and into the brain, killing the Space Marine with little pain.

The chainblades and drills fitted into narthecium allow the Apothecary to crack open even Terminator armour to reach a fallen brother's progenoid glands. It is essential that these are recovered, as they contain vital gene-seed without which the Chapter cannot survive. For this the narthecium has a carbon-alloy reductor, a tool optimally designed for the extraction of progenoid glands quickly for secure storage in the narthecium's dedicated cryo-receptacle.

Other Chapters use their own variants of this equipment. Blood Angels Sanguinary Priests carry the Acus Placidus, a wrist-mounted pistol for euthanising those Blood Angels too seriously wounded to recover. The Space Wolves' Wolf Priests bear the Fang of Morkai, a multi-bladed tool, alongside a wide assortment of potions, balms and herbs.

Pyre of Glory was boarded by secessionist forces. Master Apothecary Harath Shen won renown defending the vessel's gene-seed vaults, hacking down traitor after traitor to preserve the legacy of his Chapter's fallen.

All gene-seed is examined closely on a regular basis for faults of any description, with any failing to meet the required standard being destroyed. Nevertheless, some Chapters are forced out of desperation to use gene-seed of lower quality, while a rare few even deliberately foster deformed zygotes and implant them into their aspirants. This is a highly dangerous practice, regarded as heretical by many. In the Era Indomitus, with so many Chapters cut off from much of the Imperium, no few will have resorted to this if they deemed it necessary. To catalogue the data accrued in the stringent examinations of their gene-seed, some Chapters maintain vast memory banks, which are used in the training of future Apothecaries. In a great many respects, the future of the Chapter is in the Apothecaries' hands.

Responsible for all the Apothecarion's wide array of essential tasks is the Chief Apothecary, whose exact title will vary from Chapter to Chapter. He is one of the Chapter's most senior officers and is highly respected for his deep knowledge of the Chapter's genetics, years of battlefield experience saving his battle-brothers' lives, and the due care for his Chapter's future he oversees with meticulous diligence.

Apothecaries-in-training are under the tutelage of the Chief Apothecary and serving Apothecaries. To acquire all the nuanced and detailed knowledge an Apothecary must have to perform even their most basic functions takes many years. Many serve as Helix Adepts in Infiltrator Squads, honing their skills in trying battlefield conditions deep behind enemy lines while utilising the helix gauntlet – a scaled down version of the narthecium.

A Codex-adherent Chapter has many dozens of Apothecaries. At least one of these individuals will serve in each company on a permanent basis, with the remainder carrying out the vital tasks of the Apothecarion, such as testing gene-seed and implanting organs into aspirants. Some Chapters assign Apothecaries on a permanent basis to their fleet vessels as a part of the ships' limited Space Marine crew; fleet-based Chapters are noted to rotate Apothecaries throughout their ships to ensure that – even in the event of a catastrophic defeat in the cold depths of the void – the skills of the Apothecaries will live on.

Apothecaries are trained warriors, as adept with bolter and blade as the battle-brothers they accompany on the field. They have to be, for there is nowhere their charges go that they must not. Should a Space Marine fall it is the Apothecaries' solemn, proud duty to restore them to health or recover their gene-seed. Whilst they may never attain accolades for great victories won or enemies cast down, every battle-brother holds the Apothecaries in the highest regard for the dangers they face to reach casualties. It is a great demonstration of a Chapter's deep sense of comradeship in action.

The cultures of many Chapters have impacted on the workings of their Apothecaries. Those of the Fire Lords master the arts of cauterisation, knowing how to apply the perfect level of heat for the right duration to heal different wounds. Those of the fleet-based Rift Stalkers, often operating in enemy territory and far from Imperial supply lines, have little access to standard resources, and as such are expert improvisers.

Pain and death are illusions of the weak mind. While his gene-seed returns to the Chapter, a Space Marine cannot die. Without death, pain loses its relevance.

He that may fight, heal him.

He that may fight no more, give him peace.

He that is dead, take from him the Chapter's due.

LIBRARIUS

The Librarius is one of a Space Marine Chapter's most mysterious institutions. Its members are the Librarians, warrior-mystics and scholars who have spent decades mastering their psychic talent to lend their Chapter great wisdom as well as fearsome power in battle.

Behind locked doors warded with pentagrammic and hexagrammic symbols, the Librarius thrums with strange activity. Strange lights flash out of the cracks beneath heavy wooden doors. Hideous screams echo down dark corridors whose walls are etched with arcane symbols of shielding and containment. Serfs and scribes shuffle hurriedly about their tasks, clutching tokens and sigils of safeguarding and whispering chants of obviation with their eyes fixed on the floor. In sealed chambers the Space Marine Librarians see to their duties. Some sit in reflective meditation. Others scry the skeins of fate, beads of sweat falling down faces twisted in effort and concentration. Some fight

in practice cages, blasting apart servitors and targets with bolts of psychic power or striking them down with psychically attuned blades and axes. They must train constantly to ensure the strength of their willpower, for their greatest foes – the foul abominations of the warp – are ever watchful for weakness.

One of the functions of the Librarius is the recording of the Chapter's history. Depending on a Librarian's rank, their precise role in this regard will differ. Lexicaniums, the first rank after a Librarian has qualified, write reports of battles and wars. The Codiciers, those of the second rank, carefully scrutinise every entry into the archives. Those

who pass through these ranks become Epistolaries. The knowledge and wisdom Librarians accrue makes their counsel highly sought after, and so most strike forces include a Librarian.

By far the largest facilities in the Librarius are its vast archives, where the Chapter's recorded history is stored. Shelving units fill rooms from floor to ceiling, each stacked with ancient vellum tomes and parchment scrolls. Besides them are humming repositories and archaic catalogues full of data crystals. Hundreds of serfs toil day and night, copying from decaying codicils and tracts lest any information be lost. Only the most senior Librarians have any

'Acolytum, we of the Librarius are unique in our power, unique in our strength and unique in our vulnerability. Thus, our tools of war must be unique. We are truly blessed by the weapons we wield and that which protects our minds.

The galaxy is plagued by the Emperor's myriad foes – countless traitors, xenos and heretics. The foulness of the warp suffuses many of them with its fell power, which they will attempt to use against us. Thus we don the psychic hood. With its psionic baffles, null circuits and empyric siphons are we ever shielded from the foul witchery of our enemies.

The efficacy of the force sword, stave and axe demonstrates clearly the power of our wrath. Through them do we channel our fury, our hatred of the foe. Through their crystalline matrices does our strength flow, and with them do we lay low our enemies.'

- Epistolary Agorus Telorian of the Ultramarines

true idea of what their archives hold, or what lies behind the locked portals of their most secure areas – and even these vastly knowledgeable individuals have only a reasonable understanding of the rest of the archive. Huge quantities of information can be lost for millennia, or even forever, through sheer ignorance of its existence. Few Chapters have a complete collection of their history.

Another of the Librarians' essential functions is to screen the Chapter's aspirants for the weak-willed and those with psychic potential. They must be merciless, for to permit any weakness is to threaten the Chapter and its gene-seed with corruption. Those recruits displaying both psychic potential and the strength necessary to become Space Marines will be taken directly under the Librarians' wing to learn their arcane crafts. Other potential Librarians are sourced elsewhere, including the Scholastica Psykana. Those selected, known as Acolytum, undergo a process more arduous than even that of their brother Space Marines. They must survive the trials, training and implantations to become Space Marines, as well as learn to master their psychic gifts and protect their minds from the terrible hazards of the warp. If they fail, a fate worse than death awaits in the clutches of the immaterium's malignant entities. Such are the dangers involved with these practices that some Chapters refuse to include a Librarius in their Chapter. The Black Templars and a handful of other Chapters forbid the use of psychic arts, seeing them as blasphemous. Some Chapters tolerate their Librarians only as a necessary evil, shunning their psyker brothers as much as possible. A number embrace their Librarius wholeheartedly, such as the Blood Ravens and Silver Skulls.

Over their lives the Librarians will master myriad psychic disciplines and other subtle skills. They will learn to manipulate raging infernos with the slightest hand gestures, turn the nightmares of their foes into horrifying reality, detect the movements of Daemons through warp space and read the Emperor's Tarot. A trained Librarian can sense the shock waves and turbulence of starships arriving

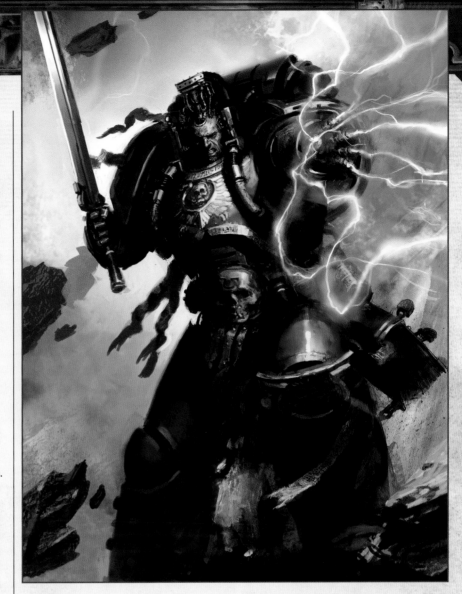

in a system from the insanity of warp space, or detect the echoes they leave from plunging into its depths. The powers of the Chapter's Chief Librarian, its most senior psyker, are truly formidable.

Librarians are as vigilant for weakness in their own number as well as the rest of the Chapter. They scour the minds of their battle-brothers, taking careful record of every deviancy, however minor. It pains many to scrutinise their brothers in such a way, but purity of mind is something that a Chapter cannot compromise on. The Librarians subject those Space Marines who have suffered particularly intense psychic trauma at the hands of nefarious xenos races or the blasphemous forces of Chaos to meticulous screening and

cleansing. The principal reason for this is to ensure the purity of the Chapter's gene-seed, for it may become corrupted, and the Librarians work closely with the Apothecarion to eradicate weakness wherever it is found.

Librarians are far more than battle-psykers. They identify other psykers, ensuring hidden threats are rendered visible. The skills of the Epistolaries in particular enable them to communicate across interstellar space in the same manner as the Astropaths of the Adeptus Astra Telepathica. They are so powerful they have no need to undertake the torturous Soul Binding ritual to do so – though to attempt such a message is enormously taxing and has been known to kill those who attempt it.

ARMOURY

Whether aboard a colossal, starfaring warship or deep within its mountainous fortress monastery, a Chapter's Armoury is where the great majority of its armoured vehicles, gunships, weapons and wargear are maintained and tended to when they are not being unleashed upon the Emperor's foes.

The Armoury is both a branch of the Chapter hierarchy and a physical location. Headed by uncanny and knowledgeable Masters of the Forge, the Chapter's Techmarines all belong to the Armoury and are responsible for thousands of serfs and servitors. Their task is to ensure that the Chapter's wargear and weaponry are repaired and their machine spirits placated so that they are ready to face the enemy in future conflicts.

Whilst every Chapter's Armoury is different in form, structure and size, they share many common traits. Each is a vast complex of immense forge-furnaces, cells and alcoves, lit by crackling braziers and cold lumen. Servo-skulls, formed from the craniums of favoured Chapter serfs upon their death and affixed with precision servo-tools or bearing important messages, fly through the air. Service to the Chapter rarely ends in death.

Each of a Chapter's vehicles and warsuits has its own antechamber that is a shrine in itself, adorned with purity seals and vows of fidelity and devotion scratched by serfs onto scraps of parchment. Every Space Marine vehicle is given a name upon its induction to the Chapter to reflect its role as a warrior, and is embraced as a battle-brother itself. Its alcove is adorned with trophies and relics from the battles it has fought in, the Space Marines it has fought alongside laying down the skulls of slaughtered foes or the sanctified weapons of enemy champions.

Thousands of serfs, techno-thralls, mecha-helots and servitors labour day and night in the scorching heat of the Armoury, all caked in ash, drenched in sweat and stained with oils. Such is the thickness of the smog and sacred incense in the air, even servitors are regularly replaced, their mechanical systems clogged and biological components choked. Human serfs breathe recycled air through rebreathers, though even this equipment fails to protect them from all of the particulates that blacken the air. The reek of burning metal, lapping powders and blessed oils add to the heavy and cloying stench. The serfs' lifespans are rendered measurably shorter than their fellows working for the Chapter elsewhere, and these labourers are often prone to terrible injuries in their work – such is the wrath of the machine spirits not treated with due care.

TECHMARINE WARGEAR

The unique role of the Techmarines means they carry bespoke wargear. No Techmarine goes to war without heavy servo-arms and supple mechadendrites. These are powerful mechanical tools with the strength to lift entire battle tanks off the ground, or with the dexterity to deftly fix the smallest components and solder shut the most minute of wounds in a vehicle's flank. Some Techmarines wear a formidable servo-harness. With a pair of servo-arms, a flamer and a plasma cutter, the servo-harness enables the wearer to fix vehicles more efficiently and better combat the foe. It also enables them to rapidly construct or reinforce defensive positions. It is not uncommon for Techmarines to carry grav pistols. In the 41st Millennium, grav weapon technology is rare, known only to a select few. When fired, grav weapons affect the local gravity field, using the victim's own mass against them to lethal effect. Heavily armoured targets are crushed as if by a mighty god, whilst vehicles are left as crumpled wrecks.

The barrage on the senses is made complete by a cacophony of industrial workings and intoned sacred rites. The clang of piston hammers striking sheet metal rings through vaulted chambers. The curt orders of the Techmarines are barely audible over the roar of adamantine grinders and plasma cutters. All this is set against the sonic backdrop of constantly droning servitors – endlessly repeating binharic chants of reverence – and the serfs' liturgies of dedication.

TECHMARINES

The Adeptus Astartes and Adeptus Mechanicus hold ancient pacts. Chapters may send those of their number most at one with technology to Mars, to learn the ways of the machine. During their long and arduous training they are inducted into the machine cult. They learn the hymnals of maintenance, the liturgies of resanctification, and rites of appeasement and awakening. If no Space Marines did this, it would be impossible for Chapters to make war, for soon their weapons, wargear and battle tanks would fall into disrepair.

Those who return from the Red Planet do so as Techmarines, now aloof from their brothers. They develop dual loyalties to the machine cult of Mars as well as their Chapter, but nevertheless fight bravely for their brotherhood, and their skills and knowledge are regarded highly. Techmarines' proficiency as drivers, gunners and pilots is especially recognised – once they have interfaced with a vehicle's machine spirit, the bond formed is lethally effective.

MASTER OF THE FORGE

The Master of the Forge is the most senior Techmarine in the Chapter. His grasp of arcane sciences and the mysteries of the Omnissiah are such that his skills are on par with those of Martian tech-magi. He calms the most belligerent of machine spirits with but a whisper of a tech-psalm, and can heal terrible wounds in a battle tank's hull at incredible speed. As with the Techmarine brethren they command, Masters of the Forge are regarded with a degree of mistrust by Chapter Command, with some shunned on matters unrelated to their specialisation. In Chapters such as the Iron Hands and Astral Knights, which are more embracing of the mysteries of technology, they are revered individuals. These exceptions are relatively few, however some Masters of the Forge earn admirable reputations.

SERVITORS

A Space Marine Chapter has thousands of these biomechanical slaves. Whether they are vat-grown in artificial nutrients, or created from failed aspirants or mind-wiped and lobotomised criminals, they are fitted with an array of mechanical tools to carry out the Chapter's work. Many have limbs replaced with infrared sensors, bionic exoskeletons, huge claws, flux-torsion drills or even heavy weapons. Servitors are made resilient by their modifications, though their minds are utterly unfeeling and incapable of coherent, independent thought. Without the guidance of a Techmarine they become mindlocked, babbling incoherent nonsense until given instructions.

DREADNOUGHTS

The Dreadnought epitomises the Space Marines' commitment to service and fighting the enemies of the Emperor. Each is piloted by a hero of the Chapter who is so grievously wounded that only the esoteric, life-extending technologies within the Dreadnought's armoured sarcophagus could preserve his life. Inside, little remains of the interred Space Marine but shrivelled biological components sloshing in life-giving fluids. Such an existence shatters the sanity of even the strongest-minded warriors, and as such they slumber for centuries at a time, preserved only for the battles in which the Chapter needs them most. As they sleep, the sepulchres in the Armoury that houses Dreadnoughts are regarded as sacred shrines, and Techmarines delicately anoint them with sacred balms and oils on a daily basis. Dreadnoughts are highly revered by their brothers for their wisdom and strength, and some Space Marines attend them to pay their respects.

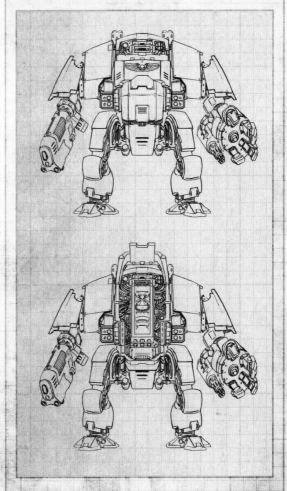

Honoured brother, long may you serve. May your wisdom ever guide us, may your hate ever bring death to our enemies.

BATTLE TANKS

A Space Marine Chapter has a formidable array of fighting vehicles, each holding a particular battlefield role laid down in the Codex Astartes that enable the Adeptus Astartes to dominate any battlefield. Each Space Marine vehicle is given a name upon its creation, and is regarded as a battle-brother by its Chapter. Though many Space Marine vehicles are designed so they can be customised with different weapons, once they have been fitted with their armaments they are rarely modified, the machine spirit growing used to and protective of its wargear. A great many vehicles in use by the Adeptus Astartes are thousands of years old, prized veterans known for their aggression or deep hatred of a particular foe.

Many Space Marine armoured assets are built on the rugged and reliable Rhino chassis. Predators are main battle tanks. Whirlwinds fire barrages of explosive or incendiary missiles. Vindicators are devastating siege tanks, whilst Hunters and Stalkers blast squadrons of enemy air assets out of the sky. Thanks to the Rhino platform, all are manoeuvrable enough to keep pace with the relentless Space Marine advance and are simple to repair for the Techmarines.

Land Raiders are mobile fortresses with a design dating back to times of myth and legend. In addition to formidable weaponry and nigh-impenetrable ceramite and adamantine armour, their machine spirits are far more potent than those of other vehicles. Thus, fewer crew are required in comparison to similar-sized vehicles, and the machine spirit can take control of the Land Raider's engines and weapons – some have been known to operate the tank even after their crew have all been killed.

Thanks to powerful anti-grav technology and turbine engines, gravitic battle tanks can traverse trench lines, boiling lava streams and treacherous waterways with impunity. These technologies are also weapons in their own right – the crew can direct pulses of gravitic force through their vehicle's ventral plates to knock foes to the ground. Different gravitic tanks have a range of sophisticated features. The Repulsor Executioner sacrifices transport space for additional capacitors, plasma cells and ballistic cogitators. The Impulsor's vectored thrusters allow it to reach much greater speeds, and its chassis is highly adaptable, capable of being fitted with all manner of upgrades.

Techmarines and Techmarine novitiates commonly pilot Space Marine gunships and battle tanks – their natural affinity for the machine suits them well to this role.

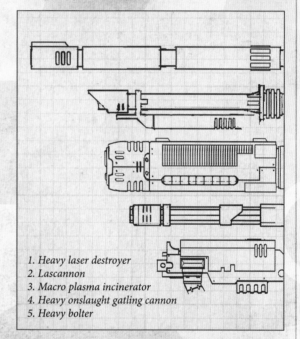

1. Heavy laser destroyer
2. Lascannon
3. Macro plasma incinerator
4. Heavy onslaught gatling cannon
5. Heavy bolter

An honoured crew member may be paired with his vehicle even in death, his skull mounted on the interior walls alongside lists of his heroic deeds.

Space Marine vehicles are awarded accolades and campaign badges just as the battle-brothers are. Crews adorn their tanks with these awards.

Few Space Marine transports are without relics and trinkets of great spiritual value. Such artefacts inspire battle-brothers as they race to war.

The Storm Speeder was developed as a part of Cawl's Primaris project, combining Arkhan Land's ancient discoveries with the uncompromising brute force of Repulsor technology. Though closely resembling the Land Speeder and performing a similar function, Storm Speeders are larger and more heavily armed without compromising on manoeuvrability.

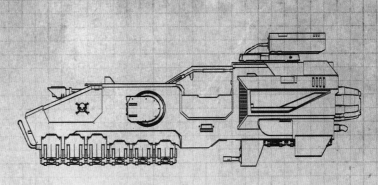

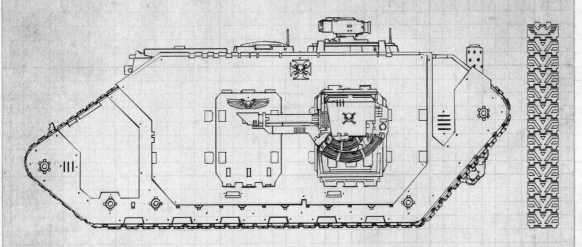

It is thought that Land Raiders were once made in enormous numbers. In the 41st Millennium, however, few forge worlds can produce them. Their scarcity and power make them highly valued, and the Techmarines believe a part of the Omnissiah's essence resides within them.

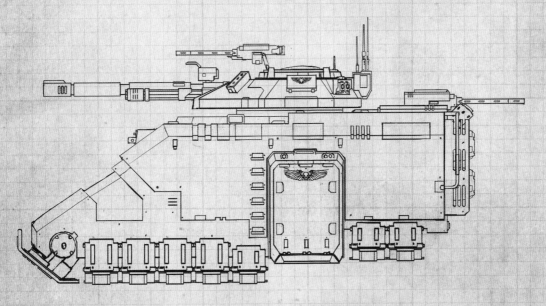

Repulsor Executioners are as adept at serving as armoured escorts for dedicated troop carriers as they are at transporting Hellblasters and other specialised squads. In either capacity, the heavy weapons of the infantry and battle tank make a lethal combination.

SPACE MARINE ARMOUR

Space Marines wage war clad in some of the finest armour in the Imperium. Suits of power armour are fully enclosed, made of thick ceramite plates and have electrically motivated fibre bundles that replicate the movements of the wearer and supplement his strength. Rather than simply being worn, a Space Marine's armour integrates with him. It can take many decades to forge a single suit of power armour, and each is maintained with absolute care and devotion by skilled Chapter serfs or even the Space Marines themselves. Each suit is a unique artefact with a spirit and history deeply valued by its Chapter.

Power armour has a range of auxiliary systems that improve the Space Marine's effectiveness, including auto-senses made up of thought-activated comms-augurs, audio filters, targeting reticules and numerous other features. Life support functions include pain suppressors, combat stimulants and anti-venoms. Reinforced greaves incorporate gyroscopic stabilisers and power units that magnetise the soles of the armour's boots.

Primaris Space Marines wear Mk X armour. This highly flexible protective system can be modified and upgraded to suit the needs of the battlefield. Mk X Tacticus is the most common variant, and is worn by Intercessors, among others. Mk X Phobos armour is lighter and heavily streamlined. With greater mobility and servo-motors engineered to be silent, it is used most optimally in stealth and infiltration missions. The Mk X Gravis variant may be bulky but is enormously sturdy, allowing the wearer to stride into the most furious firestorms and emerge unscathed.

SPACE MARINE WEAPONS

The foes of the Adeptus Astartes are myriad; thus are the Space Marines equipped with a vast array of different weapons. They include mass reactive round-firing bolt weapons, flame weapons that spew burning liquid promethium, auto weapons that fire deluges of high-velocity shot, grav weapons that affect local gravity, and melta weapons that liquidise heavy armour in moments. The Space Marines have many other kinds of weapons.

Plasma weapons work by energising photonic hydrogen fuel into a plasma state and firing it through a magnetic accelerator. On impact with the target the energy released is like that of a small sun, destroying with searing heat and explosive shock. Plasma weapons have different settings to increase their power, but are incredibly dangerous to the wielder thanks to the enormous amount of energy the armaments have to contain.

Las weapons emit a short-lasting beam of highly focused light that causes a rapid increase in the target's temperature when struck. Each shot results in a distinctive crack as the beam ionises the air. Firing pinpoint beams, las weapons must be used with great precision. The largest versions of these weapons are devastating against battle tanks and vehicles.

Missile launchers are highly versatile. The Space Marines utilise armour-breaking krak missiles with shaped charges, sky-clearing flakk missiles and frag missiles that rain shrapnel upon impact. Those used by skyspear missile launchers house interred remains of favoured Chapter serfs, their mummified brains aiding the weapon's auto-targeters.

SPACE MARINE WARSUITS

The Invictor Tactical Warsuit is a stripped down version of the Redemptor Dreadnought chassis. Instead of being piloted by a fallen hero of the Chapter, it is instead crewed by a Space Marine clad in Phobos armour. The Invictor's systems are plugged into the armour inloads of the pilot, ensuring the machine spirit is joined in binharic choral harmony with the warrior's autosenses. The Warsuit becomes an extension of the Space Marine himself, affording him significant strength, firepower and resilience vital to the far-ranging missions of Vanguard strike forces. Warsuit pilots are selected specifically with this goal in mind, and are swift and independent in thought while exhibiting a carefully protective attitude. Combined with considerable tactical autonomy, Invictors act as mobile bulwarks and line breakers.

Centurion Warsuits protect the wearer with thick ablative ceramite plates, and the powerful exoskeleton ensures that they can be fitted with the most powerful infantry-borne weapons.

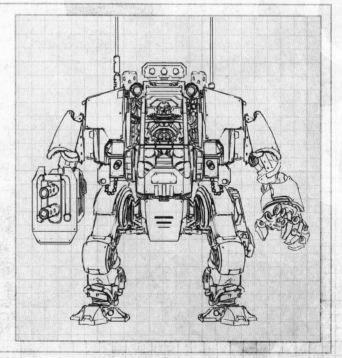

THEOD OF THE GOLDEN HALOS

At the Battle for Saint Pelagion, the cardinal world where the Golden Halos Chapter fought sadistic Drukhari raiders, Brother Theod went to battle equipped as a member of an Infiltrator Squad. Theod carried numerous weapons, all easily accessible in combat. These included the grenades attached to his chest straps, the dagger-shaped icon at his hip and the marksman bolt carbine slung over his shoulder.

Like many Space Marines, Theod has applied numerous embellishments to his armour. These are in addition to the Chapter icon he bears on his left pauldron and the vertical arrow symbol on his right pauldron, which indicates that he is a member of a battleline squad.

He has handwritten battle-oaths on the inset of the left shoulder pad in the script of his home world, Sacratis, as well as the Chapter's motto in High Gothic: 'Ex Ungue Leonem', or 'Judge the Lion by his Claws'. A single skull is illustrated on his right shoulder pad. This is in memoriam Anast, his squad brother who was slain in an earlier clash on Saint Pelagion. Each check painstakingly illuminated on the right shoulder pad represents a single slain enemy. By the end of the campaign, every unadorned area on the entire pad was marked in this way.

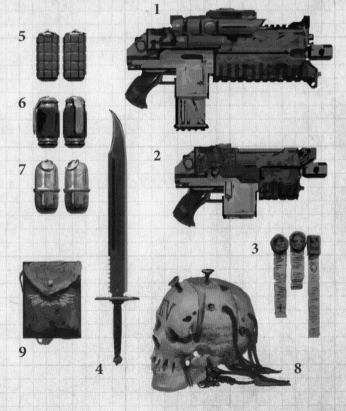

1. **Marksman bolt carbine:** Primary weapon, called Longclaw.

2. **Bolt pistol:** Sidearm, used in close-quarters fighting. Named as Hidden Roar.

3. **Purity seals:** Theod bears proof that his armour and weapons have undergone all fifty-three sanctification rituals.

4. **Combat knife:** Monomolecular edge. Serrated section. Called Smyladon.

5. **Frag grenades:** Anti-personnel weapons, explode into thousands of shards.

6. **Smoke grenades:** Emit thick chemical obscurant, provide concealment from enemy fire.

7. **Krak grenades:** Destroy armoured targets with a concentrated implosive blast.

8. **Skull:** Theod carries the skull of his birth brother, who died as a neophyte. This serves as a reminder of guilt, of the consequences of failure and as a spur to fight on through great adversity.

9. **Pouch:** Additional magazines of ammunition for both Theod's firearms are stored in pouches at his waist.

WAR ZONE: SITHOZA

HALTMOAT

SITHOZA

CALIXIS SECTOR

DRACONITH

THE EYE OF TERROR

MEDUSA

As the war for Vigilus grew in ferocity and significance, more and more Space Marine Chapters sought to deploy warriors there. Some wished to win glory on a famed battlefield, others sought penance for past misdeeds, and many drew upon deep reserves of hatred for the forces of Chaos.

Strike forces from several Chapters – the Imperial Fists, Black Templars, Mantis Warriors, Raven Guard and Fire Lords – converged at the Simiun Plateau, a region of space of surprising calm in the Imperium Nihilus and but a handful of short warp jumps from Vigilus. The Navigators of their war-worn vessels had each led them there, desperate for rest. Through sheer geographical accident a significant force had gathered. All found this to their benefit; combined they would be a hammer blow against the forces of Chaos that threatened the Nachmund Gauntlet.

Despite the Space Marines' relative numerical strength, many months of campaigning had significantly reduced their supplies of fuel and ammunition. Thus they travelled to the Sithoza System, where they could resupply at the hive world of Torikev. Upon their arrival, and without warning, defensive laser cannons opened fire on them. The Mantis Warriors hunter destroyer *Ootheca's Lament* was cut in half by the searing bolts. The Black Templars strike cruiser *His Will Be Done* detonated after its warp drive took a direct hit. The resulting explosion severely damaged the Raven Guard gladius ships *Sable Liberator* and *Shadow Claw*.

The Space Marines responded immediately, loosening the fleet's battle formation. Their vox networks were subject to a barrage of traitorous babble from all three of Sithoza's worlds. They screamed of the Imperium's doom, the end of Mankind and the glory of false gods. But among them were a handful of cries for aid from embattled Imperial forces. Regiments of Iat Mountainmen faced off against hordes of daemons summoned by the world's tribes. Preceptories of Battle Sisters held firm on Hediarth, attempting valiantly to quash rebellion after rebellion. Torikev's entire planetary leadership had fallen to heresy, and with each passing hour more and more pockets of Imperial resistance were snuffed out. The Space Marines surmised that such an important system turning against the Imperium was no coincidence. Abaddon's agents were no doubt making it all but impossible for Imperial relief forces to reach Vigilus from elsewhere in the Imperium Nihilus. The Sithoza System had to be wrested back from heretic control.

The Mantis Warriors made for Iat to relieve the Iat Mountainmen in a Drop Pod assault. The Black Templars raced to Hediarth to aid the Adepta Sororitas. On Torikev the Raven Guard began a shadow war, assassinating cult leaders and key heretic overseers. By making essential factorums vulnerable in this way, the heavy siege forces of the Imperial Fists and Fire Lords could capture them with ease and finally turn the tide.

SPACE MARINES OF WAR ZONE SITHOZA

The war for the Sithoza System was one the Space Marine Chapters fighting it were not prepared for. Battered by previous campaigns and low on supplies of all kinds, they thundered to battle in dropship and Drop Pod regardless.

IMPERIAL FISTS

SIEGEBREAKER COHORT 'ANTORUS'
Brother Vysach......................Ironclad Dreadnought
'Boreas' .... close support (Centurion Assault) squad
'Carnak' ... close support (Centurion Assault) squad
'Lohr' .... close support (Centurion Assault) squad

1ST COMPANY
'Jago'.............................. Veteran (Terminator) squad
'Hesp' .... Veteran (Relic Terminator) squad

2ND COMPANY
'Issus' ....battleline (Heavy Intercessor) squad
'Gorean' ....battleline (Heavy Intercessor) squad
'Maxim' ....fire support (Eradicator) squad
'Thane' .... fire support (Aggressor) squad

RAVEN GUARD

STRIKE FORCE 'SYRAS'
'Aevar'.......................... Veteran (Sternguard) squad
'Dariyan'......................battleline (Infiltrator) squad
'Phryn'......................battleline (Infiltrator) squad
'Orlos'.....................close support (Incursor) squad
'Kylo'.......................close support (Incursor) squad

BLACK TEMPLARS

THE UTERECHT CRUSADE
'Bharros' .... Sword Brethren Terminator Squad
'Atar'......Sword Brethren Terminator Assault Squad
'Torvoch' ....Crusader Squad
'Heoth' ....Crusader Squad
'Visaldus' ....Crusader Squad
'Theud' ....Crusader Squad
Brother Haldrac .... Dreadnought
Brother Orthuld................................... Dreadnought
'Sigismund's Hammer' ....Vindicator squadron
'Abvald'...Repulsor squadron
'The Orkbanes' .... Gladiator Reaper squadron

FIRE LORDS

BURNING SPEAR TASK FORCE 'IGNIS'
'World Scorchers'.......... Gladiator Valiant squadron
'III' ....Gladiator Lancer squadron
'Malakye' .... Stormhawk Interceptor
'Infernopike' ....Firestrike Servo-turret
'Kindis' ....batteline (Intercessor) squad
'Calkine' ....battleline (Tactical) squad
'Davon' ....batteline (Intercessor) squad

MANTIS WARRIORS

4TH COMPANY
'Atharid'.............................Company Veterans squad
'Borani'...........................battleline (Tactical) squad
'Sarus' ....battleline (Intercessor) squad
'Vitamar' ....battleline (Intercessor) squad
'Suatris' .... close support (Assault) squad
'Vandil' .... fire support (Hellblaster) squad
Brother Galindo.................Venerable Dreadnought

++ WHILST THIS DATA WAS COLLECTED IN THE IMPERIUM NIHILUS, AND IS THEREFORE UNRELIABLE AT BEST, THERE ARE FEATURES OF NOTE. THE FIRST IS THE BLACK TEMPLARS' SQUAD DESIGNATIONS, SWORD BRETHREN AND CRUSADER SQUAD IN PARTICULAR. THESE DO NOT ALIGN WITH ANY OF THE FOURTEEN VERSIONS OF THE CODEX ASTARTES WE HAVE BEEN ABLE TO SECURE. THE SECOND IS THE VARIABLE NAMING CONVENTION OF THE FIRE LORDS' VEHICLE SQUADRONS – ONE HAS YET TO EARN OR BE GIVEN A NAME OF ANY KIND, A NUMBER IN ITS PLACE. MULTIPLE OBSERVED CHAPTERS DO SIMILAR. ++

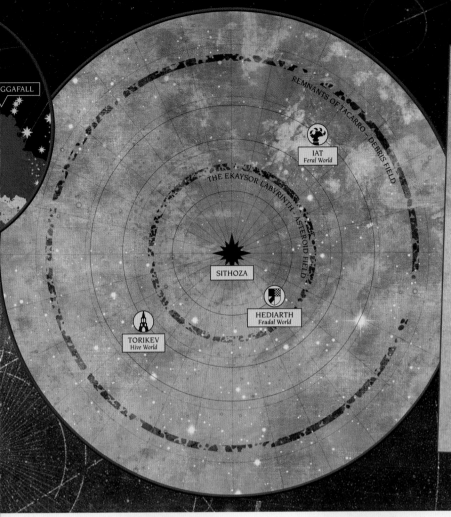

REMNANTS OF TACARRO - DEBRIS FIELD

GGAFALL

IAT
Feral World

THE EKAYSOR LABYRINTH ASTEROID FIELD

SITHOZA

HEDIARTH
Feudal World

TORIKEV
Hive World

Brother Kamar, Fire Lords 5th Company, 5th Squad. Slain in honour during the capture of Torikev's primary manufactorum complex. Seriously wounded, he fought on for five days, claiming over two thousand enemy lives.

Initiate Danatar Foth of the 6th, 'Uterecht', Crusade. First to establish contact with the Adepta Sororitas defenders of the Shrine of Saint Locrezzia; fought alongside the Order of the Burning Light for seven weeks.

Each Black Templars crusade bears its own unique seal, most frequently depicted on a shield of varying design. Every element used, from the symbols to the colours, has a range of interpretations and is carefully chosen.

An unprotected soul can no more cross the storms of the warp than a heretic can bear the gaze of an Inquisitor.

ULTRAMARINES

THE SONS OF GUILLIMAN

The Ultramarines epitomise what it means to be Adeptus Astartes. They are beacons of nobility, honour and discipline in a galaxy riven by darkness and disorder. No Chapter holds the Codex Astartes in such hallowed regard as they, and they have utilised its tenets and strategies to achieve glorious victories over ten thousand years.

Few, if any Chapters can match the efficiency, speed and skill with which the Ultramarines apply their deep learning of the Codex's tactics and strategies. On countless battlefields the Ultramarines have outwitted, outfought and outmanoeuvred their enemies, striking repeatedly with gene-wrought might until the foe is utterly vanquished.

The Ultramarines live and breathe the Codex Astartes. For ten millennia have they learned and practised its teachings, paying close attention to the most minute of details. Many Ultramarines can recite swathes of the text by heart, as well as produce lengthy treatises demonstrating a full understanding of its teachings.

They have quashed heretic uprisings, swept aside piratical raids of murderous Drukhari, purged verminous Hrud infestations and shattered voracious Tyranid invasions. They have won

victories for the ages in scorching deserts, stifling jungles, labyrinthine ruined cities and even in the depths of oceans. These they have achieved in horrific sieges, gruelling guerrilla warfare and armoured conflicts of such a scale that the wreckage fields can be seen from orbit.

The Ultramarines' home world is Macragge. A bastion of civilisation, learning and culture, it has been their base of operations since their Primarch, Roboute Guilliman, was united there with the Emperor during the Great Crusade. Heavily fortified, it is the jewel in the crown that is the Ultramarines' stellar empire, known as Ultramar. This grouping of worlds and systems pays no tithe to Terra, their resources dedicated to supporting the Ultramarines. Nonetheless, such is the skill with which this region is organised, Ultramar is able to provide troops and materiel for the aid of the beleaguered Imperium.

The Ultramarines shattered Hive Fleet Behemoth in the First Tyrannic War, many of the Chapter's greatest heroes losing their lives to halt the xenos' fury. They clashed with the Black Legion Heretic Astartes within the walls of the Fortress of Hera, their own fortress monastery, fighting with peerless zeal. All the vile might of Nurgle's Plague Legions and Mortarion's disease-ridden ranks of Death Guard have not been enough to break the Ultramarines, no matter the fell diseases and maladies thrown at them. As large and as powerful as Ultramar is, this makes it a prize hungered after by some of the Imperium's deadliest enemies, and the Ultramarines have been forced to fiercely defend it many times.

The Ultramarines are commanded by some of the greatest Space Marines in the Imperium. Marneus Calgar, the Chapter Master, is a superlative warrior and talented strategist. Long is his list of

ROBOUTE GUILLIMAN

When the Primarchs were taken from the Emperor and scattered across the galaxy, the capsule containing Roboute Guilliman landed on the world of Macragge. He was adopted by a wealthy ruling family, and his immense physical and mental powers soon became apparent. He consumed all forms of knowledge and wisdom with insatiable voraciousness, absorbing science and philosophy with ease, and developing an unparalleled talent for war and its organisation. Crushing savage tribes and insidious rebellions, he eventually became Macragge's sole ruler. Under his leadership it, and the local worlds with which it had been able to keep in contact with through Old Night, flourished. Trade boomed, Macragge's armies were made mighty and their fortifications strong. Few citizens went without, all experiencing a time of plenty unlike any in Macragge's history.

When the Emperor arrived, legend tells that Guilliman bowed the knee immediately. The XIII Legion, the force of Space Marines genetically derived from Roboute Guilliman, was assigned to the Primarch. With him at their head, the Ultramarines conquered vast swathes of space and became the largest of the Legions by some margin. During the terror of the Horus Heresy, the Word Bearers and World Eaters Legions mauled the Ultramarines in ferocious fighting across Ultramar. Such was the delay this caused that Guilliman could not reach Terra before Horus' siege of the Throneworld was defeated. In the wars that followed, known as the Scouring, Guilliman was wounded unto death by the Daemon Primarch Fulgrim. To preserve him his sons put him into stasis, where he remained for ten thousand years. It was only during the Imperium's darkest hour that fate conspired to see him restored.

victories – he crushed the Orks in the Siege of Zalathras, defeated an Aeldari Avatar at the Battle of Orar's Sepulchre and led the masterful defence of Vigilus, engaging Abaddon the Despoiler himself in single combat. Tigurius is the Ultramarines' Chief Librarian, a battle-psyker and warrior-scholar of formidable intellect and insight whose word is of greater value than armies of spies, strategists and tacticians. Ortan Cassius, the Master of Sanctity, is the Ultramarines' oldest living Space Marine. It was he who established the Ultramarines' Tyrannic War Veterans and has made it his personal mission to see the Tyranids erased from existence.

It has not gone unnoticed amongst the Imperium's highest echelons that – despite being the author of the Codex Astartes and the loudest voice for the breaking up of the huge Space Marine Legions in the very distant past – Roboute Guilliman is now the only individual in the Imperium capable of commanding the loyalty of so vast a force of arms. A great many of the Ultramarines' successor Chapters regard him as their spiritual liege. Even those that have strayed from the teachings of the Codex to some degree, or have embraced their home world's culture more, hold him in the highest regard. Those who are particularly learned believe that the combined strength of the Ultramarines' successors may well exceed that of the Ultramarines Legion at the height of the Great Crusade. Of course, no such comments are made to the Lord Commander of the Imperium in person, and little in his absence, in the event his agents hear. What Guilliman thinks of this is unknown to all but the risen Primarch himself, but an individual of such awe-inspiring intellect is unlikely to have missed such a detail.

Despite these concerns, the overwhelming view held in the Imperium is a simple one: the Ultramarines and their successors have served the Imperium, the Emperor, and all Mankind with honour and loyalty for millennia, and continue to do so. With Humanity under threat from all sides, such forces are vital to the Human race's very survival.

'We are the Ultramarines, the sons of Guilliman. Whilst we draw breath, we stand. Whilst we stand, we fight. Whilst we fight, we prevail. Nothing shall stay our wrath.'

- Chapter Master Marneus Calgar

We march for Macragge!

White Consuls

The White Consuls value wise governance and vision as much as martial skill. In order to advance to higher rank, the Chapter's battle-brothers must therefore act as local consulate rulers of Imperial worlds. In the wake of the Great Rift's opening, their Chapter Planet – Sabatine – was consumed by a warp storm, yet much of their number escaped. The White Consuls now seek a new world from which to rebuild their greatness.

Libators

The Libators are amongst the more brutal and uncompromising of the scions of Guilliman. Their name stems from their practice of letting their foes' blood and dedicating it as an offering to the Primarch and the Emperor both. The Chapter has faced censure on several occasions for its treatment of captive enemy commanders and champions, who, in the Libators' eyes, make for the worthiest offerings.

Genesis Chapter

The Genesis Chapter has the proud distinction of being first of the Primogenitors, those Chapters formed from the Ultramarines during the Second Founding. It was made from the noblest Ultramarines veterans who survived the Horus Heresy. They have always venerated Roboute Guilliman, and were one of the first Chapters to seek out the Primarch upon his revival, pledging themselves to the Lord Commander.

Praetors of Orpheus

The Praetors of Orpheus are famous for a disciplined approach to executing the Codex Astartes. This occasionally causes the Chapter to offend their allies, but means that, on the battlefield, the Praetors operate like a perfectly calibrated engine of war. Guilliman's recent revisions of the Codex have been rapidly and rigidly adopted by the Chapter, whose inflexible adherence to the word of the law continues unabated.

Aurora Chapter

The Aurora Chapter are masters of the armoured assault, and their Armoury boasts more Land Raiders and Predators than that of most Chapters. Many of these vehicles are ancient war relics that have fought for the Aurora Chapter since the Second Founding. The Chapter's home world of Firestorm features huge industrial macrofactorums whose output ensures the Aurora Chapter's guns never run dry.

Silver Skulls

Highly superstitious, the Silver Skulls believe that the Emperor himself guides their deeds. Though this means that they will only take to the field when the portents are favourable, it also leads them to fight with the absolute conviction of fanatics, which does not sit well with some Imperial commanders. After the opening of the Great Rift, the Silver Skulls have been amongst the most active of all Chapters, fighting on many fronts.

Black Consuls

The Black Consuls are among the least compromising of the Primogenitors, and brook no deviation whatsoever from the tenets laid down in the Codex. Their history is rich in battles won, although they were recently believed to have been annihilated by the Iron Warriors. Instead, the Chapter has rebuilt itself upon its home world of Cyclopia, and its warriors remain stalwart guardians of the Imperium in Segmentum Pacificus.

Iron Snakes

Hailing from the frozen ocean world of Ithaka, the Iron Snakes are a somewhat superstitious brotherhood whose squads are named after the founding leaders of the Chapter. Over the centuries, several Iron Snakes squads have accumulated particularly impressive strings of victories and glorious rolls of honours – the histories of Squads Skypio, Parthus, Veii and Thebes are the stuff of many great sagas and legends.

Novamarines

The Novamarines Chapter have a long and storied history, and are one of the most honoured Primogenitors in the Imperium. Even amongst the other firstborn Chapters, the Novamarines are noted for their consistency and unshakable faith in the Codex Astartes. The Novamarines are an exceptionally dynamic Space Marine Chapter, and they have not fought as a single force since the early years of the 37th millennium.

Silver Templars

The Silver Templars are weapon masters without compare. They form exceptional connections with their blades and guns – and in unusual cases, even tanks and spacecraft – in a ritual known as the Bond Martial. This allows the Silver Templars to fight with unbelievable skill and poise, but should a warrior of this Chapter ever lose their chosen weapons in battle, they would suffer terrible dishonour and gnawing grief.

Hawk Lords

The Hawk Lords heavily favour the use of gunships, and so are unsurprisingly the undisputed masters of aerial combat. It is not unknown for pilots from other Chapters to hone their skills while on secondment to a Hawk Lords Talon Wing. During the Noctis Aeterna, it was only the sublime efforts of the Hawk Lords' Stormtalon pilots that protected the hive world of Thesor from otherwise certain doom.

Howling Griffons

Few Chapters have won as much renown as quickly as the Howling Griffons. They fought with honour in the Badab War, the Vengeance Crusade, the Overthrowing of the Regent of Amar and a thousand other campaigns vital to the Imperium. In recent years, the Howling Griffons' home world has come under increasingly savage assault by greenskin hordes spilling from the Charadon Sector. So far, the Griffons stand firm.

Scythes of the Emperor

Once nearly obliterated in battle with Tyranids, the Scythes of the Emperor were prepared to go out fighting. However, Archmagos Cawl and the Ultima Founding gave the Chapter an unlooked for chance to return to full strength. Unusually, the Scythes of the Emperor display their company markings through the Aquila on their breastplates. Veteran status is denoted by a yellow left knee adorned with a black skull.

Iron Hounds

Renowned for their relentlessness, the Iron Hounds are ruthless warriors who pursue their enemies until every last foe has been slain. Hailing from the Ultima Segmentum and with legends of their history dating back to the Fourth Founding, they have always been firm allies of the Ultramarines and have pledged warriors to the cause of Ultramar on countless occasions, most notably in the Plague Wars and at Damnos.

Brazen Consuls

Hailing from the rich world of Aventinium, the Brazen Consuls recruit solely from the world's nobility. Such is these people's wealth that they commit their scions to training from birth. Thus, aspirants are expert fencers and precision marksmen, as finely disciplined and learned in strategic wisdom and solitary survival as they are in the complex etiquettes of the banqueting hall.

Patriarchs of Ulixis

The Patriarchs of Ulixis maintain a proud tradition of martial prowess. They especially prize the skilled and selfless defence of those they are assigned to protect. Many Patriarchs of Ulixis battle-brothers have made names for themselves amidst the ranks of the Deathwatch, and have been seconded to the honour guards of notable Imperial worthies or – on occasion – even the elite Victrix Guard of the Ultramarines.

IMPERIAL FISTS
THE SONS OF DORN

The Imperial Fists have stood as steadfast defenders of the Imperium since the Great Crusade. Strong of mind and spirit, they are the Emperor's shield, indomitable and unbreakable. Their stubbornness in the face of any enemy and their determination to hold no matter the cost is matched only by their zealous efforts to see their gene-sire's dreams for the Imperium made real.

The Primarch of the Imperial Fists was Rogal Dorn, whose name is revered throughout the Imperium, and from him stem the Chapter's proud history and traditions. After being torn from Terra and cast into the galaxy, the Emperor discovered Dorn years later on the ice world of Inwit. Like many of his brothers, he had risen to lord of his people, and he had established a stellar empire of his own. Recognising the Emperor as his father and liege, he presented the Master of Mankind with *Phalanx*, an immensely powerful and mobile space station that dated back to the Age of Technology. The Emperor handed to Dorn the Imperial Fists Legion, created using Dorn's own

genetic material. The Emperor also insisted the Primarch keep *Phalanx*, and ever since it has been the Imperial Fists' flagship and primary fortress.

Dorn discovered his sons to be peerless crusaders and resolute warriors, firm in their commitment to order, unwilling to give ground and unhesitating in making the ultimate sacrifice for victory. Their talent for siegecraft was undeniable, though they had achieved glorious victories in all manner of warfare. The Emperor later declared Dorn and his Legion to be his Praetorians, and tasked them with fortifying the Sol System, Terra and the Imperial Palace itself. Ever

since, the Imperial Fists have been known as the Defenders of Terra, a title they bear with immense pride. Their official home world, ten thousand years later, remains Terra itself, though the demands of war ensure the Imperial Fists now almost never return.

Dorn saw the Imperium being built by the Emperor's Legions as a fortress, with each world a part of a galactic system of ramparts, bulwarks and counter-guards. He laced the worlds the Imperial Fists conquered with mighty bastions and constructed vast orbital citadels around them, naming this system the Bastion Imperialis. When the Horus Heresy

SIEGE MASTERS

Apocryphal datastacks, encrusted with ten thousand years of dust deep within *Phalanx*'s Librarius, tell of the collapse of the Citadel of Behemoni, the breaching of the Unbreakable Wall of K'hartt and the construction of the Alkazar of Binding Complyance. Should these near mythological tales be believed, they suggest that the Imperial Fists have been the masters of siege warfare and erecting nigh on impregnable fortresses since even before being united with Rogal Dorn.

In the 41st Millennium, the Imperial Fists see the siege as the ultimate crucible of war, the truest test of a warrior's skill, courage, determination and resolve. They have toppled the Emperor's Children's Bastions of Pain and reduced ramshackle Ork fortresses to scrap. In turn they have stood firm on their battlements to throw back ravenous hordes of Tyranid bioforms and regimented phalanxes of Necrons. The Imperial Fists have greater reserves of siege-related assets than many other Chapters, making significant use of Vindicator tanks, Centurion warsuits and Mk X Gravis armour. To attack the Imperial Fists when they are upon their battlements, or to seek shelter when the sons of Dorn strike, is little more than suicide.

struck and world after world fell in with the traitors or was conquered by them, he saw each fall as a deep crack in his design.

The tireless efforts of Rogal Dorn and the Imperial Fists to fortify the Sol System paid dividends during the Siege of Terra, turning the Imperial Palace into one of the most formidable fortresses the Imperium had ever seen. The Imperial Fists fought unwaveringly in the fighting, holding the walls and throwing back traitor assaults. Dorn teleported with the Emperor to engage Horus aboard the traitor's flagship, but was separated from his father before the duel that decided the fate of the Imperium took place. Bitterness and a deep sense of failure came to define his character for some time, and it took much to convince him to break his Legion down into Chapters following Roboute Guilliman's publication of the Codex Astartes.

For ten thousand years the Imperial Fists have been a symbol of Imperial defiance in the face of all the myriad threats posed to Humanity. They have played a vital role in the preservation of the Imperium, thousands of their number sacrificing themselves on battlefields the galaxy over. Rarely will a warrior of the Imperial Fists boast of such deeds, however. For them the performance of such acts ranks far higher in importance than the declaring of them. Though not secretive and mysterious like the Dark Angels, they also do not possess the brash, loud and forthright nature of the Space Wolves. The Imperial Fists often appear humourless and severe to those who encounter them, but they are nonetheless passionate warriors, determined, firm and believing still in the great cause of Rogal Dorn's Bastion Imperialis. For them, it is said, the Great Crusade is yet to be completed. Whilst this goal is rarely spoken of aloud by the Imperial Fists, doubtless it is one that scarcely leaves their minds as they wage war.

Sacrifice and commitment are huge elements of the Imperial Fists' ideals. They refuse to give ground to the foe, on occasion to their detriment. *Phalanx*'s Librarius has records of many destroyed Imperial Fists forces that could well have been saved were it not for stubbornness

– though it is without any doubt that many more victories have been won thanks to this trait, which runs so deeply through them. The Imperial Fists have a deep well of recruit reserves with which to replace their fallen brothers, drawn from a multitude of worlds to allow for the high casualties they frequently suffer. While their Chaplains teach of the need to manage excessive pride to avoid catastrophic losses, the determination to never give up holds a vice-like grip over every Imperial Fist's hearts.

In terms of their combat doctrine, many Imperial Fists spend a disproportionately long period of time in fire support roles, serving in Hellblaster Squads, Devastator Squads and Aggressor Squads. This is due to their preference for heavy

firepower, the emphasis they place on marksmanship and the hellish siege battles they so often fight.

In the time of the Era Indomitus, the Imperial Fists have fought battle after battle to break the forces of the Arch-enemy, relieve populations besieged by hordes of ravening xenos and recapture fallen worlds.

BLOOD ANGELS
THE SONS OF SANGUINIUS

Resplendent in their Chapter's gleaming red, the Blood Angels have fought for the Emperor since the First Founding. They are amongst the most noble Space Marine Chapters, seeking to always protect the weak and vulnerable – yet this deep sense of integrity and honour is besmirched by a hideous curse they conceal from all outsiders and ever strive to resist.

Little is known of the Blood Angels' earliest history. Sanguinius was discovered during the Great Crusade on Baal Secundus, the second moon of the planet Baal. Though Baal and its moons were once glorious places of wealth and breathtaking architecture, during the Dark Age of Technology all was destroyed. They were left as irradiated husks, inhabited by a small Human population and savage mutants. After his pod crashed there, Sanguinius was as a god to the near feral inhabitants, a figure of incomparable nobility and beauty in a place of suffering, death and ugliness – this despite his angelic wings, which nearly led the tribes to slaughter him upon his discovery. When the Emperor finally reached the Baal System, Sanguinius accepted him as his liege without question, and took command of the IX Legion.

Little detail survives of the Legion's involvement in the Great Crusade itself, besides a handful of honorifics and generic articles praising the Blood Angels' successes, almost all from the time after Sanguinius was placed at the head of his sons. What is clear is that Sanguinius was regarded as one of the greatest of the Emperor's sons. Beautiful in body and mind, he was a warrior almost without peer and a leader who could inspire incredible feats of personal courage not just within his own Legion, but throughout the vast multitudes of the Emperor's varied servants. It is believed that the Blood Angels Legion fought by their Primarch's side throughout the Horus Heresy, though the only battle in the historical record they can be accurately placed at is the Siege of Terra – the conflict that defined the next ten thousand years of Humanity's history.

It is said that it was only after a long and arduous journey – the battles of which are now lost to history – that the Blood Angels reached Terra to defend the Throneworld from the forces of the Arch-traitor, Horus. They fought with honour and courage and slew countless foes on the battlements of the Imperial Palace. But the cost of their efforts was great. In the final, desperate attack against Horus' flagship, the *Vengeful Spirit*, Sanguinius engaged the Warmaster in personal combat. In the titanic duel that followed, he was slain.

The IX Legion shared a deep bond with their Primarch – perhaps one deeper than most of the Legiones Astartes had with their gene-sire – for all Blood Angels at that time were injected with droplets of Sanguinius' blood. Some Blood Angels believe it is this, combined with the Primarch's death, that caused the Flaw that has cursed every Blood Angel ever since. Partial fragments discovered in hidden corners of the Legion's Librarius that suggest some Blood Angels Legionaries suffered from a version of the

By the blood, we are made strong. By the blood, we are made whole. By the blood, our souls are made pure. By the blood, our spirits are fortified.

Epistolary Themizel soared over the battlefield on deep crimson wings made of pure psychic energy. To his left stormed the five Inceptors of Squad Hazazel. Their plasma exterminators glowed brightly with barely contained power, the machine spirits of the weapons as hungry for blood as their wielders.

To his right bounded the golden-armoured warriors of Sanguinary Guard Squad Castivar. Their encarmine blades gleamed even in the weak light of Ankerin's distant star, miniature bands of lightning crackling down their length.

He could feel the thirst for blood in all of their psyches, desperate to be unleashed like a starved war-beast. Behind the calm of their helms he knew they bore looks of ferocious anger.

Themizel looked down. Beneath thick clouds of smog he saw burning wrecks of once-Imperial vehicles covered with eight-pointed stars and racks of spikes upon which Human skulls had been driven. He saw a red helm among the trophies. 'The traitors will pay for this evil,' he said to himself.

Themizel reached out to his brothers' minds to communicate – the cacophony of explosions and gunfire was so loud they could not hear each other over the internal vox. +The Word Bearers' sorcerer is near. His presence feels like that of a blood-gnat on my skin.+ Acknowledgement runes blinked in his helm's visual feed.

Other Blood Angels Librarians roamed the battlefield, seeking out their own sorcerous targets. The Chapter boasted many such battle-psykers, being inheritors of Sanguinius' spiritual might. +On this day the valiant light of the Angel shall smite the darkness of traitorous evil,+ Themizel affirmed as he saw his quarry. The traitor sorcerer was clad in power armour of deepest red, every inch of the ceramite etched with runes of dead, forbidden languages. Parchments hung from the plate, scrawled with more heinous writings. Several horns had grown out of the traitor's head and his face had dark, reptilian scales in the place of skin. As one, the Blood Angels descended.

Themizel channelled his pent-up fury into a psychically conjured lance, which he raised above his head. 'This day you die, traitor!'

Flaw even before Sanguinius' death have been dismissed as false and locked away.

The Flaw takes two forms: the Red Thirst and the Black Rage. Every Blood Angel has deep within them an insatiable battle-lust and hunger for blood. This is the Red Thirst, and it afflicts every gene-son of Sanguinius in every waking moment. Though they take great pains to resist its lure, not all are successful, and no few Blood Angels succumb to it in the midst of battle; doing so renders them truly deadly, to the extent that some attempt to control it and use it. Though a curse, the Red Thirst humbles the Blood Angels. It makes them aware of their own weaknesses and thus more understanding of those in others.

For all the horror of the Red Thirst, the Black Rage is far worse. When this takes over the Blood Angel's mind, it is irreversible. The Blood Angels believe that all will succumb to it should they not die first. Death is the only cure. Ingrained

in the Blood Angels' gene-seed is the encoded experience of their Primarch, the strongest of which is his duel with Horus. On the eve of battle, an event or circumstance will trigger this memory in a Blood Angel. The battle-brother's mind is taken over by this experience, and to those around him he appears crazed with berserk fury, no longer aware of where or who he is. These brothers are assigned to the Death Company, to meet an honourable end in battle.

The worst thing of all about these twin curses is that with each passing year, more brothers succumb to them. The Blood Angels and their successors, all of whom are afflicted in the same way, are dying out. Some at a faster rate than others.

Few would be surprised if a Chapter afflicted in such a way would fall to despair, yet the Blood Angels do not. They fight on. They charge headlong into the guns of the enemy, eager to slay them in hand-to-hand combat. They

honour their Primarch's belief that the galaxy can be changed for the better. This is epitomised in the transformation of recruits into Space Marines. The rad-scarred aspirants drawn from the Baal System undergo an apotheosis. They spend a year in slumber in ancient sarcophagi, in which time they receive their implants to become Space Marines. They emerge as demigods, tall, strong of muscle, keen of sense and beautiful in body – the image of Sanguinius himself. Their desire to perfect and improve things manifests in every aspect of the Blood Angels' existence, from the elaborate embellishments many sport on their armour, the exquisite craftsmanship of their weapons and their incredible skill with bolter and blade.

In these dark times, the Blood Angels represent all that Humanity can be. Despite, or because of, their terrible flaws they are paragons of virtue and duty, serving as inspiration for all in the Imperium.

WHITE SCARS
THE SONS OF THE WARHAWK

The roaring of furious engines, deep rumbles of thundering armoured transports, screaming of heavy jump packs at full burn and ferocious Korchin war cries herald the devastating assault of the White Scars. Formidable hunters drawn from fierce tribesmen, the White Scars smash through their foes like the tip of a spear through the flank of prey.

The White Scars are masters of lightning warfare and hit-and-run attacks. They stalk their prey patiently and relentlessly, before striking at the weakest point with incredible precision, ferocity and speed. They have inherited this martial legacy from the harsh culture of their home world, as well as from their Primarch, Jaghatai Khan, known as the Warhawk, the Khagan and the Khan of Khans.

The White Scars hail from Chogoris, a world of windswept planes and jagged mountains. Its nomadic population are expert hunters and horsemen, and are persistently at war. This harsh lifestyle produces hard people, and therefore aspirants of high quality for the White Scars. It is among these people that Jaghatai grew up, learning and embodying their ways. After his discovery during the Great Crusade, he imbued the V Legion with the traditions of Chogoris, and in so doing bound his sons to him. To this day the White Scars hang furs, Chogorian trinkets and shamanistic fetishes from their armour, ritually scar their faces with tribal heraldry, and go to battle bearing the severed heads of their enemies.

Thanks to these trappings, many mistakenly believe the White Scars to be backwards, or even barbarous. The White Scars' manner of war is tightly controlled, however. As hunters they carefully observe the lay of the land, striking only when they are ready. Off the battlefield, though they train as hard as any other

Space Marines in the arts of war, they are highly cultured. Many White Scars seek mastery in one or more of the Noble Pursuits set down by the Khagan. For some this is hunting, for others Korchin calligraphy or the telling of ancient tales. A rare few embrace the challenge of *ci* verse. These skills are vital in making the White Scars better warriors. The patience required to paint a perfect character of Korchin script is the same patience that makes for an adept hunter. Even killing is an act of beauty to them, a demonstration of unity between warrior and weapon. The White Scars are also possessed of a strong sense of honour and justice, another legacy from their Primarch and the tribes of Chogoris.

Deep mysticism and superstition form an integral part of Chogorian tribal culture, and so too are they embraced by the White Scars. The Chapter's warriors place a great deal of trust in their Librarians, who they call Stormseers, calling upon these battle psykers for the enlightened wisdom they have accumulated over years of study. In battle, Stormseers command the elemental fury of the tempest. Gales flow at their instruction and lightning bolts strike the foe at their behest. This appears to have been so for

almost all of their history, according to those few with knowledge on the matter. They suggest that the White Scars argued in favour of retaining the Space Marine Legions' Librarius in the fabled Council of Nikaea during the Great Crusade. Some believe that it was here that the Emperor prohibited the Space Marines' use of psychic powers before the Horus Heresy – though the horror of that terrible conflict necessitated reinstating the Librarius.

The White Scars' battle tactics are highly fluid, the warriors of Chogoris repeatedly utilising feints, staged retreats and flanking attacks to destroy the foe. Speed is a key component of their strategies, and every White Scars strike force brings with it a host of bikes, armoured transports and jump packs. Few things give a son of the Warhawk greater joy than roaring across the battlefield, blade in hand, to bring death to the Emperor's enemies, often laughing as they strike their foes down.

At the head of every White Scars company is a khan, a mighty warrior, calculating strategist and superb duellist who has proven himself on the battlefield countless times. Where multiple khans

take to the field, they compete for overall command of the White Scars' force. In doing so they both seek to earn honour for their company – known to the White Scars as a brotherhood – as well as for the sheer pleasure of rivalry amongst brothers. Thanks to a khan's cunning tactics, a White Scars force breaks apart and scatters their enemies, putting them to flight. In this moment their hunting skills come to the fore as they pursue the foe and slaughter them all.

The White Scars battle in the Era Indomitus with all the strength available to them, taking the fight to the forces of Chaos and the xenos menace. The Yasan Sector, in which their home world resides, has come under ferocious attack by the forces of Chaos pouring from the Maelstrom. Chogoris itself was besieged by the Renegade Space Marines of the Red Corsairs, led by their warlord, Huron Blackheart. But the White Scars held firm and drove the traitors from their world, and the Chapter's brotherhoods have since fought in the Vigilus, Asmar, Chenna and Anragua Systems. Though these times are fraught with perils beyond imagining, the White Scars refuse to be cowed, just as they never have in all their glorious history.

No matter where you flee, we will find you. No matter how fast you run, we will chase you down. No matter the strength of your great armies and fine warriors, we will defeat you. We are the White Scars, and we will laugh as we mount your heads on the spikes that line the roads to Quan Zhou.

ARMOURED STEEDS

The White Scars are masters of making war from the saddle, and few embrace the fast-moving vehicles of a Space Marine Chapter's Armoury as they do. Whether it be the Invader ATV or combat bikes, the White Scars have mastered their use.

Each of the Invader ATV's four wheels is independently adaptable thanks to the vehicle's highly articulated suspension. Operated by a machine spirit, these enable the Invader to cross broken battlefield terrain with impunity. Between its robust vox aerial and ground-mapping advanced auspex, the Invader accumulates vast quantities of valuable topographical information with which the Khans formulate their highly complex

battle-plans. Before its spirit is roused, the Invader is folded into a more compact form, and transported into a battle zone hanging from the deployment racks of a gunship. Dropped into battle, the crew engage Sagittus-class hunting protocols, awaken the machine spirit and race into battle.

Often racing alongside Invader ATVs are Space Marine bikes. Only a Space Marine has the physical power needed to operate and manoeuvre these, or has the strength of will to dominate their especially bellicose machine spirits. In battle a Space Marine will form a close bond with his mount, battle-brother and machine spirit working together to achieve victory.

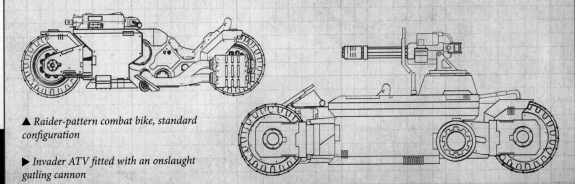

▲ *Raider-pattern combat bike, standard configuration*

▶ *Invader ATV fitted with an onslaught gatling cannon*

DARK ANGELS
THE SONS OF THE LION

The Dark Angels were the First Legion. No other Space Marine brotherhood has served the Emperor for as long as they have. Staunch defenders of Mankind, they are merciless in the attack and stubborn in the defence. They are also shrouded in mystery, however, and have secrets so shameful they are kept even from many of their own number.

The Dark Angels' name is held equally in awe and fear by those they fight for and against. They are not regarded in the same light as their brothers in the Ultramarines or Blood Angels. They are famed less for their honour and nobility than their unsettling demeanour, taciturn manner, inscrutability and solemnity. Those who have fought beside the Dark Angels observe the deliberate detachment the Chapter exhibits, and the rapid disappearance of its warriors as soon as their mission is achieved – sometimes even before the war is concluded.

The Dark Angels are a fleet-based Chapter, crossing the void in their armada of warships – and at its head, the mysterious fortress monastery known as the Rock. Few know how this colossal voidborne citadel came to be – or why the Dark Angels' former home world of Caliban no longer exists – and they would fight and die to keep the truth from the remainder of the Imperium.

To fully understand the Dark Angels it is necessary to learn of their Primarch, Lion El'Jonson, and his greatest friend, Luther. When the Emperor came to Caliban after the Lion's discovery, Luther was too old to join the I Legion as a Space Marine. The Lion left him the vital charge of defending Caliban and raising new generations of Space Marines. But Luther's heart grew bitter. When the Horus Heresy ended, and the Lion returned to Caliban, Luther and

the Dark Angels he commanded opened fire. Luther's strength was swelled by that of the Dark Gods of Chaos, and was thus the Lion's every equal in combat. Only once Luther had mortally wounded the Lion did he realise his calamitous mistake. As Luther cried out in anguish, a warp rift consumed Caliban, tearing the planet apart and sweeping thousands of the traitorous Dark Angels into the empyrean. They would later be regarded as the Fallen.

The surviving Dark Angels vowed to pursue the traitors and keep these events secret, believing the Imperium would damn them all should the truth become known. Embracing the Codex Astartes with little complaint so as to avoid suspicion, they and their successors

referred to themselves as the Unforgiven, retaining close ties with each other and fighting the Imperium's wars with distinction even as they went about their clandestine mission. Over time, the Inner Circle formed, made up of the only Dark Angels aware of the Chapter's terrible secrets. Only a battle-brother who has earned their trust and fought bravely on the battlefield may join their number, and even then they are told but a fraction of the whole damning truth.

Whilst the hunt for the Fallen is of incredible importance to the Dark Angels, the great majority of their wars have little to do with their traitorous brethren. Following the Codex in its entirety besides two specialist companies, the veteran Deathwing and the rapid-striking Ravenwing, the Dark Angels fight in the manner of most Space Marines Chapters. Lightning assaults, combined arms forces and tactical flexibility are at the core of the Dark Angels' way of war. Every battlefield is searched for sedition, however. Though only the Inner Circle understand the signs of the Fallen, the uninitiated can still recognise heresy where they see it.

In these tumultuous times, the Dark Angels have been at the forefront of some of the galaxy's most significant wars. The sons of Caliban have bled their foes in the Stygius Sector, the Vigilus System, the Prosperan Rift and numerous other war zones, upholding their name as some of the Emperor's fiercest defenders.

Mercy. Compassion. Forgiveness. These words, used only by the weak and the supine, have no place in our order. We must earn redemption through the breaking of vengeance. Any other war is heresy.

Hamied thumbed the triggers. His Storm Speeder Hailstrike's onslaught gatling cannon span into life in seconds, spitting deluges of fire at warriors of the Bloody Daggers warband. Heretic Astartes clad in ceramite of deep crimson took cover behind hastily erected defences.

But he was not here for them. Though they would slay every one of the Bloody Daggers, there was one above all he and his ebon-armoured Ravenwing brethren sought. The so-called Sower of Deceitful Truths. This traitor had cast three whole systems into traitorous anarchy. He had deactivated the watch-savants deployed to watch over the Ork empire of Gorak Thugga, meaning the neighbouring sub-sector had no warning of Waaagh! Thugga's overwhelming assault, which careened straight through the whole region, leaving no survivors. Hamied's blood boiled with hatred.

The Bloody Daggers were withdrawing, squads of the traitors covering each other's retreat with typical Space Marine discipline.

'Using those skills for their deeds of evil sickens me,' he remarked over the vox. The defeated traitors' fire was so controlled that brother Inias, the pilot, had to veer off.

'I share your anger, brother,' Inias said. 'We shall burn their corpses yet, it is but a matter of time.'

The other Storm Speeders of their squadron broke off their attack at the same time to avoid the savage volleys of accurate bolt-fire the traitors were putting down. As they regrouped, Larathiel's Storm Speeder exploded, sending burning wreckage crashing to the ashen ground. Hamied felt shrapnel patter on his Mk X Tacticus armour and heard shards dash against his own vehicle.

'Missiles,' said Inias, with all the icy calm worthy of a veteran. The two remaining Storm Speeders loosened their formation in a well-practised battle drill to make it harder for the heretics to hit them.

'This complicates the situation,' said Inias. He was right. With the Ravenwing unable to press the attack, some of the traitors could escape, and most importantly might the Sower of Deceitful Truths.

It was then that Inias saw a bright flash of energy in the near distance. Where there was once nothing, now stood ten warriors clad in bone-white Terminator plate. Their storm bolters were roaring, and one was launching bolts of explosive plasma into the unsuspecting traitors.

'The Deathwing!' he said. He had never seen these warriors fight in such a manner before. They were awe-inspiring. Their fire discipline was remarkable, their speed even in heavy armour mesmerising. The traitors were surrounded now.

Inias seized the initiative, gunning the Hailstrike's engines and turning the anti-grav vehicle towards the traitors again as they were distracted.

Hamied worked the Storm Speeder's weapons, pouring a relentless hail of fire upon the shattered traitors. Solid shot punctured the ceramite plate of one traitor in a dozen places, killing the heretic immediately. A hail of fragstorm grenades perforated half a dozen enemy warriors before they were shredded by the relentless heavy stubber fire of another Hailstrike.

Though Hamied never stopped firing at the traitors, he constantly watched for the Sower of Deceitful Truths hidden there. He eventually saw him: a warrior clad in ancient black armour and covered in a heavy cloak. But another warrior had already discerned the betrayer. In the instant it took Hamied to process the speed of the Deathwing Champion's attack, the white-armoured warrior smashed the heretic to the ground with his thunder hammer.

RAVEN GUARD
THE SONS OF CORAX

Masters of clandestine warfare and the art of the shadowed blade, when the Raven Guard engage in open warfare, it is already too late for their enemies. The bloody conclusion to a campaign of sabotage, guerrilla tactics and targeted strikes is a peerless coordination of assets by which the Raven Guard apply exactly the right amount of power to utterly destroy their foe.

A series of shocking and explosive deaths followed by the hissing roar of jump packs is often the first time a heretic or xenos force is even aware of the Raven Guard's presence. The Chapter's sable-coloured armour reflects little light, and its battle-brothers are highly skilled in using their surroundings to their advantage. Remaining unseen, they slip through twisted ruins and alien undergrowth, silently merging into pools of inky shadow.

To fight the Raven Guard is to swing blades at whorls of smoke and to fire at half-seen spectres with increasing panic. When every piece of their strategy has fallen into place, then will the Raven Guard swoop, their blades slicing deep and their heavy guns piercing the enemy lines in a dozen places at once.

The Raven Guard are one of the original brotherhoods of Space Marines who fought with the Emperor more than ten millennia ago. Under their Primarch, Corvus Corax, the Raven Guard crafted their Trifold Path of Shadow, mastering the doctrines of ambush, stealth and vigilance. These principles represent the pinnacle of the Raven Guard's way of war, those which every battle-brother seeks to perfect.

Lord Corax was withdrawn and taciturn, traits his sons inherited alongside his pallid skin and unsettling, dark eyes. The Primarch spent his early years among indentured slaves on a prison moon orbiting the industrial world of Kiavahr. Corax led the prisoners in revolt and broke the power of Kiavahr's slave guilds. The moon was renamed Deliverance and

has been the site of the Raven Guard's fortress monastery – the Ravenspire – since the Legion were united with their Primarch. It is a grim and sombre citadel. Due to near constant campaigns and a careful rate of recruitment, many enormous halls gather dust in the gloom, and certain lofty towers haunted by ancient rumour are stasis-sealed against intrusion. Yet the austere display belies the power within, and its inviolable redoubts maintain a menacing watchfulness. The Raven Guard spare no thought for displays of prestige. Function is all, and as a training ground, bulwark and memory of their gene-sire's legacy, the Ravenspire fulfills every function the Chapter requires of it.

Corax's experiences on Deliverance instilled in him a deep hatred of

'The honoured brothers of the Armoury are skilled in the mysteries they wield to repair Dirae's stabiliser fins, oil its intakes and stoke its fiery heart. Yet they know not this jump pack's pall of dread vengeance and the twinning of warrior spirits as we roar together into the ambush. Never have they felt the brooding kinship that comes when the drop-ship's armature cradle lowers Dirae onto my back and the armoured harness locks into place. With the sudden connection through armour ports, every flicker of power and growl of the pack's jets is an extension of me.

Though the Techmarines preen its plasteel planes, it is I who feel Dirae's powerful thrusters as black wings at my back, speeding me into the unknowing foe. Vector runes and engine dynamics cycle on my helm display, gifting unmatched aerial control. Dirae's precision pulse-jets slow my descent to a crushing impact. In a moment, we have killed in a flurry of talon strikes. With a silent command, Dirae roars once more and we bound onto the next ambush in a graceful curve.'

- Brother Vaen, 8th Squad, Raven Guard 3rd Company

oppressors. To this day the Raven Guard strive to liberate Humanity from heretical tyrants and xenos overlords. They break the chains that bind Mankind's sundered and enslaved worlds, though they do so from the darkness, with no expectation of glory – for the Raven Guard shun the kinds of acclaim and honours that are laid before other Chapters.

The Raven Guard's isolationist tendencies and inscrutable nature do not endear them to their allies. Their dour and laconic battle-brothers are viewed as suspicious and uncertain figures, distancing themselves even from other Space Marine Chapters. With their brooding mien and dark gaze, the Raven Guard are held by those Human survivors who owe them their lives as much in fear as in awe. Yet there is no doubting the Chapter's stalwart resistance and unwavering loyalty. For ten thousand years the Raven Guard have shielded the Imperium, fighting wars across the galaxy – from the dark heart of the Emperor's realm to the bleak fringes.

Many of the Chapter's operations are undertaken by strike forces of Vanguard and Scout Squads, supported by squads of jump pack troops and other aerial assets such as gunships and speeders. Such forces are expert at manoeuvring behind enemy lines. There, they sow confusion and destruction or prepare to sink their talons into the foe's rear lines at the very instant a more conventional Raven Guard attack strikes from another angle.

Hunting from the shadows, teams of Raven Guard snipers mercilessly cut down fiery demagogues and savage xenos warlords. Highly valued among Corax's doctrines was the belief that a leaderless enemy is an enemy already defeated. Decapitation missions and assassinations are coordinated with feigned retreats and skyborne strikes; these stunning strategies leave the enemy reeling and vulnerable to the final coup de grâce without unnecessarily exposing the Raven Guard. The Chapter's doctrine espouses stealth and swift reactions over brazen and costly onslaughts.

The Raven Guard understand first hand the consequences of terrible losses. Some of their oldest legends speak in bleak and bitter terms of the darkest days of the Horus Heresy. Along with the Iron Hands and Salamanders, Corax and the Raven Guard were brutally betrayed on the black sands of Isstvan V by former allies. Hardly anything is known for certain of those chaotic times, but the Raven Guard were massacred and almost wiped out. After that terrible day, scattered bands of Raven Guard fought a shadow war against the forces of the traitors, making them pay in blood for every step they took towards Terra.

Not all the Raven Guard's missions are undertaken subtly. After careful reconnaissance by infiltrating squads, a Shadow Captain may deem a decisive strike of sudden and precise force is necessary. Shock troops are revealed in terror-filled storms of noise and death, flights of jump troops descend from the skies, heralded by gunfire and crackling lightning claws. Such a strike shatters the foe's strength before they are aware the fight has even begun. As counter-strikes mobilise against them, these fast-moving squads have already withdrawn to strike elsewhere.

WAR ZONE:
DAMNOS

When a Necron tomb awoke on Damnos, the Ultramarines were unable to stop the deathless androids from conquering the planet. However, they were at the speartip of the Imperial assault that reclaimed Damnos and purged the xenos. Yet the Necrons were not done with that ice-locked mining world; they would return...

Severe ire was roused in those Ultramarines on Macragge when astropathic cries for aid reached their home world from Damnos. A vast new Necron invasion force had descended from space upon that much-troubled planet, and its defenders could not hold alone. With a great portion of the Ultramarines' strength committed to the Indomitus Crusade, fighting the forces of Mortarion in wider Ultramar and waging war on Vigilus, few Ultramarines were available to respond. Nonetheless, a strike force was assembled. The Ultramarines had given too much to Damnos to abandon it now.

The Ultramarines wasted no time in calling for allies, their astropathic choirs screaming out into the void to reach other sons of Guilliman. The Ultramarines knew that given their low numbers, they couldn't achieve victory through strength alone. They made all speed to Damnos, bringing with them regiments of the Ultramar Auxilia. They fully trusted their brothers to reinforce them, and were not disappointed. As the last of the auxilia regiments established a perimeter around Kellenport – the only Human settlement not yet under attack – vessels in the gunmetal and blood red of the Iron Hounds, the polished bronze of the Brazen Consuls and the gleaming amber of the Libators emerged from the warp. A brief war council saw all Adeptus Astartes forces fall under command of Ultramarines Captain Hellios of the 8th Company. He rapidly organised the Space Marines' counter-attack.

The Necrons were identified as being of the Szarekhan Dynasty, that same force reported by Battle Group Kallides of Indomitus Crusade Fleet Primus. Few of the Space Marines had fought them before, but this troubled them little. They were xenos, and xenos had to die. The Space Marines committed every vessel to the complete domination of Damnosian space as gunships delivered dozens of squads directly into battle. They relieved the beleaguered defenders of Fort Thakken, escorted refugee columns through the Northern Crags and met Necron phalanxes head-on. But for all the Space Marines' efforts, the Necrons were numberless, arriving in their thousands by tomb ship and dolmen gate to reconquer purged tomb complexes. All the while the Space Marines' casualties mounted and the war became desperate.

The Ultramarines feared the worst when the Mandeville Point flared once more. But rather than enemies, out poured highly embellished Salamanders vessels and sleek hunters of the White Scars. Thanks to the vagaries of the warp, they too had heard the Ultramarines' call for aid, and had raced to reinforce their cousins.

'Many are the legends of the Ultramarines' tenacity in Damnos' defence, and of their great victory reclaiming it for the Imperium. Their refusal to abandon that world and their hatred for the xenos are worthy of legend and praise. Without hesitation I salute them.

It would have been easy for the Ultramarines to give in to pride and seek to fight for Damnos alone. It must have stung them to learn of a world they had thought made safe under threat once again. But they did not surrender to vanity. They called for aid, knowing that serving the Emperor and preserving his realm is more important than the personal honour of any battle-brother or Chapter.

The Ultramarines have ever been held in the Salamanders' esteem. They are men of honour, loyalty and steadfastness. Their humility drew our admiration, and a burning desire in our hearts to fight alongside them and slaughter the xenos.'

- Firedrake Ko'Tan Dallor,
Salamanders 1st Company

THE THIRD WAR FOR DAMNOS

For the third time the Ultramarines fighting to secure Damnos from the android warriors of the Necrons. Numerous Space Marine Chapters stood shoulder to shoulder with them.

ULTRAMARINES

STRIKE FORCE 'TRIVINIUS'
'Quintas'.......................Veteran (Intercessor) squad
'Axio'................................Veteran (Vanguard) squad
'Acilion'...Scout squad
'Caerellio'......................................Scout squad
Brother Gabinius.............Redemptor Dreadnought

LIBATORS

8TH COMPANY
'Triferon'.................close support (Outrider) squad
'Remos'.... close support (Storm Speeder) squadron
'Salenio'.................... close support (Assault) squad
'Ubrenicus'..............close support (Inceptor) squad
'Meles'..... close support (Assault Intercessor) squad
Brother Aedinio....................Ironclad Dreadnought
Brother Attius........................Ironclad Dreadnought

IRON HOUNDS

LAND RAIDER SPEARHEAD 'CASTOR'
'Spear of Orinus'....................................Land Raider
'Canis Infernus'................... Land Raider Redeemer
'Bloodhound'....................... Land Raider Crusader

BRAZEN CONSULS

SUPPRESSION FORCE 'DIGNITOR'
'Torsus'......close support (Land Speeder) squadron
'Travian'.................................... Whirlwind squadron

ANTI-AIR DEFENCE FORCE 'TITUS'
'Gallorn'...Hunter squadron
'Tearers of the Skies'...................... Stalker squadron

6TH COMPANY
'Galetus'...........................battleline (Tactical) squad
'Tiberias'..........................battleline (Tactical) squad
'Otavio'..........................battleline (Infiltrator) squad
'Andronicus'....battleline (Heavy Intercessor) squad
Brother Thysor...................Venerable Dreadnought

SALAMANDERS

STRIKE FORCE 'SAR'TATH'
'N'pann'...........................battleline (Tactical) squad
'Hezonn'..........................battleline (Tactical) squad
'Gnirra'.............battleline (Heavy Intercessor)squad
'Tes'ssen'.................fire support (Eradicator) squad
'Hek'ulon'....................Veteran (Bladeguard) squad
'Mir'Shan'.........Veteran (Assault Intercessor) squad

WHITE SCARS

HUNTING FORCE 'KAIDU'
'Argasar'...................close support (Outrider) squad
'Gesu'.................close support (Attack Bike) squad
'Korgeljin'...................... close support (Bike) squad
'Dunei'....................................Scout Bike squad
'Ochin'....................................Scout Bike squad

STORM WING 'GHAZAR'
'Turger'................................1 Stormraven Gunship
'Khiratarr'..............................1 Stormtalon Gunship
'Illusei'..................................1 Stormtalon Gunship

++ DUE TO THE XENOTECHNOLOGICAL INTERFERENCE IN THE DAMNOS SYSTEM IN ADDITION TO STANDARD EMPYRICAL INTERFERENCE, DATA COLLECTED ON ADEPTUS ASTARTES FORCES PRESENT DEEMED 62.15% ACCURATE AT BEST. ++

++ DATA OF OTHER IMPERIAL FORCES PRESENT, NAMELY THOSE OF THE DAMNOSIAN PLANETARY DEFENCE MILITIA AND ULTRAMAR AUXILIA REGIMENTS CAN BE VIEWED IN FILE 82ΰΦ/Z3V5. TREAT WITH SIMILAR CAUTION. ++

The Space Marines engaged on Damnos sported numerous campaign badges. Some of the Ultramarines Veterans had fought in the previous Damnos Wars, and wore the adornments of those battles with great pride. These warriors swore to destroy the Necrons and cleanse Damnos forever.

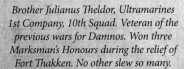

Brother Julianus Theldor, Ultramarines 1st Company, 10th Squad. Veteran of the previous wars for Damnos. Won three Marksman's Honours during the relief of Fort Thakken. No other slew so many.

Brother Tacitun Paxor, Libators 8th Company, 4th Squad. Awarded the Imperial Laurel for saving the lives of over three hundred Damnosian citizens in a single day.

Brother Constantius Remus Severinus, Brazen Consuls 6th Company, 3rd Squad. Killed in action on the tenth day of the Halaheim Reclamation. Saved seven brothers from a Wraith ambush.

SPACE WOLVES
THE SONS OF RUSS

With the fury of a winter's storm and the savagery of apex predators, the Space Wolves tear apart Humanity's foes with instinctive aggression. The Chapter is a brotherhood of heroes, hungry for glory and dedicated to defending the Imperium. Seeking to forge their sagas of honour, Space Wolves eagerly face down the most powerful enemies with ferocious snarls.

Clad in storm-grey power armour that reflects the wide tempestuous skies of their home world, bearing weapons hung with feral fetishes of atavistic power and howling their savage war cries into the wind, the Space Wolves are among the most renowned and fierce Chapters of Space Marines. With cunning strategies and hunters' instincts, they stalk the stars and seal the fate of all enemies of Mankind.

The Space Wolves are expert hunters and trackers, loping patiently after their quarry over battlefields across the galaxy. The hyper-keen senses of their battle-brothers are more refined than those of other Chapters. These are genetic traits inherited from their Primarch, Leman Russ. Also known as the Wolf King, Russ fully embraced the tribal nature of his upbringing, and this culture forms an important part of the Chapter to this day. The Space Wolves are divided amongst twelve Great Companies, each an autonomous brotherhood whose commanding Wolf Lord is answerable only to the master of the Chapter, the Great Wolf. Diverging far from the tenets of the Codex Astartes, the Great Companies are as individual as their lords, reflecting their commander's preferred methods of warfare.

Each Great Company maintains its own ships, war engines and specialist advisors that in other Chapters are often drawn from centralised institutions. Every Great Company includes warriors who fight in what adepts of the Codex would recognise as every strata of strategic designation. In this way, each Wolf Lord is capable of taking the fight to any enemy, the warriors who answer his call deploying in massed drop assaults, in roaring columns of bikes and battle tanks, in bands of heavy weapon specialists or in swift groups of close combat killers.

Space Wolves fight in tightly knit squads called packs. Maintaining their ancient traditions, most battle-brothers fight with the same pack for their entire lives, building iron-hard bonds of camaraderie and honour that see them operate fluidly and instinctively as a whole. Individual warriors may be singled out for their glorious deeds and raised to the Great Company's elite packs of Wolf Guard, or they may possess specialised skills and traits that are best employed elsewhere, such as in stealthy and taciturn packs of Wolf Scouts or among aggressive and headstrong Skyclaws.

Guided by the Chapter's priests in their totemic, lupine culture, Space Wolves appear as barbarous and feral to their allies as they are terrifying to their enemies. Their giant warriors wear wolf pelts, runic talismans and necklaces of oversized fangs, while upon their armour and leathery, weather-beaten skins are jagged icons, tribal tattoos and warding sigils redolent of their harsh home world.

The Space Wolves hail from the death world of Fenris, an icy planet of savage beauty, storm-tossed seas and lethal predators. Its tribes of nomadic hunters endure age-long ferocious winters and brief Seasons of Fire, in which the world's scattered islands disappear beneath the waves and new lands erupt after volcanic cataclysms. Only the permanently ice-bound continent of Asaheim endures and upon its mountainous peaks rises the Space Wolves fortress monastery: the Fang. Native tradition forbids the tribes of Fenrisians from attempting to reach Asaheim, viewing it as a distant land of fierce gods. They are ignorant of the wider Imperium, and know of the Space Wolves only as mythical Sky Warriors. These armoured giants, swathed in furs, may appear suddenly after a tribal battle and take with them those youths who fought with the greatest bravery and ferocity, never to be seen again.

These vanished heroes are never mourned. Though they may have been grievously wounded when taken, as good as dead, their kin know they now wage eternal war among the stars at the side of the demigods. This warlike pragmatism and indomitable spirit was instilled by Leman Russ in the Space Wolves and remains perhaps the greatest strength of his sons. The Chapter's battle-brothers are immune to the insidious tendrils of despair, apathy and discontent, for they live the warrior's dream: an existence of daily battle waged alongside their brothers, punctuated by feasting and drinking, and at its end a truly valorous death.

As the pack follows its alpha, we follow the teachings of Russ. No greater warrior sailed the Sea of Stars, no greater champion of the Emperor ever wielded blade and axe in His name. So it has been for ten thousand years. So it will be until the end, until the Wolftime.

CURSE OF THE WULFEN

The practices by which Space Marine Chapters select, genetically alter and induct new warriors have long since become esoteric mixtures of sacred rite, pseudo-religious tradition and half-understood mummery. In the Space Wolves Chapter, the shamanic spiritualism of their warrior culture dictates that aspirants undergo a ritualistic trial – one of many – in which the inductee imbibes a potent mixture of genetic material from the Cup of Wulfen. This is the Canis Helix, the deadliest of the legacies handed down by the Wolf King.

The Primarch Leman Russ passed more than keen senses onto his sons; through the Canis Helix the bestial vigour and ferocity of the Wolf King is made manifest in the Space Wolves. After drinking from the Cup of Wulfen, the aspirant undergoes changes in body and mind. He reverts to a primal state, bones buckle and skin splits, thick hair grows in a shaggy mane and the aspirant's thoughts are filled with the desire to hunt and glut on fresh meat. The youth must control the raging beast whose howls sing through his blood, lest it overwhelm him completely. Should he endure the trials to come, the Chapter's Wolf Priests will implant the remainder of the Space Wolves gene-seed, stabilising the Canis Helix. Yet some warriors never completely conquer its transformative effects; in times of great stress, some Space Wolves succumb to berserk rages and horrifying savagery, altering into the bestial state that haunts their soul. This is the Curse of the Wulfen.

SALAMANDERS
THE SONS OF VULKAN

Forged in the crucible of war, the Salamanders are flame-bearers and warrior-craftsmen who hail from the volcanic death world of Nocturne. This brotherhood of onyx-skinned guardians has fought stoically to defend the Imperium for ten millennia, wielding master-wrought weapons to hammer the foe into oblivion.

The Salamanders are the scions of the Primarch Vulkan, whose great strength, endurance and skill in the forging and wielding of magnificent weapons is legendary. These traits and many others passed into his sons, and have persisted for ten millennia. The Chapter's warriors have skin as black as flawless obsidian, thought to be an unusual reaction between their gene-seed and the as yet unexplained radiation on their home world. Coupled with the black orbs of their eyes, broken only by ruddy glows at their centre like lit coals, Salamanders Space Marines present a more terrifying appearance than warriors of other Chapters. Though they carry their unsettling appearance with a humble nobility, more than one insurrection has been quashed in its infancy by the sight of an unhelmed Salamander advancing upon the ringleaders with red eyes blazing.

Salamanders excel in short-range firefights, striding through storms of enemy shots in suits of master-forged armour. Each step forward is echoed by synchronised bursts of blistering firepower. They expertly employ large numbers of incendiary weapons such as flamers and meltaguns, with which they burn their enemies out of the shadowed places of the galaxy and carve open their places of refuge. The Salamanders prize patience and wisdom above impetuosity and haste. Against overwhelming odds, they maintain steady advances, until they meet the foe eye to eye. Then are the fires of their rage unleashed and the famed strength of their gene-sire visited upon Mankind's enemies in blows from artisan-crafted blades and immense drake-headed thunder hammers.

The Salamanders' home world of Nocturne is a fiery orb, strung with volcanoes, black plains and sulphurous seas. Its higher crags are stalked by immense fire-breathing predators from which the Salamanders take their name. It was on Nocturne where

'Death hangs over the galaxy and seeks to extinguish the fire of the Imperium. Let our strength burn brightly, brothers, to light Humanity's path and sear its enemies to ash.'

- Chapter Master Tu'Shan

THE HEAT OF THE FORGE

Every battle-brother of the Salamanders Chapter is a highly skilled craftsman. Rather than relying wholly upon the Adeptus Mechanicus, many of the Chapter's weapons are forged by the Salamanders themselves. Each of these weapons is unique, the skill of the Space Marine who forged and embellished it showing in the strength of its construction and the surety of its shot. Symbols of the Promethean Cult are recurring features of design – the smith's hammer and anvil, the fanged maw and scales of predatory reptiles and the bloom of flame.

The draconic heat of the Salamanders' Armoury radiates from its most emblematic weapons. Imperial thermal technology, used in weapons such as the melta rifle, employs sub-molecular thermal agitation, melting or evaporating matter in moments. Living tissue is horribly and explosively vaporised, while plasteel and even solid rock run like glittering wax. Salamanders claim to hear the weapons' belligerent machine spirit in the distinctive hiss of superheated air and the roaring blast of contact.

Flame weapons all work in a similar fashion. Liquid promethium, sometimes admixed with other volatile chemicals, is stored in sealed canisters and sprayed from the weapon before it is ignited, engulfing the enemy in fire. Flamers are sometimes alloyed with the sacred boltgun, to form versatile combi-weapons.

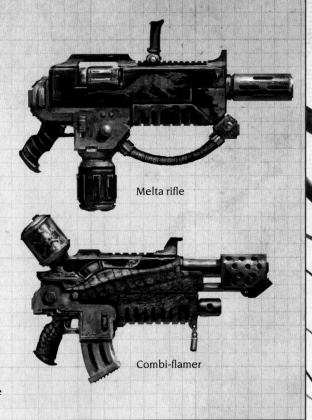

Melta rifle

Combi-flamer

Vulkan learned the art of metalworking, unlocking the secrets of fire and steel, the virtues of patience and honest labour. His sons continue to perfect these traits and each battle-brother learns to craft and maintain their own wargear with great skill. This allows the Chapter's Techmarines to focus on the repair of the Salamanders' large war machines and create technological artefacts of great beauty and perfect function.

While the Salamanders fortress monastery sits on Nocturne's barren moon of Prometheus, the Chapter's battle-brothers maintain close ties with the Human inhabitants of Nocturne. This perhaps explains why the Salamanders hold in high esteem many of the Human values that other Space Marines have distanced themselves from or simply forgotten. The Chapter's culture draws on Vulkan's formative upbringing on the planet and places great emphasis on self-reliance, loyalty and sacrifice.

The Salamanders maintain a great many technologies from ancient times, including unusually large numbers of hulking suits of Terminator armour. The Firedrakes of the Chapter's Veteran 1st Company often take to battle arrayed in such powerful wargear, and their personification of the Salamanders' ideals recalls their heroic namesakes from millennia ago. The original Firedrakes were Vulkan's elite warriors and, together with a large part of the Legion, they were betrayed during the opening stages of the Horus Heresy by those they had thought were allies. With a fraction of their Legion remaining, the Salamanders nevertheless proved a patient and enduring foe.

Official records tell of no known successors to the Salamanders Chapter prior to the Ultima Founding. It is said that at the Second Founding, when Roboute Guilliman bade every Space Marine Legion to divide its strength into separate Chapters, Vulkan secured an agreement to keep the depleted Salamanders whole. There have been many Foundings since that time, and there are several Chapters that share similarities in doctrine, organisation and physique with the sons of Vulkan. Whether these Chapters are successors of the Salamanders remains a matter of debate. During the Ultima Founding, Archmagos Belisarius Cawl used the true genetic stock of Vulkan to create Primaris battle-brothers for the Salamanders. All-Primaris Chapters were also founded from this source, their warriors plunging themselves into the fires of war with the tenacity expected of all Vulkan's sons. The Salamanders made swift contact with them, dispatching Chaplains to each to instruct them in the Promethean Cult.

IRON HANDS
THE SONS OF FERRUS MANUS

Adherents to cold logic, intolerant of weakness and utterly without mercy, the Iron Hands are implacable warriors whose resolve is as unflinching as solid adamantine. They are relentless defenders of the Imperium who seek to replace the weakness of the flesh with the unyielding strength of the machine to attain perfection.

To the Iron Hands, the flesh is weak. Though many Space Marine Chapters utilise bionics to replace body parts of their wounded that have been damaged beyond repair, the Iron Hands replace entirely functional limbs, organs and digits with mechanical augmentations. The ultimate goal for a great many Iron Hands is to be interred within a Dreadnought, which they see as the perfect alloy of the organic and the mechanical. To them no destiny is more perfect than spending an eternity of war as a living machine.

The Iron Hands inherited their disdain for weakness in part from the tribal culture of their home world, Medusa. Shrouded in a perpetual gloom, it is a death world characterised by jagged volcano ranges, rupturing geysers and toxic pollution, pumped into its atmosphere by the population's enormous land-crawlers. Medusa's inhabitants are in a constant state of war with each other, fighting furiously over the planet's scarce resources. Such a way of life breeds a hardy and remorseless people. However, the greatest cause of the Iron Hands' intolerance can be traced to their Primarch, Ferrus Manus; indeed, it was his death that set them fully down the path of affinity with the machine.

Ferrus Manus was the first Primarch to die in the Horus Heresy. When he learned of Horus' treachery he made for the Isstvan System with all haste. On the ash plains of Isstvan V he surged into the fray without hesitation, consumed with wrath. In the bloody ambush by several brother Legions that killed tens of thousands of loyalist Legionaries, he struck down traitor after traitor, and ignored the pleas to retreat issued by Vulkan of the Salamanders and Corax of the Raven Guard. For all of Manus' fury, he could not prevail against the odds stacked against him, and he was slain by the traitor Primarch Fulgrim of the Emperor's Children, who had once been amongst Ferrus' closest brothers.

The death of their indomitable gene-sire caused the surviving Iron Hands much anguish. They blamed the Salamanders and Raven Guard for failing to support Ferrus in his hour of greatest need. They blamed themselves for their own weakness, for not being able to reach their Primarch and fight by his side. They even blamed Ferrus Manus himself, for allowing his anger to consume him at the expense of sense and logic. The Iron Hands decided that they would purge this emotional weakness, embedded as it is in organic flesh, from themselves, so that they might never fall to its frailties as their Primarch did.

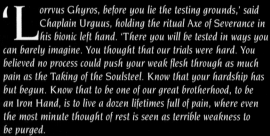

'Lorrvus Ghyros, before you lie the testing grounds,' said Chaplain Urguus, holding the ritual Axe of Severance in his bionic left hand. 'There you will be tested in ways you can barely imagine. You thought that our trials were hard. You believed no process could push your weak flesh through as much pain as the Taking of the Soulsteel. Know that your hardship has but begun. Know that to be one of our great brotherhood, to be an Iron Hand, is to live a dozen lifetimes full of pain, where even the most minute thought of rest is seen as terrible weakness to be purged.

'But ahead of you lies opportunity. If you survive, if you are strong, you will become more than the mere meat you are now. Within our brotherhood you can embrace the logic of the machine, become attuned with it, even become it.

'Tell me, Lorrvus Ghyros, formerly of Clan Avernii and now on the precipice of honoured Clan Dorrvok, the Crucible. Do you embrace the life that awaits you?'

Lorrvus looked straight ahead, his left hand outstretched and resting upon a cold metal slab. 'With steel in my soul and iron in my hearts,' he said.

'Do you vow to purge all of your fear, the greatest weakness of all?'

'Through inexorable reason and unbending rationality shall it be excised.'

'Are you prepared to begin the forgechain, that which links our core to the harshness of Medusa and to the clans with which we bring death to the Emperor's foes?'

'It will make me as everlasting as adamantine itself.'

'An Iron Hand is tempered only by the fires of battle, the inferno of war and the blood of his enemies. An Iron Hand faces these without fear, and has unbending knowledge that they strengthen him.'

'I am ready, I am willing, I will be Iron.'

In a single, swift motion, Urguus brought the axe down, severing Lorrvus' left hand. The blade went straight through to the slab beneath. The severed lump of bone and flesh flopped to the floor. Lorrvus made no response. He did not even blink.

'Welcome, brother,' said the Chaplain, his face expressionless.

As a part of this purge, the Iron Council was formed, its nominated members each granted the title of Iron Father. It has led the Iron Hands ever since. The Iron Hands have no permanent Chapter Master, instead electing a warrior to lead the Chapter if one is deemed required. The Iron Council adopted Roboute Guilliman's Codex Astartes, seeing it as the only logical course. Despite this, each of the Iron Hands' ten companies retained the clan company names of the Legion, which are in turn taken from the greatest clans of Medusa's population. The Iron Hands held on to the tradition despite its apparent superfluity.

In its pursuit of perfection by purging the weakness of flesh from their bodies, the Iron Hands in time grew more reclusive and insular. It was only with the Adeptus Mechanicus that their ties grew, bonded by their reverence for machines and scorn for the weakness of the organic. This relationship has proven beneficial to the Iron Hands – their armoured vehicles and Dreadnoughts are among the most mechanically resilient and best crafted in the Imperium, and their Techmarines are taught secrets of the Omnissiah that those of most Chapters will never learn. It is a great irony that this bond with the Machine Cults of Mars has been forged through shared passion rather than sheer logical necessity. If the Iron Hands have observed this, they have never remarked on it.

To those that encounter them, the Iron Hands almost resemble automata, apparently despising such concepts as valour that drive so many of their brother Chapters. Nonetheless, at their core they are still of Mankind, and emotion rules a part of their hearts regardless of their efforts to suppress it. In fact, such efforts merely draw it out. Their wrath is legendary. Their hatred for weakness is still hate. Their reverence of the machine is still reverence.

When the Iron Hands go to war, they select the war zones they will fight in through ruthless utilitarianism. The Iron Hands perform the Calculum Rationale, a painstakingly detailed and ruthless calculation that determines the exact resources needed for victory. If these are

not available for a campaign, they will not fight. On the battlefield itself, the Iron Hands often prioritise the destruction of the foe to the saving of the world they are fighting on. While this makes them lethal, uncompromising adversaries, for many it can make them poor, if not dangerous, allies.

As the Great Rift tore across the galaxy and the population of world after world succumbed to waves of mutation of psychic maladies, the Iron Hands tolerance for flesh only grew weaker.

They responded to threats in the manner they always had, however – with careful calculation. This has seen much of the Chapter's strength deployed to the vital world of Vigilus, where they and the warriors from their Brazen Claws and Sons of Medusa successors have fought with distinction. They have deployed with such unfeeling discernment that those they have refused aid to have deemed them aloof and unreliable. The Iron Hands care not, indifferent to what they see as nothing more than the craven mewling of the weak.

In iron, strength. In steel, fortitude. In the machine, perfection. With these shall we have victory over our weaknesses, and victory over our foes.

DEATHWATCH

SLAYERS OF THE ALIEN HORDE

It is the task of the Deathwatch to defend the Imperium from the ravages of the xenos, countless species of which threaten Mankind in every corner of the galaxy. For thousands of years the Deathwatch have remained true to their endless task. Drawing their numbers from almost every Space Marine Chapter, each is an elite alien killer of proven skill in battle.

The galaxy is inhabited with innumerable alien horrors, each non-Human race seen by the Deathwatch as a blight on Mankind's birthright. Wherever these creatures tread they taint the land, pollute the air and poison the waters. Their very existence is a crime that the Deathwatch punish with death. On a thousand fronts is the Imperium threatened by these monsters, and it is the duty of the Deathwatch to meet them wherever and whenever they raise their heads. The threats are myriad and endless, and against them the Deathwatch are the Shield that Slays, the thin black line. They are the watchmen in the void that throw back colossal xenos invasions, put planetwide nesting sites to flame and mercilessly stamp out emerging threats before they grow. They endure unimaginable terrors and fight creatures dangerous beyond measure, whether they be clouds of minute parasites or gigantic bio-titans.

The Deathwatch are puritanical in their hatred of the alien. Few understand the true repugnance of xenos species more than the Deathwatch. Such is their loathing that only in the rarest of circumstances will they consider even the most tentative truce with a xenos race, and then only if such an action will result in the destruction of a much graver threat or the saving of a vital Imperial world.

The Deathwatch are organised into small, elite companies, their strength drawn from the Space Marine Chapters who have pledged to tithe a portion of their number to the annihilation of the alien. A battle-brother can only join the Deathwatch with the approval of his Captain, an Apothecary and Chaplain of his Chapter, and must be an expert in slaying all manner of xenos creatures. Before departing to join one of the Deathwatch's watch fortresses, he will leave his battle-brothers in a solemn ceremony where his armour is painted black, for few expect him to return alive. Once a Space Marine has joined his Deathwatch brothers, he receives advanced training in anti-xenos combat techniques and in the use of a range of weapons only the Deathwatch have access to. He is also subject to all manner of psycho-conditioning. During this arduous process he absorbs the knowledge the Deathwatch have accrued in their millennia-long fight. Thus, even if he goes to war against a species he has never before encountered, he will instinctively know their weaknesses and how to exploit them.

When a Space Marine joins the Deathwatch, their rank is cast aside and he joins a kill team, a disparate group of formidable warriors from up to ten different Chapters. This squad dynamic inevitably leads to friction and rivalries, but all are sworn to the greater cause. The kill team's brotherhood is forged in combat, in the terrible adversity they face. They begin to respect each other's skills and methods of war and learn from each other. Unshakeable bonds between entire Chapters have formed via harmonious Deathwatch kill teams in which the combat doctrines of the battle-brothers have worked together seamlessly. In this way, Deathwatch kill teams are stronger than the sum of their parts, honed so finely they can devastate alien machinations with a single, well-placed attack.

The Deathwatch is no blunt instrument. Countless races infest worlds and flood space with their multitudes, too numerous to engage in open battle. Thus the Deathwatch investigate, observe, analyse and only then strike at the optimal point to cause the most catastrophic damage. Then they withdraw to strike again at the next critical vulnerability in their foe. By this method have they prevented the awakening of Necron tomb worlds, scattered Aeldari raiders, purged Tyranid tendrils and stymied Ork Waaaghs!

With the Great Rift's emergence, never has the Deathwatch's unstinting vigil been of more vital importance. The task of defeating the alien falls increasingly heavy upon them as Imperial world after Imperial world becomes embattled with the forces of the Archenemy or beset by heretical uprisings.

The Deathwatch's responsibility is a nigh on overwhelming burden to bear. To this day, however, it is one they shoulder with pride, and to this day they have proved equal to the task.

DEATHWATCH HERALDRY

The many watch fortresses of the Deathwatch – such as Talasa Prime, the Furor Shield and the Eye of Damocles – each have their own unique banners and heraldry, adorned with their sigils and symbols. Many of these bear sanctified trophies – skulls and bones of those beasts and creatures slain in defence of the Imperium. The standards recount the watch fortress' victories, the stitched on name of each battle representing a time when the Deathwatch wiped a xenos species from existence, or saved an Imperial system from a horrific end at the claws of some abominable race.

It is around these symbols, honour rolls and banners that the brotherhood of the watch fortress is formed.

With ranks replete with warriors from scores, perhaps hundreds, of different Chapters, it is essential that all brothers see themselves as part of a greater whole. The banners of the Deathwatch remind them of the legacy that has been passed down to them by brothers past, what a formidable force they are now privileged to be a part of and what glories they can win. This is not to say a warrior's history with their own Chapter is without importance – far from it. The Deathwatch are encouraged to embrace the strengths of all within a kill team to the betterment of the Imperium. The Deathwatch's incredible success in the millennia of its existence is testament to the effectiveness of this system.

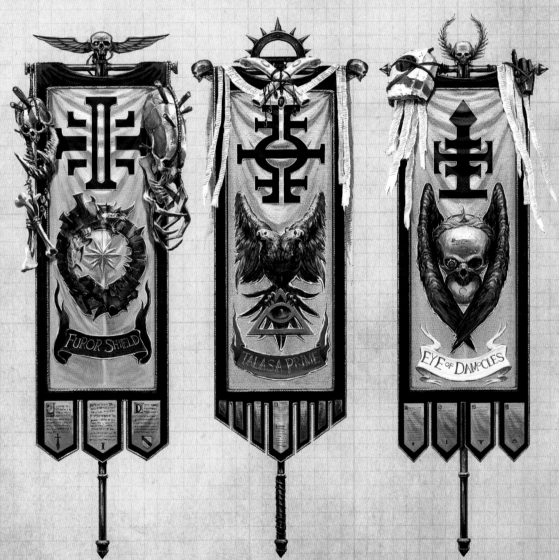

Furor Shield has the task of monitoring the Octarius Sector. Both the Ork and Tyranid race adapt and evolve in war, and whichever survives their titanic conflict will emerge deadlier than ever.

Talasa Prime is the Deathwatch's capital training world. Rather than a space station, this watch fortress is an entire world, situated in Ultramar. They have slain countless T'au and Tyranids.

The Eye of Damocles is a vast fortress that monitors the borders between Imperial and T'au space. Its kill teams are experts in vertical assaults, striking from Corvus Blackstar gunships.

We care not what the alien thinks; that we simply hate suffices.

SUCCESSOR CHAPTERS

Most Space Marine Chapters can trace their genetic lineage to one of the nine loyal Primarchs that fought for the Emperor during the Horus Heresy.

There is no singular reason as to why a certain Primarch's gene-seed is selected for a new Chapter during a Founding. Assessment of purity, availability of resource, the reasons for the Founding being declared in the first place and even political manoeuvring has had an impact on which gene-seed is used and how often.

Many successor Chapters have close bonds with their parent Chapters, as the Covenant of Fire have with the Salamanders. This is not always the case, however. Chapters have their own own histories and traditions, often developed over centuries or longer, which their battle-brothers are deeply proud of. Thus, some feel little reason to hold their parent in higher regard than others. Some successors will never encounter their parent Chapter, with both waging wars at opposite ends of the galaxy. Such a situation easily breeds indifference. Some Chapters even shun their parent Chapters for all manner of reasons.

IMPERIAL FISTS SUCCESSORS

Black Templars
The Black Templars are valiant warrior-knights and pious champions of the Emperor. They are deeply unusual among the Adeptus Astartes for venerating the Emperor as a literal god. The Chapter's fanatical devotion finds its focus in constant campaigning. A fleet-based Chapter, they divide their forces into crusades led by Marshals, and storm across the galaxy immolating and annihilating everything that stands in their path.

Crimson Fists
The Crimson Fists spent arduous decades on the brink of extinction. Crippled by the assault on their home planet of Rynn's World by Ork Waaagh! Snagrod, the Chapter held on to their planet through sheer tenacity and tactical excellence. Only with the Ultima Founding was their strength restored, and they could look to the future with some degree of hope. They now fight to overthrow xenos despots and tyrants.

Hammers of Dorn
Founded in the 41st Millennium, the Hammers of Dorn have already proven themselves during hundreds of campaigns, including the bitterly fought Achilus Crusade against the Word Bearers, and the Nightfire Wars against the T'au. The Hammers of Dorn are a stringent Codex Chapter, and uphold the precepts of Guilliman's scriptures with exacting precision.

Subjugators
Near as zealous as the Black Templars, the Subjugators are infamous for their extreme and unsubtle methods of warfare. There have been numerous documented occasions where the Subjugators have liberated a conquered Imperial world at the cost of its entire population. Of course, though the Subjugators' methods may be costly, they are also spectacularly effective.

Iron Knights
Every inch of the Iron Knights' home world of Brycantia is sheathed in the metal or hewn stone of manufactorums and bastions. The population spends its existence under the overseer's lash, producing vast quantities of weapons and ammunition for the Iron Knights. The Chapter's warriors share the harsh demeanour of the people, knowing that hardship and sacrifice are necessary if they are to win victories.

Sons of the Phoenix
Faithful to the Emperor and ritualistic in their battle cant, the Sons of the Phoenix pride themselves on plunging into the flames of battle. Their crusades are so impressive in spectacle they pave the way for the Imperial creed to spread, and hence are followed by a great many holy men and women. The Chapter fleet was scattered by the opening of the Great Rift, and now the Sons of the Phoenix crusade to gather their forces back as one.

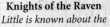

Revilers

One of the Raven Guard's few Second Founding successors, the ranks of the Revilers were drawn heavily from the survivors of the Isstvan V disaster. The Chapter's warriors have proven worthy inheritors of Corax's legacy, possessing exceptional skills in stealth and ambush. The Revilers maintain an ongoing shadow war with the traitor forces of the Alpha Legion, and have thwarted many of their insidious schemes.

Rift Stalkers

A relatively new Chapter, the Rift Stalkers are composed entirely of Primaris Space Marines. They are fleet-based, for it is their task to patrol the Cicatrix Maledictum, as many foul abominations emerge out of that great rent in reality. In addition to slaying the Emperor's enemies, they diligently seek new methods of reconnecting with the hundreds of thousands of worlds cut off in the galactic north.

Raptors

Believed to have been founded from initiates training on Deliverance at the time of the Isstvan V disaster, the Raptors are an ancient and well respected Chapter. They prize skilled marksmanship and independent thought, and view the Codex Astartes as a highly effective set of guidelines rather than absolute doctrine. The Raptors are known for fielding substantial 10th Company assets supported by waves of combat skimmers.

Iron Ravens

The Iron Ravens are specialists in sudden, shocking drop assaults. Their 10th Company elements may spend months building up local intelligence and preparing the ground so that, when the main body of the Iron Ravens force comes screaming down into battle, they strike with such decisive and destructive precision that the war is won with a single unstoppable sword-blow. The Chapter have taken to calling this 'the Blade of Corax'.

Knights of the Raven

Little is known about the Knights of the Raven. When they fight alongside other Imperial forces, they communicate only when necessary, and talk to each other in cryptic battle-tongue. The fortress monastery of the Chapter is on the feudal world of Coralax. To the inhabitants of this bleak place, the Knights of the Raven are mythological figures who descend from the heavens to spirit away their greatest young warriors.

Black Guard

This Chapter believes in the timely application of overwhelming firepower to defeat their foes. Masters of the careful ambush, the Black Guard deploy massed batteries of Thunderfire Cannons and Vindicators to annihilate their enemies in an instant. Overkill or half measures are not concepts that the Chapter's warriors understand, and they are known to leave vast cratered ruins in the wake of their many victories.

Necropolis Hawks

The Necropolis Hawks are trained extensively in close-quarters combat, and many are veterans of fierce city-fights. They additionally bear their battlefield role insignia upon their backpacks so that their comrades can identify them even in the choking smoke and dust of urban war. Although a newer Chapter, the Necropolis Hawks have earned a reputation for pragmatic brutality and relentless – if carefully measured – aggression.

Death Spectres

Stationed beyond the bounds of the Imperium, the Death Spectres keep constant vigil. Even with the Great Rift yawning wide, their thankless duty remains: ensuring that the mysterious, deathless inhabitants of the Ghoul Stars never again ascend to threaten the galaxy. They come from the Thirteenth Founding, which is known as the Dark Founding, for less is known of its creations than of any other Space Marine founding.

Marauders

The Marauders are isolationist in their tendencies. They will fight readily enough alongside other Imperial forces, but remain aloof and exchange only what information they must to prosecute their campaigns. Recognised for their particular aptitude as marksmen, the Marauders often set ambushes for their enemies and hammer them with massed firepower before sweeping down to finish off the ragged and terrified survivors.

Rampagers

The Rampagers are a Second Founding successor of the White Scars, known for their practice of facial scarring to denote rank. At the celebratory feasts that follow these rituals, the blood of those marked for elevation is mixed with drinks. The Rampagers are in the habit of claiming feral worlds as fresh recruiting grounds in the wake of conquest – providing the planet's populace test negative for any forms of spiritual or physical corruption.

Dark Hunters

The Dark Hunters were founded during the tenebrous days of the Occlusiad. That their first campaign as a Chapter saw harrowing fighting against the Daemon Engines of Warpsmith Hilghar, and the mutated Warlord Titan Repellus Maximal during the Battle of Bloodsteel, has left a deep-rooted mistrust of the machine within their psyche. Even today, the Chapter's relations with the Tech-Priests of Mars are strained at best.

Destroyers

Established during the Second Founding, the Destroyers have a troubled history. Though they have won many great victories, questions remain regarding the stability of their gene-seed. These concerns have grown despite the self-sacrificing heroics the Chapter displayed in the wake of the Daemon rampage throughout the Lhorgus Sub-sector. For their part, the Destroyers are concerned only with the next mission.

Solar Hawks

The Solar Hawks are from an unknown founding, but date back to at least M35. Aggressive and noble, they embody all that is best in the sons of the Khan, and honour their progenitor by either painting a pauldron or gauntlet white. As their name suggests, they field an especially large number of airborne assets, regularly deploying whole wings of Stormtalons, Stormravens and other gunships into battle.

Storm Reapers

There are few more battle-hungry than the Storm Reapers, the first Primaris Chapter founded from Jaghatai Khan's gene-seed. The Khan would be proud of his ferocious sons; they are wise and noble, but fight with a passion he would recognise as his own. They claimed the feral world of Jagun for their home, with its savage natives, and were commended for their spearheading of the Absolutis Crusade.

Storm Lords

As Second Founding successors of the White Scars, the Storm Lords can trace their history back to a time when Jaghatai Khan hunted across the stars. They have maintained a strong rivalry with their parent Chapter, frequently competing for glory, and have been known to go to reckless lengths in order to emerge victorious. The Storm Lords are also particularly well known for the ferocity with which they hunt Ork Waaaghs!.

Mantis Warriors

Thanks to their indiscretions during the Badab War, the Mantis Warriors have spent decades on a penitent crusade. Due to their historic crimes, the Chapter received no Greyshield reinforcements when its Torchbearer fleet reached it, leaving the Mantis Warriors terribly understrength and still on their near-ruinous crusade. Nevertheless, they have utilised the Primaris technology to as good an effect as they can.

Iron Lords

The Iron Lords are a Chapter known for their stern demeanour and lauded xenophobia. For long years now it has been the duty of the Iron Lords to watch over the Grendl Stars, encircling the vile Barghesi and preventing their destructive potential from being absorbed by Hive Fleet Kraken. Knowing the consequences of this would be dire for the Imperium, the Iron Lords have suffered greatly in upholding their oath.

Brazen Claws

Unyielding and remorseless, the Brazen Claws are noted for their stoicism and their grim determination to succeed. Since their creation during the Second Founding, they have amassed a string of glories and triumphs. Arriving too late to fight on Cadia itself, they instead bled the foe around the Cadian Gate. Riding out the cataclysmic opening of the Great Rift, they lent their might to the defence of Gudrun, Lapis VII and other worlds.

Covenant of Fire

The Covenant of Fire crave knowledge of the Imperium they fight for, seeking out lore wherever they can find it, hoping that this information can help them bring light to darkness. Conversely, they purge any sign of heretical material they find, knowing that its knowledge is a false light that leads only to ruin. The Chapter eagerly embraced the Promethean Cult, imbibing and applying the wisdom of their gene-sire swiftly.

Black Vipers

The Salamanders accidentally learned of the Black Vipers many years after they learned of their other Ultima Founding successors. Sur K'gosi, the Chaplain sent to the Chapter by the Salamanders, disappeared without trace. The Black Vipers appear to claim no world for their own, and spurn contact with allies on the rare occasion where it is seen at war. Wherever the Chapter has been identified, agents of Belisarius Cawl have never been far away…

Red Talons

The Red Talons are a Second Founding Chapter. Their home world of Raikan lies within the Segmentum Tempestus. Since their founding at the end of the Great Scouring, the Red Talons have been known for their bold style of warfare and never-ending vendetta against the Traitor Legions. Several times the Lords of Terra have tasked the Red Talons with hunting down and destroying Renegade Chapters, a duty they discharge with relish.

Sons of Medusa

The Sons of Medusa are utterly ruthless, and share the Iron Hands' reliance on the power of the machine and intolerance for the weakness of flesh. The Chapter's unorthodox organisational doctrine sees its companies divided between three war clans, and is notable for its furious aggression, large-scale use of armoured transports, and thundering armoured spearheads that it drives deep into enemy lines.

Dragonspears

A fleet-based Chapter, the Dragonspears have won renown fighting alongside the Space Wolves against the Orks at the Gnarion Reef, and have become expert Ork hunters. Being constantly on the move, it took many years for the Salamanders to make contact with them, in which time the Dragonspears developed a very strong culture of self-sacrifice and endocannibalism, to ensure their lost brothers never fall from memory.

Dark Krakens

The Dark Krakens' oceanic and night-bathed home world of Naktis only boasts one land mass capable of supporting a fortress monastery. Naktis' vast seas are replete with bioluminescent megafauna and shoal-predators, which the native population hunt for sport and nourishment. Echoing this, in battle the Dark Krakens seek out the largest foes, whether that be in terms of physical size or sheer numbers.

UNKNOWN FOUNDINGS

Not every Chapter can trace its lineage to one of the Primarchs. Over the millennia records have been lost, destroyed, tampered with or concealed. For some Chapters being ignorant of this part of their history is a source of immense frustration, and they take great pains to learn anything they can of their brotherhood's origins, waging entire wars for fragments of information. Others care little. They believe that it is their task to defeat and kill the Emperor's foes, and that knowing or recovering lost parts of their history contributes little to the successful fulfilment of their purpose. Rumours often abound around these Chapters regardless, as some demonstrate the traits of certain First Founding Chapters more than others, or even exhibit the characteristics of more than one equally.

These Unknown Founding Chapters cannot count on the brotherhood often found among Chapters descended from the same Primarch. Their alliances are hard-won, and the mystery that surrounds them sees them deemed unworthy by some. Nonetheless, they are loyal Chapters of the Adeptus Astartes, and they fight furiously for the Imperium.

Mentors
The Mentors Chapter have no official progenitor, but it is known they were created during the 26th Founding. The Mentors are distrusting of others, and prefer to work alone and unobserved. They are often referred to as the Mentor Legion, and some – highly unreliable and apocryphal – fragmentary records suggest that the Chapter has at times fielded warriors of unusual size, strength and fortitude.

Fire Lords
The Fire Lords favour a plethora of flamer weapons. Preceding their fiery assaults with barrages of incendiary missiles, they hurl themselves at the charred, bewildered foe even before the flames have burned out. Their home world is Mundus Pyra, a planet far out on the Eastern Fringe, and they are known for the strange flamecraft they use in Chapter rituals, which many find reminiscent of the Salamanders.

Blood Ravens
The Blood Ravens originate from an unknown founding and have an unknown gene-sire. They have operated as a solely fleet-based Chapter ever since the loss of their home planet. Their own records have been expunged, and the ones kept by the Ordo Malleus are sealed. Perhaps because of this, the Blood Ravens hunger for knowledge, and are particularly obsessive about discovering the truth behind their creation.

Black Dragons
It is believed that the Black Dragons were created in the so-called Cursed Founding, but their gene-sire is unknown. Rumours abound of a genetic mutation that can cause osseous blades to protrude from their limbs. Their name appears in battle records fighting alongside other Chapters, but their presence is brief. Only the turmoil of the Great Rift has halted the latest Inquisition investigation into the Black Dragons.

Exorcists
The Exorcists are speculated to have come from the Thirteenth Founding. Their progenitor is known only to the highest-ranking members of the Ordo Malleus, and details of their creation have been placed under Inquisitorial seal. The Exorcists maintain two additional Scout Companies, for a total of twelve companies – their esoteric training requires a high influx of recruits in order to ensure the Chapter's continuation.

Star Dragons
The Star Dragons practise ritual scarification, inlaying the deep cuts with electro circuitry that causes them to glow like caged stars. There has been speculation that they are the scions of Ferrus Manus, but if this is so they display little of their erstwhile brothers' relentless logic. Instead, the Star Dragons are guided by their furious passions, unleashing their wrath upon any who threaten the Emperor's realm.

Storm Giants

The Storm Giants have fought in several of the Imperium's greatest and most pivotal wars, not least amongst them the Third War for Armageddon. They display heightened physical strength, even for Space Marines, and there is some debate that their gene-seed may have mutated to enhance their biscopea. Several magos-genitors have made requests to study the Chapter's gene-seed, but the Storm Giants have refused on each occasion.

White Templars

Hailing from the world of Sanctum, the White Templars are stoic and relentless in their prosecution of the foe. Though for a time it was thought that they were Imperial Fists successors, recent discoveries by Administratum genetoria-logi have thrown substantial doubt upon this claim. The White Templars have been shaken by this revelation, and have launched a star-spanning crusade to discover the truth.

Dragon Lords

All contact was lost with the Dragon Lords even before the emergence of the Great Rift. By immense and costly efforts, a torchbearer task force discovered them fighting still, having been nearly annihilated by successive Hrud invasions that reduced their fortress monastery to dust. The Dragon Lords vowed to rebuild and have been reinforced by their Primaris brethren. They now wage war anew in the Imperium Nihilus.

Brazen Skulls

Though the Brazen Skulls are known to have been destroyed during the Sabbat Worlds Crusade, their name, colours and heraldry were reinstated during the Ultima Founding, and thus all of their number are Primaris Space Marines. The Brazen Skulls are determined to live up to the honour of their forebears and have swiftly earned a reputation for heroism, tenacity and all-consuming hatred for the forces of Chaos.

Tigers Argent

With their home world perilously close to the Great Rift as well as the Pariah Nexus, the Tigers Argent are extremely hard-pressed. Their battered strike forces have repulsed incursion after incursion pouring from the Cicatrix Maledictum and have yet to be bested. Icefang, their home world, has become a beacon of hope, drawing all manner of refugees and scattered Imperial forces seeking sanctuary.

Red Scorpions

The fleet-based crusaders of the Red Scorpions believe in the Emperor's divinity without question and are staunch followers of the Codex Astartes, which they see as holy writ. Fanatical in their pursuit of purity, their gene-seed's sanctity is essential to their core beliefs; as a result, they have more Apothecaries than most Chapters, and their Master of the Apothecarion is second in command of the whole Chapter.

Carcharodons

Mysterious prowlers of the outer dark, the Carcharodons are ever on the move, seeking out the Emperor's foes beyond the Imperium's borders. Few have ever fought alongside them. Those who have report their unsettling savagery, their preference for rapid strikes using stealth or extreme speed, and their deadly skill in close-quarters actions using a range of bayonets, blades, chain weapons and point-blank weapons fire.

Minotaurs

The Minotaurs' history beyond a thousand years ago has been deliberately concealed by edicts that even Inquisitors cannot circumvent with ease. In battle they are possessed of a berserk fury and are willing to sustain heavy losses to ensure victory. How they are able to maintain the rapid influx of aspirants and war machinery to replace those lost is another mystery. More than one Imperial agent has been found dead whilst researching such subjects.

The Damnation of Tybilos' *laser blaster exploded in a colossal azure fireball.* The heretic Titan was staggered by the force of the blast, much of its night-blue armour scorched to a deep, coal black. The groans of tortured metal were like the moans of a wounded prey-beast, and the god-machine responded like a cornered, desperate animal. Blue flames danced around the joint socket where the *Damnation*'s laser blaster had been. Fat sparks fizzled and popped, raining to the ground.

Ultramarines Captain Galenus saw the Titan's gatling blaster spin to life at a speed that looked impossible for such a gargantuan weapon. '*Macragge's Javelin, Primarch's Thunder,* evasive pattern Theta, now!' he roared over the vox. The Titan unleashed a stream of high explosive shells at the Repulsor Executioners that had wounded it so sorely. Both were erased from existence by the barrage – all that remained of the once proud battle tanks were scraps of burnt and twisted metal.

Galenus cursed. 'Not swift enough,' he breathed. Honourable brothers and noble machine spirits were lost. The Executioners were his primary assets for dealing with the Titan. He was not without brave warriors who could be counted on, but even for Space Marine infantry toppling a god-machine was a difficult prospect.

The *Damnation of Tybilos* was isolated. Galenus' warriors had pushed back the throngs of deranged cultists that worshipped the Titan, cutting down swathes of the hooded, malnourished masses that fought like lunatics as they screamed the name of their false god. More than half his strike force was engaged to keep the *Damnation* without support.

Oh, to be on the front lines, he thought. But he could not go there. His power sword, as beautiful and deadly a relic as it was, was useless against the Titan. On this day he was tactician and strategist, a coordinator of the finest warriors in the galaxy in pursuit of the destruction of the heretical abomination that blighted Vackenides.

This battle is far from over, he thought. The Titan had to be destroyed. The space port of Helice was only a few score miles away, where hundreds of thousands were being evacuated from the doomed world. They had to be protected.

'Brothers,' said Galenus into the strike-force-wide vox. 'Cordio, Bassus, we need your Land Speeders. Allecto, your Centurions are to provide covering fire – target whatever you deem fit, and do not cease firing. Aelius, have *Hera's Arrow* on aerial overwatch at all times. Raldor, do the same with the *Lightning of Ultramar*. Remember, the engine's plasma generators are built into the rear of its carapace.' The acknowledgement runes built into his tactical display blinked green.

Galenus looked up and saw the *Arrow* and *Lightning* storm overhead, the Stormraven and Stormtalon flying in loose formation. Within seconds they opened fire, launching streams of missiles and searing plasma blasts at the Titan's head. Such fire would have reduced most foes to wrecked shells or bloody paste, but against the *Damnation* they simply rippled over the god-machine's void shields, which had already partially restored following the destruction of its laser blaster. Nonetheless, the Ultramarine pilots continued firing whilst moving at high speed, avoiding the hails of missiles fired back at them. The spiralling warheads explosives detonated harmlessly across the city, causing the stagnant water Galenus stood in to tremble. Much of the city was partially flooded, the Mathineion Dam having been breached by another traitor god-engine scant weeks before.

'Everyone else, keep moving. Antoninus, Decimus, move your squads closer but remain out of sight. You may be needed to advance within the engine's void shields.'

On the tactica-cartographicus built into his helmet's display, Galenus saw all his squads' movements. He saw the rough line where Intercessors and Dreadnoughts held back droves of cultists desperate to reach their adamantine deity. He saw Antoninus' Eradicators and Decimus' Hellblasters moving concentrically towards the god-machine, hugging what cover they could and taking advantage where the Titan was distracted by the *Arrow*, the *Lightning* and Land Speeders. Galenus maintained his distance from the fighting, keeping himself obscured from the *Damnation*'s view where he could, but in a position to watch the battle as it unfolded with his own eyes. His command squad and Chaplain Tavian shadowed his movements.

The *Damnation* kept moving, refusing to present its vulnerable plasma generators to any one direction for too long, its gigantic adamantine feet crushing what little remained of the structures around it. With the Ultramarines focusing on speed, it was clearly struggling to find targets, but that changed when Sergeant Allecto's Centurion Devastators opened fire. Lascannon beams evaporated against the Titan's void shields. Krak missiles simply bounced off them. Though the Centurions were already redeploying after having fired, it was too late. The god-engine launched a storm of apocalypse missiles that struck their positions, wreathing them in terrible flames.

'Sergeant Allecto,' Galenus said over the vox. 'Report.'

Hissing static was his only reply. There was no more weapons fire.

Undoubtedly the Titan's corrupted machine spirit was enraged by the insect-like irritation the Space Marines provided. It began firing in all directions, apparently determined to kill through sheer weight of fire. Barrages of missiles and salvoes of high-explosive rounds tore the landscape apart. Casualty reports came through swiftly. Life-sign markers turned from green to red. Land Speeders were destroyed. The Ultramarines maintained their manoeuvres and attacks. Casualties were a part of Space Marine life, an inevitable price that had to be paid for victory. Nonetheless, Galenus' list of options was growing shorter.

It would grow shorter yet.

'Heretic Astartes identified,' declared Lieutenant Lato over the vox. He was leading the forces keeping the cultists at bay. 'Fist of Guilliman is damaged. Cultist forces resurging. Request reinforcements. Chance of enemy breakthrough increased by a factor of four.' His voice was calm, measured, as it should be.

Fist of Guilliman, damaged, thought Galenus incredulously. The relic Land Raider had served the Ultramarines since the Great Crusade. It was a wondrous treasure, beyond priceless.

'The heretics cannot be allowed to capture or destroy the Fist,' said Chaplain Tavian.

'Agreed, brother-Chaplain. Take my command squad, along with a Repulsor and a Razorback.'

The Chaplain saluted and left. Within minutes, Hera's Steed and Hamerixis had thundered off to relieve the other part of the company.

'Caltar, take your Eliminators to Lieutenant Lato. He has need of you,' Galenus said over the vox.

'Aye, Captain,' Caltar replied.

Galenus' vox chimed into life again within seconds. It was Raldor, piloting the Lightning.

'Captain, the Titan's fire grows–'

The vox suddenly cut out. Galenus looked up. The rear half of the Lightning had been sheared off completely and the gunship was plummeting to the ground in a dizzying spin. Out of control, it smashed into the Arrow. The heretic engine's gods must be conspiring against us, he thought. Together the Stormtalon and Stormraven veered and tumbled through the air, but somehow not without purpose. 'Throne,' Galenus said under his breath in disbelief. 'They can't be…'.

The flyers crashed into the Titan, causing a horrific explosion that engulfed the wrecked gunships in a raging inferno as their fuel tanks ignited and ammunition hoppers detonated. The god-engine still stood, though was visibly damaged. 'Thank you, brothers,' he said. He nonetheless clenched his jaw in frustration. His warriors were dying, and they were no closer to victory.

We have to get within the void shields, he thought. Exploit the damage caused, make their sacrifice worth it.

'Cordio, Bossus, keep close to the Damnation,' he ordered over the vox. 'Make it impossible for it to hit you. Antoninus, Decimus, we have to kill the engine at its heart. I am coming to you, but do not slow down.'

He ran as fast as he could through the water, each stride working against the volume of stale liquid. He was a Space Marine – no such minor obstacle would ever slow him down. He took care to keep in the shadows of those buildings that remained, lest his form appear in the Titan's targeting reticules. Not encumbered by heavy Gravis armour or plasma incinerators as his warriors were, Galenus soon gained ground with and reached his Eradicators and Hellblasters. He saw that many of those who had begun the battle were missing.

The Titan emitted furious blasts from its warhorn. It was enraged. It wanted them dead. The thunderous booming of its enormous tread reverberated through the ground. It was hunting them.

'Keep the monster distracted,' Galenus voxed to his Land Speeder pilots. 'I'm moving in with squads Antoninus and Decimus.'

Galenus advanced. He had no need to give orders to his warriors. They moved with him, in formations they had drilled countless times. The Space Marines advanced as rapidly as they could, taking cover when stray rounds exploded nearby. Thanks to their armour they shrugged off flying chunks of ferrocrete the size of their helmets.

The *Damnation* was less than a hundred metres away.

'Onwards, brothers, for Ultramar!' Galenus yelled, upping his pace to a sprint.

'We march for Macragge!' came the response. As one, the twelve Space Marines ran.

'Victory and revenge will be ours!'

'For Guilliman and the Emperor!'

As he ran, Galenus watched the distance counter to the Titan drop.

Ninety metres...

Seventy metres...

Fifty metres...

The Titan turned. It saw them. It fired. A trio of missiles shot towards them. Their best chance of survival was to keep charging, to get inside the god-engine's guard.

Primarch, bring my warriors through the tempest, Galenus thought. Though the Primarch had returned, old habits died hard. He still invoked Roboute Guilliman in times of need. He saw the missiles fly towards his battle-brothers, superhuman reflexes allowing him to note the malignant symbols scratched on their flanks. He saw the corruption that had consumed them, the same that had consumed the heretic god-machine's crew. The taint infected it all. Galenus saw the missiles fly over his head, so close he noted his armour's temperature regulator's attempts to account for the intense heat it was subject to as the missiles' exhaust washed over him.

The missiles detonated. The shock waves threw him to the floor another dozen metres forward. More red icons filled his tactical display, five Ultramarines slain in the blasts. As he staggered to his feet, he was helped up by Erasman, one of the Hellblasters. He could tell Erasman was badly wounded. More of the survivors rallied around him – the others had to have been driven unconscious.

The *Damnation* was attempting to move away. *We must be too close for it to engage,* Galenus thought. It was slow – much of its power must have been lost when its arm had been

destroyed earlier. Galenus sprinted towards the Titan, throwing every ounce of his strength into every step. 'You will not escape my wrath,' he vowed. 'The Imperium will have its vengeance.' His warriors followed him, some limping but advancing nonetheless.

At last they crossed the point where the Titan's void shields met the ground. But their battle was far from done. The god-machine raised one of its feet, meaning to crush them beneath its immense adamantine tread. Galenus leaped to one side to avoid it. After the *Damnation* had driven its foot down, a miniature tidal wave washed over the Ultramarines, knocking many of them over again. They rose swiftly to their feet. 'Get behind it, find its generator and destroy it,' he ordered.

Their agility was his strength here. The Titan could not keep up with them. It attempted to crush the Ultramarines twice more before finally enough could make the shot against its plasma generators. The adamantine casing that shielded them was damaged where the *Arrow* and the *Lightning* had crashed into it earlier. 'Thank you again, brothers,' he said.

'Brothers, fire at will, bring the monster down. For Macragge!' He raised his bolt pistol and opened fire alongside his warriors, if for nothing else than the

satisfaction of having shot at the heretic engine. Bolts of super-charged blue light struck the plasma generators over and over again as the Space Marines fired. They kept moving as they fired, the Titan still attempting to shake them off, but their focus was pure. Plasma boiled from the rents in the generators and soon smoke billowed from the god-machine's armour joints. So damaged, there would inevitably be an apocalyptic explosion when the generators detonated.

'Pull back, brothers,' ordered Galenus. They ran. They had been moving for six seconds when the Titan detonated. An augmented Human would have not covered enough ground in that time. A fully armoured Space Marine was beyond such limitations. Once again, Galenus was thrown by the concussive shock waves that left him winded and wracked in pain. His armour was peppered with shards of corrupted adamantine that were embedded deep into his armour plate. But he lived, and the Titan was dead.

INSIGNIUM ASTARTES

The Space Marine Chapters march to battle proudly bearing their traditional colours and heraldry. Powerful, semi-autonomous armies, their ranks are made up of myriad squad and warrior types, each designed for a single purpose: to make war upon the enemies of the Imperium, and in so doing purge them from the galaxy without mercy. These pages show example warriors and vehicles of the most famous Chapters of these Angels of Death.

The Codex Astartes makes significant provision for how squads, vehicles, Dreadnoughts, gunships and other assets should display Chapter heraldry and organisational markings. Many Chapters, such as the Ultramarines and a multitude of their successors, follow these to the letter. Other Chapters deviate through choice. This may be due to the influence of being descended from another Primarch, the cultural influences of their home world, or other traditions whose origins have long since been lost to history. Others deviate through accidents of time. Over the millennia, the Codex Astartes has been copied many times, with deviations, mistranslations and reinterpretations slowly leaking into the innumerable different versions. Many Space Marine Chapters claim to be fully Codex-compliant when it comes to their organisation and markings, but vary considerably with others who claim the same. Combined with the guidance of the Codex that Space Marine forces can and indeed should alter their markings in a war zone in order to confuse the enemy, Space Marine forces have enormous variety in how they adorn their armour.

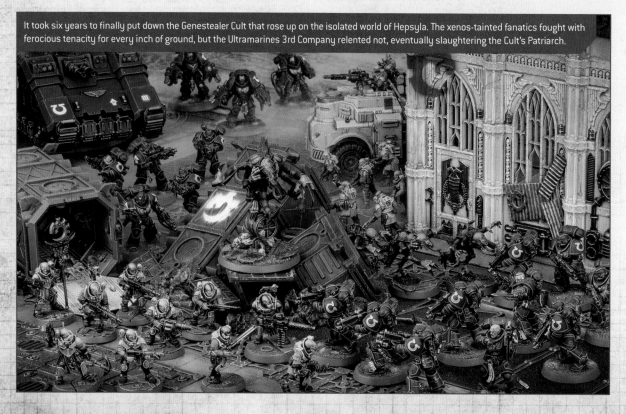

It took six years to finally put down the Genestealer Cult that rose up on the isolated world of Hepsyla. The xenos-tainted fanatics fought with ferocious tenacity for every inch of ground, but the Ultramarines 3rd Company relented not, eventually slaughtering the Cult's Patriarch.

The Ultramarines are strict adherents to the Codex Astartes, their Primarch's Magnum Opus. The Codex is replete with wily tactics and war-winning strategies, all of which the Ultramarines put to use purging the hated Word Bearers Heretic Astartes from Besel V.

FILE: ULTRA//3356XA – ULTRAMARINES CODEX DESIGNATION

Battlefield Role
A Space Marine's battlefield role is typically indicated by a symbol displayed on his right pauldron.

 Battleline

 Close Support

 Fire Support

 Veteran

 Command

Company Colours
Company colours are displayed on the edges of an Ultramarine's pauldrons.

1st Company
2nd Company
3rd Company
4th Company
5th Company
6th Company
7th Company
8th Company
9th Company
10th Company

Ultramarines Intercessor

Ultramarines
Intercessor Sergeant

Rank

 Battle-brother

 Sergeant

 Veteran

 Veteran Sergeant

 Lieutenant

 Captain

Squad Markings

A company's squads can be numbered from one to twenty. Most commonly a Space Marine's squad number is displayed as a High Gothic numeral on his right pauldron, superimposed above a symbol that specifies their strategic designation.

One	Two	Three	Four	Five
I	II	III	IV	V
Six	**Seven**	**Eight**	**Nine**	**Ten**
VI	VII	VIII	IX	X
Eleven	**Twelve**	**Thirteen**	**Fourteen**	**Fifteen**
XI	XII	XIII	XIV	XV
Sixteen	**Seventeen**	**Eighteen**	**Nineteen**	**Twenty**
XVI	XVII	XVIII	XIX	XX

Imperial Fists Intercessor

Imperial Fists Aggressor

Imperial Fists Hellblaster Sergeant

FILE: SQUAD//HG1114F – ASTARTES SQUAD DESIGNATION

Masters of stealth, infiltration and the hit-and-run attack, when the Raven Guard strike it is to inflict maximum damage in the shortest time possible, bringing their assets of war to the enemy at high speed with unstoppable fury.

On Obstinax, the Imperial Fists 5th Company withstood the assaults of wave after wave of Szarekhan Dynasty Necron Warriors and Canoptek constructs, their incomparable skills in the art of siegecraft ensuring not one of the world's ten mega-fortresses fell.

Transport Designation

Troop transports, warsuits and armoured vehicles carry the same heraldry and organisational squad markings as the Space Marines who crew them.

Battleline

Close Support

Fire Support

Veteran

Command

FILE: TRANSPORT // IMPULSOR 6632XS-00

Impulsor with ironhail skytalon array, ironhail heavy stubber and storm bolters

Space Marine Chapters have access to a wide array of formidable tanks with which to dominate any field of battle. During the Plague Wars, the Ultramarines unleashed dozens of these devastating vehicles to smash Death Guard siege lines at the Relief of Kurinon City.

82

Vehicle Company Markings

When a vehicle is attached to a Codex-compliant company, a small roundel displaying the company's colour and number and is placed on the vehicle's hull.

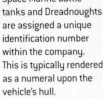

Space Marine battle tanks and Dreadnoughts are assigned a unique identification number within the company. This is typically rendered as a numeral upon the vehicle's hull.

Space Marine Chapters award campaign badges to their warriors. Sometimes, this will be ahead of a major conflict, the badge given out before on the eve of glorious battle. On other occasions, they are awarded upon war's end.

Invictor Tactical Warsuit with twin ironhail autocannon

Few Space Marines deplore weakness as much as the Iron Hands do, and their warriors are renowned for their formidable endurance. On Krajnov, the Iron Hands withstood dozens of gruelling Drukhari ambushes, slaughtering thousands of the depraved xenos.

FILE: CODEX VARIATION REF/7345-00-223

Although the Raven Guard follow much of Codex convention for their squad markings, they all trim one pauldron in black.

Raven Guard Intercessor,
2nd Company, 2nd Squad

White Scars Intercessor Sergeant,
3rd Company, 16th Squad

The squad a White Scar belongs to is identified by the patterns on his left knee plate.

1st	2nd	3rd
4th	5th	6th
7th	8th	9th etc.

Each Iron Hands clan company has its own symbol, borne on the right pauldron. The Chapter symbol is borne on the left.

Iron Hands Intercessor Sergeant,
Clan Raukaan (3rd), 6th Squad

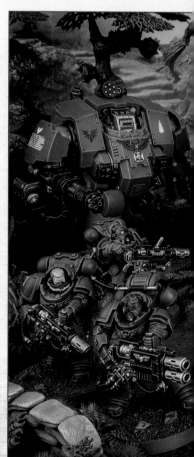

Dark Angels Intercessor Sergeant, 5th Company, 2nd Squad

Rather than by pauldron trim, the Dark Angels denote the company they belong to by the marking on their left knee pad.

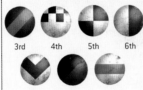

3rd   4th   5th   6th

7th   8th   9th

 Veteran/Command   Battleline

Fire Support   Close Support

The Blood Angels denote battlefield role by helmet colour.

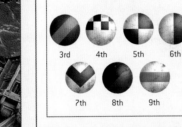

Blood Angels Heavy Intercessor, 2nd Company, 2nd Squad

Space Wolves Hellblaster, the Blackmanes Great Company

Space Wolves wear pack markings on their right shoulder. These indicate whether they belong to Wolf Scouts, hunter packs, fang packs or claw packs.

Some of the Imperium's wars are so savage, the worlds involved so strategically vital, that Space Marine Chapters work together to achieve victory. On Dekidua, the Blood Angels and Dark Angels fought side by side to prevent the total slaughter of the world's inhabitants.

85

Hailing from a volcanic death world, the Salamanders are perfectly at home making war in forbiddingly hostile environments. When Necrons of the Novokh Dynasty assaulted the magma mines of Kouliaas III, the Salamanders responded with the fury of a vengeful drake.

FILE: PR44500001 · CODEX ASTARTES COMMAND AND VETERANS

Ranks and Honours

Higher-ranking Space Marines and specialists often bear alternative markings. These indicate their specialisms and ranks for easy identification in the heat of battle by their warriors and allies.

Ultramarines Captain, 2nd Company

Imperial Fists Captain, 3rd Company

Raven Guard Lieutenant, 3rd Company

Ultramarines Ancient, 1st Company

Captain with Master-crafted Heavy Bolt Rifle

Ultramarines Primaris Techmarine

Ultramarines Primaris Chaplain

The Pariah Nexus was a threat of a kind the Imperium had never encountered before. Regardless, the brave souls of Battle Group Kallides led the charge to sunder the region and the fell xenos that created it. The Ultramarines led the way, determined to thwart the aliens' plans.

Bladeguard Veterans

Each Bladeguard Veteran displays their personal heraldry on their tilting plate. The wide array of symbols and colours used reflects the Veteran's years of service, companies they were promoted from and many other details.

Bladeguard Veteran Sergeant

Primaris Lieutenant

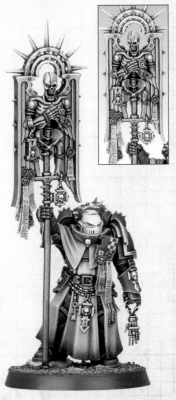

Bladeguard Ancient

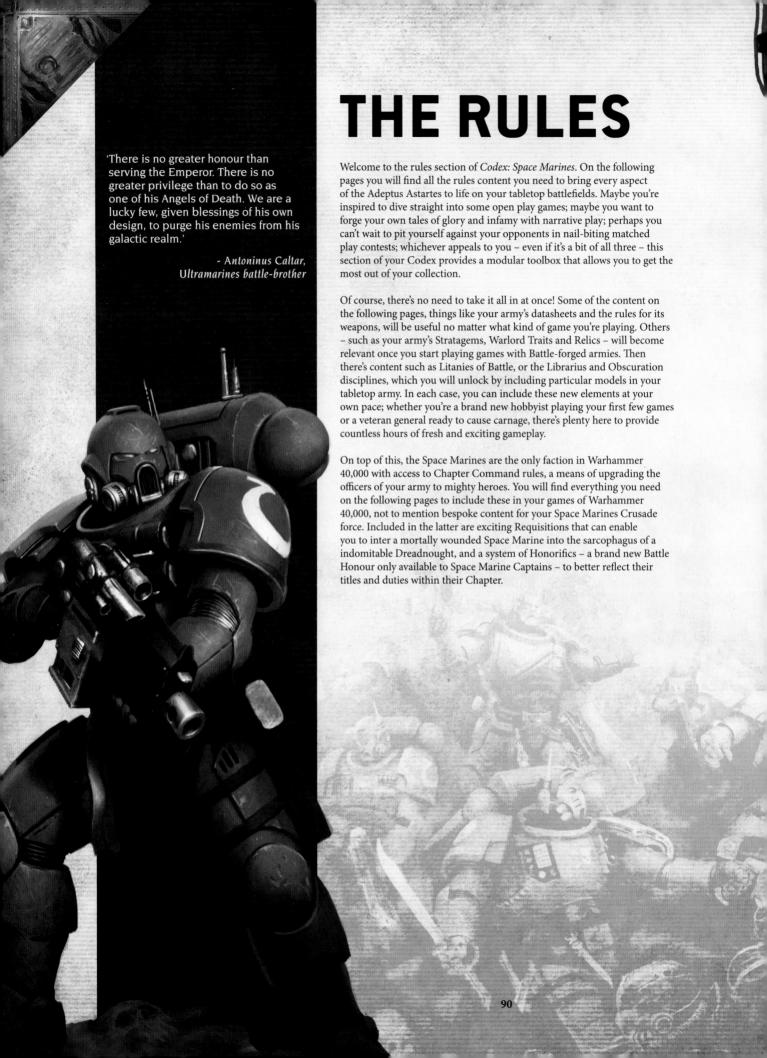

'There is no greater honour than serving the Emperor. There is no greater privilege than to do so as one of his Angels of Death. We are a lucky few, given blessings of his own design, to purge his enemies from his galactic realm.'

- Antoninus Caltar,
Ultramarines battle-brother

THE RULES

Welcome to the rules section of *Codex: Space Marines*. On the following pages you will find all the rules content you need to bring every aspect of the Adeptus Astartes to life on your tabletop battlefields. Maybe you're inspired to dive straight into some open play games; maybe you want to forge your own tales of glory and infamy with narrative play; perhaps you can't wait to pit yourself against your opponents in nail-biting matched play contests; whichever appeals to you – even if it's a bit of all three – this section of your Codex provides a modular toolbox that allows you to get the most out of your collection.

Of course, there's no need to take it all in at once! Some of the content on the following pages, things like your army's datasheets and the rules for its weapons, will be useful no matter what kind of game you're playing. Others – such as your army's Stratagems, Warlord Traits and Relics – will become relevant once you start playing games with Battle-forged armies. Then there's content such as Litanies of Battle, or the Librarius and Obscuration disciplines, which you will unlock by including particular models in your tabletop army. In each case, you can include these new elements at your own pace; whether you're a brand new hobbyist playing your first few games or a veteran general ready to cause carnage, there's plenty here to provide countless hours of fresh and exciting gameplay.

On top of this, the Space Marines are the only faction in Warhammer 40,000 with access to Chapter Command rules, a means of upgrading the officers of your army to mighty heroes. You will find everything you need on the following pages to include these in your games of Warhammer 40,000, not to mention bespoke content for your Space Marines Crusade force. Included in the latter are exciting Requisitions that can enable you to inter a mortally wounded Space Marine into the sarcophagus of a indomitable Dreadnought, and a system of Honorifics – a brand new Battle Honour only available to Space Marine Captains – to better reflect their titles and duties within their Chapter.

BATTLE-FORGED RULES

DETACHMENT ABILITIES (PG 93)
Units in Space Marine Detachments gain additional abilities to better reflect how Space Marine armies operate together and wage war on the battlefield, including Chapter Tactics to describe individual fighting styles of the different Space Marine Chapters. You can find out more about Detachment abilities in the Battle-forged Armies section of the Warhammer 40,000 Core Book.

CHAPTER COMMAND (PG 98-101)
Certain character models in your Space Marine army can be upgraded to be part of the Chapter Command. In being so, these high-ranking officers will gain powerful new abilities.

STRATAGEMS (PG 102-105)
Space Marine armies have access to unique battlefield strategies and tactics that they can utilise to best their foes in any theatre of war; these are represented by the Stratagems in this section, which you can spend Command points to use in your games. You can find out more about Stratagems and Command points in the Warhammer 40,000 Core Book.

ARMY RULES

WARLORD TRAITS (PG 106-107)
The Warlord of a Space Marine army can have one of the traits presented in this section. These help to personalise the leader of your force and better reflect their individual combat prowess and command style on the battlefield.

RELICS (PG 108-109)
Space Marine heroes can take powerful artefacts and venerated weapons called Chapter Relics into battle; these Relics and the rules they bestow are described in this section.

LIBRARIUS DISCIPLINE (PG 110)
If your army includes any Librarians, they can be given additional psychic powers from the Librarius discipline. This represents the different arcane lore and particular talents of each individual Librarian. You can find out more about psychic powers in the Warhammer 40,000 Core Book.

OBSCURATION DISCIPLINE (PG 111)
Librarians clad in Phobos armour can be granted additional psychic powers from the Obscuration discipline. This psychic discipline is bespoke to those Librarians who have trained in the psychic arts of illusion, and are well suited to the Vanguard operations such individuals are seconded to.

LITANIES OF BATTLE (PG 112)
On the battlefield, Chaplains recite rousing Litanies of Battle to inspire their comrades to feats of heroism. The list of different litanies that each Chaplain in your army can choose from can be found in this section.

MATCHED PLAY RULES

CHAPTER APPROVED RULES (PG 113)
If you are playing a battle that instructs you to select secondary objectives, then you will be able to choose from the additional Adeptus Astartes ones printed here. These represent the tactical and strategic goals unique to Space Marine armies. You can find out more about selecting secondary objectives in many matched play mission packs, including the Eternal War mission pack found in the Warhammer 40,000 Core Book.

CRUSADE RULES

CRUSADE (PG 114-123)
Space Marines have access to a host of additional rules that further personalise your Crusade force. These include bespoke Requisitions, Agendas, Crusade Relics and Battle Tactics that reflect the rich background of the Adeptus Astartes. Amongst the rules presented in this section are Honorifics, a new type of Battle Honour that Space Marine Captains can take to better reflect their individual roles within their Chapter.

DATASHEETS

DATASHEETS (PG 124-194)
This section is essential to all Space Marine players, regardless of preferred play style, containing as it does the datasheets for Space Marine units. Each datasheet describes, among other things, the profiles of its models, the wargear they can be equipped with and the abilities they have. You can find out more about datasheets in the Warhammer 40,000 Core book.

WARGEAR

WEAPON PROFILES (PG 195-201)
This section provides wargear lists referenced in the wargear options of certain Space Marine datasheets, as well as profiles for all of the weapons that Space Marine units can be equipped with.

POINTS

POINTS VALUES (PG 202-206)
If you are playing a game that uses points values, you can use the alphabetised lists in this section to determine the cost of each unit in your army. These will be reviewed annually.

RULES REFERENCE

GLOSSARY (PG 207)
In this section you will find a glossary of rules terms used in this Codex that is designed to aid in resolving any complex rules interactions that may arise.

REFERENCE (PG 208)
Here you will find a handy bullet-pointed rules reference that summarises some common Space Marine rules.

COMBAT PATROL

Combat Patrol is the smallest size game, and the Space Marine force below is a great way to start – regardless of whether you want to play an open play game, forge a narrative with a Crusade army, or compete in a matched play mission.

Created from the contents of the Warhammer 40,000 Elite Edition Starter Set, this force can be used in a Battle-forged army, and in itself comprises a Patrol Detachment, as described in the Warhammer 40,000 Core book.

On the battlefield, the Assault Intercessors are a resilient and hard-hitting Troops unit, more than able to contend with the warriors of other armies. As part of a Battle-forged army, this unit will also gain the Objective Secured ability, as described on page 93, enabling them to hold on to objectives even when outnumbered by the foe – a likely prospect for an elite army such as Space Marines.

When the Assault Intercessors are bolstered by the Primaris Captain's Rites of Battle ability, they become a truly formidable force in melee. The Primaris Captain is himself equipped to excel in the cut and thrust of close combat, capable of slaying all but the most titanic of foes whilst his relic shield affords him some of the best protection available.

The Outriders make for a rapid response force that can dash forwards to grab objectives, or rush in to support your slower-paced infantry forces. Though few in number, these bikers are an incredibly deadly blend of firepower and close combat punch.

The Invader ATV is equipped with this Combat Patrol's heaviest weaponry. With a choice of an anti-infantry onslaught gatling cannon or an anti-tank multi-melta, it is a versatile and mobile weapon platform that is best used in conjunction with the Outriders to threaten your opponent's most prized assets and obliterate them.

DETACHMENT ABILITIES

An **ADEPTUS ASTARTES** Detachment is one that only includes models with the **ADEPTUS ASTARTES** keyword (excluding models with the **AGENT OF THE IMPERIUM** or **UNALIGNED** keyword).

- **ADEPTUS ASTARTES** Detachments gain the Company Command ability.
- **ADEPTUS ASTARTES** units in **ADEPTUS ASTARTES** Detachments gain the Chapter Tactics ability.
- Troops units in **ADEPTUS ASTARTES** Detachments gain the Objective Secured ability (this ability is described in the Warhammer 40,000 Core Book).

COMPANY COMMAND

When Space Marines are deployed to battle, the honour of leading them often falls to the Captain of a company and his esteemed Lieutenants.

You can include a maximum of one **CAPTAIN** model and two **LIEUTENANT** models in each Detachment in your army.

CHAPTER TACTICS

Each Chapter has its own combat philosophy suited to the unique skills of its battle-brothers.

All **ADEPTUS ASTARTES** units (other than **SERVITOR** and **BEAST** units) with this ability, and all the models in them, gain a Chapter Tactic so long as every unit in their Detachment is from the same Chapter. The tactic gained depends upon which Chapter they are from, as shown on the following pages.

Example: *An **ULTRAMARINES** unit with the Chapter Tactics ability gains the Codex Discipline tactic.*

If your Chapter does not have an associated Chapter Tactic, you must instead select Successor Tactics for them, as described on page 96; this allows you to customise the rules for your successor Chapter. In either case, write down all of your Detachments' Chapter Tactics/Successor Tactics on your army roster.

CHAPTER TACTICS

DARK ANGELS: GRIM RESOLVE

The stalwart descendants of the Lion are renowned for their unshakeable resolve, enduring tenacity and strict fire discipline in battle.

- Each time a model with this tactic makes an attack, unless that model's unit has moved this turn (excluding pile-in and consolidation moves), add 1 to that attack's hit roll.
- Each time a Combat Attrition test is taken for a unit with this tactic, it is automatically passed.

WHITE SCARS: LIGHTNING ASSAULT

The White Scars are the Masters of high speed, hit-and-run warfare. Theirs is the fury of the storm, the scent of prey upon the wind. They do battle on the move, wrong-footing their enemies with breakneck manoeuvres and melting away one moment only to crash home like a lightning strike elsewhere the next.

- Units with this tactic are eligible to declare a charge with in a turn in which they Advanced or Fell Back.
- Models with this tactic do not suffer the penalty incurred to their hit rolls for firing Assault weapons in the same turn their unit Advanced.

SPACE WOLVES: HUNTERS UNLEASHED

The Space Wolves train their whole lives for the moment when battle is joined. After a long hunt tensed for the kill, they spring forward to devastating effect.

- Each time a model with this tactic makes a melee attack, if that model's unit made a charge move, was charged or performed a Heroic Intervention this turn, add 1 to that attack's hit roll.
- Units with this tactic are eligible to perform Heroic Interventions as if they were **Characters**.

IMPERIAL FISTS: SIEGE MASTERS

The Imperial Fists drill tirelessly with their armaments, perfecting the art of purging their foes from behind ramparts with hails of pinpoint fire.

- Each time a model with this tactic makes a ranged attack, the target does not receive the benefits of Light Cover against that attack.
- Each time a model with this tactic makes an attack with a bolt weapon (pg 195), an unmodified hit roll of 6 scores 1 additional hit.

CRIMSON FISTS: NO MATTER THE ODDS

Even when faced with seemingly insurmountable odds, the Crimson Fists emerge bloodied but victorious with bolters roaring.

- Each time a model with the tactic makes a ranged attack against a unit that contained at least 5 more models than the attacker's unit when it was selected to shoot, add 1 to that attack's hit roll. For the purposes of this tactic, **Vehicle** models each count as 5 models.
- Each time a model with this tactic makes an attack with a bolt weapon (pg 195), an unmodified hit roll of 6 scores 1 additional hit.

BLACK TEMPLARS: RIGHTEOUS ZEAL

Hot burns the hatred of the Black Templars for the mutant, the witch and the heretic, and bright blazes their faith in the immortal Emperor of Mankind. With furious cries do these crusading warriors hurl themselves into battle against their reviled foes, and with fervent prayers do they shrug off even the most grievous wounds.

- You can re-roll Advance rolls and charge rolls made for units with this tactic.
- Each time a model with this tactic would lose a wound as a result of a mortal wound, roll one D6: on a 5+, that wound is not lost.

BLOOD ANGELS: RED THIRST

Though they strive to restrain it, the murderous ferocity of the Blood Angels simmers beneath the surface of their thoughts. In battle, this rage drives [the]m towards the foe and lends great strength to their blows.

- Add 1 to Advance rolls and charge rolls made for units with this tactic.
- Each time a model with this tactic makes a melee attack, if that model's unit made a charge move, was charged or performed a Heroic Intervention this turn, add 1 to that attack's wound roll.

FLESH TEARERS: FURY WITHIN

The Flesh Tearers are possessed of a bloodthirsty recklessness. When controlled and focused, however, this murderous ferocity makes [the]m unstoppable.

[Ea]ch time a model with this tactic makes a melee attack:

- [I]f that model's unit made a charge move, was charged or [p]erformed a Heroic Intervention this turn, add 1 to that [a]ttack's wound roll.
- [O]n an unmodified wound roll of 6, improve the Armour [P]enetration characteristic of that attack by 1. This is [c]umulative with the bonus from the Assault Doctrine if it is [a]ctive for your army (pg 125).

IRON HANDS: THE FLESH IS WEAK

Most Iron Hands are heavily augmented with ultra-durable cybernetic limbs and organs that render them extremely difficult to kill, while their [veh]icles have been upgraded with all manner of secret Adeptus [Me]chanicus technologies that make them incredibly resilient.

- [Ea]ch time a model with this tactic would lose a wound, roll [o]ne D6: on a 6, that wound is not lost.
- [M]odels with this tactic whose characteristics can change as [t]hey suffer damage are considered to have double the number [o]f wounds remaining for the purposes of determining what [t]hose characteristics are.

'Each of us belongs to a proud brotherhood, with our own traditions, histories, heroes and conventions. Each of us would die for our Chapters and all they represent a hundred times over without hesitation. We may differ on all manner of philosophy, culture and way of war, but we are all Space Marines, we are all battle-brothers, and we will all lay down out lives for the Emperor and the Imperium.'

- Marneus Calgar, Chapter Master of the Ultramarines

ULTRAMARINES: CODEX DISCIPLINE

The sons of Guilliman hold the tenets of the Codex Astartes as sacrosanct, its wisdom guiding them to discipline and measured strategic responses even amidst the hottest-burning flames of battle.

- Add 1 to the Leadership characteristic of models with this tactic.
- Units with this tactic are eligible to shoot in a turn in which they Fell Back, but if they do, then until the end of the turn, each time a model in that unit makes a ranged attack, subtract 1 from that attack's hit roll.

SALAMANDERS: FORGED IN BATTLE

To the Salamanders, war is the anvil upon which their strength is wrought, every battle a test in which to prove themselves and the superior craftsmanship of their weapons and armour.

- Each time a unit with this tactic is selected to shoot or fight, you can re-roll one wound roll when resolving that unit's attacks.
- Each time an attack with an Armour Penetration characteristic of -1 is allocated to a model with this tactic, that attack has an Armour Penetration characteristic of 0 instead.

RAVEN GUARD: SHADOW MASTERS

The Raven Guard slip through the shadows, half-seen spectres barely visible to the foe. Enemies blaze away into the gloom with increasing panic, their shots flying wide as the sons of Corax encircle their victims and prepare to level the killing blow. By the time the prey is close enough to direct their fire with any real chance of accuracy, they are caught within the Raven's talons.

- Each time a ranged attack is made against a unit with this tactic, if the attacker is more than 18" away, then the unit with this tactic is treated as having the benefits of light cover against that attack (see the Warhammer 40,000 Core Book).
- Each time a ranged attack is made against an **INFANTRY** unit with this tactic that is entirely on or within a terrain feature, if the attacker is more than 12" away, then the unit with this tactic is treated as having the benefits of dense cover against that attack (see the Warhammer 40,000 Core Book).

DEATHWATCH: XENOS HUNTERS

Warriors of the Deathwatch are psycho-conditioned even beyond other Space Marines, rapidly learning about the hundreds of xenos species that threaten Mankind. This, combined with their incredible martial skill and strict discipline, makes them unparalleled xenos hunters; when fighting these enemies they are frighteningly effective.

- Each time a model with this tactic makes a melee attack against a **TYRANIDS, AELDARI, ORK, NECRONS** or **T'AU EMPIRE** unit, re-roll a hit roll of 1.
- After both sides have finished deploying their armies, select [one Battlefield Role. Until the end of the battle, each time a]

SUCCESSOR CHAPTER TACTICS

If your chosen Chapter does not have an associated Chapter Tactic on pages 94-95, you must instead create their Chapter Tactic by selecting rules from the list here. Unless otherwise stated, your Chapter has two Successor Tactics from the following list:

Bolter Fusillades
With rigorous drilling and singular focus, this Chapter trains its battle-brothers to optimise the killing fury of their bolt weaponry and annihilate their enemies in firefights.

Each time a model with this tactic makes a ranged attack with a bolt weapon (pg 195), re-roll a hit roll of 1.

Born Heroes
Like demigods of war do the champions of this Chapter bestride the battlefield, taking their blades to any foe who dares challenge them and leaving nought but bloodied corpses in their wake.

Each time a model with this tactic makes a melee attack, if that model's unit made a charge move this turn, add 1 to that attack's hit roll.

Duellists
This Chapter prizes skill and precision in close-quarters combat above simple ferocity. Its warriors are deadly combatants, their attacks flowing around their enemies' guard like smoke.

Each time a model with this tactic makes a melee attack against an **INFANTRY** or **BIKER** unit, an unmodified hit roll of 6 automatically wounds the target.

You cannot select this tactic if you have already selected the Whirlwind of Rage tactic (see opposite).

Fearsome Aspect
Whether through ominous trappings and iconography, deafening vox-amplified war cries or simply the sheer force of their presence, this Chapter's warriors sow terror amongst the enemy ranks.

Units with this tactic have the following ability: '**Fearsome Aspect (Aura):** While an enemy unit is within 3" of this unit, subtract 1 from the Leadership characteristic of models in that enemy unit.'

Hungry for Battle
For this Chapter's warriors, all else is but a prelude to the glorious moment in which their warriors' charge crashes home.

Add 1 to Advance rolls and charge rolls made for units with this tactic.

Indomitable
No matter what horrors they face, nor what catastrophic losses they might suffer, this Chapter's warriors stand immovable and fearless before even the most ghastly foe.

Each time a Combat Attrition test is taken for a unit with this tactic, it is automatically passed.

Inheritors of the Primarch
So closely do this Chapter's warriors cleave to the strategic doctrines of their genetic forebears that only their heraldry marks them out as unique from the First Founding Chapter they emulate.

You cannot select this Successor Tactic if you have selected any other Successor Tactic, and if you select this tactic you cannot select a second. Select one of the following Chapters and use the Chapter Tactic of that Chapter as listed on pages 94-95: Dark Angels, White Scars, Space Wolves, Imperial Fists, Blood Angels, Iron Hands, Ultramarines, Salamanders or Raven Guard.

Designer's Note: *If, in the background of our publications, your Chapter is a known successor of a specific First Founding Chapter (pg 94-95), then if you select this Successor Tactic you must select the Chapter Tactic of that First Founding Chapter.*

Knowledge is Power
Vast are the data-stacks and Librarius cloisters of this Chapter, and esoteric is the knowledge possessed by its psykers. In battle, they swiftly establish empyric dominance.

Each time a Psychic test or Deny the Witch test is taken for a **PSYKER** unit with this tactic, re-roll any or all dice results of 1.

Long-range Marksmen
This Chapter's warriors are able to extend the maximum effective range of their firearms through a combination of modified targeting rituals and precision adjustments by their skilled armourers.

Add 3" to the Range characteristic of Rapid Fire and Heavy weapons (excluding Flame weapons, see page 195) models with this tactic are equipped with.

Master Artisans
Far and wide spreads the fame of this Chapter's craftsmen, who fashion the finest masterwork weaponry for their battle-brothers.

Each time a unit with this tactic is selected to shoot or fight, you can re-roll one hit roll when resolving that unit's attacks.

Preferred Enemy
Time and time again, the warriors of this Chapter have faced the same foes. Through bloody defeat and hate-fuelled victory they have learned their enemies' weaknesses well.

When you select this tactic, select one of the following Faction keywords: **CHAOS KNIGHTS; TYRANIDS; AELDARI; ORK; HERETIC ASTARTES; NECRONS; T'AU EMPIRE.** Each time a model with this tactic makes a melee attack against a unit with that Faction keyword, re-roll a hit roll of 1.

Rapid Assault
Firing from the hip, tracking their targets with enhanced runic displays that flicker lightning-fast across their auto-senses, the warriors of this Chapter lay down punishing fusillades even as they close with the foe.

Models with this tactic do not suffer the penalty incurred to their hit rolls for firing Assault weapons in the same turn their unit Advanced.

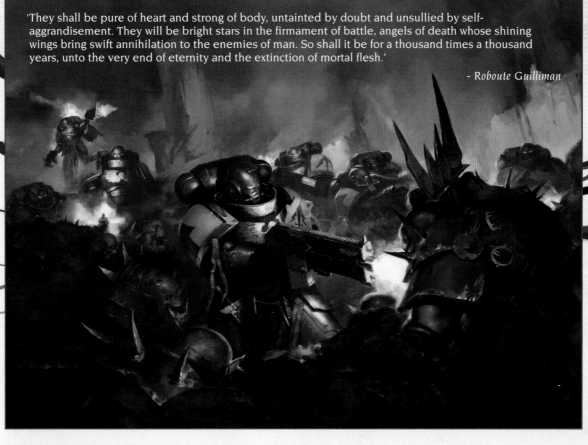

'They shall be pure of heart and strong of body, untainted by doubt and unsullied by self-aggrandisement. They will be bright stars in the firmament of battle, angels of death whose shining wings bring swift annihilation to the enemies of man. So shall it be for a thousand times a thousand years, unto the very end of eternity and the extinction of mortal flesh.'

– Roboute Guilliman

Scions of the Forge

This Chapter's warriors are expert armourers, their tanks and Dreadnoughts maintained to levels that even the Adeptus Mechanicus would admire.

Models with this tactic whose characteristics can change as they suffer damage are considered to have double the number of wounds remaining for the purposes of determining what those characteristics are.

Stalwart

How does one defeat warriors whose willpower and determination are so ferocious that they can shrug off even the most catastrophic injuries and keep on fighting?

Each time an attack is made against a unit with this tactic, an unmodified wound roll of 1 or 2 always fails, irrespective of any abilities that the weapon or the attacker may have.

Stealthy

This Chapter makes a virtue of deception and cunning, and drills its battle-brothers in evasive techniques that allow them to hug the shadows and close upon their foes unseen and unsuspected.

Each time a ranged attack is made against a unit with this tactic, if the attacker is more than 18" away, the unit with this tactic is treated as having the benefits of light cover against that attack (see the Warhammer 40,000 Core Book).

Stoic

Bravery runs in the blood of this Chapter's battle-brothers.

Add 1 to the Leadership characteristic of models with this tactic.

Tactical Withdrawal

This Chapter's warriors are well drilled in the art of disengaging only to hurl themselves back into the fray with fresh impetus.

Units with this tactic are eligible to declare a charge with even if they Fell Back this turn.

Warded

Whether through latent psychic talent, personal energy shielding, enhanced reflexes or sheer zealotry, the battle-brothers of this Chapter can shrug off even the most devastating attacks.

Each time a model with this tactic would lose a wound as a result of a mortal wound, roll one D6: on a 5+, that wound is not lost.

Whirlwind of Rage

Like ravening beasts this Chapter's battle-brothers fall upon the foe.

Each time a model with this tactic makes a melee attack, if that model's unit made a charge move, was charged or performed a Heroic Intervention this turn, an unmodified hit roll of 6 scores 1 additional hit.

You cannot select this tactic if you have already selected the Duellists tactic (see opposite).

With the blade, banish; with the bolter, smite; with fire, purify; with hate, purge.

CHAPTER COMMAND

If your army is Battle-forged and includes any **Adeptus Astartes** Detachments (excluding Auxiliary Support, Super-heavy Auxiliary or Fortification Network Detachments), then when you muster your army, you can upgrade any of the following **Adeptus Astartes Character** units in your army: **Captain, Chaplain, Librarian, Techmarine, Apothecary, Ancient, Company Champion**.

Each time you upgrade one of the aforementioned units, its Power Rating is increased, as shown in the table to the right. If you are playing a matched play game, or a game that uses a points limit, then the points value of that unit is also increased by the amount shown in the same table. Make a note on your army roster each time you upgrade a unit using these rules.

Each time you upgrade a unit, it gains a new keyword, as shown in the Chapter Command Keyword column of the table to the right. It also gains one or more additional abilities, as shown in the appropriate section over the following pages, as well as access to bespoke Warlord Traits and Relics (these are considered to be Chapter Relics for all rules purposes). These units are still considered to be the same datasheet for the purposes of any mission rules that limit the number of times any particular datasheet can be included in your army.

A Crusade force cannot start with any upgraded **Character** units – to include one in a Crusade force, you must use the Chapter Command Requisition (pg 116).

You cannot upgrade named characters using these rules. An army (and a Crusade force) cannot contain more than one model from the same Chapter that has the same Chapter Command keyword (e.g. it cannot contain two **Ultramarines Chapter Masters**, or two **Salamanders Chief Librarians** etc.). A **Black Templars Company Champion** cannot be upgraded to be a **Chapter Champion**. A **Deathwatch Captain** cannot be upgraded to be a **Chapter Master**. A **Blood Angels Ancient** cannot be upgraded to be a **Chapter Ancient**.

MASTERS OF THE CHAPTER

CHARACTER	CHAPTER COMMAND KEYWORD	POWER	POINTS
Captain	Chapter Master	+2	+40
Chaplain	Master of Sanctity	+1	+25
Techmarine	Master of the Forge	+1	+20
Librarian	Chief Librarian	+1	+25
Apothecary	Chief Apothecary	+1	+15
Ancient	Chapter Ancient	+1	+20
Company Champion	Chapter Champion	+1	+15

CHAPTER MASTER

Chapter Masters are some of the greatest military minds in the galaxy. There are few elements of strategy and tactics they have not studied and mastered, and they have tested their skills against innumerable enemies. They are magnificent leaders able to inspire their warriors to acts of legendary valour. There is no task to which they will set their battle-brothers that they have not completed themselves, and when they lead from the front, they wield their blades with incomparable ability, slaughtering more of the foe than any of their warriors.

ABILITIES
A **Chapter Master** model gains the following ability:

'**Chapter Master:** In your Command phase, select one friendly **<Chapter> Core** or **<Chapter> Character** unit within 6" of this model. Until the start of your next Command phase, each time a model in that unit makes an attack, you can re-roll the hit roll.'

A **Chapter Master** is excluded from the Company Command rule (pg 93). This means a Detachment can include both one **Chapter Master** unit and one other **Captain** unit.

RELICS AND WARLORD TRAITS
You can give a **Chapter Master** model the Angel Artifice Relic, instead of giving them a Chapter Relic. In addition, you can give them the Master of the Codex Warlord Trait instead of giving them another Warlord Trait.

Master of the Codex (Warlord Trait)
Chapter Masters have spent centuries studying the hallowed pages of the Codex Astartes, poring over its wisdom and analysing its teachings in detail. Many commit its content to memory word for word, ready to draw upon what they have learned even when battle is raging at its fiercest.

At the start of your Command phase, if this **Warlord** is on the battlefield, roll one D6: on a 4+, you gain 1 Command point.

Angel Artifice (Relic)
The surface of this exquisite battle plate is woven with a super-dense alloy, the exact nature of which has been lost to history. Whatever its origin, it absorbs and refracts incoming energy, rendering the wearer all but invulnerable. Such a priceless relic is bestowed upon only the greatest heroes of the Adeptus Astartes.

- The bearer has a Save characteristic of 2+.
- Add 1 to the bearer's Wounds and Toughness characteristics.

MASTER OF SANCTITY

Masters of Sanctity are the High Chaplains of the Space Marine Chapters. They maintain the spiritual well-being of their brothers, ensuring none falter in their responsibilities. Their mere presence inspires fervent aggression amongst their kin, though they are just as capable of delivering retribution first-hand. With word and deed a Master of Sanctity guides his brothers to glory.

ABILITIES

A **Master of Sanctity** model has the following ability:

'**Master of Sanctity:** This model knows one additional litany from the Litanies of Battle (pg 112). In your Command phase, if this model is on the battlefield, it can recite one additional litany it knows that has not already been recited by a friendly model that turn.'

RELICS AND WARLORD TRAITS

You can give a **Master of Sanctity** model the Emperor's Judgement Relic, instead of giving them a Chapter Relic. In addition, you can give them the Wise Orator Warlord Trait instead of giving them another Warlord Trait:

Wise Orator (Warlord Trait)

A veteran of the battlefield and of the sermon, this warlord intones his litanies and galvanises his brothers with every word.

- Each time this **Warlord** recites a litany, add 1 to the roll to see if it is inspiring.
- Each time this **Warlord** is selected to use the Commanding Oratory Stratagem (pg 103), that Stratagem costs 1 Command point.

The Emperor's Judgement (Relic)

Legend has it that the golden, skull-faced death mask known as the Emperor's Judgement was crafted in the years following the Horus Heresy, and its crimson, crystal eye lenses are imbued with droplets of his own lifeblood. Regardless of the truth of its origins, several influential Masters of Sanctity have been granted the honour of wearing the Emperor's Judgement in battle. Both heretics and xenos cower in the face of its grim majesty.

- Each time an attack is made against the bearer, your opponent cannot re-roll the hit roll, cannot re-roll the wound roll and cannot re-roll the damage roll.
- The bearer has the following ability: '**The Emperor's Judgement (Aura):** While an enemy unit is within 6" of the bearer, each time a Morale test is taken for that unit, roll one additional D6 and discard the lowest result.'

MASTER OF THE FORGE

Masters of the Forge are the chief artificers of the Space Marines, responsible for maintaining the arms, armour and vehicles of their Chapter. Peerless mechanics and technicians, they are the foremost experts within the Adeptus Astartes on the intricacies that surround the machine. Having distinguished themselves from their brother Techmarines, Masters of the Forge oversee the Chapter's armoury, and have an intimate knowledge of its workings and the machine spirits that reside there.

ABILITIES

A **Master of the Forge** model has the following ability:

'**Master of the Forge:** Each time this model repairs a model using its Blessing of the Omnissiah ability, that model regains up to 3 lost wounds instead of up to D3'.

RELICS AND WARLORD TRAITS

You can give a **Master of the Forge** model the Mortis Machina Relic, instead of giving them a Chapter Relic. In addition, you can give them the Warden of the Ancients Warlord Trait instead of giving them another Warlord Trait.

Warden of the Ancients (Warlord Trait, Aura)

This warlord has an affinity with the Dreadnoughts of his Chapter. He meticulously tends to his bellicose, ill-tempered charges, ensuring that when the time comes for them to take to the battlefield, they fight with unrivalled fury.

While a friendly **<Chapter> Dreadnought** is within 6" of this **Warlord**, add 1 to its Strength and Attacks characteristics.

Mortis Machina (Relic)

Forged deep within the subterranean vaults of Mars, this axe hews through not just the metal armour of war engines and vehicles, but through their very machine spirit. Even a glancing blow can gut an enemy tank or walker.

Model equipped with an Omnissian power axe only. This Relic replaces an Omnissian power axe and has the following profile:

WEAPON	RANGE	TYPE	S	AP	D
Mortis Machina	Melee	Melee	+3	-2	3

Abilities: Each time an attack is made with this weapon against a **Vehicle** unit, if the saving throw is failed, the target suffers 1 mortal wound in addition to any normal damage.

CHIEF LIBRARIAN

At head of each Chapter's Librarius can be found the Chief Librarian. Battle scholars with vast experience and immense psychic power, they are as much invaluable warriors as they are dependable advisors. When mastery of the warp is required, none are better equipped to deal with its turbulent nature. On the battlefield, Chief Librarians direct the energies of the immaterium with unrivalled precision and power.

ABILITIES

A **Chief Librarian** model gains the following ability:

'**Chief Librarian:** This model knows one additional psychic power from their chosen discipline and can attempt to deny one additional psychic power in your opponent's Psychic phase.'

RELICS AND WARLORD TRAITS

You can give a **Chief Librarian** model the Neural Shroud Relic, instead of giving them a Chapter Relic. In addition, you can give them the Psychic Mastery Warlord Trait instead of giving them another Warlord Trait.

Psychic Mastery (Warlord Trait)

This Librarian has reached a level of psychic mastery that allows him to delve deep into the warp, to depths that would cause lesser psykers to be consumed by its ravenous energies.

Add 1 to Psychic tests taken for this **Warlord**.

Neural Shroud (Relic)

A neural shroud is a specially modified psychic hood sometimes worn by the most senior members of a Chapter's Librarius. The resonating crystals within its neurokinetic housing have been supercharged with empyric energy. Though wearing such a device demands incredible focus and willpower, it projects an extremely potent anti-psychic field.

Increase the range of the bearer's Psychic Hood ability to 24".

CHIEF APOTHECARY

Chief Apothecaries are the most senior surgeons and battle medics available to Space Marine Chapters. Calm and resolute, they maintain the life force of their battle-brothers on and off the battlefield. Most importantly, they are responsible for their Chapter's future in the preservation of Space Marine gene-seed. With vast experience to draw upon, a Chapter's Chief Apothecary is its ultimate practitioner of the healer's art.

ABILITIES

A **Chief Apothecary** model gains the following ability:

'**Chief Apothecary:** At the end of your Movement phase, this model can use its Combat Restoratives ability twice instead of once.'

RELICS AND WARLORD TRAITS

You can give a **Chief Apothecary** model the Acquittal Relic, instead of giving them a Chapter Relic. In addition, you can give them the Selfless Healer Warlord Trait instead of giving them another Warlord Trait.

Selfless Healer (Warlord Trait)

This altruistic warlord will go to any lengths to heal his brothers.

- Each time this **Warlord** uses its Combat Restoratives ability, the model being healed regains up to 3 lost wounds instead of D3.
- Each time this **Warlord** is selected to return a destroyed model to a unit by using the Combat Revival Stratagem (pg 103), that Stratagem costs 0 Command points.

Acquittal (Relic)

Acquittal is a master-crafted pistol equipped with a powerful bio-auspex scope. This allows the wielder to both dispatch his foes with surgical precision and grant swift and painless oblivion to his wounded battle-brothers.

Model equipped with a bolt pistol or absolvor bolt pistol only. This Relic replaces a bolt pistol or absolvor bolt pistol and has the following profile:

WEAPON	RANGE	TYPE	S	AP	D
Acquittal	18"	Pistol 1	5	-3	2

Abilities: Each time an attack is made with this weapon against an **Infantry** unit, that attack always wounds on an unmodified wound roll of 2+ and has a Damage characteristic of 4.

Guns and warriors are useful, but it is our indomitable will that promises the ultimate victory.

CHAPTER ANCIENT

Only the most distinguished Space Marines are granted the title of Chapter Ancient. Given the sacred task of bearing the Chapter's standard to war, they selflessly fly the colours even as they slay their foes. The sight of such a holy relic flying high above the battlefield inspires the Ancients' brethren to give their all. The mere presence of the Chapter's standard is worth a fortified bastion to the warriors of the Adeptus Astartes.

ABILITIES

A **Chapter Ancient** model gains the following ability:

'**Chapter Banner:** In your Command phase, select one friendly **<Chapter> Core** unit within 6" of this model. Until the start of your next Command phase, each time a model in that unit makes a melee attack, add 1 to that attack's hit roll.'

RELICS AND WARLORD TRAITS

You can give a **Chapter Ancient** model the Pennant of the Fallen Relic, instead of giving them a Chapter Relic. In addition, you can give them the Steadfast Example Warlord Trait instead of giving them another Warlord Trait.

Steadfast Example (Warlord Trait, Aura)

This warlord vows to secure victory no matter the cost, and inspires his brethren to take a similar oath.

While a friendly **<Chapter> Core** unit is within 6" of this **Warlord**, that unit has the Objective Secured ability (see the Warhammer 40,000 Core Book). If a model in such a unit already has this ability, that model counts as one additional model when determining control of an objective marker.

Pennant of the Fallen (Relic)

This hallowed standard records the names of legendary Space Marines of the Chapter, mighty heroes who have fallen in glorious battle against the xenos and the heretic. The last stands of these warriors are grand tales of defiance in the face of overwhelming odds. Warring in the shadow of such a proud legacy inspires battle-brothers to fight until their final breath.

Each time a friendly model is destroyed and makes attacks as a result of the bearer's Astartes Banner ability (pg 146), that model can make 2 attacks with one of its melee weapons instead of 1.

CHAPTER CHAMPION

The honorific of Chapter Champion is bestowed only upon the mightiest of Adeptus Astartes warriors. These martial masters fight for the glory and honour of their battle-brothers. In combat, they will seek out worthy opponents to cross blades with, and can single-handedly turn the tide of conflict. Only the most noble and accomplished of warriors ascend to this rank, each a shining example of their Chapter's glory and martial capabilities.

ABILITIES

A **Chapter Champion** model gains the following abilities:

'**Skilful Parry:** Each time a melee attack is made against this model, subtract 1 from the hit roll.'

'**Exquisite Swordsman:** Each time this model makes a melee attack against an enemy **Character** unit, you can re-roll the wound roll.'

'**Chapter Champion:** This model has an Attacks characteristic of 5 and a Leadership characteristic of 9.'

RELICS AND WARLORD TRAITS

You can give a **Chapter Champion** model the Blade of Triumph Relic, instead of giving them a Chapter Relic. In addition, you can give them the Martial Exemplar Warlord Trait instead of giving them another Warlord Trait.

Martial Exemplar (Warlord Trait, Aura)

This warlord is an exquisite warrior and an exemplar of the Chapter, whose deeds inspire those around him.

While a friendly **<Chapter> Core** or **<Chapter> Character** unit is within 6" of this **Warlord**, you can re-roll charge rolls made for that unit.

Blade of Triumph (Relic)

This gleaming broadsword is a masterpiece of artifice and a weapon befitting any Chapter Champion. Its perfectly weighted blade is etched with the names of its previous wielders and a catalogue of their most magnificent deeds. By pressing an indentation in the sword's electrum grip the wielder can overcharge its power field with a surge of fiery energy, allowing the Blade of Triumph to cleave through even the thickest armour.

Model with master-crafted power sword only. This Relic replaces a master-crafted power sword and has the following profile:

WEAPON	RANGE	TYPE	S	AP	D
Blade of Triumph	Melee	Melee	+3	-3	3

STRATAGEMS

If your army includes any **ADEPTUS ASTARTES** Detachments (excluding Auxiliary Support, Super-heavy Auxiliary or Fortification Network Detachments), you have access to these Stratagems, and can spend CPs to use them. When one of these Stratagems instructs you to select a unit from your army, replace all instances of **<CHAPTER>** on that Stratagem (if any) with the name of the Chapter that your selected unit is drawn from.

DEATH TO THE TRAITORS!   1CP

Adeptus Astartes – Battle Tactic Stratagem

Of all Humanity's foes, none are as hated as the Heretic Astartes, for they have betrayed their ancient oaths.

Use this Stratagem in the Fight phase, when an **ADEPTUS ASTARTES** unit from your army is selected to fight. Until the end of the phase, each time a model in that unit makes a melee attack against a **HERETIC ASTARTES** unit, you can re-roll the hit roll.

HONOUR THE CHAPTER   2CP

Adeptus Astartes – Battle Tactic Stratagem

Every Chapter has forged its own tales of heroism, and none of its battle-brothers would see that noble record besmirched.

Use this Stratagem at the end of the Fight phase. Select one **ASSAULT INTERCESSOR SQUAD** unit from your army that is within Engagement Range of any enemy units; that unit can fight again.

FURY OF THE FIRST   1CP

Adeptus Astartes – Battle Tactic Stratagem

When the fighting is at its fiercest, the Terminator-armoured warriors of the Chapter truly show their quality.

Use this Stratagem in your Shooting phase, when an **ADEPTUS ASTARTES** unit from your army is selected to shoot, or in the Fight phase, when an **ADEPTUS ASTARTES** unit from your army is selected to fight. Until the end of the phase, each time a **TERMINATOR** model in that unit makes an attack, add 1 to that attack's hit roll.

TRANSHUMAN PHYSIOLOGY   1CP/2CP

Adeptus Astartes – Battle Tactic Stratagem

Space Marines can fight through even the most grievous of wounds.

Use this Stratagem in any phase, when a **PRIMARIS** unit from your army is selected as the target of an attack. Until the end of the phase, each time an attack is made against that unit, an unmodified wound roll of 1-3 for that attack fails, irrespective of any abilities that the weapon or the model making the attack may have. If that unit contains 5 or fewer models, this Stratagem costs 1CP; otherwise, it costs 2CP.

RAPID FIRE   2CP

Adeptus Astartes – Battle Tactic Stratagem

The combination of superhuman reflexes and bolter drills means Space Marine Intercessors can produce a devastating rate of fire.

Use this Stratagem at the end of your Shooting phase. Select one **INTERCESSOR SQUAD** or **VETERAN INTERCESSOR SQUAD** unit from your army; that unit can shoot again.

GENE-WROUGHT MIGHT   1CP

Adeptus Astartes – Battle Tactic Stratagem

Blessed with incredible strength, Primaris Space Marines deliver blows that inflict terrifying damage.

Use this Stratagem in the Fight phase, when a **PRIMARIS** unit from your army is selected to fight. Until the end of the phase, each time a model in that unit makes a melee attack, an unmodified hit roll of 6 automatically wounds the target.

UNYIELDING IN THE FACE OF THE FOE   1CP

Adeptus Astartes – Battle Tactic Stratagem

Those clad in Gravis armour are walking ceramite strongpoints.

Use this Stratagem in any phase, when a **MK X GRAVIS** unit from your army selected as the target of an attack. Until the end of the phase, each time an attack with a Damage characteristic of 1 is allocated to a model in that unit, add 1 to any armour saving throw made against that attack.

ONLY IN DEATH DOES DUTY END   2CP

Adeptus Astartes – Epic Deed Stratagem

Imminent death does not prevent a Space Marine from enacting his final justice upon the enemies of the Imperium.

Use this Stratagem in the Fight phase, when an **ADEPTUS ASTARTES CHARACTER** model from your army that has not already been selected to fight this phase is destroyed. Do not remove that model from play – it can fight after the attacking model's unit has finished making attacks. After resolving the destroyed model's attacks, it is then removed.

ARMOUR OF CONTEMPT   1CP

Adeptus Astartes – Epic Deed Stratagem

The belligerency of some Adeptus Astartes machine spirits makes them unyielding foes to face.

Use this Stratagem in any phase, when an **ADEPTUS ASTARTES VEHICLE** model from your army would lose a wound as the result of a mortal wound. Until the end of the phase, each time that model would lose a wound as the result of a mortal wound, roll one D6: on a 5+, that wound is not lost.

No matter the foe, we are its better. No matter the challenge, we shall overcome it. Our skills and our weapons are gifts of the Primarch and the Emperor – forces impossible for the mutant, traitor or alien to match.

POWER OF THE MACHINE SPIRIT — 2CP

Adeptus Astartes – Epic Deed Stratagem

There are many tales of machine spirits wreaking havoc on the foe, even after their crew are slain and critical systems are failing.

Use this Stratagem in your Command phase. Select one **ADEPTUS ASTARTES MACHINE SPIRIT** model from your army. Until the start of your next Command phase, that model is considered to have its full wounds remaining for the purposes of determining what characteristics on its profile to use.

WISDOM OF THE ANCIENTS — 1CP

Adeptus Astartes – Epic Deed Stratagem

Each fallen champion who rests within the sarcophagus of a Dreadnought has seen a thousand battles and slain foes beyond counting. All such noble warriors are immensely inspiring to their battle-brothers.

Use this Stratagem in your Command phase. Select one **ADEPTUS ASTARTES DREADNOUGHT** model from your army (excluding **WULFEN** and **DEATH COMPANY** models). Until the start of your next Command phase, that model gains either the Rites of Battle ability or the Tactical Precision ability, as shown below:

- **Rites of Battle (Aura):** While a friendly **<CHAPTER> CORE** unit is within 6" of this model, each time a model in that unit makes an attack, re-roll a hit roll of 1.
- **Tactical Precision (Aura):** While a friendly **<CHAPTER> CORE** unit is within 6" of this model, each time a model in that unit makes an attack, re-roll a wound roll of 1.

COMMANDING ORATORY — 2CP

Adeptus Astartes – Epic Deed Stratagem

Fuelled by battlefield adrenaline, the Chaplain recites his litanies with even greater fervour, inspiring the warriors around him.

Use this Stratagem at the start of any of your phases other than your Command phase. Select one **ADEPTUS ASTARTES CHAPLAIN** unit from your army that has not recited a litany this turn. That model can recite one litany that has not already been recited by a friendly model this turn. That litany is automatically inspiring (do not roll) and takes effect until the start of your next Command phase.

COMBAT REVIVAL — 1CP

Adeptus Astartes – Epic Deed Stratagem

With decades of experience, the Apothecary confidently works with at high speed to return wounded brothers to the fray.

Use this Stratagem at the end of your Movement phase. Select one **<CHAPTER> APOTHECARY** unit from your army and then select one friendly **<CHAPTER> INFANTRY** or **<CHAPTER> BIKER** unit that is not at its Starting Strength and is within 3" of that **APOTHECARY**. One of the selected unit's destroyed models is returned to its unit with its full wounds remaining.

RELIC OF THE CHAPTER — 1CP

Adeptus Astartes – Requisition Stratagem

In times of great need, the Space Marine Chapters will unleash the full power of their armouries, equipping their battle-brothers with artefacts of extraordinary power.

Use this Stratagem before the battle, when you are mustering your army, if your **WARLORD** has the **ADEPTUS ASTARTES** keyword. Select one **ADEPTUS ASTARTES CHARACTER** model from your army and give them one Chapter Relic (this must be a Relic they could have). Each Relic in your army must be unique, and you cannot use this Stratagem to give a model two Relics. You can only use this Stratagem once, unless you are playing a Strike Force battle (in which case, you can use this Stratagem twice) or an Onslaught battle (in which case, you can use this Stratagem three times).

HERO OF THE CHAPTER — 1CP

Adeptus Astartes – Requisition Stratagem

Every Space Marine is a champion in their own right, a post-human demigod who stands between Mankind and the darkness.

Use this Stratagem before the battle, when you are mustering your army, if your **WARLORD** has the **ADEPTUS ASTARTES** keyword. Select one **ADEPTUS ASTARTES CHARACTER** model from your army (excluding named characters) and determine one Warlord Trait for it (this must be a Warlord Trait it can have); that model it is only regarded as your **WARLORD** for the purposes of that Warlord Trait. Each Warlord Trait in your army must be unique (if randomly generated, re-roll duplicate results), and you cannot use this Stratagem to give a model two Warlord Traits. You can only use this Stratagem once, unless you are playing a Strike Force battle (in which case, you can use this Stratagem twice) or an Onslaught battle (in which case, you can use this Stratagem three times).

HIT-AND-RUN WARFARE — 1CP

Adeptus Astartes – Strategic Ploy Stratagem

Space Marine pilots receive advanced training in handling their vehicles, and have preternatural reaction speeds.

Use this Stratagem in your Movement phase, when an **ADEPTUS ASTARTES BIKER, LAND SPEEDER** or **STORM SPEEDER** unit from your army Falls Back. That unit is still eligible to shoot this turn even though it Fell Back.

HAMMER OF WRATH — 1CP

Adeptus Astartes – Strategic Ploy Stratagem

Space Marines with jump packs crash into combat with bone-breaking force.

Use this Stratagem in your Charge phase, when an **ADEPTUS ASTARTES JUMP PACK** unit from your army finishes a charge move. Select one enemy unit within Engagement Range of that **JUMP PACK** unit and roll one D6 for each model in that **JUMP PACK** unit that is within Engagement Range of that enemy unit. For each dice result that equals or exceeds that enemy unit's Toughness characteristic, it suffers 1 mortal wound.

SKILLED RIDERS — 1CP

Adeptus Astartes – Strategic Ploy Stratagem

Space Marine riders and pilots rely on their post-human reflexes to weave around incoming fire.

Use this Stratagem in your opponent's Shooting phase, when an **Adeptus Astartes Biker, Land Speeder** or **Storm Speeder** unit from your army that Advanced is selected as the target of a ranged attack. Until the end of the phase, each time an attack is made against that unit, subtract 1 from that attack's hit roll.

UNCOMPROMISING FIRE — 2CP

Adeptus Astartes – Strategic Ploy Stratagem

Switching weapons to full auto, the Space Marines unleash a short-lived but inescapable hail of fire.

Use this Stratagem in your Shooting phase. Select one **Adeptus Astartes Infantry** unit from your army that is performing an action. That unit can shoot this phase without that action failing.

STEADY ADVANCE — 2CP

Adeptus Astartes – Strategic Ploy Stratagem

A measured advance allows Space Marines to unleash a steady stream of fire.

Use this Stratagem in your Movement phase, when an **Adeptus Astartes Infantry** unit from your army makes a Normal Move. Until the end of the turn, that unit is considered to have Remained Stationary.

ADAPTIVE STRATEGY — 2CP

Adeptus Astartes – Strategic Ploy Stratagem

The tenets of the Codex Astartes allow for unorthodox use of combat tactics and the employment of divergent strategic doctrines if doing so will lead to victory.

Use this Stratagem in your Command phase, if a **<Chapter> Warlord** from your army is on the battlefield and a combat doctrine is active for your army. Select one **<Chapter> Core** unit from your army that is on the battlefield. Until the start of your next Command phase, each time a model in that unit makes an attack, the Devastator Doctrine, Tactical Doctrine and Assault Doctrine are considered to be active for that attack.

SUPPRESSION FIRE — 1CP

Adeptus Astartes – Strategic Ploy Stratagem

Few indeed are the foes who can hope to escape the savage barrage of Space Marine artillery with their wits intact.

Use this Stratagem in your Shooting phase, when a **Whirlwind** model from your army is selected to shoot. Until the end of the phase, each time that model makes an attack with a weapon that has the Blast ability, if a hit is scored for that attack, then until the start of your next turn the target cannot fire Overwatch or Set to Defend, and cannot be selected to fight until all eligible units from your army have done so.

TERROR TROOPS — 2CP

Adeptus Astartes – Strategic Ploy Stratagem

At the most critical time, Reivers engage their armour's enhanced features to terrify and disrupt the enemy as much as possible.

Use this Stratagem in your Command phase. Select one **Reiver** unit from your army.

- That unit gains the following ability: '**Terror Troops (Aura):** Until the start of your next Command phase, while an enemy unit is within 3" of that unit, it loses the Objective Secured ability and any similar abilities that allow them to control an objective marker regardless of the number of enemy models within range of that objective marker.
- Until the end of the turn, each time that **Reiver** unit ends a Normal Move, an Advance or a charge move within 3" of an enemy unit that is performing an action, roll 2D6: if the total exceeds that enemy unit's Leadership characteristic, the action the unit is attempting to perform immediately fails.

GUERILLA TACTICS — 1CP

Adeptus Astartes – Strategic Ploy Stratagem

At the opportune moment, Space Marine infiltration units slip away from battle, only to relocate and strike the foe again.

Use this Stratagem in your Movement phase, when a **Phobos** unit from your army that is more than 6" from any enemy models is selected to move. If the mission you are playing is using the Strategic Reserves rule, place that unit into Strategic Reserves.

ORBITAL BOMBARDMENT — 3CP

Adeptus Astartes – Strategic Ploy Stratagem

The Chapter's orbiting star ships stand ready to unleash hell.

Use this Stratagem in your Command phase, if an **Adeptus Astartes Warlord** from your army is on the battlefield. Select one point on the battlefield and place a marker on that point. At the start of your next Command phase, roll one D6 for each unit within 6" of the centre of that marker, adding 1 if the unit being rolled for is within 3" of the centre of the marker and subtracting 1 if the unit being rolled for is a **Character**. On a 2-5, that unit suffers D3 mortal wounds, and on a 6+, that unit suffers D6 mortal wounds. The marker is then removed. You can only use this Stratagem once.

AUSPEX SCAN — 2CP

Adeptus Astartes – Wargear Stratagem

Nearby motion and radiation signatures are detected by a handheld device, forewarning the bearer of ambushes.

Use this Stratagem at the end of the Reinforcements step of your opponent's Movement phase. Select one **Adeptus Astartes Infantry** unit from your army that is not within Engagement Range of any enemy units. That unit can shoot as if it were your Shooting phase, but its models can only target a single eligible enemy unit that was set up as Reinforcements this turn and that is within 12" of their unit when doing so.

TREMOR SHELLS   1CP

Adeptus Astartes – Wargear Stratagem

*These shells burrow deep into the ground before detonating;
though the force of the blast is reduced, the resulting shock wave is
sufficient to hurl the foe from their feet.*

Use this Stratagem in your Shooting phase, when selecting a
target for a **THUNDERFIRE CANNON** model from your army. Until
the end of the phase, each time that model makes a ranged
attack, subtract 1 from that attack's wound roll, and, if a hit is
scored against a target that is not **TITANIC** and cannot **FLY**, then
until the start of your next Movement phase, halve the Move
characteristic of models in the target unit and subtract 2 from
Advance rolls and charge rolls made for that unit.

SHOCK AND AWE   1CP

Adeptus Astartes – Wargear Stratagem

*Space Marine forces use shock grenades and similar weapons to
stun and distract the enemy with blinding light and raucous noise.*

Use this Stratagem in your Shooting phase, when an **ADEPTUS
ASTARTES SHOCK GRENADES** or **LAND SPEEDER STORM** unit from
your army is selected to shoot. Select one enemy unit within 6"
of that unit. Until the start of your next turn:

- The selected unit cannot fire Overwatch or Set to Defend.
- Each time a model in the selected unit makes an attack,
  subtract 1 from that attack's hit roll.

ASSAULT LAUNCHERS   1CP

Adeptus Astartes – Wargear Stratagem

*Assault launchers fire salvoes of explosive charges at the enemy,
causing horrific damage to those who are caught out of cover.*

Use this Stratagem at the start of your Charge phase. Select one
ADEPTUS ASTARTES ASSAULT LAUNCHERS unit from your army and
one enemy unit (excluding **VEHICLE** or **MONSTER** units) within 9"
of that unit. That enemy unit can either brace or duck for cover.

- If that unit braces, it suffers D3 mortal wounds.
- If that unit ducks for cover, then until the end of the turn,
  subtract 1 from the Attacks characteristic of models in that
  unit, and that unit cannot fire Overwatch or Set to Defend.

MELTA BOMB   1CP

Adeptus Astartes – Wargear Stratagem

*Melta bombs are fusion charges designed to burn through an
armoured hull in a matter of seconds.*

Use this Stratagem in the Fight phase, when an **ADEPTUS
ASTARTES MELTA BOMB** unit from your army is selected to fight.
Select one model in that unit; that model can only make one
attack this phase, and must target an enemy **VEHICLE** unit with
that attack, but if a hit is scored, that unit suffers 2D3 mortal
wounds and the attack sequence ends.

GRAV PULSE   1CP

Adeptus Astartes – Wargear Stratagem

*Crews of gravitic battle tanks can discharge directed pulses of
gravitic force through their ventral plates.*

Use this Stratagem in either:

- Your Movement phase, when an **ADEPTUS ASTARTES REPULSOR
  FIELD** unit from your army Falls Back. Until the end of the
  turn, that unit is still eligible to shoot even though it Fell Back.
- Your opponent's Charge phase, when an **ADEPTUS ASTARTES
  REPULSOR FIELD** unit from your army is selected as a target of
  a charge. Until the end of the phase, subtract 2 from charge
  rolls made for any unit that declares a charge against that
  REPULSOR FIELD unit.

HELLFIRE SHELLS   1CP

Adeptus Astartes – Wargear Stratagem

*Originally devised to counter large Tyranid bio-forms, hellfire
rounds fill the target with mutagenic acid upon detonation.*

Use this Stratagem in your Shooting phase, when an **ADEPTUS
ASTARTES INFANTRY** model from your army shoots with a heavy
bolter, a hellstorm heavy bolter or an executor heavy bolter. You
can only make one attack with that weapon this phase, but if a
hit is scored, the target suffers D3 mortal wounds and the attack
sequence ends (if a hit is scored against a **MONSTER** unit, that
unit suffers 3 mortal wounds instead of D3).

FLAKK MISSILE   1CP

Adeptus Astartes – Wargear Stratagem

*Flakk missiles are designed to eliminate aircraft by unleashing a
payload of shrapnel that shreds armour and vital systems.*

Use this Stratagem in your Shooting phase, when an **ADEPTUS
ASTARTES INFANTRY** model from your army targets an **AIRCRAFT**
unit with a missile launcher. You can only make one attack with
that weapon this phase, but add 1 to that attack's hit roll. If a hit
is scored, the target suffers 2D3 mortal wounds and the attack
sequence ends.

SMOKESCREEN   1CP

Adeptus Astartes – Wargear Stratagem

*Throwing down a hail of smoke grenades or deploying their smoke
launchers, the Space Marines screen themselves from the enemy.*

Use this Stratagem in your opponent's Shooting phase, when an
ADEPTUS ASTARTES SMOKESCREEN unit from your army is selected
as the target of an attack. Until the end of the phase, each time
an attack is made against that unit, subtract 1 from that attack's
hit roll.

WARLORD TRAITS

If an **Adeptus Astartes Character** model is your **Warlord**, you can use the Space Marines Warlord Traits table below to determine what Warlord Trait they have. You can either roll one D6 to randomly generate one, or you can select one. If a **Phobos Character** model is your **Warlord**, you can instead use the Vanguard Warlord Traits table below to determine what Warlord Trait they have in the same manner. If you wish, instead of selecting a Warlord Trait from either of the tables below, you can select a Chapter Warlord Trait for your **Warlord**, but only if they are from the relevant Chapter.

When you have determined a Warlord Trait for an **Adeptus Astartes Character** model, replace all instances of the **<Chapter>** keyword in their Warlord Trait (if any) with the name of the Chapter that your model is drawn from.

SPACE MARINES WARLORD TRAITS

1. FEAR MADE MANIFEST (AURA)
The Emperor's enemies quail beneath this champion's wrathful gaze.

While an enemy unit is within 6" of this **Warlord**:
- Subtract 1 from the Leadership characteristic of models in that unit.
- Each time a Combat Attrition test is taken for that unit, subtract 1 from that Combat Attrition test.

2. THE IMPERIUM'S SWORD
This warlord hurls himself forwards with unbridled ferocity, cutting down the foe like a reaping whirlwind.

- You can re-roll charge rolls made for this **Warlord**.
- Each time this **Warlord** fights, if it made a charge move or performed a Heroic Intervention this turn, then until that fight is resolved, add 1 to its Strength and Attacks characteristics.

3. IRON RESOLVE
Faith and duty drive this warlord relentlessly onwards as he shrugs off injuries that would lay lesser warriors low.

- Add 1 to the Wounds characteristic of this **Warlord**.
- Each time this **Warlord** would lose a wound, roll one D6: on a 6, that wound is not lost.

4. CHAMPION OF HUMANITY
This commander has slain enemy generals beyond counting.

- Each time this **Warlord** fights, if it is within Engagement Range of any enemy **Character** units, then until that fight is resolved, add 1 to this **Warlord**'s Attacks characteristic.
- Each time this **Warlord** makes a melee attack against a **Character** unit, add 1 to that attack's hit roll and wound roll.

5. STORM OF FIRE (AURA)
This warlord expertly guides his warriors' fire.

While a friendly **<Chapter> Core** unit is within 6" of this **Warlord**, each time a model in that unit makes a ranged attack, on an unmodified wound roll of 6, improve the Armour Penetration characteristic of that attack by 1.

6. RITES OF WAR (AURA)
This commander and his warriors have vowed to secure victory.

While a friendly **<Chapter> Core** or **<Chapter> Character** unit is within 6" of this **Warlord**, that unit has the Objective Secured ability (see the Warhammer 40,000 Core Book).

VANGUARD WARLORD TRAITS

1. SHOOT AND FADE
This warrior harries the foe before returning to the shadows.

Once per turn, in your Shooting phase, after shooting with a friendly **<Chapter> Phobos** unit within 6" of this **Warlord**, that unit can make a Normal Move or it can Advance; in either case, if it does, that unit is not eligible to declare a charge with this turn.

2. LORD OF DECEIT
This leader is adept at subterfuge and spreading misinformation.

After both players have deployed their armies, select up to three **<Chapter> Phobos** units from your army and redeploy them. If the mission uses the Strategic Reserves rules, any of those units can be placed into Strategic Reserves without having to spend any additional CPs, regardless of how many units are already in Strategic Reserves. If both players have abilities that redeploy units, roll off; the winner chooses who redeploys their units first.

3. MASTER OF THE VANGUARD (AURA)
This living legend of the Vanguard is an inspiration to his brothers.

While a friendly **<Chapter> Phobos** unit is within 6" of this **Warlord**:

- Add 1 to charge rolls made for that unit.
- Each time that unit is selected to make a Normal Move, Advance or Fall Back, add 1" to that unit's Move characteristic until the end of the phase.

4. STEALTH ADEPT
This warlord slips through enemy territory like a spectre.

Unless this **Warlord** is the closest eligible target, enemy models cannot target it with ranged attacks.

5. TARGET PRIORITY
This tactician is constantly seeking prime targets.

In your Command phase, you can select one friendly **<Chapter> Phobos** unit within 6" of this **Warlord**. Until the start of your next Command phase, each time a model in that unit makes a ranged attack, add 1 to that attack's hit roll.

6. MASTER MARKSMAN
This warlord is one of the finest sharpshooters in the galaxy.

Add 1 to the Damage characteristic of ranged weapons this **Warlord** is equipped with (excluding Grenades and Relics).

A commander leads always from the front. He must make no order he cannot carry out himself. His hatred for the foe must burn more fiercely than the brightest star. He must inspire. He must instil deep discipline. His first goal is victory – without these things, that can never be attained.

CHAPTER WARLORD TRAITS

DARK ANGELS: BRILLIANT STRATEGIST
The commanders of the Dark Angels share a measure of their Primarch's vaunted strategic brilliance.

In your Command phase, you can select one friendly **DARK ANGELS** unit within 6" of this **WARLORD**. Until the start of your next Command phase, if the Tactical Doctrine is active for your army, then each time a model in that unit makes an attack, the Devastator Doctrine is considered to be active for that attack instead; if the Assault Doctrine is active for your army, then each time a model in that unit makes an attack, the Tactical Doctrine is considered to be active for that attack instead.

WHITE SCARS: DEADLY HUNTER
This son of the Warhawk strikes swiftly, a predator whose first kill is claimed before the foe are even aware of their peril.

After this **WARLORD** makes a charge move, you can select one enemy unit within 1" of it and roll one D6: on a 2+, that unit suffers 1 mortal wound.

SPACE WOLVES: BEASTSLAYER
This warlord has slain some of the worst creatures that the galaxy has to offer. Such a hero embodies Russ' ferocity and courage.

- While this **WARLORD** is within Engagement Range of any enemy **MONSTER** or **VEHICLE** units, add 1 to its Attacks characteristic.
- Each time this **WARLORD** makes an attack against a **MONSTER** or **VEHICLE** unit, add 1 to that attack's hit roll and add 1 to that attack's wound roll.

IMPERIAL FISTS: ARCHITECT OF WAR (AURA)
Imperial Fist leaders have a gift for bolstering defensive positions.

While a friendly **IMPERIAL FISTS CORE** unit that is receiving the benefits of cover is within 6" of this **WARLORD**, each time an attack with an Armour Penetration characteristic of -1 is allocated to a model in that unit, that attack has an Armour Penetration characteristic of 0 instead.

CRIMSON FISTS: REFUSE TO DIE
This Crimson Fists champion defies death against all odds.

The first time this **WARLORD** is destroyed, you can choose to roll one D6 at the end of the phase instead of using any rules that are triggered when a model is destroyed (e.g. the Only in Death Does Duty End Stratagem, page 102). If you do, then on a 4+, set this **WARLORD** back up on the battlefield as close as possible to where they were destroyed and more than 1" away from any enemy models, with D3 wounds remaining.

BLACK TEMPLARS: OATHKEEPER
The fury of a Black Templars warlord carries him headlong into battle no matter the hardships, the foe or the challenge he faces.

- This **WARLORD** is eligible to perform a Heroic Intervention if it is within 6" horizontally and 5" vertically of any enemy unit.
- Each time this **WARLORD** makes a Heroic Intervention move, it can move up to 6" instead of 3". All other rules for Heroic Interventions still apply.

BLOOD ANGELS: SPEED OF THE PRIMARCH
Honouring the memory of Sanguinius on the field of battle, this warlord strikes as fast as the mighty angel of Baal once did.

At the start of the Fight phase, if this **WARLORD** is within Engagement Range of any enemy units, it can fight first that phase.

FLESH TEARERS: MERCILESS BUTCHER
In battle, this warlord loses themselves in the pursuit of slaughter, hacking apart all before them with unrelenting savagery.

Each time this **WARLORD** fights, if there are 5 or more enemy models within 3" of it, it can make D3 additional attacks.

IRON HANDS: ADEPT OF THE OMNISSIAH
This warlord is a master of war and the rites of the machine.

- At the end of your Movement phase, unless this **WARLORD** is a **TECHMARINE**, it can repair one friendly **IRON HANDS VEHICLE** model within 1" of it. That **VEHICLE** model regains 1 lost wound. Each model can only be repaired once per turn.
- If this **WARLORD** is a **TECHMARINE**, then each time it uses its Blessing of the Omnissiah ability, the model it is repairing regains up to D3+1 lost wounds instead of D3.

ULTRAMARINES: ADEPT OF THE CODEX
Ultramarines warlords are peerless masters of tactics and strategy, epitomising the teachings of the Codex Astartes.

While this **WARLORD** is on the battlefield, each time you spend a Command point to use a Stratagem you can roll one D6: on a 5+, that Command point is refunded.

SALAMANDERS: ANVIL OF STRENGTH
Vulkan was renowned as the strongest of the Primarchs, and his genetic heritage lends this son of Nocturne great physical might.

Add 2 to the Strength characteristic of this **WARLORD**.

RAVEN GUARD: ECHO OF THE RAVENSPIRE
This warlord can vanish from sight with supernatural skill.

Once per battle, at the end of your Movement phase, this **WARLORD** can vanish into the gloom if it is more than 6" from any enemy models. If it does, remove it from the battlefield and then, in the Reinforcements step of your subsequent Movement phase, set up this **WARLORD** anywhere on the battlefield that is more than 9" away from any enemy models. If the battle ends and this **WARLORD** is not on the battlefield, it is destroyed.

DEATHWATCH: VIGILANCE INCARNATE
In standing sentinel over a vital swathe of the Imperium, this warlord always knows the appropriate tactics to defeat a foe.

In your Command phase, you can select one friendly **DEATHWATCH CORE** unit within 6" of this **WARLORD**. Each time you do, select one Battlefield Role; until the start of your next Command phase, each time a model in that unit makes an attack against an enemy unit with that Battlefield Role, re-roll a wound roll of 1.

RELICS

If your army is led by an **ADEPTUS ASTARTES WARLORD**, you can, when mustering your army, give one of the following Chapter Relics to an **ADEPTUS ASTARTES CHARACTER** model from your army. Named characters and **VEHICLE** models cannot be given any of the following Relics.

When a model from your army is given a Chapter Relic, replace all instances of the **<CHAPTER>** keyword in that Relic's rules (if any) with the name of the Chapter that your model is drawn from.

Note that some Relics replace one of the model's existing items of wargear. Where this is the case, you must, if you are using points values, still pay the cost of the wargear that is being replaced. Write down any Chapter Relics your models have on your army roster.

THE ARMOUR INDOMITUS

The Armour Indomitus was forged long before the Horus Heresy. Unlike the plasteel and ceramite of normal power armour, the artefact is made from plates of raw adamantine, making it all but unbreachable by conventional weaponry. When rained upon with heavier fire, the Armour Indomitus manifests a shimmering force field, the secrets of which have long been lost to modern artificers.

- Add 1 to the Wounds characteristic of the bearer.
- The bearer has a Save characteristic of 2+.
- Once per battle, before making a saving throw for the bearer, it can activate its armour's force field. If it does, then until the end of the phase, the bearer has a 3+ invulnerable save.

THE SHIELD ETERNAL

The Shield Eternal was a gift from Rogal Dorn to his seneschal during the dark days of the Horus Heresy. This magnificently worked storm shield is a bulwark against which all the wrath of a hateful galaxy can crash. Its warding powers turn aside the maleficent attentions of the witch and the daemon, safeguarding its wearer from mortal blows and perfidious warpcraft alike.

Model with a storm shield, relic shield or combat shield only. This Relic replaces a storm shield, relic shield or combat shield.

- The bearer has a 4+ invulnerable save.
- Add 1 to armour saving throws made for the bearer.
- Each time the bearer would lose a wound, roll one D6: on a 5+, that wound is not lost.

STANDARD OF THE EMPEROR ASCENDANT

Woven from threads of spun adamantine in the early days of the Unification of Terra, this banner was carried at the head of the Emperor's guard. It is said that its constant proximity to the Master of Mankind has imbued within it indelible traces of his psychic signature. Whatever the truth of this, its presence is a constant inspiration to those loyal to the Emperor's cause, instilling them with valour and determination even as their foes quail in its presence.

ANCIENT model only.

- Add 3" to the range of the bearer's Astartes Banner ability.
- Each time a Morale test is taken for a friendly **<CHAPTER> CORE** unit within range of the bearer's Astartes Banner ability, you can re-roll that test.

TEETH OF TERRA

The origins of the Teeth of Terra lie shrouded in mystery. Mentions of this large, obsidian-toothed chainsword can be found dotted throughout the histories of many Space Marine Chapters, yet the weapon itself can be traced to no artisan's hand, nor can it be found in any Chapter's Armoury save in times of the greatest need. What is certain is that, when wielded in battle by a true hero of the Imperium, the Teeth of Terra strikes with the force of a thunderbolt, leaving a bloody trail of broken bodies in its wake.

Model equipped with an Astartes chainsword only. This Relic replaces an Astartes chainsword and has the following profile:

WEAPON	RANGE	TYPE	S	AP	D
Teeth of Terra	Melee	Melee	+1	-2	2

Abilities: Each time the bearer fights, it makes 3 additional attacks with this weapon.

PRIMARCH'S WRATH

The ancient boltgun known as the Primarch's Wrath is believed to have come from the personal weapons collection of Roboute Guilliman himself. Perhaps the finest example of its kind ever crafted, it has dispensed thunderous death to the foes of Mankind for millennia. Chased in Theldrite moonsilver and inscribed in microscopic lettering with every treatise on tactics that Guilliman ever penned, this weapon's quality is such that it allows its wielder to sweep away great swathes of the enemy with a storm of armour-piercing, fragmenting bolts.

Model equipped with a boltgun, master-crafted boltgun or special issue bolt carbine only. This Relic replaces a boltgun, master-crafted boltgun or special issue bolt carbine and has the following profile:

WEAPON	RANGE	TYPE	S	AP	D
Primarch's Wrath	24"	Rapid Fire 2	5	-2	2

THE BURNING BLADE

This ancient broadsword is so large and dense that no mere Human could lift it, let alone wield it in battle. It was recovered from the wreckage of Horus' battle barge, the only unblemished artefact in a chamber crawling with the filthy taint of Chaos. Some artificers have posited that it is the Master of Mankind's greatness that shines out from its sacred steel. In the heat of battle, the sword blazes so brightly that it can melt through even the thickest armour.

Model equipped with a power sword or master-crafted power sword only. This Relic replaces a power sword or master-crafted power sword, and has the following profile:

WEAPON	RANGE	TYPE	S	AP	D
The Burning Blade	Melee	Melee	+3	-5	2

By honouring our relics we honour those who served, bled and won before us. By this we honour our legacy. By this we honour our Primarch. By this we honour the Emperor.

PURGATORUS

This bolt pistol is a true work of the artificer's art. Since its forging in M35, many battle-brothers have used the pistol to purge traitors, tyrants and heretics from the Emperor's realm. The weapon's machine spirit is wrathful, its aim inescapable; in many ways, Purgatorus epitomises the very warriors who wield it.

Model equipped with a bolt pistol, heavy bolt pistol, master-crafted special issue bolt pistol or absolvor bolt pistol only. This Relic replaces a bolt pistol, heavy bolt pistol, master-crafted special issue bolt pistol or absolvor bolt pistol and has the following profile:

WEAPON	RANGE	TYPE	S	AP	D
Purgatorus	18"	Pistol 3	5	-3	2

RELIQUARY OF GATHALAMOR

By the time the Indomitus Crusade reached the world of Gathalamor, daemonic hordes had already carved a bloody path across much of the planet. Its final defence was led by Knight Centura Ordela Grendoth, whose null-field was anathema to the warp creatures. Gathalamor was liberated by Guilliman, but Grendoth was slain in the battle. Her bones have since been placed inside a reliquary that now possesses a fraction of her power.

PRIMARIS model only. The bearer has the following ability: 'Reliquary of Gathalamor (Aura): While an enemy **PSYKER** unit is within 18" of the bearer, subtract 1 from Psychic tests taken for that unit, and each time a Psychic test is failed for that unit, roll one D6: on a 4+, that unit suffers D3 mortal wounds.'

BELLICOS BOLT RIFLE

The forge world of Bellicos was a hidden weapons-testing facility given dispensation to practise near heretical levels of technological innovation. Before it was swallowed by the Great Rift, the planet managed to dispatch a single cargo hauler containing prototype bolt rifles of an incredibly advanced pattern. These weapons are regarded with a borderline religious reverence for their bellicose lethality, and to wield one is considered a paramount honour.

Model equipped with a master-crafted auto bolt rifle only. This Relic replaces a master-crafted auto bolt rifle and has the following profile:

WEAPON	RANGE	TYPE	S	AP	D
Bellicos bolt rifle	24"	Assault 4	5	-1	2

LAMENT

Dark rumours abound that this weapon is so cruel of essence that those who wield it doom themselves as surely as those who fall under their sights. It is telling of the Space Marines' selfless courage that they utilise the weapon regardless.

Model equipped with a master-crafted stalker bolt rifle only. This Relic replaces a master-crafted stalker bolt rifle and has the following profile:

WEAPON	RANGE	TYPE	S	AP	D
Lament	36"	Heavy 1	5	-2	3

Abilities: Each time an attack is made with this weapon, if the attack successfully wounds the target, it inflicts 1 mortal wound on the target in addition to any normal damage.

GHOSTWEAVE CLOAK

Hand-stitched by blinded servitors and anointed with the distilled blood of a thousand sentries who failed at their posts, this cloak contains strands of mnemothread spun from a thrice-blessed dataloom imbued with obfuscatory data-spirits. It throws up a field of techno-spiritual dissonance that veils its wearer from sight and sensors, allowing them to slip across the battlefield like a wraith.

PHOBOS model with a camo cloak only.

- Each time the bearer makes a Normal Move, Advances or Falls Back, it can move across models as if they were not there.
- Each time an attack is made against the bearer, subtract 1 from that attack's hit roll.

TOME OF MALCADOR

Malcador the Sigillite was the trusted aide of the Emperor himself. The most potent Human psyker of the time, the tome he penned on the nature of reality enhances the mind of the reader.

LIBRARIAN model only. The bearer knows one additional psychic power from any discipline it has access to.

BENEDICTION OF FURY

Borne on a dozen bloody and hard-fought crusades, this weapon's unique empathokinetic circuitry has absorbed the bellicosity and righteous wrath of every Chaplain who has ever wielded it. As a result, it now strikes with the force of a thunderbolt.

CHAPLAIN model only. This Relic replaces a Crozius Arcanum and has the following profile:

WEAPON	RANGE	TYPE	S	AP	D
Benediction of Fury	Melee	Melee	+2	-2	3

Abilities: Each time an attack is made with this weapon, an unmodified wound roll of 6 inflicts 1 mortal wound on the target in addition to any normal damage.

THE HONOUR VEHEMENT

A single stanza of script, the original of which was said to have been penned by the Emperor himself, the Honour Vehement is inscribed on thrice-blessed parchment and affixed with a purity seal upon its bearer's armour. So potent is the inspirational value of the Emperor's own evocation that not only those who bear it, but all their battle-brothers are driven into a relentless killing fury.

The bearer has the following ability: 'The Honour Vehement (Aura): While a friendly **<CHAPTER> CORE** unit is within 6" of the bearer, each time that unit fights, until that fight is resolved, add 1 to the Attacks characteristic of models in that unit. This is not cumulative with the additional attack granted by the Shock Assault ability (pg 125).'

THE VOX ESPIRITUM

Developed by Archmagos Cawl, the Vox Espiritum is a powerful neural amplifier that causes its wearer's voxed utterances to resonate on a modulated and heavily warded frequency. Though still highly experimental and not altogether safe, it allows its user to project their bellowed commands – and sometimes even unspoken mental imperatives – directly into the minds of friend and foe alike.

PRIMARIS model only. Add 3" to the range of the bearer's aura abilities (to a maximum of 9"). This does not increase the range of aura abilities that are psychic powers.

LIBRARIUS DISCIPLINE

Before the battle, generate the psychic powers for **Psyker** models from your army that know powers from the Librarius discipline using the table below. You can either roll one D6 to generate each power randomly (re-rolling duplicate results), or you can select which powers the psyker knows.

When a **Psyker** unit from your army manifests a psychic power from this discipline, replace all instances of the **<Chapter>** keyword on that psychic power (if any) with the name of the Chapter that your **Psyker** is drawn from.

1. VEIL OF TIME
The psyker projects his will beyond the regular passage of time, altering the temporal flow to sway the tide of battle.

Blessing: *Veil of Time* has a warp charge value of 6. If manifested, select one friendly **<Chapter>** unit within 18" of this **Psyker**.

- Until the start of your next Psychic phase, you can re-roll Advance rolls and charge rolls made for that unit.
- Until the start of your next Psychic phase, if that unit starts the Fight phase within Engagement Range of an enemy unit, it fights first that phase.

2. MIGHT OF HEROES
The psyker cages the immense power of the immaterium within the physical form of one of his brothers, making the blessed warrior the Emperor's vengeance made manifest.

Blessing: *Might of Heroes* has a warp charge value of 6. If manifested, select one friendly **<Chapter> Core** or **<Chapter> Character** model within 12" of this **Psyker**. Until the start of your next Psychic phase, add 1 to that model's Strength, Toughness and Attacks characteristics (if a unit has more than one Toughness characteristic, use the lowest Toughness characteristic in that unit when resolving any rules).

3. NULL ZONE
The psyker unleashes the full might of his mind to cast down his opponent's defences, both technological and mystical, rendering them vulnerable to the retribution of the Adeptus Astartes.

Blessing (Aura): *Null Zone* has a warp charge value of 7. If manifested, then:

- Until the start of your next Psychic phase, while a unit is within 6" of this **Psyker**, each time an attack is made against that unit, invulnerable saving throws cannot be made against that attack.
- Until the start of your next Psychic phase, while an enemy **Psyker** unit is within 6" of this **Psyker**, halve the total of Psychic tests taken for that unit.

4. PSYCHIC SCOURGE
The psyker pits his superhuman willpower against that of his enemies in a battle of mental fortitude, seeking to destroy their minds in a burst of psychic fury.

Witchfire: *Psychic Scourge* has a warp charge value of 6. If manifested, select one enemy unit within 18" of and visible to this **Psyker**. Then, roll one D6 and add this **Psyker**'s Leadership characteristic to the result. Your opponent then rolls one D6 and adds that unit's Leadership characteristic to the result. If your total is higher than your opponent's, the selected unit suffers D3 mortal wounds; if it is equal to your opponent's total, the selected unit suffers 1 mortal wound; if it is less than your opponent's total, nothing happens.

5. FURY OF THE ANCIENTS
Calling upon the myths of his Chapter's home world, the psyker sends forth a terrifying monstrosity wrought from psychic energy.

Witchfire: *Fury of the Ancients* has a warp charge value of 6. If manifested, select one enemy model that is within 18" of and visible to this **Psyker**. Draw a line between any part this **Psyker**'s base and any part of the selected model's base (or hull); the selected model's unit, and every other enemy unit that this line passes over or through, suffers 1 mortal wound.

6. PSYCHIC FORTRESS
Drawing on boundless reserves of inner strength, the psyker constructs a powerful field of shimmering psychic energy around himself as well as any nearby battle-brothers, protecting them from harm.

Blessing (Aura): *Psychic Fortress* has a warp charge value of 6. If manifested, then until the start of your next Psychic phase, while a friendly **<Chapter>** unit is within 6" of this **Psyker**, models in that unit have a 5+ invulnerable save.

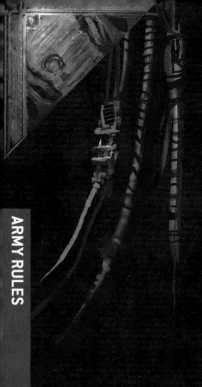

A closed mind is as a mighty fortress prepared for siege, its drawbridge raised, battlements manned and gates barred.

OBSCURATION DISCIPLINE

Before the battle, generate the psychic powers for **PSYKER** models that know powers from the Obscuration discipline using the table below. You can either roll one D6 to generate each power randomly (re-rolling duplicate results), or you can select which powers the psyker knows.

When a **PSYKER** unit from your army manifests a psychic power from this discipline, replace all instances of the **<CHAPTER>** keyword on that psychic power (if any) with the name of the Chapter that your **PSYKER** is drawn from.

1. SHROUDING
The psyker uses his mastery of the warp to fog the minds of his enemies, clouding their senses so that his allies appear as nothing more than indistinct shadows.

Blessing: *Shrouding* has a warp charge value of 6. If manifested, select one friendly **<CHAPTER> PHOBOS** unit within 18" of this **PSYKER**. Until the start of your next Psychic phase, unless that unit is the closest eligible target, enemy models cannot target that unit with ranged attacks.

2. SOUL SIGHT
The psyker shares his warp-sight with his brethren, causing their eyes to glow with an ethereal light. So empowered, no foe can escape their omniscient gaze; the souls of their targets flare like flaming beacons in the dark.

Blessing: *Soul Sight* has a warp charge value of 6. If manifested, select one friendly **<CHAPTER> PHOBOS** unit within 18" of this **PSYKER**. Until the start of your next Psychic phase, each time a model in that unit makes a ranged attack, you can re-roll the hit roll and the target does not receive the benefits of cover against that attack.

3. MIND RAID
The psyker peers into the mind of the foe, raiding their thoughts for secret codes, battle plans, the location of hidden forces and any other tactical information that might be useful. Such brute psychic interrogation doubtless inflicts severe cerebral trauma on its victim.

Witchfire: *Mind Raid* has a warp charge value of 6. If manifested, select one enemy model within 18" of and visible to this **PSYKER**.

- That model's unit suffers 1 mortal wound.
- If that model is a **CHARACTER**, roll 3D6: if the result is equal to or greater than that model's Leadership characteristic, you gain 1 Command point.

4. HALLUCINATION
The psyker instils terror and panic within his foes by conjuring images out of their memories – from past allies seemingly returned from the dead, to apparitions wrought from nightmares.

Malediction: *Hallucination* has a warp charge value of 6. If manifested, select one enemy unit within 18" of and visible to this **PSYKER**.

- Until the start of your next Psychic phase, subtract 1 from the Leadership characteristic of models in that unit.
- Until the start of your next Psychic phase, each time a model in that unit makes an attack, subtract 1 from that attack's hit roll.

5. TENEBROUS CURSE
As the psyker twists his hand, a psychic bolt lances through the minds of his enemies. As they reel from the assault, their own shadows seemingly come to life, pulling their casters to the ground with frenzied determination.

Malediction: *Tenebrous Curse* has a warp charge value of 7. If manifested, select one enemy unit that cannot **FLY** and is within 18" of and visible to this **PSYKER**.

- That unit suffers 1 mortal wound.
- Until the start of your next Psychic phase, halve that unit's Move characteristic and subtract 2 from Advance rolls and charge rolls made for it.

6. TEMPORAL CORRIDOR
The psyker creates an invisible corridor in which the passage of time is altered, allowing his allies to traverse the battlefield with supernatural swiftness.

Blessing: *Temporal Corridor* has a warp charge value of 5. If manifested, select one friendly **<CHAPTER> PHOBOS** unit within 6" of this **PSYKER**.

- That unit cannot shoot or fight this turn.
- If that unit is not within Engagement Range of any enemy models, it can either make a Normal Move or it can Advance as if it were your Movement phase (if it Advances, do not make an Advance roll; instead, until the end of the phase, add 6" to the Move characteristic of models in that unit).

ARMY RULES

111

LITANIES OF BATTLE

All **CHAPLAINS** know the *Litany of Hate* (see below). In addition, before the battle, generate the additional litanies for **PRIEST** models from your army that know litanies from the Litanies of Battle using the table below. You can either roll one D6 to generate each litany randomly (re-rolling duplicate results), or you can select which litanies the priest knows.

When a **PRIEST** unit from your army recites a litany, replace all instances of the **<CHAPTER>** keyword on that litany (if any) with the name of the Chapter that your **PRIEST** is drawn from.

LITANY OF HATE (AURA)
The Chaplain fuels his battle-brothers with hatred and exhorts them to strike the foe harder and harder, without mercy.

If this litany is inspiring, then while a friendly **<CHAPTER> CORE** or **<CHAPTER> CHARACTER** unit is within 6" of this **PRIEST**, each time a model in that unit makes a melee attack, you can re-roll the hit roll.

1. LITANY OF FAITH (AURA)
The Chaplain exhorts his charges to steel themselves against even the most dangerous weapons the enemy can bring to bear.

If this litany is inspiring, then while a friendly **<CHAPTER> CORE** or **<CHAPTER> CHARACTER** unit is within 6" of this **PRIEST,** each time a model in that unit would lose a wound as the result of a mortal wound, roll one D6: on a 5+, that wound is not lost.

2. CATECHISM OF FIRE
The Chaplain calls upon his brothers to unleash a relentless storm of close-range firepower.

If this litany is inspiring, select one friendly **<CHAPTER> CORE** or **<CHAPTER> CHARACTER** unit within 6" of this **PRIEST**. Each time a model in that unit makes a ranged attack against the closest eligible target, add 1 to that attack's wound roll.

3. EXHORTATION OF RAGE
The Chaplain bellows his fury at the enemy, his brothers surging forwards to strike them down.

If this litany is inspiring, select one friendly **<CHAPTER> CORE** or **<CHAPTER> CHARACTER** unit within 6" of this **PRIEST**. Each time a model in that unit makes a melee attack, add 1 to that attack's wound roll.

4. MANTRA OF STRENGTH
The Chaplain focuses his mind on the purity of the blood that runs through his veins, bestowed upon him by the Primarch himself.

If this litany is inspiring:

- Add 1 to this **PRIEST**'s Attacks and Strength characteristics.
- Add 1 to the Damage characteristic of melee weapons this **PRIEST** is equipped with.

5. RECITATION OF FOCUS
The Chaplain recites creeds that focus the minds of his brothers to ensure their shots strike true.

If this litany is inspiring, select one friendly **<CHAPTER> CORE** or **<CHAPTER> CHARACTER** unit within 6" of this **PRIEST**. Each time a model in that unit makes a ranged attack, add 1 to that attack's hit roll.

6. CANTICLE OF HATE (AURA)
Bellowing his hatred of the foe, the Chaplain leads his brothers in the wholesale destruction of the enemy.

If this litany is inspiring, then while a friendly **<CHAPTER> CORE** or **<CHAPTER> CHARACTER** unit is within 6" of this **PRIEST**:

- Add 2 to charge rolls made for that unit. This is not cumulative with any other rule that adds to a unit's charge roll.
- Each time a model in that unit makes a pile-in or consolidation move, it can move up to an additional 3". This is not cumulative with any other rule that increases the distance models can pile in or consolidate.

CHAPTER APPROVED RULES

If every model in your army (excluding **Agent of the Imperium** and **Unaligned** models) has the **Adeptus Astartes** keyword, and your **Warlord** has the **Adeptus Astartes** keyword, you can, if you are playing a matched play battle that instructs you to select secondary objectives (e.g. a mission from the Eternal War mission pack in the Warhammer 40,000 Core Book), select one of them to be from the **Adeptus Astartes** secondary objectives listed below.

Like all other secondary objectives, each of the secondary objectives listed below has a category, and they follow all the normal rules for secondary objectives (for example, when you select secondary objectives, you cannot choose more than one from each category, you can score no more than 15 victory points from each secondary objective you select during the mission etc.).

PURGE THE ENEMY

CODEX WARFARE

End Game Objective

The Codex Astartes has proven its worth as a superb treatise on warfare over countless battlefields, and has remained so even after ten thousand years. Many Space Marines hold its teachings in awe, following its guidance in all ways, trusting in its ability to give them victory. Their belief has been rewarded on battlefield after battlefield.

If you select this objective, you score victory points as follows:

- Score 1 victory point at the end of the battle (to a maximum of 5 victory points) for each enemy unit that was destroyed as the result of an attack made with a Heavy or Grenade weapon by an **Adeptus Astartes** unit from your army while the Devastator Doctrine was active for your army.

- Score 1 victory point at the end of the battle (to a maximum of 5 victory points) for each enemy unit that was destroyed as the result of an attack made with a Rapid Fire or Assault weapon by an **Adeptus Astartes** unit from your army while the Tactical Doctrine was active for your army.

- Score 1 victory point at the end of the battle (to a maximum of 5 victory points) for each enemy unit that was destroyed as the result of an attack made with a Pistol or Melee weapon by an **Adeptus Astartes** unit from your army while the Assault Doctrine was active for your army.

BATTLEFIELD SUPREMACY

SHOCK TACTICS

Progressive Objective

The Space Marines are the Emperor's finest shock troops, striking at the foe before they can react or even know they are under threat. In their lightning assaults, Space Marines smash aside the enemy, slaughtering them without mercy, to achieve their goals.

Score 3 victory points at the end of the battle round if you control one or more objective markers that were controlled by your opponent at the start of the battle round, and an **Adeptus Astartes** unit from your army is within range of that objective marker.

NO MERCY, NO RESPITE

OATHS OF MOMENT

Progressive Objective

Before battle, Space Marines take all manner of oaths. They swear to never falter, to never give up, to never yield and to fight until their last breath. Made before their battle-brothers, commanders and Chaplains, the Space Marines take fewer things more seriously.

If you select this objective, you score victory points at the end of each battle round for achieving the following three Oaths:

- **Oath of Valour:** Score 1 victory point if any **Character**, **Vehicle** or **Monster** unit was destroyed by an **Adeptus Astartes** unit from your army during that battle round.

- **Oath of Honour:** Score 1 victory point at the end of the battle round so long as no **Adeptus Astartes** units from your army failed a Morale test, and provided no **Adeptus Astartes** units from your army Fell Back during that battle round.

- **Oath of Duty:** Score 2 victory points at the end of the battle round if an **Adeptus Astartes** unit from your army is wholly within 6" of the centre of the battlefield.

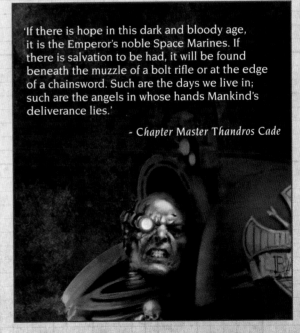

'If there is hope in this dark and bloody age, it is the Emperor's noble Space Marines. If there is salvation to be had, it will be found beneath the muzzle of a bolt rifle or at the edge of a chainsword. Such are the days we live in; such are the angels in whose hands Mankind's deliverance lies.'

- Chapter Master Thandros Cade

A Space Marine's word is as unbreakable as the armour he wears.

CRUSADE RULES

In this section you'll find additional rules for playing Crusade battles with Space Marines, such as Agendas, Battle Traits and Crusade Relics that are bespoke to Adeptus Astartes units. You can find out more about Crusade armies in the Warhammer 40,000 Core Book.

This section contains the following additional rules:

AGENDAS

Adeptus Astartes units attempt to achieve unique Agendas in Crusade battles, which can be found on the page opposite. These Agendas reflect the unique goals of Space Marine armies on the battlefield and help to reflect their particular methods of waging war. You can find out more about Agendas in Crusade mission packs, such as that presented in the Warhammer 40,000 Core Book.

REQUISITIONS

Space Marine armies have access to a number of additional Requisitions, suited to their methods for waging war. You can find these on page 116.

BATTLE TRAITS

Space Marine units can be given one of the Battle Traits presented on page 117 as they gain experience and are promoted in your Crusade force. These help to better reflect the unique upgrades and Battle Honours that are bestowed to Space Marine units.

HONORIFICS

The Honorifics presented on pages 118-119 is a new category of Battle Honour that can be bestowed to Space Marine Captains. They help to reflect the particular honours, duties and skills associated with leading a company of Space Marines, and further personalise the Captains in your Crusade force.

CRUSADE RELICS

In addition to the Crusade Relics presented in the Warhammer 40,000 Core Book, Space Marine characters can quest to search for one of the Crusade Relics described on page 120-121; these Relics are unique to the Adeptus Astartes, and are highly prized by any aspiring Space Marine hero.

SHOWCASE CRUSADE ARMY

On pages 122-123 you will find Darren Latham's superb Silver Skulls Space Marines Crusade army, with a description of the force and its upgrades, and details of its exploits on the battlefield.

Both the Silver Skulls and enigmatic craftworld Aeldari pay close attention to portents, omens and the skeins of fate when making war. On Xenrick, the Silver Skulls were one of the few Imperial forces who could in any way respond in strength to the dozens of unpredictable Biel-Tan raids.

AGENDAS

If your Crusade army includes any **ADEPTUS ASTARTES** units, you can select one Agenda from the Adeptus Astartes Agendas listed below. This is a new category of Agendas, and follows all the normal rules for Agendas (for example, when you select Agendas, you cannot choose more than one from each category).

ANGELS OF DEATH

Adeptus Astartes Agenda

For the Space Marines, only the total destruction of the Emperor's enemies is acceptable.

At the end of the battle, if there are no models from the enemy army remaining on the battlefield, each **ADEPTUS ASTARTES** unit from your army that is on the battlefield gains 3 experience points.

KNOW NO FEAR

Adeptus Astartes Agenda

The Space Marines know no fear. Superhuman courage in the face of terrifying horrors and overwhelming odds are expected from each and every battle-brother. Fleeing from the conflict is as anathema to them as allowing the enemies of the Emperor to draw breath.

Keep a Know No Fear tally for each **ADEPTUS ASTARTES** unit in your army. Each time a unit passes a Morale test, add 1 to its Know No Fear tally. If a unit fails a Morale test, reset its tally back to 0. At the end of the battle, each unit gains 2 experience points for every mark on its Know No Fear tally.

QUEST OF ATONEMENT

Adeptus Astartes Agenda

The warriors of the Chapter who bear the Mark of Censure have submitted themselves to the reclusiam for their failures, and been set upon a quest for absolution in their Chapter's eyes. Only by striking down the mightiest foes of the Emperor will their shame be absolved.

When you select this Agenda, select one **ADEPTUS ASTARTES** unit in your army that has one of the following Battle Scars: Loss of Reputation, Disgraced or Mark of Shame. At the end of the battle, if a melee attack made by that unit during the battle destroyed an enemy **CHARACTER** with a Power Rating of 5 or more, or a **WARLORD**, **MONSTER** or **VEHICLE** unit, then the selected unit loses one of the aforementioned Battle Scars and gains 5 experience points.

HONOUR THE STANDARD

Adeptus Astartes Agenda

The standards of the Space Marines are inspirational icons and symbols of the Emperor's dominance. To plant one is to claim that ground in the name of the Imperium.

Keep an Honour the Standard tally for each **ADEPTUS ASTARTES** unit in your army. At the end of each of your turns, if a **CORE** unit is wholly within 6" of a model from the same Chapter whose standard has been planted (see below), add 1 to that unit's Honour the Standard tally.

If you selected this Agenda, then **ADEPTUS ASTARTES ANCIENT** units in your army can attempt the following action:

Plant the Standard (Action): At the end of your Movement phase, one **ADEPTUS ASTARTES ANCIENT** unit from your army that is within 6" of the centre of the battlefield can start to perform this action. The action is completed at the end of your turn. Once completed the Ancient's Standard has been planted, and remains so until that model makes a Normal Move, Advances, Falls Back or makes a charge move.

Each unit gains a number of experience points equal to their Honour the Standard tally.

RECOVER GENE-SEED

Adeptus Astartes Agenda

In the confusion of battle, the fallen body of a mighty hero was left on the field, his progenoids not recovered. It is of vital import this precious resource is found.

If you selected this Agenda, then after both sides have finished deploying, your opponent must set up one objective marker anywhere on the battlefield that is not within their own deployment zone. This objective marker represents the fallen Space Marine hero, but does not count as an objective marker for any rules purposes other than for this Agenda. **ADEPTUS ASTARTES APOTHECARY** units in your army can attempt the following action:

Recover Progenoids (Action): At the end of your Movement phase, one **ADEPTUS ASTARTES APOTHECARY** unit from your army that is within 3" of the fallen Space Marine hero objective marker can start to perform this action if no enemy units (excluding **AIRCRAFT** units) are within 3" of that objective marker. The Action is completed at the end of your turn. If completed, remove the fallen Space Marine hero objective marker from the battlefield. If an **APOTHECARY** unit successfully performs this action, it gains 5 experience points and your Crusade force gains 1 bonus Requisition point.

By the way of their death we shall know them.

Through blood and fire I march. In war eternal, my hearts thunder. I am an angel born of violence, a soldier forged of legend. I am the blade in the Emperor's hand, the holy ceramite of his armour.

REQUISITIONS

If your Crusade force includes any ADEPTUS ASTARTES units, you can spend Requisition points (RPs) on any of the following Requisitions in addition to those presented in the Warhammer 40,000 Core Book.

EVEN IN DEATH I STILL SERVE   1RP

A mortally wounded Space Marine may be interred in the sarcophagus of a Dreadnought, allowing him to bring death to his foes in a new form.

Purchase this Requisition when an ADEPTUS ASTARTES CHARACTER unit (excluding VEHICLE units) from your Crusade force gains their second or subsequent Battle Scar. Remove that CHARACTER from your Order of Battle and replace it with a DREADNOUGHT (excluding named characters) from the same Chapter. You can only add a PSYKER DREADNOUGHT if the CHARACTER it is replacing was a PSYKER. You cannot purchase this Requisition if doing so would cause your total Power Level to exceed your Crusade force's Supply Limit. The new DREADNOUGHT starts with the same number of experience points as the CHARACTER it replaced and gains the appropriate number of Battle Honours for its rank.

CHAPTER COMMAND   1RP

Through heroism on the field of battle and unwavering commitment to duty, Space Marines can ascend the ranks.

Purchase this Requisition when a CAPTAIN, LIBRARIAN, CHAPLAIN, APOTHECARY, ANCIENT, COMPANY CHAMPION or TECHMARINE from your Crusade force gains the Heroic or Legendary rank. That model is upgraded to the Chapter Command (pg 98); increase its Power Rating accordingly and make a note on its Crusade card. You cannot purchase this Requisition if doing so would cause your total Power Level to exceed your Crusade force's Supply Limit.

INDOMITUS CRUSADE VETERANS   1RP

Many Primaris Space Marines served as part of the Indomitus Crusade before joining their Chapters, bringing vital experience of the fractured Imperium.

Purchase this Requisition when you add a PRIMARIS CORE unit (excluding CHARACTER units) to your Order of Battle that has the Elites Battlefield Role. That unit gains 6 experience points (and therefore gains the Blooded rank). Select one Battle Honour for them as normal.

RUBICON PRIMARIS   1RP

To cross the Rubicon Primaris is not a decision taken lightly, for not all warriors survive the transformation. Those who do become even more potent avatars of war.

Purchase this Requisition at any time. Select one CAPTAIN, LIBRARIAN, CHAPLAIN, APOTHECARY, ANCIENT or TECHMARINE unit from your Crusade force that does not have the PRIMARIS keyword and roll one D6. On a 1, that unit is removed from your Order of Battle. On a 2+, replace that unit with a PRIMARIS unit with the same keyword drawn from the same Chapter. You cannot purchase this requisition if doing so would cause your total Power Level to exceed your Crusade force's Supply Limit. The new PRIMARIS unit has the same number of experience points and the same Battle Honours and Battle Scars as the unit it replaced. If a Battle Honour cannot be applied (e.g. a Weapon Enhancement for a weapon that PRIMARIS model cannot be equipped with), select a new Battle Honour to replace it.

Faust's Mk X Tacticus armour was chipped, charred and caked in stinking filth. He, Galla and Kyral stood in parade formation. Their armour was as battered as his. Three dozen of their brothers were ranked around them, witnessing the proceedings.

Captain Zonoros, who stood before them, had ordered they make no attempt to clean or repair their armour ahead of the ceremony, except for one thing – their left shoulder pauldron, upon which their Chapter symbol was painted.

'To tell all of your achievements, the hardships you have endured and that you belong to our brotherhood,' the Captain had explained to them earlier.

They had fought against the Death Guard on the sludge-fields of Rhagabe for more than two local months. The traitors had unleashed the Plague That Walks upon the population of the once paradisical world, and millions of once-Humans, hungering for flesh, shuffled tirelessly across the planet's surface. Thick smog hung in the air that burned exposed flesh. Rains of mucus lashed the landscape in a ceaseless deluge of sticking slime.

'Brothers Faust, Galla and Kyral,' said the Captain. 'Today we honour you. Today we recognise your valiant efforts. Let all those who bear our colours know your names and your deeds. It was you who held the bridge over the Thoter river for seven

days, holding back the Dead That Walk whilst Tetuna was evacuated. It was you who stormed the traitors' bunker complex at the Pihar Oasis, purging it of foes and cleansing its taint. It was you who waged a guerrilla war against our hated enemies for three weeks in the tunnel maze beneath the city of Airon, inflicting crippling damage and confusion. Without your efforts, victory may never have been achieved here. For this, you have your Chapter's admiration. For this, I award you all the laurels of victory.'

The dead deserve far more than this, Faust thought. Each of his seven dead squad-brothers had suffered a hideous fate at the hands of the enemy. Virtually nothing remained of them to recover, their gene-seed mutated by the enemy or consumed by them. Faust's hearts pumped harder as his anger grew at the thought.

Captain Zonoros placed the laurels, made from once-pristine leaves taken from the Golden Halos' home world, upon Faust, Galla and Kyral's helmets. Faust could see the laurels were already beginning to wilt in the horrific environment.

'You have achieved more than this, brothers,' said the Captain. 'Your victories are great indeed, your commitment to our Chapter without doubt. I will be recommending all of you to join the honoured ranks of our First Company. They have a grievous need for warriors after what happened at Teremo. I've no doubt they will welcome you.'

BATTLE TRAITS

When an **ADEPTUS ASTARTES** unit gains a Battle Trait, you can use one of the tables below instead of one of the tables in the Warhammer 40,000 Core Book to determine what Battle Trait the unit has gained. To do so, roll one D6 and consult the appropriate table, or choose a Battle Trait from the appropriate table that tells the best narrative for your unit. If a unit gains one of these Battle Traits, replace all instances of the **<CHAPTER>** keyword on that Battle Trait (if any) with the name of the Chapter that your unit is drawn from. All the normal rules for Battle Traits apply (e.g. a unit cannot have the same Battle Trait more than once). As with any Battle Honour, make a note on the unit's Crusade card when it gains a Battle Trait and increase its Crusade points accordingly, as described in the Warhammer 40,000 Core Book.

ADEPTUS ASTARTES MACHINE SPIRIT UNITS

D6	TRAIT
1-2	**Bellicose Machine Spirit** *This machine spirit seeks to grind its foes beneath it.* Improve this model's Weapon Skill characteristic by 3.
3-4	**Focused Machine Spirit** *Even under duress, the attacks of this machine remain precise.* This model does not suffer the penalty incurred to its hit rolls for firing at enemy units that are within Engagement Range of it.
5-6	**Resilient Machine Spirit** *This machine spirit's indomitable might is legendary.* Add 2 to this model's Wounds characteristic.

TECHMARINE UNITS

D6	TRAIT
1-3	**Expert Mechanic** *This Techmarine displays a natural ability to make even the most seriously damaged vehicle ready to wage war again.* If this model is part of your Crusade army, and if it was not destroyed during the battle, then at the end of the battle you can ignore one failed Out of Action test taken for a **<CHAPTER> VEHICLE** unit – that test is treated as having been passed instead.
4-6	**Bionic Extremis** *This Techmarine is more akin to his mechanical charges than he is to a flesh and blood battle-brother.* This Techmarine has a 5+ invulnerable save.

APOTHECARY UNITS

D6	TRAIT
1-3	**Master of Physiology** *This skilled physician is able to return even the most seriously-wounded battle-brother to the field with all speed.* If this model is part of your Crusade army, and if it was not destroyed during the battle, then at the end of the battle you can ignore one failed Out of Action test taken for a **<CHAPTER>** unit (excluding **VEHICLE** and **BEAST** units) – that test is treated as having been passed instead.
4-6	**Custodian of the Future** *This Apothecary fights with the fury of their Primarch when a battle-brother falls, lest their gene-seed be lost.* Each time this model fights, if any friendly **<CHAPTER> INFANTRY** or **<CHAPTER> BIKER** models have been destroyed this turn, then until that fight is resolved, add 3 to this model's attacks characteristic.

ADEPTUS ASTARTES UNITS (EXCLUDING VEHICLES)

D6	TRAIT
1	**Marksman's Honours** *Awarded to those warriors who prove their accuracy in combat, these badges are constructed by coating spent bolter shell casings, ejected from the weapons of great heroes, in gold.* Improve the Ballistic Skill of each model in this unit by 1.
2	**Aquila Imperialis** *Awarded to those who have shown great resolve, this eagle emblem is emblazoned on the warrior's chest plate.* Each time a Morale test is taken for this unit, it is automatically passed. In addition, each time an Out of Action test is failed for this unit, re-roll that test.
3	**Purity Seals** *Purity seals record not so much honours as blessings given by the Chapter's Chaplains before battle. When a battle-brother receives a seal, the Chaplains chant litanies before affixing it to the Space Marine's armour.* Once per turn, this unit can attempt to Deny the Witch as if it were a **PSYKER**. If this unit is a **PSYKER**, then in each enemy Psychic phase, it can instead attempt to Deny the Witch one additional time.
4	**Bladesman's Honour** *Awarded to the most superlative duellists of the Chapter, this honour badge is shaped like a dagger and proclaims the bearer's skill at arms.* Improve the Weapon Skill of each model in this unit by 1.
5	**Terminator Honours** *Veterans who have earned the honour of waging war in Terminator armour are permitted to wear these badges – smaller representations of the Crux Terminatus – when fighting in their power armour.* Select one model in this unit (if the unit has a unit champion, such as a Space Marine Sergeant, you must select that model). Add 1 to the Attacks and Leadership characteristic of the selected model. In addition, unless the selected model is a **CHARACTER**, you also add 1 to the selected model's Wounds characteristic.
6	**Centurios Service Studs** *These rivets are stamped into a warrior's cranium to record ten, fifty or a hundred years' service. Though described in the Codex, the awarding of studs is not officially required.* At the start of your Command phase, select the Devastator, Tactical or Assault Doctrine (pg 125). Until the start of your next Command phase, each time a model in this unit makes an attack, the doctrine you selected is considered to be active for that attack instead of whatever doctrine is actually active for your army.

HONORIFICS

Honorifics are a new type of Battle Honour that can be given to **Adeptus Astartes Captain** units. When such a unit from your army would gain a Battle Honour, you can instead choose for it to gain one of the Honorifics listed below. You cannot give an Honorific to a unit from the Deathwatch Chapter or the Space Wolves Chapter (or any of its successor Chapters).

Each **Captain** unit can only have a single Honorific, and your Order of Battle cannot include more than one such unit from the same Chapter with the same Honorific (e.g. you cannot have two **Blood Angels Captain** units with the Master of the Watch Honorific, or two **Silver Skulls Captain** units with the Master of Recruits Honorific). As with any Battle Honour, make a note on the unit's Crusade card when it gains an Honorific, and increase its Crusade points total by 1.

If a **Captain** unit from your army is upgraded to be a Chapter Master using the Chapter Command Requisition (pg 116), that unit loses any Honorific it has (if so, its Crusade points are reduced by 1).

MASTER OF THE KEEP

In some Chapters the 1st Company Captain serves as Master of the Keep. These mighty warriors may serve as the Chapter Master's second in command, be responsible for the Chapter's fortress monastery and speak for the Chapter Master in his absence.

Once per battle, if this unit is on the battlefield, when you use an Adeptus Astartes Battle Tactic Stratagem (pg 102), that Stratagem costs 0 Command points.

MASTER OF THE WATCH

The Captain of the 2nd Company is often responsible for the defence of the Chapter's home world. They are heavily involved with system-wide defence and intelligence assessment of threats to their Chapter's seat of power. Regardless of how much a Chapter involves itself in the affairs of its home world's population, the Master of the Watch takes a keen interest in them.

If this unit is part of your Crusade army and you are the Defender, then you start the battle with an additional 2 Command points.

MASTER OF THE ARSENAL

This Captain, often of the 3rd Company, is responsible for managing and overseeing the Chapter's vast inventory of munitions.

Once per battle, if this unit is on the battlefield, when you use an Adeptus Astartes Wargear Stratagem (pg 104-105), that Stratagem costs 0 Command points.

MASTER OF THE FLEET

The Master of the Fleet is often the Captain of the 4th Company, and is responsible for the Chapter's armada of spacefaring warships. He is expected to be highly skilled not only in commanding a single ship in battle, but also in coordinating all of the Chapter's vessels in the highly complex matters of ship-to-ship combat.

- If this unit is on the battlefield, you can use the Orbital Bombardment Stratagem (pg 104) twice during the battle instead of once.
- While this unit is on the battlefield, each time you use the Orbital Bombardment Stratagem (pg 104), it costs 1 Command point instead of 3.

MASTER OF THE MARCHES

This warrior oversees the deployment of all the Chapter's assets, in addition to their role as Captain of the 5th Company. In so doing they hear all pleas for the Chapter's aid, dismissing those he deems the most unworthy before presenting those that remain to the Chapter Master.

If this unit is part of your Crusade army and you are using the Strategic Reserves rule, you can halve the Command point cost required to place units into Strategic Reserves (rounding fractions down). You can find out more about the Strategic Reserves rule in the Warhammer 40,000 Core Book.

MASTER OF THE RITES

The Master of the Rites is often the Captain of the 6th Company. Among his many duties he is often responsible for preserving and recording the Chapter's martial traditions and ceremonial conventions.

If this unit is part of your Crusade force, then the Warlord Trait Requisition costs 0 Requisition points if the model being given the Warlord Trait is from the same Chapter as this unit.

CHIEF VICTUALLER

Traditionally held by the Captain of the 7th Company, a warrior with this title is responsible for the non-armament provisions the Chapter requires to continue its operations, as well as thousands of serfs and servitors. In this role, a battle-brother must prove himself a master logistician.

If this unit is part of your Crusade force, then the Rearm and Resupply Requisition costs 0 Requisition points if the unit selected for that Requisition is from the same Chapter as this unit.

LORD EXECUTIONER

The Captain of the 8th Company is a martial example to his Chapter's warriors. As Lord Executioner, he dispenses the Chapter's justice – whether that be to the Chapter's hated foes or those within its ranks who fail to meet enormously stringent disciplinary requirements.

If this unit is part of your Crusade army and you are the Attacker, then you start the battle with an additional 2 Command points.

MASTER OF RELICS

The Captain of the 9th Company is often responsible for the maintenance, security and care of the Chapter's priceless relics, as well as the recovery of relics that lie as yet undiscovered throughout the galaxy.

If this unit is part of your Crusade force, then the Relic Requisition costs 0 Requisition points if the model gaining the Relic is from the same Chapter as this unit.

MASTER OF RECRUITS AND MASTER OF RECONNAISSANCE

The 10th Company Captain is responsible for training the Chapter's future generations. With ten Vanguard squads at his command, he also serves as the Chapter Master's eyes and ears, and possesses vast amounts of intelligence.

If this unit is part of your Crusade force, then the Fresh Recruits Requisition costs 0 Requisition points if the unit gaining the Fresh Recruits is from the same Chapter as this unit.

'The gauntlet of Maurik reminds us of the sacrifices our brothers made in the Meatgrinder. The Auranescant Banner depicts glories won over four thousand years of history. The blood of ten-score Hrud still sheens the blade of the Leonine Axe. And these are but three of hundreds of ancient artefacts we hold. Each tells a story of our oathsworn duty, of our honour, of our untarnished service. May we add many more.'

- Luko Phrant, Master of Relics, Golden Halos

Hailing from the feral world of Varsavia, the Silver Skulls have adopted the head-taking traditions of their planet's tribal populace. Storming an Ork fortress on the world of Trazolya, the Silver Skulls were eager to slay the Bad Moons Orks, the long-fanged greenskins making for excellent trophies.

CRUSADE RELICS

When an **Adeptus Astartes Character** gains a Crusade Relic, you can instead select one of the Relics listed below. All the usual rules for selecting Crusade Relics, as described in the Warhammer 40,000 Core Book, apply.

When a model from your army is given a Crusade Relic, replace all instances of the **<Chapter>** keyword on that Crusade Relic's rules (if any) with the name of the Chapter that your model is drawn from.

ARTIFICER RELICS

An **Adeptus Astartes Character** model can be given one of the following Artificer Relics instead of one of the ones presented in the Warhammer 40,000 Core Book.

Halo Indomitus

This Iron Halo protects the bearer from harm, whilst proclaiming them to be a mighty hero of the Imperium.

- The bearer has a 4+ invulnerable save.
- Each time the bearer would lose a wound as the result of a mortal wound, roll one D6: on a 4+, that wound is not lost.

Adamantine Cuirass

This chest plate bears an Aquila crest wrought in adamantine, rendering it proof against even the mightiest blow.

Add 1 to the bearer's Wounds and Toughness characteristics.

Astartes Teleportation Transponder

Incorporating arcane technology found in suits of Terminator armour, this unassuming device allows the bearer to be teleported accurately into the thick of battle from their orbiting spacecraft.

The bearer has the Teleport Strike ability (pg 125).

ANTIQUITY RELICS

An **Adeptus Astartes Character** model of Heroic rank or higher can be given one of the following Antiquity Relics instead of one of the ones presented in the Warhammer 40,000 Core Book. Add 1 to a unit's total Crusade points for each Antiquity Relic it has – this is in addition to the +1 from gaining a Battle Honour, for a total of +2.

Paragon Blade

This blade is a relic of the Great Crusade and is rumoured to have been crafted on Terra. It is now borne by only the greatest heroes of the Space Marine Chapters.

Model with a power sword, master-crafted power sword, relic blade, xenophase blade or executioner relic blade only. This Relic replaces the model's power sword, master-crafted power sword, relic blade, xenophase blade or executioner relic blade and has the following profile:

WEAPON	RANGE	TYPE	S	AP	D
Paragon blade	Melee	Melee	+2	-4	3

Standard of Righteous Hatred

This bloodstained banner lists the atrocities and injustices committed by the Emperor's foes, a reminder of the duty of the Adeptus Astartes to purge the stars of the heretic and the alien.

Ancient model only. Each time a friendly model is destroyed and make an attack as a result of the bearer's Astartes Banner ability (pg 146), that attack scores a hit on a hit roll of 2+, irrespective of any modifiers.

LEGENDARY RELICS

An **Adeptus Astartes Character** model of Legendary rank can be given one of the following Legendary Relics instead of one of the ones presented in the Warhammer 40,000 Core Book. In addition, in order to give a model a Legendary Relic, you must also pay 1 Requisition point (if you do not have enough Requisition points, you cannot give that model a Legendary Relic). Add an additional 2 to a unit's total Crusade points for each Legendary Relic it has – this is in addition to the +1 from gaining a Battle Honour, for a total of +3.

Vortex Bolts

Crafted long ago in forges lost to the mist of time, these immensely rare rounds create a miniature vortex within the target upon their detonation. Such an event causes catastrophic damage to even the largest enemies, and psykers who miraculously survive are driven mad by the creatures of the warp that flow from the tear in reality.

Model with a bolt weapon (pg 195) only. When you select this Relic, select one bolt weapon the bearer is equipped with. Once per battle, when the bearer shoots with that weapon, you can choose for it to fire a vortex bolt. If you do, you can only make one attack with that weapon, but if it scores a hit, the target suffers D3+3 mortal wounds and the attack sequence ends. In addition, until the end of the battle, subtract 1 from Psychic tests taken for a **Psyker** unit hit by a vortex bolt.

Relic of the Primarch

In the deepest vaults of every Chapter are ancient relics inherited from the personal wargear of their gene-father. Only in the direst circumstances are these brought to the battlefield to inspire battle-brothers to even greater deeds; if these relics were to be lost, it would be a tragedy on par with the blackest days in the Chapter's history.

Once per battle, in your Command phase, the bearer can unveil the Relic of the Primarch. If it does so, then until the start of your next Command phase:

- Add 1 to the Attacks characteristic of models in **<Chapter>** units (excluding **Primarch** models) that were within 6" of this model when it unveiled the relic.
- Each time a model in a **<Chapter>** unit (excluding **Primarch** models) that was within 6" of this model when it unveiled the relic makes a melee attack, add 1 to that attack's hit roll.

If the bearer is destroyed, then after removing it from play, replace it with an additional objective marker to represent the Relic of the Primarch (set it up as close as possible to the centre of the model's base before it is removed). You immediately gain the Recover the Relic Agenda (below), in addition to any other Agendas that are being used for this battle:

RECOVER THE RELIC

Adeptus Astartes Agenda

The loss of one of the Primarch's priceless relics is an unthinkable shame that cannot be allowed to pass.

If you control the Relic of the Primarch objective marker at the end of the battle, you can select one unit that is within 3" of that objective marker; that unit gains 3 experience points. If you do not control that objective marker at the end of the battle, then you lose 10 victory points (to a minimum of 0).

Thick smoke hung in the Reclusiam's air, issuing from a dozen censers swayed by hideous robotic cherubim. Twenty Golden Halos lined each side of a long amber-coloured carpet threaded with shimmering black gemstones, their armour and weapons gleaming in the intense firelight of scores of braziers fuelled with lumen-accelerants.

At the head of the aisle, Chaplain Eustakius stood at the top of a series of marble steps, where the carpet ended, next to a vacant stasis casket. His charcoal-black armour was perfectly polished. He had a noble bearing, which deeply contrasted with the savage visage given him by his skull-helm. He read from a large volume, which was bound in gold and Human bone. Its pages had been made from the skin of the most loyal Reclusiam's serfs.

'And so we welcome the Palamas Blade into the Chapter's heart. Many were the foes that it slew. Much was the blood that it spilled. Countless were the Emperor's peoples made safe by its fury. May it serve with its incomparable wrath until Mankind has reclaimed the stars and Humanity has purged the galaxy clean.'

Four Space Marines walked along the carpet, bearing a velvet litter of deep violet. Upon it was a two-handed power sword. Oaths of banishment and protection were etched into its long blade. Its grip was wrapped with black leather inlaid with fine gold thread that depicted haloed lions slaughtering monsters of legend. Its crossguard and pommel were inlaid with rubies, emeralds and sapphires, each stone perfectly cut. They caught the light, bathing the chamber in radiant colour. Ten robed serfs followed the litter bearers, their heads bowed and hands clasped together in prayer. Their mouths moved as they chanted near silent oaths and wards.

Truly magnificent, Eustakius thought, even as he intoned.

'The Palamas Blade slew the Aeldari reaver-king that terrorised Elikis. It beheaded the Aeldari witch that threatened to throw the world of Paiwesh into the empyrean. With great sweeps it slaughtered hundreds of the Great Devourer on the plains of Uzash. Now we lay it to rest until once more its service is needed.'

When the litter reached him, Eustakius lifted the weapon carefully with two hands, its blade in one open palm, its grip in the other. The litter-bearing Space Marines and the following serfs moved to allotted positions.

'Hail the Palamas Blade!' bellowed the Chaplain.

'Hail!' echoed all those in the chamber.

Eustakius turned to the casket. Its arma-glass panels were bordered by strips of gold encrusted with black diamonds. The stones were so well polished Eustakius could see his nightmarish reflection in them. Flat, carved bone images of the Chapter's legendary figures had been placed in the corners of each panel.

He placed the sword into the casket with the care of a mother placing her firstborn in its crib. He closed the case. He pressed the runed code-keys of the stasis field. It thrummed into life.

CRUSADE ARMY

This glorious host of Silver Skulls Space Marines are part of a larger collection belonging to Citadel Miniatures Designer and former 'Eavy Metal painter Darren Latham.

The Silver Skulls are renowned for taking the heads of their fallen enemies as trophies, and for their reverence for their Librarians, who they call Prognosticators. Darren was inspired by these cool themes, as well as the Chapter's striking yet simple colour scheme. He has chosen to build his army around a solid core of Intercessors, strongly supported by heavy weapon-wielding Hellblasters and relic sword-bearing Bladeguard Veterans. A squad of implacable Aggressors incinerate all foes they encounter as a formidable Redemptor Dreadnought rains torrents of fire at the enemy. At their command is the skilled Captain Argentus and a Chaplain, who stirs the Silver Skulls' 3rd Company to battle with his powerful oratory as an Ancient holds the company banner high. Combined, this force represents the undeniable flexibility of Space Marine armies!

This impressive collection is based around the 3rd Company. Crucially, each warrior has his Chapter symbol on his left shoulder pad. Each warrior's company is recognised by the number on his left knee and by the colour of the battlefield role icon on his right shoulder. Squad numbers are applied to the back of powerpacks using transfers. In keeping with the Silver Skulls' background, every warrior's helmet has been painted a brighter silver than the rest of their armour. With very little conversion work, Darren has created a highly coherent force that is true to the background.

Often hobbyists will pay particular attention to centrepiece models such as heroic champions or mighty armoured vehicles. Darren is no exception. Argentus, his Captain, has been converted using a Reiver head. The terrifying skull mask is certainly in keeping with the Chapter's name! Additionally, Darren has taken the opportunity to paint lettering onto the scroll details on the model. The Captain's bolt weapon is named 'Argent', and, ominously, 'Mortis' has been painted on Argentus' shoulder pad. As befitting the army's Ancient, Darren has paid particular attention to the glorious banner the warrior carries, all to better inspire his battle-brothers! He has painted the Ultramarines symbol to honour the Silver Skulls' parent Chapter, and also made sure that the company number is prominent. Lazarius is the strike force's Redemptor Dreadnought, his name proudly emblazoned on his sarcophagus' carapace. The Dreadnought's armour is covered with battle damage, showing that this Chapter hero has thrown himself into the most furious fighting and survived!

Darren plans to add plenty more to this army! He is busy at work converting a Librarian, well in keeping with the Chapter's theme. He also is readying a deadly squad of Eradicators, warriors perfectly equipped to reduce his opponents' tanks to pools of molten metal. Such a squad will only make this force even more versatile.

DATASHEETS

This section contains the datasheets that you will need to fight battles with your Space Marines miniatures, as well as an explanation of the selectable keywords found on those datasheets and details of army-specific abilities. You can find out how to use datasheets in the Warhammer 40,000 Core Book.

THE <CHAPTER> KEYWORD

Every datasheet in this section has the <CHAPTER> keyword. This is a keyword that you can select for yourself, as described in the Warhammer 40,000 Core Book, with the guidance detailed below.

All **ADEPTUS ASTARTES** units are drawn from a Chapter. When you include such a unit in your army, you must nominate which Chapter it is from and then replace the <CHAPTER> keyword in every instance on its datasheet with the name of your chosen Chapter. This could be one of the Chapters detailed in a Warhammer 40,000 publication, or one of your own design.

Example: If you include a Captain in your army, and you decide he is from the Blood Ravens Chapter, his <CHAPTER> keyword becomes **BLOOD RAVENS** *and his Rites of Battle ability reads 'While a friendly* **BLOOD RAVENS CORE** *unit is within 6" of this model, each time a model in that unit makes an attack, re-roll a hit roll of 1.'*

If your army is Battle-forged, you cannot include units from two different Chapters in the same Detachment. You can find out more about Battle-forged armies in the Warhammer 40,000 Core Book.

Non-Codex Compliant Chapters
You cannot select Grey Knights or Legion of the Damned when nominating which Chapter a unit is from. In addition, the following restrictions apply:

- **Black Templars:** **LIBRARIAN** units cannot be from the Black Templars Chapter.

- **Dark Angels:** **STERNGUARD VETERAN SQUAD** and **VANGUARD VETERAN SQUAD** units cannot be from the Dark Angels Chapter (or any of their successor Chapters).

- **Deathwatch:** The following units cannot be from the Deathwatch Chapter: **ASSAULT SQUAD; ATTACK BIKE SQUAD; BIKE SQUAD; DEVASTATOR SQUAD; STERNGUARD VETERAN SQUAD; TACTICAL SQUAD; SCOUT** units.

- **Space Wolves:** The following units cannot be from the Space Wolves Chapter (or any of their successor Chapters): **APOTHECARY; ASSAULT SQUAD; DEVASTATOR SQUAD; STERNGUARD VETERAN SQUAD; TACTICAL SQUAD; VANGUARD VETERAN SQUAD.**

Successor Chapters
Some rules refer to successor Chapters. If your unit is not from the Deathwatch or a First Founding Chapter (Dark Angels, White Scars, Space Wolves, Imperial Fists, Blood Angels, Iron Hands, Ultramarines, Salamanders or Raven Guard), it is from a successor Chapter, and you must decide which of the aforementioned First Founding Chapters it is a successor of. If the successor Chapter you have chosen is one established in the background, its founding Chapter will often be known (e.g. the Howling Griffons Chapter is a successor of the Ultramarines).

If your successor Chapter does not have a known founding Chapter but has the Inheritors of the Primarch Successor Tactic (pg 96), it is a successor of the Chapter whose Chapter Tactic you selected. Otherwise, select a First Founding Chapter that best fits your Chapter's character. In any case, write down on your army roster which of the First Founding Chapters your Chapter is a successor of.

WARGEAR & WEAPON LISTS

The weapon profiles found on a unit's datasheet describe the primary weapons that models in that unit can be equipped with. Some weapons are only referenced on a datasheet; profiles for these, and all other weapons, can be found on pages 196-201. In addition, some datasheets reference one or more weapon lists (e.g. *Melee Weapons* list); these can be found on page 195.

ABILITIES

A unit's datasheet will list all the abilities it has. Certain abilities that are common to many units are only referenced on the datasheets rather than described in full. These are described below.

ANGELS OF DEATH
Space Marines are amongst the finest warriors in the Imperium.

This unit has the following abilities, which are described below: And They Shall Know No Fear; Bolter Discipline; Shock Assault; Combat Doctrines.

And They Shall Know No Fear
Space Marines stand unafraid before the terrors of the galaxy.

Each time a Combat Attrition test is taken for this unit, ignore any or all modifiers.

Bolter Discipline
To a Space Marine, the boltgun is more than a weapon – it is an instrument of Mankind's divinity, the bringer of death to his foes.

Instead of following the normal rules for Rapid Fire weapons, models in this unit shooting Rapid Fire bolt weapons make double the number of attacks if any of the following apply:

- The shooting model's target is within half the weapon's range.
- The shooting model is **INFANTRY** (excluding **CENTURION** models) and its unit Remained Stationary in your previous Movement phase.
- The shooting model is a **TERMINATOR** or **BIKER**.

For the purposes of this ability, a Rapid Fire bolt weapon is any bolt weapon (as defined on page 195) with the Rapid Fire type.

Shock Assault

The Adeptus Astartes are elite troops who strike with the fury of a thunderbolt. Few opponents can withstand this onslaught.

Each time this unit fights, if it made a charge move, was charged, or performed a Heroic Intervention this turn, then until that fight is resolved, add 1 to the Attacks characteristic of models in this unit.

Combat Doctrines

When the Adeptus Astartes fight, they employ a set of combat doctrines to eliminate the enemy. After pounding the foe with heavy weapons, warriors advance to lay down a hail of bolter fire before charging forth with chainswords roaring to finish the foe.

If every unit from your army has the **ADEPTUS ASTARTES** keyword (excluding **AGENT OF THE IMPERIUM** and **UNALIGNED** units), this unit gains a bonus (see below) depending on which combat doctrine is active for your army, as follows:

- During the first battle round, the Devastator Doctrine is active for your army.

- During the second battle round, the Tactical Doctrine is active for your army.

- At the start of the third battle round, select either the Tactical Doctrine or Assault Doctrine: until the end of that battle round, the doctrine you selected is active for your army.

- During the fourth and subsequent battle rounds, the Assault Doctrine is active for your army.

Unless specified otherwise, this bonus is not cumulative with any other rules that improve the Armour Penetration characteristic of a weapon (e.g. the Storm of Fire Warlord Trait).

Devastator Doctrine

The Codex Astartes explains in detail the strategic value of overwhelming firepower applied to key targets at the optimal time in order to eliminate threats and create tactical openings.

While this combat doctrine is active, improve the Armour Penetration characteristic of every Heavy and Grenade weapon that models in this unit are equipped with by 1.

Tactical Doctrine

As the warring armies close upon one another and vicious firefights erupt, the Codex lays out strategies for swiftly seizing the initiative and combining versatility with firepower.

While this combat doctrine is active, improve the Armour Penetration characteristic of every Rapid Fire and Assault weapon that models in this unit are equipped with by 1.

Assault Doctrine

The Codex Astartes leaves no doubt that the killing blow in most engagements must be delivered with a decisive close-quarters strike. It presents plentiful tactical means to achieve this end.

While this combat doctrine is active, improve the Armour Penetration characteristic of every Pistol and Melee weapon that models in this unit are equipped with by 1.

DEPLOYMENT ABILITIES

The following abilities, which are used during deployment, are common to many **ADEPTUS ASTARTES** units.

Combat Squads

Space Marine squads can break down into smaller, tactically flexible formations known as combat squads.

At the start of deployment, before any units have been set up, if this unit contains the maximum number of models that it can, then it can be split into two units containing as equal a number of models as possible. When splitting a unit using this ability, make a note of which models form each of the two new units.

Death From Above

The Angels of Death launch their attack from all directions. Troops equipped with jump packs and grav-chutes descend from the heavens, guns blazing as they slam into battle.

During deployment, if every model in this unit has this ability, then you can set up this unit high in the skies instead of setting it up on the battlefield. If you do, then in the Reinforcements step of one of your Movement phases you can set up this unit anywhere on the battlefield that is more than 9" away from any enemy models.

Concealed Positions

Vanguard forces often infiltrate the battlefield ahead of the main advance, taking up forward positions to ambush the foe.

During deployment, when you set up this unit, if every model in this unit has this ability then it can be set up anywhere on the battlefield that is more than 9" away from the enemy deployment zone and any enemy models.

Outflank

When necessary, Space Marine units can operate behind enemy lines indefinitely, awaiting the perfect opportunity to appear on the enemy's flank and wreak havoc.

During deployment, if every model in this unit has this ability, then you can set up this unit behind enemy lines instead of setting it up on the battlefield. If you do, then in the Reinforcements step of one of your Movement phases you can set up this unit wholly within 6" of any battlefield edge and more than 9" away from any enemy models.

Teleport Strike

Space Marine strike cruisers and battle barges contain baroque chambers fitted with ancient technologies that can teleport the Angels of Death into the very heart of battle.

During deployment, if every model in this unit has this ability, then you can set up this unit in a teleportarium chamber instead of setting it up on the battlefield. If you do, then in the Reinforcements step of one of your Movement phases you can set up this unit anywhere on the battlefield that is more than 9" away from any enemy models.

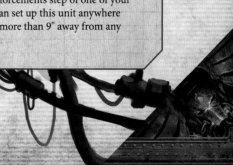

PRIMARIS CAPTAIN

No.	Name	M	WS	BS	S	T	W	A	Ld	Sv
1	Primaris Captain	6"	2+	2+	4	4	6	5	9	3+

A Primaris Captain is equipped with: bolt pistol; master-crafted auto bolt rifle; frag grenades; krak grenades.

WEAPON	RANGE	TYPE	S	AP	D	ABILITIES
Bolt pistol	12"	Pistol 1	4	0	1	-
Heavy bolt pistol	18"	Pistol 1	4	-1	1	-
Master-crafted auto bolt rifle	24"	Assault 3	4	0	2	-
Master-crafted stalker bolt rifle	36"	Heavy 1	4	-2	3	-
Special issue bolt carbine	24"	Assault 2	4	-2	2	-
Master-crafted power sword	Melee	Melee	+1	-3	2	-

OTHER WARGEAR	ABILITIES
Relic shield	Add 1 to armour saving throws made for the bearer. In addition, each time the bearer would lose a wound as the result of a mortal wound, roll one D6: on a 4+, that wound is not lost.

WARGEAR OPTIONS

- If this model is not equipped with a master-crafted power sword, its bolt pistol and master-crafted auto bolt rifle can be replaced with one of the following:
  - 1 plasma pistol and 1 power fist.
  - 1 heavy bolt pistol, 1 master-crafted power sword and 1 relic shield.
- This model's master-crafted auto bolt rifle can be replaced with 1 master-crafted stalker bolt rifle.
- If this model is equipped with either a master-crafted auto bolt rifle or a master-crafted stalker bolt rifle, it can be equipped with 1 master-crafted power sword.
- If this model is from the Dark Angels Chapter (or one of its successor Chapters), its master-crafted auto bolt rifle can be replaced with 1 special issue bolt carbine.
- If this model is equipped with a special issue bolt carbine and it is not equipped with a master-crafted power sword, it can be equipped with 1 power fist.

ABILITIES

Angels of Death (pg 124-125)

Iron Halo: This model has a 4+ invulnerable save.

Rites of Battle (Aura): While a friendly <CHAPTER> CORE unit is within 6" of this model, each time a model in that unit makes an attack, re-roll a hit roll of 1.

FACTION KEYWORDS: **IMPERIUM, ADEPTUS ASTARTES, <CHAPTER>**
KEYWORDS: **INFANTRY, CHARACTER, PRIMARIS, CAPTAIN**

Leading strike forces of Space Marines from the front lines, Captains exemplify the strength and skill of the warriors under their command. They are paragons of strategic genius with centuries of battlefield experience, and their great deeds are often rewarded with ancient artefacts drawn from the Chapter's vaults.

Master-crafted stalker bolt rifle

Master-crafted auto bolt rifle

Ultramarines Primaris Captain with master-crafted stalker bolt rifle and master-crafted power sword

Dark Angels Primaris Captain with special issue bolt carbine and power fist

Imperial Fists Primaris Captain with master-crafted auto bolt rifle

CAPTAIN WITH MASTER-CRAFTED HEAVY BOLT RIFLE

6 POWER

No.	Name	M	WS	BS	S	T	W	A	Ld	Sv
1	Captain with Master-crafted Heavy Bolt Rifle	5"	2+	2+	4	5	7	5	9	3+

A Captain with Master-crafted Heavy Bolt Rifle is equipped with: master-crafted heavy bolt rifle; master-crafted power sword; frag grenades; krak grenades.

WEAPON	RANGE	TYPE	S	AP	D	ABILITIES
Master-crafted heavy bolt rifle	36"	Rapid Fire 1	5	-1	2	-
Master-crafted power sword	Melee	Melee	+1	-3	2	-

ABILITIES

Angels of Death (pg 124-125)

Rites of Battle (Aura): While a friendly <CHAPTER> CORE unit is within 6" of this model, each time a model in that unit makes an attack, re-roll a hit roll of 1.

Iron Halo: This model has a 4+ invulnerable save.

FACTION KEYWORDS: **IMPERIUM, ADEPTUS ASTARTES, <CHAPTER>**
KEYWORDS: **INFANTRY, CHARACTER, PRIMARIS, MK X GRAVIS, CAPTAIN**

Space Marines on the defence fight with a tenacious fury. Captains will take up heavy bolt rifles so as to lay down punishing fire, and bear Gravis armour to withstand the foe's best attempts to dislodge them. Fighting in such a way, they are a symbol of the Space Marines' indomitable will to never fall.

CAPTAIN IN PHOBOS ARMOUR

5 POWER

No.	Name	M	WS	BS	S	T	W	A	Ld	Sv
1	Captain in Phobos Armour	6"	2+	2+	4	4	6	5	9	3+

A Captain in Phobos Armour is equipped with: bolt pistol; master-crafted instigator bolt carbine; combat knife; frag grenades; krak grenades; camo cloak.

WEAPON	RANGE	TYPE	S	AP	D	ABILITIES
Bolt pistol	12"	Pistol 1	4	0	1	-
Master-crafted instigator bolt carbine	30"	Assault 1	4	-2	3	Each time you select a target for this weapon, you can ignore the Look Out, Sir rule.
Combat knife	Melee	Melee	User	0	1	Each time the bearer fights, it makes 1 additional attack with this weapon.

OTHER WARGEAR	ABILITIES
Camo cloak	Each time a ranged attack is allocated to the bearer while it is receiving the benefits of cover, add an additional 1 to any armour saving throw made against that attack.

ABILITIES

Angels of Death, Concealed Positions (pg 124-125)

Rites of Battle (Aura): While a friendly <CHAPTER> CORE unit is within 6" of this model, each time a model in that unit makes an attack, re-roll a hit roll of 1.

Iron Halo: This model has a 4+ invulnerable save.

Omni-scrambler: Enemy units that are set up on the battlefield as reinforcements cannot be set up within 12" of this model.

FACTION KEYWORDS: **IMPERIUM, ADEPTUS ASTARTES, <CHAPTER>**
KEYWORDS: **INFANTRY, CHARACTER, PRIMARIS, PHOBOS, CAPTAIN**

All Primaris Space Marines are trained in reconnaissance, stealth and sabotage while in the 10th Company. Donning his Phobos armour, a Captain will combine these skills with his incredible martial prowess and hard-won strategic expertise to lead strike forces of Vanguard warriors on dangerous covert missions.

CAPTAIN IN GRAVIS ARMOUR

6 POWER

No.	Name	M	WS	BS	S	T	W	A	Ld	Sv
1	Captain in Gravis Armour	5"	2+	2+	4	5	7	5	9	3+

A Captain in Gravis Armour is equipped with: boltstorm gauntlet; master-crafted power sword.

WEAPON	RANGE	TYPE	S	AP	D	ABILITIES
Boltstorm gauntlet (shooting)	12"	Pistol 3	4	-1	1	-
Boltstorm gauntlet (melee)	Melee	Melee	x2	-3	2	Each time an attack is made with this weapon, subtract 1 from that attack's hit roll.
Master-crafted power sword	Melee	Melee	+1	-3	2	-

ABILITIES

Angels of Death (pg 124-125)

Rites of Battle (Aura): While a friendly <Chapter> Core unit is within 6" of this model, each time a model in that unit makes an attack, re-roll a hit roll of 1.

Iron Halo: This model has a 4+ invulnerable save.

FACTION KEYWORDS: Imperium, Adeptus Astartes, <Chapter>
KEYWORDS: Infantry, Character, Primaris, Mk X Gravis, Captain

Clad in a suit of indomitable Gravis armour, a Space Marine Captain can fearlessly stride into the very fiercest battlefield firestorms. To don Gravis armour is to demonstrate the greatest determination to crush the enemy, no matter how deeply they are entrenched.

CAPTAIN IN TERMINATOR ARMOUR

6 POWER

No.	Name	M	WS	BS	S	T	W	A	Ld	Sv
1	Captain in Terminator Armour	5"	2+	2+	4	4	6	4	9	2+

A Captain in Terminator Armour is equipped with: storm bolter; power sword.

WEAPON	RANGE	TYPE	S	AP	D	ABILITIES
Storm bolter	24"	Rapid Fire 2	4	0	1	-
Wrist-mounted grenade launcher	12"	Assault D3	4	-1	1	Blast
Power sword	Melee	Melee	+1	-3	1	-
Relic blade	Melee	Melee	+3	-3	2	-

OTHER WARGEAR	ABILITIES
Storm shield	The bearer has a 4+ invulnerable save. In addition, add 1 to armour saving throws made for the bearer.

WARGEAR OPTIONS

- This model's storm bolter can be replaced with one of the following: 1 combi-bolter; 1 lightning claw; 1 power fist; 1 thunder hammer; 1 storm shield (maximum 1 per model); 1 weapon from the *Combi-weapons* list.
- This model's power sword can be replaced with one of the following: 1 chainfist; 1 lightning claw; 1 power axe; 1 power fist; 1 power maul; 1 relic blade; 1 thunder hammer; 1 storm shield (maximum 1 per model).
- If this model is equipped with 1 or more power fists, it can be equipped with 1 wrist-mounted grenade launcher.

ABILITIES

Angels of Death, Teleport Strike (pg 124-125)

Deathwing: If this unit is from the Dark Angels Chapter (or one of its successor Chapters), it has the **Deathwing** keyword.

Iron Halo: This model has a 4+ invulnerable save.

Rites of Battle (Aura): While a friendly <Chapter> Core unit is within 6" of this model, each time a model in that unit makes an attack, re-roll a hit roll of 1.

FACTION KEYWORDS: Imperium, Adeptus Astartes, <Chapter>
KEYWORDS: Infantry, Character, Terminator, Captain

Space Marine Captains are expected to fight from the front, and few kinds of armour enable them to do so as effectively as Terminator plate. Formidably resilient, such a suit protects the Captain against all but the most devastating enemy fire and enables him to deploy by teleport strike right into the heart of the foe.

CAPTAIN

5 POWER

No.	Name	M	WS	BS	S	T	W	A	Ld	Sv
1	Captain	6"	2+	2+	4	4	5	4	9	3+

A Captain is equipped with: bolt pistol; master-crafted boltgun; Astartes chainsword; frag grenades; krak grenades.

WEAPON	RANGE	TYPE	S	AP	D	ABILITIES
Bolt pistol	12"	Pistol 1	4	0	1	-
Master-crafted boltgun	24"	Rapid Fire 1	4	-1	2	-
Astartes chainsword	Melee	Melee	User	-1	1	Each time the bearer fights, it makes 1 additional attack with this weapon.
Relic blade	Melee	Melee	+3	-3	2	-
Xenophase blade	Melee	Melee	+1	-4	1	Each time an attack is made with this weapon, invulnerable saving throws cannot be made against that attack.

OTHER WARGEAR	ABILITIES
Jump pack	The bearer has a Move characteristic of 12", the Death From Above ability and the **FLY** and **JUMP PACK** keywords.
Storm shield	The bearer has a 4+ invulnerable save. In addition, add 1 to armour saving throws made for the bearer.

WARGEAR OPTIONS

- This model's master-crafted boltgun can be replaced with one of the following: 1 storm shield (maximum 1 per model); 1 weapon from the *Combi-weapons* list; 1 weapon from the *Pistols* list; 1 weapon from the *Melee Weapons* list.
- This model's Astartes chainsword can be replaced with one of the following: 1 relic blade; 1 weapon from the *Melee Weapons* list; 1 storm shield (maximum 1 per model).
- If this model is from the Deathwatch Chapter, its Astartes chainsword can be replaced with 1 xenophase blade.
- This model can be equipped with 1 jump pack **(Power Rating +1)**.

ABILITIES

Angels of Death (pg 124-125)

Iron Halo: This model has a 4+ invulnerable save.

Rites of Battle (Aura): While a friendly <CHAPTER> CORE unit is within 6" of this model, each time a model in that unit makes an attack, re-roll a hit roll of 1.

FACTION KEYWORDS: IMPERIUM, ADEPTUS ASTARTES, <CHAPTER>
KEYWORDS: INFANTRY, CHARACTER, CAPTAIN

Space Marine Captains have spent centuries with their Chapter. They expect nothing but utter dedication from those they command. Each Space Marine lives up to this standard willingly, knowing there is no sacrifice their Captains haven't made, no enemy they have not slain and no hardship they have not endured.

CAPTAIN ON BIKE

6 POWER

No.	Name	M	WS	BS	S	T	W	A	Ld	Sv
1	Captain on Bike	14"	2+	2+	4	5	6	4	9	3+

A Captain on Bike is equipped with: bolt pistol; twin boltgun; Astartes chainsword; frag grenades; krak grenades.

WEAPON	RANGE	TYPE	S	AP	D	ABILITIES
Bolt pistol	12"	Pistol 1	4	0	1	-
Master-crafted boltgun	24"	Rapid Fire 1	4	-1	2	-
Twin boltgun	24"	Rapid Fire 2	4	0	1	-
Astartes chainsword	Melee	Melee	User	-1	1	Each time the bearer fights, it makes 1 additional attack with this weapon.

OTHER WARGEAR	ABILITIES
Storm shield	The bearer has a 4+ invulnerable save. In addition, add 1 to armour saving throws made for the bearer.

WARGEAR OPTIONS

- This model's bolt pistol can be replaced with one of the following: 1 master-crafted boltgun; 1 weapon from the *Combi-weapons* list; 1 weapon from the *Pistols* list; 1 weapon from the *Melee Weapons* list.
- This model's Astartes chainsword can be replaced with one of the following: 1 weapon from the *Melee Weapons* list; 1 storm shield.

ABILITIES

Angels of Death (pg 124-125)

Rites of Battle (Aura): While a friendly <Chapter> Core unit is within 6" of this model, each time a model in that unit makes an attack, re-roll a hit roll of 1.

Iron Halo: This model has a 4+ invulnerable save.

Ravenwing: If this unit is from the Dark Angels Chapter (or one of its successor Chapters), it has the **Ravenwing** keyword.

Turbo-boost: Each time this model Advances, do not make an Advance roll. Instead, until the end of the phase, add 6" to the Move characteristic of this model.

FACTION KEYWORDS: Imperium, Adeptus Astartes, <Chapter>
KEYWORDS: Biker, Character, Captain

When a Captain thunders to war on a Space Marine bike, he can race to the most critical locations on the battlefield. He smashes foes aside, cuts down countless fleeing enemies, or joins his Outriders to carry out reconnaissance missions in person so as to best develop his battle plans with first-hand knowledge.

War after war. Journey after journey. The Space Marines are relentless. They itch for battle, itch to draw their blades. They seek no rest, and barely recognise that those who serve them, yet who are not of them, cannot possibly keep pace.

Again and again the Fists order me to plunge my mind into the madness. Demand I linger in its churning morass for longer and longer. What do you see, they demand. What do you hear? They seek everything. News of battles, news of their comrades. Calls for aid, clues to enemy presences. I give it all to them. The starkest, most terrifying images, the most indecipherable and incoherent visions. And it is never enough. Dorn's sons ask more of me, just as they ask more of themselves with each passing time unit. They are never satisfied. The strain of my efforts draws blood on each occasion I conduct my work. I am left shaking, perspiring, drained, exhausted. My Telepathica colleagues fair no better. Were it not for the fact that Humanity's cause is so great, some of us may have yet given up. Only by force of will are some of us alive.

But the Space Marines should not be satisfied. Their task is great. The Imperium reels in every quarter. If Mankind is to survive they must tolerate no complacency, in themselves or in others. They must always fight harder. They must not stop. For all our sakes.

- Helicta Chemin, Astropath

PRIMARIS LIEUTENANT

4 POWER

No.	Name	M	WS	BS	S	T	W	A	Ld	Sv
1	Primaris Lieutenant	6"	2+	2+	4	4	5	4	8	3+

A Primaris Lieutenant is equipped with: bolt pistol; master-crafted auto bolt rifle; frag grenades; krak grenades.

WEAPON	RANGE	TYPE	S	AP	D	ABILITIES
Bolt pistol	12"	Pistol 1	4	0	1	-
Master-crafted auto bolt rifle	24"	Assault 3	4	0	2	-
Master-crafted stalker bolt rifle	36"	Heavy 1	4	-2	3	-
Neo-volkite pistol	15"	Pistol 2	5	0	2	Each time an attack is made with this weapon, an unmodified wound roll of 6 inflicts 1 mortal wound on the target in addition to any normal damage.
Special issue bolt carbine	24"	Assault 2	4	-2	2	-
Master-crafted power axe	Melee	Melee	+2	-2	2	-

OTHER WARGEAR	ABILITIES
Storm shield	The bearer has a 4+ invulnerable save. In addition, add 1 to armour saving throws made for the bearer.

WARGEAR OPTIONS

- This model's bolt pistol and master-crafted auto bolt rifle can be replaced with one of the following:
  - 1 bolt pistol and 1 master-crafted stalker bolt rifle.
  - 1 bolt pistol and 1 master-crafted power sword.
  - 1 neo-volkite pistol, 1 master-crafted power sword and 1 storm shield **(Power Rating +1)**.
- If this model is from the Dark Angels Chapter (or one of its successor Chapters), its bolt pistol can be replaced with 1 plasma pistol.
- If this model is from the Space Wolves Chapter (or one of its successor Chapters), its master-crafted auto bolt rifle can be replaced with 1 special issue bolt carbine and 1 master-crafted power axe.

ABILITIES

Angels of Death (pg 124-125)

Company Heroes: If your army is Battle-forged, then for each **LIEUTENANT** unit included in a Detachment, a second **LIEUTENANT** unit can be included in that Detachment without taking up an additional Battlefield Role slot.

Tactical Precision (Aura): While a friendly **<CHAPTER>** **CORE** unit is within 6" of this model, each time a model in that unit makes an attack, re-roll a wound roll of 1.

Wolf Guard: If this unit is from the Space Wolves Chapter (or one of its successor Chapters), it has the **WOLF GUARD** keyword.

FACTION KEYWORDS: IMPERIUM, ADEPTUS ASTARTES, <CHAPTER>
KEYWORDS: INFANTRY, CHARACTER, PRIMARIS, LIEUTENANT

Primaris Lieutenants, in addition to being extremely able tacticians and strategists, are highly skilled warriors. Experts in all the lethal firearms of the Intercessors they so often command and fight alongside, they lay down impressive volleys of bolts even as they bellow orders and coordinate their brothers' fire.

Ultramarines Primaris Lieutenant with master-crafted auto bolt rifle and bolt pistol

Space Wolves Primaris Lieutenant with special issue bolt carbine and master-crafted power axe

Dark Angels Primaris Lieutenant with plasma pistol and master-crafted power sword

LIEUTENANT IN REIVER ARMOUR

4 POWER

No.	Name	M	WS	BS	S	T	W	A	Ld	Sv
1	Lieutenant in Reiver Armour	6"	2+	2+	4	4	5	4	8	3+

A Lieutenant in Reiver Armour is equipped with: master-crafted special issue bolt pistol; combat knife; frag grenades; krak grenades.

WEAPON	RANGE	TYPE	S	AP	D	ABILITIES
Master-crafted special issue bolt pistol	12"	Pistol 1	4	-2	2	-
Combat knife	Melee	Melee	User	0	1	Each time the bearer fights, it makes 1 additional attack with this weapon.

ABILITIES

Angels of Death (pg 124-125)

Tactical Precision (Aura): While a friendly <CHAPTER> CORE unit is within 6"of this model, each time a model in that unit makes an attack, re-roll a wound roll of 1.

Terror Troops (Aura): While an enemy unit is within 3" of this model, subtract 2 from the Leadership characteristic of models in that unit.

Company Heroes: If your army is Battle-forged, then for each LIEUTENANT unit included in a Detachment, a second LIEUTENANT unit can be included in that Detachment without taking up an additional Battlefield Role slot.

Wolf Guard: If this unit is from the Space Wolves Chapter (or one of its successor Chapters), it has the WOLF GUARD keyword.

FACTION KEYWORDS: IMPERIUM, ADEPTUS ASTARTES, <CHAPTER>
KEYWORDS: INFANTRY, CHARACTER, PRIMARIS, PHOBOS, REIVER, SHOCK GRENADE, SMOKESCREEN, LIEUTENANT

When a Space Marine commander needs the enemy broken in terror, he unleashes detachments led by Lieutenants clad in the wargear of the Reiver Squads. With the masterful leadership of the Lieutenant, these forces become more powerful than the sum of their parts, and drive contingents of the foe to flight.

LIEUTENANT

4 POWER

No.	Name	M	WS	BS	S	T	W	A	Ld	Sv
1	Lieutenant	6"	2+	2+	4	4	4	3	8	3+

A Lieutenant is equipped with: bolt pistol; master-crafted boltgun; Astartes chainsword; frag grenades; krak grenades.

WEAPON	RANGE	TYPE	S	AP	D	ABILITIES
Bolt pistol	12"	Pistol 1	4	0	1	-
Master-crafted boltgun	24"	Rapid Fire 1	4	-1	2	-
Astartes chainsword	Melee	Melee	User	-1	1	Each time the bearer fights, it makes 1 additional attack with this weapon.

OTHER WARGEAR	ABILITIES
Jump pack	The bearer has a Move characteristic of 12", the Death From Above ability (pg 125) and the FLY and JUMP PACK keywords.

WARGEAR OPTIONS

- This model's master-crafted boltgun can be replaced with one of the following: 1 weapon from the *Combi-weapons* list; 1 weapon from the *Pistols* list; 1 weapon from the *Melee* Weapons list.
- This model's Astartes chainsword can be replaced with 1 weapon from the *Melee* Weapons list.
- This model can be equipped with 1 jump pack **(Power Rating +1)**.

ABILITIES

Angels of Death (pg 124-125)

Company Heroes: If your army is Battle-forged, then for each LIEUTENANT unit included in a Detachment, a second LIEUTENANT unit can be included in that Detachment without taking up an additional Battlefield Role slot.

Tactical Precision (Aura): While a friendly <CHAPTER> CORE unit is within 6" of this model, each time a model in that unit makes an attack, re-roll a wound roll of 1.

Wolf Guard: If this unit is from the Space Wolves Chapter (or one of its successor Chapters), it has the WOLF GUARD keyword.

FACTION KEYWORDS: IMPERIUM, ADEPTUS ASTARTES, <CHAPTER>
KEYWORDS: INFANTRY, CHARACTER, LIEUTENANT

Lieutenants constitute a supporting layer of leadership and strategic implementation within Space Marine strike forces. In addition to their own formidable combat prowess, they act as a force multiplier, their tactical capabilities allowing their warriors to adapt far more fluidly to changing situations.

LIEUTENANT IN PHOBOS ARMOUR

4 POWER

No.	Name	M	WS	BS	S	T	W	A	Ld	Sv
1	Lieutenant in Phobos Armour	6"	2+	2+	4	4	5	4	8	3+

A Lieutenant in Phobos Armour is equipped with: bolt pistol; master-crafted occulus bolt carbine; paired combat blades; frag grenades; krak grenades.

WEAPON	RANGE	TYPE	S	AP	D	ABILITIES
Bolt pistol	12"	Pistol 1	4	0	1	-
Master-crafted occulus bolt carbine	24"	Rapid Fire 1	4	0	2	Each time an attack is made with this weapon, the target does not receive the benefits of cover against that attack.
Paired combat blades	Melee	Melee	User	-1	1	-

ABILITIES

Angels of Death, Death From Above (pg 124-125)

Tactical Precision (Aura): While a friendly <Chapter> Core unit is within 6" of this model, each time a model in that unit makes an attack, re-roll a wound roll of 1.

Company Heroes: If your army is Battle-forged, then for each Lieutenant unit included in a Detachment, a second Lieutenant unit can be included in that Detachment without taking up an additional Battlefield Role slot.

Wolf Guard: If this unit is from the Space Wolves Chapter (or one of its successor Chapters), it has the Wolf Guard keyword.

FACTION KEYWORDS: Imperium, Adeptus Astartes, <Chapter>
KEYWORDS: Infantry, Character, Primaris, Phobos, Lieutenant

Highly capable combat commanders, Lieutenants can lead independent reconnaissance, sabotage and assassination forces far beyond Imperial lines. They are deadly warriors, and the last sensation of countless foes has been the cold press of a Space Marine Lieutenant's knife to their neck.

PRIMARIS LIBRARIAN

5 POWER

No.	Name	M	WS	BS	S	T	W	A	Ld	Sv
1	Primaris Librarian	6"	3+	3+	4	4	5	4	9	3+

A Primaris Librarian is equipped with: bolt pistol; force sword; frag grenades; krak grenades.

WEAPON	RANGE	TYPE	S	AP	D	ABILITIES
Bolt pistol	12"	Pistol 1	4	0	1	-
Force sword	Melee	Melee	+1	-3	D3	-

ABILITIES

Angels of Death (pg 124-125)

Psychic Hood: Each time a Deny the Witch test is taken for this model, if the unit attempting to manifest the psychic power is within 12" of this model, add 1 to that Deny the Witch test.

Deathwing: If this unit is from the Dark Angels Chapter (or one of its successor Chapters), it has the Deathwing keyword.

PSYKER

This model can attempt to manifest two psychic powers in your Psychic phase and attempt to deny one psychic power in your opponent's Psychic phase. It knows *Smite* and two psychic powers from the Librarius discipline (pg 110).

FACTION KEYWORDS: Imperium, Adeptus Astartes, <Chapter>
KEYWORDS: Infantry, Character, Primaris, Psyker, Librarian

The physical improvements granted by Primaris implants greatly benefits Librarians. Immense strength and endurance enables them to sustain their furious psychic powers for longer, and in battle their entire bodies crackle with mind-melting energies that they launch at their foes.

Librarians are the Space Marines' battle-psykers and keepers of lore. Wielding terrifying empyric energies, with but a thought they can crush a foe's skull, throw up force shields to protect their brethren from incoming fire, and hurl blasts of psychic power.

LIBRARIAN

5 POWER

No.	Name	M	WS	BS	S	T	W	A	Ld	Sv
1	Librarian	6"	3+	3+	4	4	4	3	9	3+

A Librarian is equipped with: bolt pistol; force stave; frag grenades; krak grenades.

WEAPON	RANGE	TYPE	S	AP	D	ABILITIES
Bolt pistol	12"	Pistol 1	4	0	1	-
Force axe	Melee	Melee	+2	-2	D3	-
Force stave	Melee	Melee	+3	-1	D3	-
Force sword	Melee	Melee	+1	-3	D3	-

OTHER WARGEAR	ABILITIES
Jump pack	The bearer has a Move characteristic of 12", the Death From Above ability (pg 125) and the **FLY** and **JUMP PACK** keywords.

WARGEAR OPTIONS

- This model's bolt pistol can be replaced with one of the following: 1 boltgun; 1 weapon from the *Combi-weapons* list; 1 weapon from the *Pistols* list.
- This model's force stave can be replaced with one of the following: 1 force axe; 1 force sword.
- This model can be equipped with 1 jump pack (**Power Rating +1**).

ABILITIES

Angels of Death (pg 124-125)

Deathwing: If this unit is from the Dark Angels Chapter (or one of its successor Chapters), it has the **DEATHWING** keyword.

Psychic Hood: Each time a Deny the Witch test is taken for this model, if the unit attempting to manifest the psychic power is within 12" of this model, add 1 to that Deny the Witch test.

PSYKER

This model can attempt to manifest two psychic powers in your Psychic phase and attempt to deny one psychic power in your opponent's Psychic phase. It knows *Smite* and two psychic powers from the Librarius discipline (pg 110).

FACTION KEYWORDS: IMPERIUM, ADEPTUS ASTARTES, <CHAPTER>
KEYWORDS: INFANTRY, CHARACTER, PSYKER, LIBRARIAN

LIBRARIAN IN PHOBOS ARMOUR

5 POWER

No.	Name	M	WS	BS	S	T	W	A	Ld	Sv
1	Librarian in Phobos Armour	6"	3+	3+	4	4	5	4	9	3+

A Librarian in Phobos Armour is equipped with: bolt pistol; force sword; frag grenades; krak grenades, camo cloak.

WEAPON	RANGE	TYPE	S	AP	D	ABILITIES
Bolt pistol	12"	Pistol 1	4	0	1	-
Force sword	Melee	Melee	+1	-3	D3	-

OTHER WARGEAR	ABILITIES
Camo cloak	Each time a ranged attack is allocated to the bearer while it is receiving the benefits of cover, add an additional 1 to any armour saving throw made against that attack.

ABILITIES

Angels of Death, Concealed Positions (pg 124-125)

Psychic Hood: Each time a Deny the Witch test is taken for this model, if the unit attempting to manifest the psychic power is within 12" of this model, add 1 to that Deny the Witch test.

Deathwing: If this unit is from the Dark Angels Chapter (or one of its successor Chapters), it has the DEATHWING keyword.

PSYKER

This model can attempt to manifest two psychic powers in your Psychic phase and attempt to deny one psychic power in your opponent's Psychic phase. It knows *Smite* and two psychic powers from the Obscuration discipline (pg 111).

FACTION KEYWORDS: IMPERIUM, ADEPTUS ASTARTES, <CHAPTER>
KEYWORDS: INFANTRY, CHARACTER, PRIMARIS, PHOBOS, PSYKER, LIBRARIAN

Many Librarians learn the arcane arts of obscuration and illusion as part of their long and dangerous training. Donning Phobos armour, they take to the field and use these skills to fog the minds of their enemies, prise vital battle plans from their foes' minds, and turn the enemy's shadows against them.

LIBRARIAN IN TERMINATOR ARMOUR

6 POWER

No.	Name	M	WS	BS	S	T	W	A	Ld	Sv
1	Librarian in Terminator Armour	5"	3+	3+	4	4	5	3	9	2+

A Librarian in Terminator Armour is equipped with: force stave.

WEAPON	RANGE	TYPE	S	AP	D	ABILITIES
Force axe	Melee	Melee	+2	-2	D3	-
Force stave	Melee	Melee	+3	-1	D3	-
Force sword	Melee	Melee	+1	-3	D3	-

WARGEAR OPTIONS

- This model can be equipped with 1 weapon from the *Combi-weapons* list.
- This model's force stave can be replaced with one of the following: 1 force axe; 1 force sword.

ABILITIES

Angels of Death, Teleport Strike (pg 124-125)

Deathwing: If this unit is from the Dark Angels Chapter (or one of its successor Chapters), it has the DEATHWING keyword.

Crux Terminatus: This model has a 5+ invulnerable save.

Psychic Hood: Each time a Deny the Witch test is taken for this model, if the unit attempting to manifest the psychic power is within 12" of this model, add 1 to that Deny the Witch test.

PSYKER

This model can attempt to manifest two psychic powers in your Psychic phase and attempt to deny one psychic power in your opponent's Psychic phase. It knows *Smite* and two psychic powers from the Librarius discipline (pg 110).

FACTION KEYWORDS: IMPERIUM, ADEPTUS ASTARTES, <CHAPTER>
KEYWORDS: INFANTRY, CHARACTER, TERMINATOR, PSYKER, LIBRARIAN

The powers of a Chapter's Librarians lend a lethal psychic edge to its elite infantry spearheads. Whether it be gruelling boarding actions, ferocious urban combat or on the front line against overwhelming enemy numbers, Librarians in Terminator armour blast at the foe with their powerful psychic energies.

PRIMARIS CHAPLAIN

5 POWER

No.	Name	M	WS	BS	S	T	W	A	Ld	Sv
1	Primaris Chaplain	6"	2+	3+	4	4	5	4	9	3+

A Primaris Chaplain is equipped with: absolvor bolt pistol; crozius arcanum; frag grenades; krak grenades.

WEAPON	RANGE	TYPE	S	AP	D	ABILITIES
Absolvor bolt pistol	18"	Pistol 1	5	-1	2	-
Crozius arcanum	Melee	Melee	+2	-1	2	-

ABILITIES

Angels of Death (pg 124-125)

Spiritual Leaders (Aura): While a friendly <CHAPTER> CORE unit is within 6" of this model, models in that unit can use this model's Leadership characteristic instead of their own.

Rosarius: This model has a 4+ invulnerable save.

Wolf Priest: If this unit is from the Space Wolves Chapter (or one of its successor Chapters), it has the WOLF PRIEST keyword.

PRIEST

This model knows the *Litany of Hate* and one other litany from the Litanies of Battle (pg 112). In your Command phase, if this model is on the battlefield, it can recite one litany it knows that has not already been recited by a friendly model this turn. Roll one D6: on a 3+, the recited litany is inspiring and takes effect until the start of your next Command phase.

FACTION KEYWORDS: IMPERIUM, ADEPTUS ASTARTES, <CHAPTER>
KEYWORDS: INFANTRY, CHARACTER, PRIMARIS, PRIEST, CHAPLAIN

Cloak billowing in the heat of battle and absolvor pistol flaring, Primaris Chaplains stride purposefully into battle, the boom of their oration audible even over the furious din of conflict. Without rest they exhort their brothers to victory, steeling their hearts, minds and souls no matter the savagery of the enemy.

PRIMARIS CHAPLAIN ON BIKE

6 POWER

No.	Name	M	WS	BS	S	T	W	A	Ld	Sv
1	Primaris Chaplain on Bike	14"	2+	3+	4	5	7	4	9	3+

A Primaris Chaplain on Bike is equipped with: absolvor bolt pistol; twin bolt rifle, crozius arcanum; frag grenades; krak grenades.

WEAPON	RANGE	TYPE	S	AP	D	ABILITIES
Absolvor bolt pistol	18"	Pistol 1	5	-1	2	-
Twin bolt rifle	30"	Rapid Fire 2	4	-1	1	-
Crozius arcanum	Melee	Melee	+2	-1	2	-

ABILITIES

Angels of Death (pg 124-125)

Rosarius: This model has a 4+ invulnerable save.

Spiritual Leaders (Aura): While a friendly <CHAPTER> CORE unit is within 6" of this model, models in that unit can use this model's Leadership characteristic instead of their own.

Turbo-boost: Each time this model Advances, do not make an Advance roll. Instead, until the end of the phase, add 6" to the Move characteristic of this model.

Wolf Priest: If this unit is from the Space Wolves Chapter (or one of its successor Chapters), it has the WOLF PRIEST keyword.

Ravenwing: If this unit is from the Dark Angels Chapter (or one of its successor Chapters), it has the RAVENWING keyword.

PRIEST

This model knows the *Litany of Hate* and one other litany from the Litanies of Battle (pg 112). In your Command phase, if this model is on the battlefield, it can recite one litany it knows that has not already been recited by a friendly model this turn. Roll one D6: on a 3+, the recited litany is inspiring and takes effect until the start of your next Command phase.

FACTION KEYWORDS: IMPERIUM, ADEPTUS ASTARTES, <CHAPTER>
KEYWORDS: BIKER, CHARACTER, PRIMARIS, PRIEST, CHAPLAIN

When a Chaplain takes to the field on a Raider-pattern bike, he is able to keep pace with even the swiftest armoured advance or spearhead breakthrough. Fighting in such an action, he will urge his brothers to victory as he bellows his catechisms and charges headlong into the foe, crozius arcanum swinging.

CHAPLAIN IN TERMINATOR ARMOUR

6 POWER

No.	Name	M	WS	BS	S	T	W	A	Ld	Sv
1	Chaplain in Terminator Armour	5"	2+	3+	4	4	5	3	9	2+

A Chaplain in Terminator Armour is equipped with: storm bolter; crozius arcanum.

WEAPON	RANGE	TYPE	S	AP	D	ABILITIES
Storm bolter	24"	Rapid Fire 2	4	0	1	-
Crozius arcanum	Melee	Melee	+2	-1	2	-

WARGEAR OPTIONS

- This model's storm bolter can be replaced with 1 weapon from the *Combi-weapons* list.

ABILITIES

Angels of Death, Teleport Strike (pg 124-125)

Rosarius: This model has a 4+ invulnerable save.

Spiritual Leaders (Aura): While a friendly **<CHAPTER> CORE** unit is within 6" of this model, models in that unit can use this model's Leadership characteristic instead of their own.

Deathwing: If this unit is from the Dark Angels Chapter (or one of its successor Chapters), it has the **DEATHWING** keyword.

Wolf Priest: If this unit is from the Space Wolves Chapter (or one of its successor Chapters), it has the **WOLF PRIEST** keyword.

PRIEST

This model knows the *Litany of Hate* and one other litany from the Litanies of Battle (pg 112). In your Command phase, if this model is on the battlefield, it can recite one litany it knows that has not already been recited by a friendly model this turn. Roll one D6: on a 3+, the recited litany is inspiring and takes effect until the start of your next Command phase.

FACTION KEYWORDS: IMPERIUM, ADEPTUS ASTARTES, <CHAPTER>
KEYWORDS: INFANTRY, CHARACTER, PRIEST, TERMINATOR, CHAPLAIN

Every Space Marine is roused to war by the litanies of their Chaplains, and never is this spiritual fortification more vital than amidst the blood and horror of boarding actions and beachhead strikes. Thus, Chaplains are trained to wear formidable Terminator armour so they can fight alongside Veteran battle-brothers.

CHAPLAIN

5 POWER

No.	Name	M	WS	BS	S	T	W	A	Ld	Sv
1	Chaplain	6"	2+	3+	4	4	4	3	9	3+

A Chaplain is equipped with: bolt pistol; crozius arcanum; frag grenades; krak grenades.

WEAPON	RANGE	TYPE	S	AP	D	ABILITIES
Bolt pistol	12"	Pistol 1	4	0	1	-
Crozius arcanum	Melee	Melee	+2	-1	2	-

OTHER WARGEAR	ABILITIES
Jump pack	The bearer has a Move characteristic of 12", the Death From Above ability (pg 125) and the **FLY** and **JUMP PACK** keywords.

WARGEAR OPTIONS

- This model's bolt pistol can be replaced with one of the following: 1 boltgun; 1 weapon from the *Combi-weapons* list; 1 weapon from the *Pistols* list; 1 power fist.
- This model can be equipped with 1 jump pack **(Power Rating +1)**.

ABILITIES

Angels of Death (pg 124-125)

Spiritual Leaders (Aura): While a friendly **<CHAPTER> CORE** unit is within 6" of this model, models in that unit can use this model's Leadership characteristic instead of their own.

Rosarius: This model has a 4+ invulnerable save.

Wolf Priest: If this unit is from the Space Wolves Chapter (or one of its successor Chapters), it has the **WOLF PRIEST** keyword.

PRIEST

This model knows the *Litany of Hate* and one other litany from the Litanies of Battle (pg 112). In your Command phase, if this model is on the battlefield, it can recite one litany it knows that has not already been recited by a friendly model this turn. Roll one D6: on a 3+, the recited litany is inspiring and takes effect until the start of your next Command phase.

FACTION KEYWORDS: IMPERIUM, ADEPTUS ASTARTES, <CHAPTER>
KEYWORDS: INFANTRY, CHARACTER, PRIEST, CHAPLAIN

Chaplains are the guardians of their Chapter's spirit and protectors of its warriors' souls. They uphold the traditions of their brotherhood and keep its relics safe, while on the battlefield they bellow litanies of hatred and faith, their fiery sermons giving grim inspiration to the warriors they accompany.

PRIMARIS TECHMARINE

4 POWER

No.	Name	M	WS	BS	S	T	W	A	Ld	Sv
1	Primaris Techmarine	6"	3+	2+	4	4	5	4	8	2+

A Primaris Techmarine is equipped with: forge bolter; grav-pistol; Omnissian power axe; servo-arm; mechadendrite; frag grenades; krak grenades.

WEAPON	RANGE	TYPE	S	AP	D	ABILITIES
Forge bolter	24"	Assault 3	5	-1	2	Each time the bearer shoots, it can make attacks with this weapon even if it also makes attacks with Pistols or Grenades.
Grav-pistol	12"	Pistol 1	5	-3	1	Each time an attack made with this weapon is allocated to a model with a Save characteristic of 3+ or better, that attack has a Damage characteristic of 2.
Mechadendrite	Melee	Melee	+1	0	1	Each time the bearer fights, it makes 2 additional attacks with this weapon.
Omnissian power axe	Melee	Melee	+2	-2	2	-
Servo-arm	Melee	Melee	x2	-2	3	Each time the bearer fights, no more than one attack can be made with each servo-arm.

ABILITIES

Angels of Death (pg 124-125)

Blessing of the Omnissiah: At the end of your Movement phase, this model can repair one friendly <Chapter> Vehicle model within 3" of it. That Vehicle model regains up to D3 lost wounds. Each model can only be repaired once per turn.

Awaken the Machine Spirits: In your Command phase, this model can awaken one friendly <Chapter> Vehicle model within 3" of it. Until the start of your next Command phase, each time that Vehicle model makes a ranged attack, add 1 to that attack's hit roll. Each model can only be awakened once per turn.

FACTION KEYWORDS: Imperium, Adeptus Astartes, <Chapter>
KEYWORDS: Infantry, Character, Primaris, Techmarine

Primaris Techmarines stride selflessly through oncoming fire to soothe the machine spirits of wounded war engines, deftly peeling back damaged armour plates to repair burnt-out cabling and bending warped panels back into shape with his servo-arm and mechadendrite.

SERVITORS

2 POWER

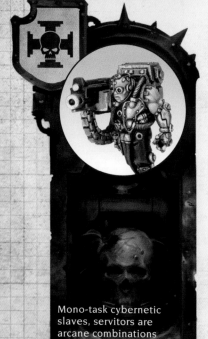

No.	Name	M	WS	BS	S	T	W	A	Ld	Sv
4	Servitor	5"	5+	5+	3	3	1	1	6	4+

Every model is equipped with: servo-arm.

WEAPON	RANGE	TYPE	S	AP	D	ABILITIES
Heavy bolter	36"	Heavy 3	5	-1	2	-
Multi-melta	24"	Heavy 2	8	-4	D6	Each time an attack made with this weapon targets a unit within half range, that attack has a Damage characteristic of D6+2.
Plasma cannon		Before selecting targets, select one of the profiles below to make attacks with.				
- Standard	36"	Heavy D3	7	-3	1	Blast
- Supercharge	36"	Heavy D3	8	-3	2	Blast. If any unmodified hit rolls of 1 are made for attacks with this weapon profile, the bearer is destroyed after shooting with this weapon.
Servo-arm	Melee	Melee	x2	-2	3	Each time the bearer fights, no more than one attack can be made with each servo-arm.

WARGEAR OPTIONS

- Up to 2 Servitors can each have their servo-arm replaced with one of the following: 1 heavy bolter; 1 multi-melta; 1 plasma cannon.

ABILITIES

Mindlock: While this unit is within 6" of any friendly <Chapter> Techmarine units, models in this unit have a Weapon Skill and Ballistic Skill characteristic of 4+ and a Leadership characteristic of 9. In addition, if your army is Battle-forged, then for each <Chapter> Techmarine unit included in a Detachment, one <Chapter> Servitors unit can be included in that Detachment without taking up a Battlefield Role slot.

FACTION KEYWORDS: Imperium, Adeptus Astartes, <Chapter>
KEYWORDS: Infantry, Servitors

Mono-task cybernetic slaves, servitors are arcane combinations of lobotomised Human and machine. Fitted with an array of mechanical augmentations, in battle servitors assist Techmarines, either by laying down torrents of covering fire or by carrying out additional repair work with their servo-arms.

TECHMARINE

No.	Name	M	WS	BS	S	T	W	A	Ld	Sv
1	Techmarine	6"	3+	2+	4	4	4	3	8	2+

A Techmarine is equipped with: bolt pistol; Omnissian power axe; servo-arm; frag grenades; krak grenades.

WEAPON	RANGE	TYPE	S	AP	D	ABILITIES
Bolt pistol	12"	Pistol 1	4	0	1	-
Helfrost pistol	Before selecting targets, select one of the profiles below to make attacks with.					
- Dispersed	12"	Pistol D3	4	-2	1	Blast
- Focussed	12"	Pistol 1	6	-4	3	-
Plasma cutter	Before selecting targets, select one of the profiles below to make attacks with.					
- Standard	12"	Assault 1	7	-3	1	-
- Supercharge	12"	Assault 1	8	-3	2	If any unmodified hit rolls of 1 are made for attacks with this weapon profile, the bearer is destroyed after shooting with this weapon.
Omnissian power axe	Melee	Melee	+2	-2	2	-
Servo-arm	Melee	Melee	x2	-2	3	Each time the bearer fights, no more than one attack can be made with each servo-arm.
Tempest hammer	Melee	Melee	x2	-3	3	Each time an attack is made with this weapon, subtract 1 from that attack's hit roll.

WARGEAR OPTIONS

- This model's bolt pistol can be replaced with one of the following: 1 boltgun; 1 weapon from the *Combi-weapons* list; 1 weapon from the *Pistols* list.
- This model's Omnissian power axe can be replaced with 1 weapon from the *Melee Weapons* list.
- If this model is not equipped with a helfrost pistol, it can be equipped with 1 flamer, 1 plasma cutter, and 1 servo-arm (**Power Rating +1**).
- If this model is from the Space Wolves Chapter (or one of its successor Chapters) and it is not equipped with a plasma cutter, its bolt pistol and Omnissian power axe can be replaced with 1 helfrost pistol and 1 tempest hammer.

ABILITIES

Angels of Death (pg 124-125)

Blessing of the Omnissiah: At the end of your Movement phase, this model can repair one friendly <Chapter> Vehicle model within 3" of it. That VEHICLE model regains up to D3 lost wounds. Each model can only be repaired once per turn.

Awaken the Machine Spirits: In your Command phase, this model can awaken one friendly <Chapter> Vehicle model within 3"of it. Until the start of your next Command phase, each time that VEHICLE model makes a ranged attack, add 1 to that attack's hit roll. Each model can only be awakened once per turn.

FACTION KEYWORDS: **Imperium, Adeptus Astartes, <Chapter>**
KEYWORDS: **Infantry, Character, Techmarine**

Possessing knowledge of the Omnissiah's deeper mysteries, Techmarines are responsible for the maintenance of their Chapter's arsenal of armoured vehicles. Equipped with a servo-arm and plasma cutter, they can repair terrible battlefield damage, ensuring the Chapter's vehicles continue to wage war.

INTERCESSOR SQUAD

5 POWER

No.	Name	M	WS	BS	S	T	W	A	Ld	Sv
4-9	Intercessor	6"	3+	3+	4	4	2	2	7	3+
1	Intercessor Sergeant	6"	3+	3+	4	4	2	3	8	3+

If this unit contains 6 or more models, it has **Power Rating 10**. Every model is equipped with: bolt pistol; bolt rifle; frag grenades; krak grenades.

WEAPON	RANGE	TYPE	S	AP	D	ABILITIES
Auto bolt rifle	24"	Assault 3	4	0	1	-
Astartes grenade launcher	Before selecting targets, select one of the profiles below to make attacks with.					
- Frag grenade	30"	Assault D6	3	0	1	Blast
- Krak grenade	30"	Assault 1	6	-1	D3	-
Bolt pistol	12"	Pistol 1	4	0	1	-
Bolt rifle	30"	Rapid Fire 1	4	-1	1	-
Stalker bolt rifle	36"	Heavy 1	4	-2	2	-

WARGEAR OPTIONS

- All of the models in the unit can have their bolt rifle replaced with 1 auto bolt rifle each.
- All of the models in the unit can have their bolt rifle replaced with 1 stalker bolt rifle each.
- If the Intercessor Sergeant is not equipped with an Astartes chainsword, a power sword, a power fist or a thunder hammer, its bolt rifle, auto bolt rifle or stalker bolt rifle can be replaced with one of the following: 1 hand flamer; 1 plasma pistol; 1 Astartes chainsword; 1 power sword.
- If the Intercessor Sergeant is not equipped with an Astartes chainsword or a power sword, it can be equipped with one of the following: 1 Astartes chainsword; 1 power fist; 1 power sword; 1 thunder hammer.
- For every 5 models in this unit, 1 model equipped with a bolt rifle, auto bolt rifle or stalker bolt rifle can be equipped with 1 Astartes grenade launcher.

ABILITIES

Angels of Death, Combat Squads (pg 124-125)

FACTION KEYWORDS: IMPERIUM, ADEPTUS ASTARTES, <CHAPTER>
KEYWORDS: INFANTRY, CORE, PRIMARIS, INTERCESSORS, INTERCESSOR SQUAD

Intercessor Squads are capable of laying down punishing fire while advancing or holding ground against the enemy. They have access to a range of bolt weaponry suited to varied battlefield assignments, from engaging enemies at long range to cleansing bunker complexes.

Stalker bolt rifle

Auto bolt rifle

Astartes grenade launcher

Bolt rifle

Deathwatch Intercessor with bolt rifle

Crimson Fists Intercessor with auto bolt rifle

Imperial Fists Intercessor Sergeant with bolt pistol and power fist

Raven Guard Intercessor Sergeant with stalker bolt rifle

ASSAULT INTERCESSOR SQUAD

5 POWER

No.	Name	M	WS	BS	S	T	W	A	Ld	Sv
4-9	Assault Intercessor	6"	3+	3+	4	4	2	2	7	3+
1	Assault Intercessor Sergeant	6"	3+	3+	4	4	2	3	8	3+

If this unit contains 6 or more models, it has **Power Rating 10**. Every model is equipped with: heavy bolt pistol; Astartes chainsword; frag grenades; krak grenades.

WEAPON	RANGE	TYPE	S	AP	D	ABILITIES
Heavy bolt pistol	18"	Pistol 1	4	-1	1	-
Astartes chainsword	Melee	Melee	User	-1	1	Each time the bearer fights, it makes 1 additional attack with this weapon.

WARGEAR OPTIONS

- The Assault Intercessor Sergeant's heavy bolt pistol can be replaced with one of the following: 1 hand flamer; 1 plasma pistol.
- The Assault Intercessor Sergeant's Astartes chainsword can be replaced with one of the following; 1 power fist; 1 power sword; 1 thunder hammer.

ABILITIES

Angels of Death, **Combat Squads** (pg 124-125)

FACTION KEYWORDS: **IMPERIUM, ADEPTUS ASTARTES, <CHAPTER>**
KEYWORDS: **INFANTRY, CORE, PRIMARIS, INTERCESSORS, ASSAULT INTERCESSOR SQUAD**

Assault Intercessors are amongst the most widespread close support units in a Chapter's arsenal. Firing their heavy bolt pistols as they close upon the foe, they charge into the fray, where they make short work of their enemies with brutal swings of their chainswords.

HEAVY INTERCESSOR SQUAD

7 POWER

No.	Name	M	WS	BS	S	T	W	A	Ld	Sv
4-9	Heavy Intercessor	5"	3+	3+	4	5	3	2	7	3+
1	Heavy Intercessor Sergeant	5"	3+	3+	4	5	3	3	8	3+

If this unit contains 6 or more models, it has **Power Rating 14**. Every model is equipped with: bolt pistol; heavy bolt rifle; frag grenades; krak grenades.

WEAPON	RANGE	TYPE	S	AP	D	ABILITIES
Executor bolt rifle	42"	Heavy 1	5	-2	2	-
Executor heavy bolter	42"	Heavy 2	5	-2	3	-
Heavy bolt rifle	36"	Rapid Fire 1	5	-1	1	-
Heavy bolter	36"	Heavy 3	5	-1	2	-
Hellstorm bolt rifle	30"	Assault 3	5	0	1	-
Hellstorm heavy bolter	30"	Heavy 4	5	0	2	-

WARGEAR OPTIONS

- If no model in this unit is equipped with a heavy bolter, you can take one of the following options:
  - All of the models in the unit can have their heavy bolt rifles replaced with 1 hellstorm bolt rifle each.
  - All of the models in the unit can have their heavy bolt rifles replaced with 1 executor bolt rifle each.
- For every 5 models in this unit, 1 Heavy Intercessor's heavy bolt rifle can be replaced with 1 heavy bolter, 1 Heavy Intercessor's heavy auto bolt rifle can be replaced with 1 hellstorm heavy bolter, or 1 Heavy Intercessor's heavy stalker bolt rifle can be replaced with 1 executor heavy bolter.

ABILITIES

Angels of Death, **Combat Squads** (pg 124-125)

FACTION KEYWORDS: **IMPERIUM, ADEPTUS ASTARTES, <CHAPTER>**
KEYWORDS: **INFANTRY, CORE, PRIMARIS, INTERCESSORS, MK X GRAVIS, HEAVY INTERCESSOR SQUAD**

Clad in thick Gravis armour, Heavy Intercessors secure ground and are immovable in the defence. Always ready for any sign of enemy counter-attack, they stand firm, laying down volleys of heavy fire that keep all but the most determined or foolhardy enemies at bay.

INFILTRATOR SQUAD

6 POWER

No.	Name	M	WS	BS	S	T	W	A	Ld	Sv
4-9	Infiltrator	6"	3+	3+	4	4	2	2	7	3+
1	Infiltrator Sergeant	6"	3+	3+	4	4	2	3	8	3+

If this unit contains 6 or more models, it has **Power Rating 12**. Every model is equipped with: bolt pistol; marksman bolt carbine; frag grenades; krak grenades.

WEAPON	RANGE	TYPE	S	AP	D	ABILITIES
Bolt pistol	12"	Pistol 1	4	0	1	-
Marksman bolt carbine	24"	Rapid Fire 1	4	0	1	Each time an attack is made with this weapon, an unmodified hit roll of 6 automatically wounds the target.

OTHER WARGEAR	ABILITIES
Helix gauntlet	Once per turn, the first time a saving throw is failed for the bearer's unit, the Damage characteristic of that attack is changed to 0.
Infiltrator comms array	The bearer's unit is always considered to be within range of the following aura abilities of any friendly **\<Chapter\> Phobos** units that are on the battlefield: Rites of Battle; Tactical Precision.

WARGEAR OPTIONS

- 1 Infiltrator can be equipped with one of the following: 1 helix gauntlet; 1 Infiltrator comms array.

ABILITIES

Angels of Death, Combat Squads, Concealed Positions (pg 124-125)

Omni-scrambler: Enemy units that are set up on the battlefield as reinforcements cannot be set up within 12" of this unit.

FACTION KEYWORDS: Imperium, Adeptus Astartes, \<Chapter\>
KEYWORDS: Infantry, Core, Primaris, Phobos, Smokescreen, Infiltrator Squad

Infiltrator Squads are experts in covert operations and are drilled extensively in self-sufficiency and survival skills. Equipped with omni-scramblers that cripple enemy communications, they wreak havoc among their foes before cutting them down with hails of accurate bolt fire.

INCURSOR SQUAD

5 POWER

No.	Name	M	WS	BS	S	T	W	A	Ld	Sv
4-9	Incursor	6"	3+	3+	4	4	2	2	7	3+
1	Incursor Sergeant	6"	3+	3+	4	4	2	3	8	3+

If this unit contains 6 or more models, it has **Power Rating 10**. Every model is equipped with: bolt pistol; occulus bolt carbine; paired combat blades; frag grenades; krak grenades.

WEAPON	RANGE	TYPE	S	AP	D	ABILITIES
Bolt pistol	12"	Pistol 1	4	0	1	-
Occulus bolt carbine	24"	Rapid Fire 1	4	0	1	Each time an attack is made with this weapon, the target does not receive the benefits of cover against that attack.
Paired combat blades	Melee	Melee	User	-1	1	-

OTHER WARGEAR	ABILITIES
Haywire mine	Once per battle, when an enemy unit finishes a charge move within Engagement Range of the bearer's unit, the bearer can use its Haywire mine. If it does, roll one D6: on a 2+, that enemy unit suffers D3 mortal wounds (if it has the **Vehicle** keyword, it suffers 3 mortal wounds instead). *We recommend placing a Haywire Mine model next to the bearer as a reminder, removing it once this ability has been used (a Haywire Mine does not count as a model for any rules purposes).*

WARGEAR OPTIONS

- 1 Incursor can be equipped with 1 haywire mine.

ABILITIES

Angels of Death, Combat Squads, Concealed Positions (pg 124-125)

Multi-spectrum Array: Each time a model in this unit makes a ranged attack, you can ignore any or all hit roll and Ballistic Skill modifiers.

FACTION KEYWORDS: Imperium, Adeptus Astartes, \<Chapter\>
KEYWORDS: Infantry, Core, Primaris, Phobos, Smokescreen, Incursor Squad

Aggressive light infantry, Incursors specialise in storming enemy defences and destroying essential assets. With a formidable array of auspexes and sensory equipment, they can see their enemies through walls and predict their movements – and with a burst of carbine fire or knife thrusts, cut them down.

TACTICAL SQUAD

5 POWER

No.	Name	M	WS	BS	S	T	W	A	Ld	Sv
4-9	Space Marine	6"	3+	3+	4	4	2	1	7	3+
1	Space Marine Sergeant	6"	3+	3+	4	4	2	2	8	3+

If this unit contains 6 or more models, it has **Power Rating 10**. Every model is equipped with: bolt pistol; boltgun; frag grenades; krak grenades.

WEAPON	RANGE	TYPE	S	AP	D	ABILITIES
Bolt pistol	12"	Pistol 1	4	0	1	-
Boltgun	24"	Rapid Fire 1	4	0	1	-

WARGEAR OPTIONS

- The Space Marine Sergeant's bolt pistol can be replaced with one of the following: 1 weapon from the *Pistols* list; 1 weapon from the *Melee Weapons* list.
- The Space Marine Sergeant's boltgun can be replaced with one of the following: 1 weapon from the *Combi-weapons* list; 1 weapon from the *Pistols* list; 1 weapon from the *Melee Weapons* list.
- If this unit contains 9 or fewer models, 1 Space Marine's boltgun can be replaced with one of the following: 1 weapon from the *Heavy Weapons* list; 1 weapon from the *Special Weapons* list.
- If this unit contains 10 models, 1 Space Marine's boltgun can be replaced with 1 weapon from the *Special Weapons* list.
- If this unit contains 10 models, 1 Space Marine's boltgun can be replaced with 1 weapon from the *Heavy Weapons* list.

ABILITIES

Angels of Death, **Combat Squads** (pg 124-125)

FACTION KEYWORDS: **Imperium, Adeptus Astartes, <Chapter>**
KEYWORDS: **Infantry, Core, Melta Bombs, Tactical Squad**

Tactical Squads have formed the backbone of Space Marine Chapters for ten thousand years. With access to a wide range of weapons, they can purge swathes of enemy infantry, scour battlefields clean of heavily armoured foes or punch burning holes through tanks.

COMPANY CHAMPION

3 POWER

No.	Name	M	WS	BS	S	T	W	A	Ld	Sv
1	Company Champion	6"	2+	3+	4	4	4	4	8	3+

A Company Champion is equipped with: bolt pistol; master-crafted power sword; frag grenades; krak grenades; combat shield.

WEAPON	RANGE	TYPE	S	AP	D	ABILITIES
Bolt pistol	12"	Pistol 1	4	0	1	-
Master-crafted power sword	Melee	Melee	+1	-3	2	-

OTHER WARGEAR	ABILITIES
Combat shield	The bearer has a 5+ invulnerable save. In addition, add 1 to armour saving throws made for the bearer.

ABILITIES

Angels of Death (pg 124-125)

Honour or Death: This model is eligible to perform a Heroic Intervention if it is within 6" horizontally and 5" vertically of any enemy unit, instead of 3" horizontally and 5" vertically. Each time this model makes a Heroic Intervention move, so long as it ends that move either closer to the closest enemy model or within Engagement Range of an enemy **Character** unit, it can move up to 6". All other rules for Heroic Interventions still apply.

Martial Superiority: At the start of the Fight phase, if this model is within Engagement Range of any enemy **Character** units, it can fight first that phase.

Command Squad: For each **<Chapter> Company Veterans** unit included in a Detachment, one **<Chapter> Command Squad Company Champion** unit can be included in that Detachment without taking up a Battlefield Role slot.

Wolf Guard: If this unit is from the Space Wolves Chapter (or one of its successor Chapters), it has the **Wolf Guard** keyword.

FACTION KEYWORDS: **Imperium, Adeptus Astartes, <Chapter>**
KEYWORDS: **Infantry, Character, Command Squad, Company Champion**

Masterful swordsmen, Company Champions meet the foe's greatest warriors in single combat to defend the honour of their Chapter. In doing this they free up their commanders to carry out the business of leading and coordinating the strike force in the fires of war.

SCOUT SQUAD

No.	Name	M	WS	BS	S	T	W	A	Ld	Sv
4-9	Scout	6"	3+	3+	4	4	1	1	7	4+
1	Scout Sergeant	6"	3+	3+	4	4	1	2	8	4+

If this unit contains 6 or more models, it has **Power Rating 8**. Every model is equipped with: bolt pistol; boltgun; frag grenades; krak grenades.

WEAPON	RANGE	TYPE	S	AP	D	ABILITIES
Astartes shotgun	18"	Assault 2	4	0	1	-
Bolt pistol	12"	Pistol 1	4	0	1	-
Boltgun	24"	Rapid Fire 1	4	0	1	-
Heavy bolter	36"	Heavy 3	5	-1	2	-
Missile launcher		Before selecting targets, select one of the profiles below to make attacks with.				
- Frag missile	48"	Heavy D6	4	0	1	Blast
- Krak missile	48"	Heavy 1	8	-2	D6	-
Scout sniper rifle	36"	Heavy 1	4	-1	1	Each time you select a target for this weapon, you can ignore the Look Out, Sir rule. Each time an attack is made with this weapon, an unmodified wound roll of 6 inflicts 1 mortal wound on the target in addition to any normal damage.
Combat knife	Melee	Melee	User	0	1	Each time the bearer fights, it makes 1 additional attack with this weapon.

OTHER WARGEAR	ABILITIES
Camo cloak	Each time a ranged attack is allocated to the bearer while it is receiving the benefits of cover, add an additional 1 to any armour saving throw made against that attack.

WARGEAR OPTIONS

- The Scout Sergeant's bolt pistol can be replaced with one of the following: 1 weapon from the *Pistols* list; 1 weapon from the *Melee Weapons* list.
- The Scout Sergeant's boltgun can be replaced with one of the following: 1 weapon from the *Combi-weapons* list; 1 weapon from the *Pistols* list; 1 weapon from the *Melee Weapons* list.
- Any number of models can each have their boltgun replaced with one of the following: 1 Astartes shotgun; 1 Scout sniper rifle; 1 combat knife.
- 1 Scout's boltgun can be replaced with one of the following: 1 heavy bolter; 1 missile launcher; 1 weapon from the *Special Weapons* list. A model can only take a weapon from the *Special Weapons* list if it is from the Space Wolves Chapter (or one of its successor Chapters).
- If this unit is from the Space Wolves Chapter (or one of its successor Chapters), 1 Scout's boltgun and bolt pistol can be replaced with one of the following:
  - 1 bolt pistol and 1 power axe.
  - 1 bolt pistol and 1 power sword.
  - 1 boltgun and 1 plasma pistol.
- Any number of models can each be equipped with 1 camo cloak.

ABILITIES

Angels of Death, Combat Squads, Concealed Positions, Outflank (pg 124-125)

FACTION KEYWORDS: IMPERIUM, ADEPTUS ASTARTES, <CHAPTER>
KEYWORDS: INFANTRY, CORE, SCOUT, SMOKESCREEN, SCOUT SQUAD

Space Marine neophytes, Scouts learn their deadly craft in daring missions independent of the main force. Led by seasoned Veteran Sergeants, they infiltrate enemy positions, clear potential drop zones, set ambushes, sabotage supply lines and complete all manner of other objectives to weaken the foe.

PRIMARIS APOTHECARY

4 POWER

No.	Name	M	WS	BS	S	T	W	A	Ld	Sv
1	Primaris Apothecary	6"	3+	3+	4	4	5	4	8	3+

A Primaris Apothecary is equipped with: absolvor bolt pistol; reductor pistol; frag grenades; krak grenades.

WEAPON	RANGE	TYPE	S	AP	D	ABILITIES
Absolvor bolt pistol	18"	Pistol 1	5	-1	2	-
Reductor pistol	3"	Pistol 1	4	-4	2	-

ABILITIES

Angels of Death (pg 124-125)

Combat Restoratives: At the end of your Movement phase, this model can heal one friendly <Chapter> Infantry or <Chapter> Biker model whose unit is within 3" of it. That model regains up to D3 lost wounds. Each model can only be healed once per turn.

Narthecium (Aura): While a friendly <Chapter> Infantry or <Chapter> Biker unit is within 3" of this model, each time a model in that unit would lose a wound, roll one D6: on a 6, that wound is not lost.

FACTION KEYWORDS: Imperium, Adeptus Astartes, <Chapter>
KEYWORDS: Infantry, Character, Primaris, Primaris Apothecary

In addition to battlefield surgery, it is the Apothecary's duty to recover the gene-seed of the fallen, and thus preserve the Chapter for later generations. For this task the Primaris Apothecary is equipped to bring peace to those too wounded to save, and efficiently extract their precious progenoid glands.

APOTHECARY

4 POWER

No.	Name	M	WS	BS	S	T	W	A	Ld	Sv
1	Apothecary	6"	3+	3+	4	4	4	3	8	3+

An Apothecary is equipped with: bolt pistol; Astartes chainsword; frag grenades; krak grenades.

WEAPON	RANGE	TYPE	S	AP	D	ABILITIES
Bolt pistol	12"	Pistol 1	4	0	1	-
Astartes chainsword	Melee	Melee	User	-1	1	Each time the bearer fights, it makes 1 additional attack with this weapon.

ABILITIES

Angels of Death (pg 124-125)

Combat Restoratives: At the end of your Movement phase, this model can heal one friendly <Chapter> Infantry or <Chapter> Biker model whose unit is within 3" of it. That model regains up to D3 lost wounds. Each model can only be healed once per turn.

Narthecium (Aura): While a friendly <Chapter> Infantry or <Chapter> Biker unit is within 3" of this model, each time a model in that unit would lose a wound, roll one D6: on a 6, that wound is not lost.

Command Squad: For each <Chapter> Company Veterans unit included in a Detachment, one <Chapter> Command Squad Apothecary unit can be included in that Detachment without taking up a Battlefield Role slot.

FACTION KEYWORDS: Imperium, Adeptus Astartes, <Chapter>
KEYWORDS: Infantry, Character, Command Squad, Apothecary

Experts in Space Marine physiology, Apothecaries serve as front-line medics, performing emergency surgery, carrying out transfusions and any other task required. Over the millennia countless lives have been saved by their heroics, with many Apothecaries placing their body between the wounded and the foe.

COMPANY ANCIENT

4 POWER

No.	Name	M	WS	BS	S	T	W	A	Ld	Sv
1	Company Ancient	6"	3+	3+	4	4	4	3	8	3+

A Company Ancient is equipped with: bolt pistol; frag grenades; krak grenades.

WEAPON	RANGE	TYPE	S	AP	D	ABILITIES
Bolt pistol	12"	Pistol 1	4	0	1	-
Boltgun	24"	Rapid Fire 1	4	0	1	-

WARGEAR OPTIONS

- This model's bolt pistol can be replaced with one of the following: 1 boltgun; 1 weapon from the *Combi-weapons* list; 1 weapon from the *Melee Weapons* list; 1 weapon from the *Pistols* list.

ABILITIES

Angels of Death (pg 124-125)

Astartes Banner (Aura): While a friendly <Chapter> Core unit is within 6" of this model, add 1 to the Leadership characteristic of models in that unit. In addition, each time a model in such a unit is destroyed by an attack made by an enemy model, roll one D6. On a 4+, do not remove the destroyed model from play – it can, after the attacking model's unit has finished making its attacks, either shoot with one of its ranged weapons as if it were your Shooting phase, or make one attack with one of its melee weapons as if it were the Fight phase. After resolving these attacks, the destroyed model is then removed.

Command Squad: For each <Chapter> Company Veterans unit included in a Detachment, one <Chapter> Command Squad Company Ancient unit can be included in that Detachment without taking up a Battlefield Role slot.

Wolf Guard: If this unit is from the Space Wolves Chapter (or one of its successor Chapters), it has the Wolf Guard keyword.

FACTION KEYWORDS: Imperium, Adeptus Astartes, <Chapter>
KEYWORDS: Infantry, Character, Ancient, Command Squad, Company Ancient

No act can bring greater shame to an Ancient than letting the standard fall from their grip. Such a failure dishonours not just the bearer but their entire company. Thus, those awarded the privilege of bearing their standards into battle are excellent warriors, who well deserve the trust invested in them by their battle-brothers.

PRIMARIS ANCIENT

4 POWER

No.	Name	M	WS	BS	S	T	W	A	Ld	Sv
1	Primaris Ancient	6"	3+	3+	4	4	5	4	8	3+

A Primaris Ancient is equipped with: bolt pistol; bolt rifle; frag grenades; krak grenades.

WEAPON	RANGE	TYPE	S	AP	D	ABILITIES
Bolt pistol	12"	Pistol 1	4	0	1	-
Bolt rifle	30"	Rapid Fire 1	4	-1	1	-

ABILITIES

Angels of Death (pg 124-125)

Wolf Guard: If this unit is from the Space Wolves Chapter (or one of its successor Chapters), it has the Wolf Guard keyword.

Astartes Banner (Aura): While a friendly <Chapter> Core unit is within 6" of this model, add 1 to the Leadership characteristic of models in that unit. In addition, each time a model in such a unit is destroyed by an attack made by an enemy model, roll one D6. On a 4+, do not remove the destroyed model from play – it can, after the attacking model's unit has finished making its attacks, either shoot with one of its ranged weapons as if it were your Shooting phase, or make one attack with one of its melee weapons as if it were the Fight phase. After resolving these attacks, the destroyed model is then removed.

FACTION KEYWORDS: Imperium, Adeptus Astartes, <Chapter>
KEYWORDS: Infantry, Character, Primaris, Ancient

Ancients bear the Chapter's precious standards. These glorious relics have been present in some of the Chapter's most notable battles, their finely worked designs commemorating countless campaigns and heroic deeds. They are symbols of selfless commitment and the unbreakable loyalty of brothers.

BLADEGUARD ANCIENT

5 POWER

No.	NAME	M	WS	BS	S	T	W	A	Ld	Sv
1	Bladeguard Ancient	6"	3+	3+	4	4	5	4	9	3+

A Bladeguard Ancient is equipped with: heavy bolt pistol; frag grenades; krak grenades.

WEAPON	RANGE	TYPE	S	AP	D	ABILITIES
Heavy bolt pistol	18"	Pistol 1	4	-1	1	-

ABILITIES

Angels of Death (pg 124-125)

Astartes Banner (Aura): While a friendly <Chapter> Core unit is within 6" of this model, add 1 to the Leadership characteristic of models in that unit. In addition, each time a model in such a unit is destroyed by an attack made by an enemy model, roll one D6. On a 4+, do not remove the destroyed model from play – it can, after the attacking model's unit has finished making its attacks, either shoot with one of its ranged weapons as if it were your Shooting phase, or make one attack with one of its melee weapons as if it were the Fight phase. After resolving these attacks, the destroyed model is then removed.

Deeds of Heroism (Aura): While a friendly <Chapter> Bladeguard unit is within 6" of this model, each time a model in that unit makes an attack, add 1 to that attack's hit roll.

Deathwing: If this unit is from the Dark Angels Chapter (or one of its successor Chapters), it has the **Deathwing** keyword.

Wolf Guard: If this unit is from the Space Wolves Chapter (or one of its successor Chapters), it has the **Wolf Guard** keyword.

FACTION KEYWORDS: Imperium, Adeptus Astartes, <Chapter>
KEYWORDS: Infantry, Character, Primaris, Ancient, Bladeguard, Bladeguard Ancient

Bladeguard Ancients bear the honour of carrying their Chapter's precious standards into battle. The most revered of these incorporate the remains of fallen heroes of the Chapter; in their presence, battle-brothers are inspired to emulate the legendary deeds of these paragons of old.

ANCIENT IN TERMINATOR ARMOUR

6 POWER

No.	Name	M	WS	BS	S	T	W	A	Ld	Sv
1	Ancient in Terminator Armour	6"	3+	3+	4	4	5	3	8	2+

An Ancient in Terminator Armour is a equipped with: storm bolter; power fist.

WEAPON	RANGE	TYPE	S	AP	D	ABILITIES
Storm bolter	24"	Rapid Fire 2	4	0	1	-
Power fist	Melee	Melee	x2	-3	2	Each time an attack is made with this weapon, subtract 1 from that attack's hit roll.

OTHER WARGEAR	ABILITIES
Storm shield	The bearer has a 4+ invulnerable save. In addition, add 1 to armour saving throws made for the bearer.

WARGEAR OPTIONS

- If this model is from the Blood Angels Chapter (or one of its successor Chapters), its storm bolter and power fist can be replaced with one of the following: 1 lightning claw; 1 storm bolter; 1 thunder hammer.
- If this model is from the Dark Angels Chapter (or one of its successor Chapters), its power fist can be replaced with 1 chainfist.
- If this model is from the Dark Angels Chapter (or one of its successor Chapters), its storm bolter and power fist can be replaced with one of the following: 2 lightning claws; 1 thunder hammer and 1 storm shield.

ABILITIES

Angels of Death, Teleport Strike (pg 124-125)

Crux Terminatus: This model has a 5+ invulnerable save.

Deathwing Command Squad: If this unit is from the Dark Angels Chapter (or one of its successor Chapters), it has the **DEATHWING** keyword. For each **DEATHWING COMMAND SQUAD** unit included in a Detachment, one **DEATHWING ANCIENT** unit can be included in that Detachment without taking up a Battlefield Role slot.

Wolf Guard: If this unit is from the Space Wolves Chapter (or one of its successor Chapters), it has the **WOLF GUARD** keyword.

Astartes Banner (Aura): While a friendly **<CHAPTER> CORE** unit is within 6" of this model, add 1 to the Leadership characteristic of models in that unit. In addition, each time a model in such a unit is destroyed by an attack made by an enemy model, roll one D6. On a 4+, do not remove the destroyed model from play – it can, after the attacking model's unit has finished making its attacks, either shoot with one of its ranged weapons as if it were your Shooting phase, or make one attack with one of its melee weapons as if it were the Fight phase. After resolving these attacks, the destroyed model is then removed.

FACTION KEYWORDS: IMPERIUM, ADEPTUS ASTARTES, <CHAPTER>
KEYWORDS: INFANTRY, CHARACTER, TERMINATOR, ANCIENT

Carrying the Space Marines' sacred banners is a most vital task. Symbols of the Chapter's might, Space Marines will gladly die to preserve them. This makes Ancients frequent targets. Clad in Terminator armour, they are near impervious to enemy fire, ensuring the standard always flies proud.

VETERAN INTERCESSOR SQUAD

6 POWER

No.	Name	M	WS	BS	S	T	W	A	Ld	Sv
4-9	Veteran Intercessor	6"	3+	3+	4	4	2	3	8	3+
1	Veteran Intercessor Sergeant	6"	3+	3+	4	4	2	4	9	3+

If this unit contains 6 or more models, it has **Power Rating 12**. Every model is equipped with: bolt pistol; bolt rifle; frag grenades; krak grenades.

WEAPON	RANGE	TYPE	S	AP	D	ABILITIES
Auto bolt rifle	24"	Assault 3	4	0	1	-
Astartes grenade launcher	Before selecting targets, select one of the profiles below to make attacks with.					
- Frag grenade	30"	Assault D6	3	0	1	Blast
- Krak grenade	30"	Assault 1	6	-1	D3	-
Bolt pistol	12"	Pistol 1	4	0	1	-
Bolt rifle	30"	Rapid Fire 1	4	-1	1	-
Heavy bolt pistol	18"	Pistol 1	4	-1	1	-
Stalker bolt rifle	36"	Heavy 1	4	-2	2	-
Astartes chainsword	Melee	Melee	User	-1	1	Each time the bearer fights, it makes 1 additional attack with this weapon.

WARGEAR OPTIONS

- All of the models in the unit can have their bolt rifle replaced with 1 auto bolt rifle each.
- All of the models in the unit can have their bolt rifle replaced with 1 stalker bolt rifle each.
- All of the models in the unit can have their bolt pistol and bolt rifle replaced with 1 heavy bolt pistol and 1 Astartes chainsword each (maximum 1 Astartes chainsword per model).
- The Veteran Intercessor Sergeant's heavy bolt pistol can be replaced with 1 of the following: 1 hand flamer; 1 plasma pistol.
- If the Veteran Intercessor Sergeant is equipped with a heavy bolt pistol, a plasma pistol or a hand flamer, then its Astartes chainsword can be replaced with one of the following: 1 power fist; 1 power sword; 1 thunder hammer.
- If the Veteran Intercessor Sergeant is not equipped with an Astartes chainsword, a power sword, a power fist or a thunder hammer, its bolt rifle, auto bolt rifle or stalker bolt rifle can be replaced with one of the following: 1 hand flamer; 1 plasma pistol; 1 Astartes chainsword; 1 power sword.
- If the Veteran Intercessor Sergeant is not equipped with an Astartes chainsword or a power sword, it can be equipped with one of the following: 1 Astartes chainsword; 1 power fist; 1 power sword; 1 thunder hammer.
- For every 5 models in this unit, 1 model equipped with a bolt rifle, auto bolt rifle or stalker bolt rifle can be equipped with 1 Astartes grenade launcher.

ABILITIES

Angels of Death, **Combat Squads** (pg 124-125)

Wolf Guard: If this unit is from the Space Wolves Chapter (or one of its successor Chapters), it has the **WOLF GUARD** keyword.

FACTION KEYWORDS: IMPERIUM, ADEPTUS ASTARTES, <CHAPTER>
KEYWORDS: INFANTRY, CORE, PRIMARIS, INTERCESSORS, VETERAN INTERCESSOR SQUAD

Since the Ultima Founding, Primaris Space Marines have wrought illustrious records as their tallies of victories have grown longer. Whether they have crossed the Rubicon Primaris, were forged on Mars or recruited directly by their Chapter, they now fight as part of their 1st Company.

BLADEGUARD VETERAN SQUAD

5 POWER

No.	Name	M	WS	BS	S	T	W	A	Ld	Sv
2-5	Bladeguard Veteran	6"	3+	3+	4	4	3	3	8	3+
1	Bladeguard Veteran Sergeant	6"	3+	3+	4	4	3	4	9	3+

If this unit contains 4 or more models, it has **Power Rating 10**. Every model is equipped with: heavy bolt pistol; master-crafted power sword; frag grenades; krak grenades; storm shield.

WEAPON	RANGE	TYPE	S	AP	D	ABILITIES
Heavy bolt pistol	18"	Pistol 1	4	-1	1	-
Neo-volkite pistol	15"	Pistol 2	5	0	2	Each time an attack is made with this weapon, an unmodified wound roll of 6 inflicts 1 mortal wound on the target in addition to any normal damage.
Master-crafted power sword	Melee	Melee	+1	-3	2	-

OTHER WARGEAR	ABILITIES
Storm shield	The bearer has a 4+ invulnerable save. In addition, add 1 to armour saving throws made for the bearer.

WARGEAR OPTIONS

- The Bladeguard Veteran Sergeant's heavy bolt pistol can be replaced with one of the following: 1 neo-volkite pistol; 1 plasma pistol.

ABILITIES

Angels of Death, Combat Squads (pg 124-125)

Deathwing: If this unit is from the Dark Angels Chapter (or one of its successor Chapters), it has the **DEATHWING** keyword.

Wolf Guard: If this unit is from the Space Wolves Chapter (or one of its successor Chapters), it has the **WOLF GUARD** keyword.

FACTION KEYWORDS: IMPERIUM, ADEPTUS ASTARTES, <CHAPTER>
KEYWORDS: INFANTRY, CORE, PRIMARIS, BLADEGUARD, BLADEGUARD VETERAN SQUAD

Bladeguard Veterans are inexorable warriors, advancing relentlessly with blades held high – the very image of noble knights of myth. Members of their Chapter's elite 1st Company of Veterans, each of these vastly experienced Space Marines has fought to preserve the Imperium across uncounted worlds.

Black Templars Bladeguard Veteran

Ultramarines Bladeguard Veteran Sergeant with neo-volkite pistol

White Scars Bladeguard Veteran

COMPANY VETERANS

3 POWER

No.	Name	M	WS	BS	S	T	W	A	Ld	Sv
1-4	Company Veteran	6"	3+	3+	4	4	2	2	8	3+
1	Company Veteran Sergeant	6"	3+	3+	4	4	2	3	9	3+

If this unit contains 3 or more models, it has **Power Rating 8**. Every model is equipped with: bolt pistol; boltgun; frag grenades; krak grenades.

WEAPON	RANGE	TYPE	S	AP	D	ABILITIES
Bolt pistol	12"	Pistol 1	4	0	1	-
Boltgun	24"	Rapid Fire 1	4	0	1	-

OTHER WARGEAR	ABILITIES
Combat shield	The bearer has a 5+ invulnerable save. In addition, add 1 to armour saving throws made for the bearer.
Storm shield	The bearer has a 4+ invulnerable save. In addition, add 1 to armour saving throws made for the bearer.

WARGEAR OPTIONS

- Any number of models can each have their bolt pistol replaced with one of the following: 1 weapon from the *Pistols* list; 1 weapon from the *Melee Weapons* list; 1 storm shield (maximum 1 per model).
- Any number of models can each have their boltgun replaced with one of the following: 1 weapon from the *Combi-weapons* list; 1 weapon from the *Melee Weapons* list; 1 storm shield (maximum 1 per model).
- Any number of Company Veterans can each have their boltgun replaced with 1 weapon from the *Special Weapons* list.
- If this unit contains 5 models, 1 Company Veteran's boltgun can be replaced with 1 weapon from the *Heavy Weapons* list.
- If this unit is from the Dark Angels Chapter (or one of its successor Chapters), any number of its models that are not equipped with a storm shield can each be equipped with 1 combat shield.

ABILITIES

Angels of Death (pg 124-125)

Bodyguard: While a friendly <CHAPTER> CHARACTER unit that has a Wounds characteristic of 9 or less is within 3" of this unit, enemy models cannot target that CHARACTER unit with ranged attacks.

Command Squad: If a Detachment includes a <CHAPTER> CAPTAIN, then one <CHAPTER> COMPANY VETERANS unit can be included in that Detachment without taking up a Battlefield Role slot.

Wolf Guard: If this unit is from the Space Wolves Chapter (or one of its successor Chapters), it has the WOLF GUARD keyword.

FACTION KEYWORDS: IMPERIUM, ADEPTUS ASTARTES, <CHAPTER>
KEYWORDS: INFANTRY, CORE, COMMAND SQUAD, COMPANY VETERANS

Company Veterans are elite warriors and highly experienced fighters. They are their Captain's bodyguard, closest advisors and the core of his command squad. They equip themselves for any battlefield situation, leading offensives or reinforce weakening elements of the battle line.

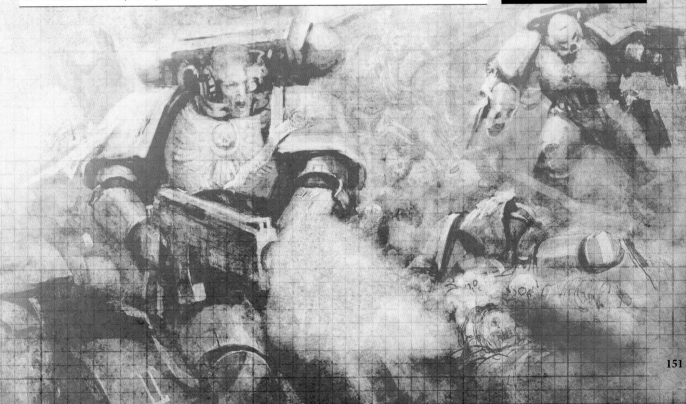

VANGUARD VETERAN SQUAD

6 POWER

No.	NAME	M	WS	BS	S	T	W	A	Ld	Sv
4-9	Vanguard Veteran	6"	3+	3+	4	4	2	2	8	3+
1	Vanguard Veteran Sergeant	6"	3+	3+	4	4	2	3	9	3+

If this unit contains 6 or more models, it has **Power Rating 12**. Every model is equipped with: bolt pistol; Astartes chainsword; frag grenades; krak grenades.

WEAPON	RANGE	TYPE	S	AP	D	ABILITIES
Bolt pistol	12"	Pistol 1	4	0	1	-
Astartes chainsword	Melee	Melee	User	-1	1	Each time the bearer fights, it makes 1 additional attack with this weapon.
Heavy thunder hammer	Melee	Melee	x2	-3	4	Each time an attack is made with this weapon, subtract 1 from that attack's hit roll.
Relic blade	Melee	Melee	+3	-3	2	-

OTHER WARGEAR	ABILITIES
Jump pack	The bearer has a Move characteristic of 12", the Death From Above ability (pg 125) and the **FLY** and **JUMP PACK** keywords.
Storm shield	The bearer has a 4+ invulnerable save. In addition, add 1 to armour saving throws made for the bearer.

WARGEAR OPTIONS

- Any number of models can each have their bolt pistol replaced one of the following: 1 weapon from the *Pistols* list; 1 weapon from the *Melee Weapons* list; 1 storm shield (maximum 1 per model).
- Any number of models can each have their Astartes chainsword replaced with one of the following: 1 weapon from the *Pistols* list; 1 weapon from the *Melee Weapons* list; 1 storm shield (maximum 1 per model).
- If this unit is from the Deathwatch Chapter, any number of its models can each have their bolt pistol and Astartes chainsword replaced with 1 heavy thunder hammer.
- The Vanguard Veteran Sergeant's Astartes chainsword can be replaced with one 1 relic blade.
- All of the models in the unit can be equipped with 1 jump pack each (**Power Rating +1** if the unit contains 5 models, **Power Rating +2** if the unit contains 6 or more models).

ABILITIES

Angels of Death, **Combat Squads** (pg 124-125)

FACTION KEYWORDS: IMPERIUM, ADEPTUS ASTARTES, <CHAPTER>
KEYWORDS: INFANTRY, CORE, MELTA BOMBS, VANGUARD VETERAN SQUAD

Vanguard Veterans are close combat experts with decades of experience. They arm themselves with the finest melee weapons from their Chapter's armouries. On the battlefield they are peerless rapid-response troops, using their jump packs to arrive at the perfect time to ensure victory.

Power axe

Thunder hammer

Power fist

Storm shield

Plasma pistol

Raven Guard Vanguard Veteran with lightning claws

Ultramarines Vanguard Veteran Sergeant with grav-pistol and relic blade

Ultramarines Vanguard Veteran with Astartes chainsword and bolt pistol

STERNGUARD VETERAN SQUAD

6 POWER

No.	NAME	M	WS	BS	S	T	W	A	Ld	Sv
4-9	Sternguard Veteran	6"	3+	3+	4	4	2	2	8	3+
1	Sternguard Veteran Sergeant	6"	3+	3+	4	4	2	3	9	3+

If this unit contains 6 or more models, it has **Power Rating 12**. Every model is equipped with: bolt pistol; special issue boltgun; frag grenades; krak grenades.

WEAPON	RANGE	TYPE	S	AP	D	ABILITIES
Bolt pistol	12"	Pistol 1	4	0	1	-
Special issue boltgun	30"	Rapid Fire 1	4	-2	1	-

WARGEAR OPTIONS

- Any number of models can each have their special issue boltgun replaced with 1 weapon from the *Combi-weapons* list.
- The Sternguard Veteran Sergeant's bolt pistol can be replaced with one of the following: 1 weapon from the *Pistols* list; 1 Astartes chainsword; 1 lightning claw; 1 power axe; 1 power fist; 1 power maul; 1 power sword.
- The Sternguard Veteran Sergeant's special issue boltgun can be replaced with one of the following: 1 weapon from the *Pistols* list; 1 Astartes chainsword; 1 lightning claw; 1 power axe; 1 power fist; 1 power maul; 1 power sword.
- Up to 2 Sternguard Veterans can each have their special issue boltgun replaced with one of the following: 1 heavy flamer; 1 weapon from the *Heavy Weapons* list; 1 weapon from the *Special Weapons* list.

ABILITIES

Angels of Death, **Combat Squads** (pg 124-125)

FACTION KEYWORDS: **Imperium, Adeptus Astartes, <Chapter>**
KEYWORDS: **Infantry, Core, Sternguard Veteran Squad**

Sternguard Veterans are possessed of an unshakeable calm, and are renowned among their brothers for their exemplary marksmanship in the fiercest battles. Proficient in all of the Chapter's ranged weaponry, they can always be found where their pinpoint volleys will best shatter the foe.

JUDICIAR

5 POWER

No.	NAME	M	WS	BS	S	T	W	A	Ld	Sv
1	Judiciar	6"	2+	3+	4	4	5	4	9	3+

A Judiciar is equipped with: absolvor bolt pistol; executioner relic blade; frag grenades; krak grenades.

WEAPON	RANGE	TYPE	S	AP	D	ABILITIES
Absolvor bolt pistol	18"	Pistol 1	5	-1	2	-
Executioner relic blade	Melee	Melee	+3	-3	2	Each time an attack is made with this weapon, an unmodified wound roll of 6 inflicts 1 mortal wound on the target in addition to any normal damage.

ABILITIES

Angels of Death (pg 124-125)

Blade Parry: This model has a 4+ invulnerable save against melee attacks.

Tempormortis: At the start of the Fight phase, you can select one enemy unit within 3" of this model. That unit is not eligible to fight this phase until after all eligible units from your army have done so.

FACTION KEYWORDS: **Imperium, Adeptus Astartes, <Chapter>**
KEYWORDS: **Infantry, Character, Primaris, Judiciar**

Sworn to silence, Judiciars do not preach aloud, but instead their deeds are a litany of fury. Wielding a tempormortis in one hand and an immense blade in the other, they must prove their worth in battle to join the Chaplaincy proper, doing so through acts of devotion and the slaying of enemies.

REIVER SQUAD

5 POWER

No.	Name	M	WS	BS	S	T	W	A	Ld	Sv
4-9	Reiver	6"	3+	3+	4	4	2	2	7	3+
1	Reiver Sergeant	6"	3+	3+	4	4	2	3	8	3+

If this unit contains 6 or more models, it has **Power Rating 10**. Every model is equipped with: special issue bolt pistol; combat knife; frag grenades; krak grenades.

WEAPON	RANGE	TYPE	S	AP	D	ABILITIES
Bolt carbine	24"	Assault 2	4	0	1	-
Special issue bolt pistol	12"	Pistol 1	4	-2	1	-
Combat knife	Melee	Melee	User	0	1	Each time the bearer fights, it makes 1 additional attack with this weapon.

OTHER WARGEAR	ABILITIES
Grapnel launcher	The bearer has the Outflank ability (pg 125). When the bearer's unit makes a Normal Move, Advances or Falls Back, the bearer does not count any vertical distance it moves against the total that it can move this turn.
Reiver grav-chute	The bearer has the Death From Above ability (pg 125).

WARGEAR OPTIONS

- All of the models in the unit can have their combat knife replaced with 1 bolt carbine each.
- If the Reiver Sergeant is equipped with a bolt carbine, it can be equipped with 1 combat knife.
- All of the models in the unit can be equipped with 1 Reiver grav-chute each.
- All of the models in the unit can be equipped with 1 grapnel launcher each.

ABILITIES

Angels of Death, Combat Squads (pg 124-125)

Terror Troops (Aura): While an enemy unit is within 3" of this unit, subtract 2 from the Leadership characteristic of models in that unit.

FACTION KEYWORDS: IMPERIUM, ADEPTUS ASTARTES, <CHAPTER>
KEYWORDS: INFANTRY, CORE, PRIMARIS, PHOBOS, REIVER, SHOCK GRENADES, REIVER SQUAD

Rapid-insertion terror troops, Reiver Squads often deploy using grav-chutes and directional fins to land with pinpoint accuracy. Operating with near perfect stealth to reach the optimum location to strike from, when ready they unleash their fury, surging forward with augmented guttural roars and blasts of weapons fire.

Special issue bolt pistol

Bolt carbine

Grapnel launcher

Combat knife

Grav-chute

Space Wolves Reiver with special issue bolt pistol and combat knife

Ultramarines Reiver with grapnel launcher and combat knife

Salamanders Reiver with bolt carbine

Raven Guard Reiver with special issue bolt pistol and grav-chute

AGGRESSOR SQUAD

6 POWER

No.	Name	M	WS	BS	S	T	W	A	Ld	Sv
2-5	Aggressor	5"	3+	3+	4	5	3	3	7	3+
1	Aggressor Sergeant	5"	3+	3+	4	5	3	4	8	3+

If this unit contains 4 or more models, it has **Power Rating 12**. Every model is equipped with: 2 flamestorm gauntlets.

WEAPON	RANGE	TYPE	S	AP	D	ABILITIES
Auto boltstorm gauntlet (shooting)	18"	Assault 3	4	0	1	-
Flamestorm gauntlet (shooting)	12"	Assault D6	4	0	1	Each time an attack is made with this weapon, that attack automatically hits the target.
Fragstorm grenade launcher	18"	Assault D6	4	0	1	Blast
Auto boltstorm gauntlet (melee)	Melee	Melee	x2	-3	2	Each time an attack is made with this weapon, subtract 1 from that attack's hit roll.
Flamestorm gauntlet (melee)	Melee	Melee	x2	-3	2	Each time an attack is made with this weapon, subtract 1 from that attack's hit roll.

WARGEAR OPTIONS

- All of the models in the unit can have their 2 flamestorm gauntlets replaced with: 2 auto boltstorm gauntlets and 1 fragstorm grenade launcher each.

ABILITIES

Angels of Death, **Combat Squads** (pg 124-125)

FACTION KEYWORDS: IMPERIUM, ADEPTUS ASTARTES, \<CHAPTER\>
KEYWORDS: INFANTRY, CORE, PRIMARIS, MK X GRAVIS, AGGRESSOR SQUAD

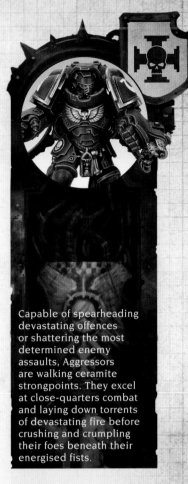

Capable of spearheading devastating offences or shattering the most determined enemy assaults, Aggressors are walking ceramite strongpoints. They excel at close-quarters combat and laying down torrents of devastating fire before crushing and crumpling their foes beneath their energised fists.

Ultramarines Aggressor with auto boltstorm gauntlets and fragstorm grenade launcher

Salamanders Aggressor with flamestorm gauntlets

Imperial Fists Aggressor with auto boltstorm gauntlets and fragstorm grenade launcher

TERMINATOR ASSAULT SQUAD

9 POWER

No.	NAME	M	WS	BS	S	T	W	A	Ld	Sv
4-9	Assault Terminator	5"	3+	3+	4	4	3	2	8	2+
1	Assault Terminator Sergeant	5"	3+	3+	4	4	3	3	9	2+

If this unit contains 6 or more models, it has **Power Rating 18**. Every model is equipped with: thunder hammer; storm shield.

WEAPON	RANGE	TYPE	S	AP	D	ABILITIES
Lightning claw	Melee	Melee	User	-2	1	Each time the bearer fights, it makes 1 additional attack with this weapon. Each time an attack is made with this weapon, you can re-roll the wound roll.
Thunder hammer	Melee	Melee	x2	-2	3	Each time an attack is made with this weapon, subtract 1 from that attack's hit roll.

OTHER WARGEAR	ABILITIES
Storm shield	The bearer has a 4+ invulnerable save. In addition, add 1 to armour saving throws made for the bearer.
Teleport homer	Once per battle, at the start of your Movement phase, you can remove this unit from the battlefield and then, in the Reinforcements step of your next Movement phase, you can set this unit back up on the battlefield, anywhere wholly within your own deployment zone and more than 9" from any enemy models, or anywhere within 3" of a friendly <CHAPTER> model and more than 9" from any enemy models. If the battle ends and this unit is not on the battlefield, it is destroyed. If this unit has split into two units because of its Combat Squads ability (pg 125), only one of those units can use the Teleport Homer ability.
	We recommend placing a Teleport Homer model next to the unit as a reminder, removing it once this ability has been used (a Teleport Homer does not count as a model for any rules purposes).

WARGEAR OPTIONS

- Any number of models can each have their thunder hammer and storm shield replaced with 2 lightning claws.
- The unit can be equipped with 1 teleport homer.

ABILITIES

Angels of Death, Combat Squads, Teleport Strike (pg 124-125)

Deathwing: If this unit is from the Dark Angels Chapter (or one of its successor Chapters), it has the **DEATHWING** keyword.

Crux Terminatus: Every model in this unit has a 5+ invulnerable save.

Wolf Guard: If this unit is from the Space Wolves Chapter (or one of its successor Chapters), it has the **WOLF GUARD** keyword.

FACTION KEYWORDS: IMPERIUM, ADEPTUS ASTARTES, <CHAPTER>
KEYWORDS: INFANTRY, CORE, TERMINATOR, TERMINATOR ASSAULT SQUAD

Terminator Assault Squads are armed with devastating close combat weaponry perfect for ferocious vanguard assaults and savage boarding actions. They rush to engage the enemy's greatest warriors, shredding the foe with lightning claws or shattering their skulls with thunder hammers.

TERMINATOR SQUAD

9 POWER

No.	NAME	M	WS	BS	S	T	W	A	Ld	Sv
4-9	Terminator	5"	3+	3+	4	4	3	2	8	2+
1	Terminator Sergeant	5"	3+	3+	4	4	3	3	9	2+

If this unit contains 6 or more models, it has **Power Rating 18**. The Terminator Sergeant is equipped with: storm bolter; power sword. Every Terminator is equipped with: storm bolter; power fist.

WEAPON	RANGE	TYPE	S	AP	D	ABILITIES
Assault cannon	24"	Heavy 6	6	-1	1	-
Cyclone missile launcher		Before selecting targets, select one of the profiles below to make attacks with.				
- Frag missile	36"	Heavy 2D6	4	0	1	Blast
- Krak missile	36"	Heavy 2	8	-2	D6	-
Heavy flamer	12"	Heavy D6	5	-1	1	Each time an attack is made with this weapon, that attack automatically hits the target.
Storm bolter	24"	Rapid Fire 2	4	0	1	-
Chainfist	Melee	Melee	x2	-4	D3	Each time an attack is made with this weapon, subtract 1 from that attack's hit roll, and if that attack is allocated to a **VEHICLE** model, that attack has a Damage characteristic of 3.
Power fist	Melee	Melee	x2	-3	2	Each time an attack is made with this weapon, subtract 1 from that attack's hit roll.
Power sword	Melee	Melee	+1	-3	1	-

OTHER WARGEAR	ABILITIES
Teleport homer	Once per battle, at the start of your Movement phase, you can remove this unit from the battlefield and then, in the Reinforcements step of your next Movement phase, you can set this unit back up on the battlefield, anywhere wholly within your own deployment zone and more than 9" from any enemy models, or anywhere within 3" of a friendly **<CHAPTER>** model and more than 9" from any enemy models. If the battle ends and this unit is not on the battlefield, it is destroyed. If this unit has split into two units because of its Combat Squads ability (pg 125), only one of those units can use the Teleport Homer ability. *We recommend placing a Teleport Homer model next to the unit as a reminder, removing it once this ability has been used (a Teleport Homer does not count as a model for any rules purposes).*

WARGEAR OPTIONS

- For every 5 models this unit contains, 1 Terminator's storm bolter can be replaced with one of the following: 1 assault cannon; 1 heavy flamer; 1 storm bolter and 1 cyclone missile launcher.
- Any number of models can each have their power fist replaced with 1 chainfist.
- The unit can be equipped with 1 teleport homer.

ABILITIES

Angels of Death, **Combat Squads**, **Teleport Strike** (pg 124-125)

Crux Terminatus: Every model in this unit has a 5+ invulnerable save.

Deathwing: If this unit is from the Dark Angels Chapter (or one of its successor Chapters), it has the **DEATHWING** keyword.

Wolf Guard: If this unit is from the Space Wolves Chapter (or one of its successor Chapters), it has the **WOLF GUARD** keyword.

FACTION KEYWORDS: IMPERIUM, ADEPTUS ASTARTES, <CHAPTER>
KEYWORDS: INFANTRY, CORE, TERMINATOR, TERMINATOR SQUAD

Terminator armour is a marvel of technology that enables its wearer to survive anything, from the stresses of teleportation to earth-shaking artillery bombardments. So equipped, Terminator Squads can appear in the midst of the foe or stride unstoppably across the field towards them, firing their weapons all the while.

RELIC TERMINATOR SQUAD

9 POWER

No.	NAME	M	WS	BS	S	T	W	A	Ld	Sv
4-9	Relic Terminator	5"	3+	3+	4	4	3	2	8	2+
1	Relic Terminator Sergeant	5"	3+	3+	4	4	3	3	9	2+

If this unit contains 6 or more models, it has **Power Rating 18**. Every model is equipped with: combi-bolter; power fist.

WEAPON	RANGE	TYPE	S	AP	D	ABILITIES
Combi-bolter	24"	Rapid Fire 2	4	0	1	-
Grenade harness	12"	Assault D6	4	-1	1	Blast
Heavy flamer	12"	Heavy D6	5	-1	1	Each time an attack is made with this weapon, that attack automatically hits the target.
Plasma blaster		Before selecting targets, select one of the profiles below to make attacks with.				
- Standard	18"	Assault 2	7	-3	1	-
- Supercharge	18"	Assault 2	8	-3	2	If any unmodified hit rolls of 1 are made for attacks with this weapon profile, the bearer is destroyed after shooting with this weapon.
Reaper autocannon	36"	Heavy 4	7	-2	1	-
Volkite charger	20"	Heavy 2	5	0	2	Each time an attack is made with this weapon, an unmodified wound roll of 6 inflicts 1 mortal wound on the target in addition to any normal damage.
Chainfist	Melee	Melee	x2	-4	D3	Each time an attack is made with this weapon, subtract 1 from that attack's hit roll, and if that attack is allocated to a **Vehicle** model, that attack has a Damage characteristic of 3.
Lightning claw	Melee	Melee	User	-2	1	Each time the bearer fights, it makes 1 additional attack with this weapon. Each time an attack is made with this weapon, you can re-roll the wound roll.
Power fist	Melee	Melee	x2	-3	2	Each time an attack is made with this weapon, subtract 1 from that attack's hit roll.
Power sword	Melee	Melee	+1	-3	1	-

WARGEAR OPTIONS

- For every 5 models in this unit, 1 Relic Terminator's combi-bolter can be replaced with one of the following: 1 heavy flamer; 1 reaper autocannon.
- For every 5 models in this unit, 1 model can be equipped with 1 grenade harness.
- Any number of models can each have their combi-bolter replaced with 1 lightning claw.
- Any number of models can each have their power fist replaced with one of the following: 1 chainfist; 1 lightning claw.
- The Relic Terminator Sergeant's combi-bolter can be replaced with one of the following: 1 plasma blaster; 1 volkite charger.
- The Relic Terminator Sergeant's power fist can be replaced with 1 power sword.

ABILITIES

Angels of Death, **Combat Squads**, **Teleport Strike** (pg 124-125)

Crux Terminatus: Every model in this unit has a 5+ invulnerable save.

Deathwing: If this unit is from the Dark Angels Chapter (or one of its successor Chapters), it has the **Deathwing** keyword.

Wolf Guard: If this unit is from the Space Wolves Chapter (or one of its successor Chapters), it has the **Wolf Guard** keyword.

FACTION KEYWORDS: Imperium, Adeptus Astartes, <Chapter>
KEYWORDS: Infantry, Core, Terminator, Relic Terminator Squad

Many Chapters possess suits of Terminator armour – such as those of the Cataphractii or Tartaros variety – that date back to the Great Crusade. Each is revered as a relic of the Chapter, and those privileged enough to wear them fight all the harder knowing the legacy of glory and sacrifice they bear.

CENTURION ASSAULT SQUAD 9 POWER

No.	NAME	M	WS	BS	S	T	W	A	Ld	Sv
2-5	Assault Centurion	5"	3+	3+	5	5	4	3	7	2+
1	Assault Centurion Sergeant	5"	3+	3+	5	5	4	4	8	2+

If this unit contains 4 or more models, it has **Power Rating 18**. Every model is equipped with: 2 flamers; siege drills; Centurion assault launchers.

WEAPON	RANGE	TYPE	S	AP	D	ABILITIES
Flamer	12"	Assault D6	4	0	1	Each time an attack is made with this weapon, that attack automatically hits the target.
Hurricane bolter	24"	Rapid Fire 6	4	0	1	-
Siege drills	Melee	Melee	x2	-4	3	-

OTHER WARGEAR	ABILITIES
Centurion assault launcher	While the bearer is on the battlefield, its unit has the **ASSAULT LAUNCHERS** keyword.

WARGEAR OPTIONS

- Any number of models can each have their 2 flamers replaced with 2 meltaguns.
- Any number of models can each have their Centurion assault launcher replaced with 1 hurricane bolter.

ABILITIES

Angels of Death, **Combat Squads** (pg 124-125)

Omniscope: Each time a model in this unit makes a ranged attack, if this unit contains a Centurion Sergeant, then the target does not receive the benefits of cover against that attack.

FACTION KEYWORDS: IMPERIUM, ADEPTUS ASTARTES, <CHAPTER>
KEYWORDS: INFANTRY, CENTURION, CENTURION ASSAULT SQUAD

There are few technologies better adapted for siege warfare than the Centurion Warsuit. Wading into thunderous storms of enemy fire, Centurion Assault Squads use their roaring siege drills to crack open armoured bunkers and tear apart tanks.

INVICTOR TACTICAL WARSUIT 8 POWER

Some of this model's characteristics change as it suffers damage, as shown below:

No.	Name	M	WS	BS	S	T	W	A	Ld	Sv
1	Invictor Tactical Warsuit (7+ wounds remaining)	10"	3+	3+	7	6	13	4	8	3+
	Invictor Tactical Warsuit (4-6 wounds remaining)	8"	4+	4+	7	6	N/A	4	8	3+
	Invictor Tactical Warsuit (1-3 wounds remaining)	6"	5+	5+	7	6	N/A	4	8	3+

An Invictor Tactical Warsuit is equipped with: fragstorm grenade launcher; heavy bolter; incendium cannon; twin ironhail heavy stubber; Invictor fist.

WEAPON	RANGE	TYPE	S	AP	D	ABILITIES
Fragstorm grenade launcher	18"	Assault D6	4	0	1	Blast
Heavy bolter	36"	Heavy 3	5	-1	2	-
Incendium cannon	12"	Heavy 2D6	5	-1	1	Each time an attack is made with this weapon, that attack automatically hits the target.
Twin ironhail heavy stubber	36"	Heavy 8	4	-1	1	-
Twin ironhail autocannon	48"	Heavy 6	7	-1	2	-
Invictor fist	Melee	Melee	x2	-3	3	-

WARGEAR OPTIONS

- This model's incendium cannon can be replaced with 1 twin ironhail autocannon.

ABILITIES

Angels of Death, **Concealed Positions** (pg 124-125)

Explodes: When this model is destroyed, roll one D6 before removing it from play. On a 6 it explodes, and each unit within 6" suffers D3 mortal wounds.

FACTION KEYWORDS: IMPERIUM, ADEPTUS ASTARTES, <CHAPTER>
KEYWORDS: VEHICLE, INVICTOR TACTICAL WARSUIT

Outfitted with silent reactors and servos, the Invictor Tactical Warsuit is a combat walker ideally suited to support Vanguard operations and function independently from a main Space Marine strike force. In battle they are piloted by hand-picked warriors dedicated to defending their battle-brothers.

Dreadnoughts are bipedal combat walkers piloted by centuries-old fallen heroes of the Chapter, kept alive by esoteric technologies in an ancient sarcophagus at the Dreadnought's heart. Equipped with devastating heavy weapons, they can annihilate the enemy from afar or crush them to paste in brutal melee.

DREADNOUGHT 7 POWER

No.	Name	M	WS	BS	S	T	W	A	Ld	Sv
1	Dreadnought	6"	3+	3+	6	7	8	4	8	3+

A Dreadnought is equipped with: assault cannon; storm bolter; Dreadnought combat weapon.

WEAPON	RANGE	TYPE	S	AP	D	ABILITIES
Assault cannon	24"	Heavy 6	6	-1	1	-
Storm bolter	24"	Rapid Fire 2	4	0	1	-
Dreadnought combat weapon	Melee	Melee	x2	-3	3	-
Great wolf claw	Melee	Melee	+4	-2	3	Each time an attack is made with this weapon, you can re-roll the wound roll.

WARGEAR OPTIONS

- This model's assault cannon can be replaced with 1 weapon from the *Dreadnought Weapons* list.
- This model's Dreadnought combat weapon and storm bolter can be replaced with one of the following:
  - 1 missile launcher.
  - 1 Dreadnought combat weapon and 1 heavy flamer.
- If this model is from the Space Wolves Chapter (or one of its successor Chapters), its Dreadnought combat weapon can be replaced with 1 great wolf claw.

ABILITIES

Angels of Death (pg 124-125)

Duty Eternal: Each time an attack is allocated to this model, subtract 1 from the Damage characteristic of that attack (to a minimum of 1).

Explodes: When this model is destroyed, roll one D6 before removing it from play. On a 6 it explodes, and each unit within 3" suffers 1 mortal wound.

FACTION KEYWORDS: IMPERIUM, ADEPTUS ASTARTES, <CHAPTER>
KEYWORDS: VEHICLE, CORE, SMOKESCREEN, DREADNOUGHT

During the Great Crusade, hundreds of Contemptor Dreadnoughts strode the battlefield in the Emperor's name. Now but a handful remain. They are no less powerful for this, fitted with atomantic field generators that shield them from harm while wielding weapons that can annihilate infantry and armour alike.

CONTEMPTOR DREADNOUGHT 8 POWER

No.	Name	M	WS	BS	S	T	W	A	Ld	Sv
1	Contemptor Dreadnought	8"	3+	3+	7	7	9	4	8	3+

A Contemptor Dreadnought is equipped with: combi-bolter; multi-melta; Dreadnought combat weapon.

WEAPON	RANGE	TYPE	S	AP	D	ABILITIES
Combi-bolter	24"	Rapid Fire 2	4	0	1	-
Kheres-pattern assault cannon	24"	Heavy 6	7	-1	1	-
Multi-melta	24"	Heavy 2	8	-4	D6	Each time an attack made with this weapon targets a unit within half range, that attack has a Damage characteristic of D6+2.
Dreadnought combat weapon	Melee	Melee	x2	-3	3	-

WARGEAR OPTIONS

- This model's multi-melta can be replaced with 1 kheres-pattern assault cannon.

ABILITIES

Angels of Death (pg 124-125)

Atomantic Shielding: This model has a 5+ invulnerable save.

Duty Eternal: Each time an attack is allocated to this model, subtract 1 from the Damage characteristic of that attack (to a minimum of 1).

Explodes: When this model is destroyed, roll one D6 before removing it from play. On a 6 it explodes, and each unit within 3" suffers 1 mortal wound.

FACTION KEYWORDS: IMPERIUM, ADEPTUS ASTARTES, <CHAPTER>
KEYWORDS: VEHICLE, CORE, DREADNOUGHT, CONTEMPTOR DREADNOUGHT

VENERABLE DREADNOUGHT

8 POWER

No.	Name	M	WS	BS	S	T	W	A	Ld	Sv
1	Venerable Dreadnought	6"	2+	2+	6	7	8	4	8	3+

A Venerable Dreadnought is equipped with: assault cannon; storm bolter; Dreadnought combat weapon.

WEAPON	RANGE	TYPE	S	AP	D	ABILITIES
Assault cannon	24"	Heavy 6	6	-1	1	-
Storm bolter	24"	Rapid Fire 2	4	0	1	-
Dreadnought combat weapon	Melee	Melee	x2	-3	3	-
Fenrisian great axe	Each time an attack is made with this weapon, select one of the profiles below to make that attack with.					
- Cleave	Melee	Melee	+4	-3	D3+3	Each time an attack is made with this weapon profile, subtract 1 from that attack's hit roll.
- Scythe	Melee	Melee	User	-3	1	Each time an attack is made with this weapon profile, make 2 hit rolls instead of 1.
Great wolf claw	Melee	Melee	+4	-2	3	Each time an attack is made with this weapon, you can re-roll the wound roll.

OTHER WARGEAR	ABILITIES
Blizzard shield	The bearer has a 4+ invulnerable save.

WARGEAR OPTIONS

- This model's assault cannon can be replaced with 1 weapon from the *Dreadnought Weapons* list.
- This model's Dreadnought combat weapon and storm bolter can be replaced with one of the following:
  - 1 missile launcher.
  - 1 Dreadnought combat weapon and 1 heavy flamer.
- If this model is from the Space Wolves Chapter (or one of its successor Chapters), its Dreadnought combat weapon can be replaced with 1 great wolf claw.
- If this model is from the Space Wolves Chapter (or one of its successor Chapters), its assault cannon and Dreadnought combat weapon can be replaced with 1 Fenrisian great axe and 1 blizzard shield.

ABILITIES

Angels of Death (pg 124-125)

Explodes: When this model is destroyed, roll one D6 before removing it from play. On a 6 it explodes, and each unit within 3" suffers 1 mortal wound.

Duty Eternal: Each time an attack is allocated to this model, subtract 1 from the Damage characteristic of that attack (to a minimum of 1).

Unyielding Ancient: Each time this model would lose a wound, roll one D6: on a 6, that wound is not lost.

FACTION KEYWORDS: IMPERIUM, ADEPTUS ASTARTES, <CHAPTER>
KEYWORDS: VEHICLE, CORE, DREADNOUGHT, SMOKESCREEN, VENERABLE DREADNOUGHT

Among the most ancient war machines fighting upon the battlefields of the 41st Millennium, Venerable Dreadnoughts are holders of knowledge all but lost and maintainers of traditions all but forgotten. Every battle-brother of their Chapter reveres them, and all take heed when they lend their invaluable wisdom and might.

IRONCLAD DREADNOUGHT

8 POWER

No.	NAME	M	WS	BS	S	T	W	A	Ld	Sv
1	Ironclad Dreadnought	6"	3+	3+	6	8	8	4	8	3+

An Ironclad Dreadnought is equipped with: meltagun; storm bolter; Ironclad combat weapon; seismic hammer.

WEAPON	RANGE	TYPE	S	AP	D	ABILITIES
Hurricane bolter	24"	Rapid Fire 6	4	0	1	-
Meltagun	12"	Assault 1	8	-4	D6	Each time an attack made with this weapon targets a unit within half range, that attack has a Damage characteristic of D6+2.
Storm bolter	24"	Rapid Fire 2	4	0	1	-
Dreadnought chainfist	Melee	Melee	x2	-4	2D3	Each time an attack made with this weapon is allocated to a **VEHICLE** model, that attack has a Damage characteristic of 6.
Ironclad combat weapon	Melee	Melee	x2	-3	3	-
Seismic hammer	Melee	Melee	x2	-4	5	Each time an attack is made with this weapon, subtract 1 from that attack's hit roll.

OTHER WARGEAR	ABILITIES
Ironclad assault launchers	The bearer has the **ASSAULT LAUNCHERS** keyword.

WARGEAR OPTIONS

- This model's seismic hammer can be replaced with 1 Dreadnought chainfist.
- This model's Ironclad combat weapon and storm bolter can be replaced with 1 hurricane bolter.
- This model's storm bolter can be replaced with 1 heavy flamer.
- This model's meltagun can be replaced with 1 heavy flamer.
- This model can be equipped with up to 2 hunter-killer missiles.
- This model can be equipped with 1 Ironclad assault launchers.

ABILITIES

Angels of Death (pg 124-125)

Wrecker: Each time this model makes a melee attack, if it is equipped with an Ironclad combat weapon, re-roll a hit roll of 1.

Duty Eternal: Each time an attack is allocated to this model, subtract 1 from the Damage characteristic of that attack (to a minimum of 1).

Explodes: When this model is destroyed, roll one D6 before removing it from play. On a 6 it explodes, and each unit within 3" suffers 1 mortal wound.

FACTION KEYWORDS: IMPERIUM, ADEPTUS ASTARTES, <CHAPTER>
KEYWORDS: VEHICLE, CORE, DREADNOUGHT, SMOKESCREEN, IRONCLAD DREADNOUGHT

Clad with slabs of ceramite plating and equipped to rend ferrocrete or reduce thick walls to rubble, the Ironclad Dreadnought has been perfected for siege warfare. It is akin to a giant battering ram, pummelling through enemy positions while flooding them with burning promethium and torrents of mass-reactive bolts.

REDEMPTOR DREADNOUGHT

9 POWER

Some of this model's characteristics change as it suffers damage, as shown below:

No.	Name	M	WS	BS	S	T	W	A	Ld	Sv
1	Redemptor Dreadnought (7+ wounds remaining)	8"	3+	3+	7	7	13	4	8	3+
	Redemptor Dreadnought (4-6 wounds remaining)	6"	4+	4+	7	7	N/A	4	8	3+
	Redemptor Dreadnought (1-3 wounds remaining)	4"	5+	5+	7	7	N/A	4	8	3+

A Redemptor Dreadnought is equipped with: 2 fragstorm grenade launchers; heavy flamer; heavy onslaught gatling cannon; Redemptor fist.

WEAPON	RANGE	TYPE	S	AP	D	ABILITIES
Fragstorm grenade launcher	18"	Assault D6	4	0	1	Blast
Heavy flamer	12"	Heavy D6	5	-1	1	Each time an attack is made with this weapon, that attack automatically hits the target.
Heavy onslaught gatling cannon	30"	Heavy 12	6	-1	1	-
Icarus rocket pod	24"	Heavy D3	7	-1	2	Blast. Each time an attack is made with this weapon against an **Aircraft** unit, add 1 to that attack's hit roll.
Macro plasma incinerator		Before selecting targets, select one of the profiles below to make attacks with.				
- Standard	36"	Heavy D6	8	-4	2	Blast
- Supercharge	36"	Heavy D6	9	-4	3	Blast. Each time an unmodified hit roll of 1 is made for an attack with this weapon profile, the bearer suffers 1 mortal wound after shooting with this weapon.
Onslaught gatling cannon	24"	Heavy 8	5	-1	1	-
Storm bolter	24"	Rapid Fire 2	4	0	1	-
Redemptor fist	Melee	Melee	x2	-3	D3+3	-

WARGEAR OPTIONS

- This model can be equipped with 1 Icarus rocket pod.
- This model's heavy flamer can be replaced with 1 onslaught gatling cannon.
- This model's heavy onslaught gatling cannon can be replaced with 1 macro plasma incinerator.
- This model's 2 fragstorm grenade launchers can be replaced with 2 storm bolters.

ABILITIES

Angels of Death (pg 124-125)

Duty Eternal: Each time an attack is allocated to this model, subtract 1 from the Damage characteristic of that attack (to a minimum of 1).

Explodes: When this model is destroyed, roll one D6 before removing it from play. On a 6 it explodes, and each unit within 6" suffers D3 mortal wounds.

FACTION KEYWORDS: **Imperium, Adeptus Astartes, <Chapter>**
KEYWORDS: **Vehicle, Core, Dreadnought, Redemptor Dreadnought**

Redemptor Dreadnoughts are some of the largest of their kind ever fielded by the Adeptus Astartes. Armed to the teeth, they can be equipped to utterly destroy virtually any kind of battlefield target with hails of solid shot or super-heated plasma.

ASSAULT SQUAD

5 POWER

No.	NAME	M	WS	BS	S	T	W	A	Ld	Sv
4-9	Assault Marine	6"	3+	3+	4	4	2	1	7	3+
1	Assault Marine Sergeant	6"	3+	3+	4	4	2	2	8	3+

If this unit contains 6 or more models, it has **Power Rating 10**. Every model is equipped with: bolt pistol; Astartes chainsword; frag grenades; krak grenades.

WEAPON	RANGE	TYPE	S	AP	D	ABILITIES
Bolt pistol	12"	Pistol 1	4	0	1	-
Astartes chainsword	Melee	Melee	User	-1	1	Each time the bearer fights, it makes 1 additional attack with this weapon.
Eviscerator	Melee	Melee	+3	-4	2	Each time an attack is made with this weapon, subtract 1 from that attack's hit roll.

OTHER WARGEAR	ABILITIES
Jump pack	The bearer has a Move characteristic of 12", the Death From Above ability (pg 125) and the **FLY** and **JUMP PACK** keywords.
Combat shield	The bearer has a 5+ invulnerable save. In addition, add 1 to armour saving throws made for the bearer.

WARGEAR OPTIONS

- The Assault Marine Sergeant's bolt pistol can be replaced with one of the following: 1 weapon from the *Pistols* list; 1 weapon from the *Melee Weapons* list.
- The Assault Marine Sergeant's Astartes chainsword can be replaced with 1 weapon from the *Melee Weapons* list.
- The Assault Marine Sergeant can be equipped with 1 combat shield.
- Up to 2 Assault Marines can each have their bolt pistol and Astartes chainsword replaced with one of the following:
  - 1 plasma pistol and 1 Astartes chainsword.
  - 1 flamer.
- For every 5 models in this unit, 1 model's Astartes chainsword can be replaced with 1 eviscerator.
- All of the models in the unit can be equipped with 1 jump pack each (**Power Rating +1** if the unit contains 5 models, **Power Rating +2** if the unit contains 6 or more models).

ABILITIES

Angels of Death, **Combat Squads** (pg 124-125)

FACTION KEYWORDS: IMPERIUM, ADEPTUS ASTARTES, <CHAPTER>
KEYWORDS: INFANTRY, CORE, MELTA BOMBS, ASSAULT SQUAD

Experts in brutal close-quarters fighting, Assault Squads take pride in drawing the most gruelling battlefield assignments. Thanks to their powerful jump packs they soar over the battlefield, slamming into the foe and cutting them down before shooting off to the next.

Bolt pistol

Ultramarines Assault Marine with jump pack and flamer

Ultramarines Sergeant with jump pack and eviscerator

Blood Angels Sergeant with thunder hammer, bolt pistol and combat shield

Dark Angels Sergeant with plasma pistol and power sword

OUTRIDER SQUAD

6 POWER

No.	Name	M	WS	BS	S	T	W	A	Ld	Sv
2	Outrider	14"	3+	3+	4	5	4	2	7	3+
1	Outrider Sergeant	14"	3+	3+	4	5	4	3	8	3+

Every model is equipped with: heavy bolt pistol; twin bolt rifle; Astartes chainsword, frag grenades; krak grenades.

WEAPON	RANGE	TYPE	S	AP	D	ABILITIES
Heavy bolt pistol	18"	Pistol 1	4	-1	1	-
Twin bolt rifle	30"	Rapid Fire 2	4	-1	1	-
Astartes chainsword	Melee	Melee	User	-1	1	Each time the bearer fights, it makes 1 additional attack with this weapon.

ABILITIES

Angels of Death (pg 124-125)

Devastating Charge: Each time this unit fights, if it made a charge move this turn, then until that fight is resolved, add 2 to the Attacks characteristic of models in this unit.

Turbo-boost: Each time this unit Advances, do not make an Advance roll. Instead, until the end of the phase, add 6" to the Move characteristic of models in this unit.

Ravenwing: If this unit is from the Dark Angels Chapter (or one of its successor Chapters), it has the **RAVENWING** keyword.

FACTION KEYWORDS: IMPERIUM, ADEPTUS ASTARTES, <CHAPTER>
KEYWORDS: BIKER, CORE, PRIMARIS, OUTRIDER SQUAD

Outrider Squads advance ahead of the main Space Marine lines, guard flanks of larger formations and hunt down enemy infiltrators. When battle is joined, they conduct lightning fast hit-and-run attacks on defended positions, and run down those who would try to escape the vengeance of the Chapter.

INVADER ATV SQUAD

4 POWER

No.	Name	M	WS	BS	S	T	W	A	Ld	Sv
1-3	Invader ATV	14"	3+	3+	4	5	8	4	7	3+

If this unit contains 2 models, it has **Power Rating 8**. If this unit contains 3 models, it has **Power Rating 12**. Every model is equipped with: bolt pistol; onslaught gatling cannon; twin auto bolt rifle; frag grenades; krak grenades.

WEAPON	RANGE	TYPE	S	AP	D	ABILITIES
Bolt pistol	12"	Pistol 1	4	0	1	-
Multi-melta	24"	Heavy 2	8	-4	D6	Each time an attack made with this weapon targets a unit within half range, that attack has a Damage characteristic of D6+2.
Onslaught gatling cannon	24"	Heavy 8	5	-1	1	-
Twin auto bolt rifle	24"	Assault 6	4	0	1	-

WARGEAR OPTIONS

- Any number of models can each have their onslaught gatling cannon replaced with 1 multi-melta.

ABILITIES

Angels of Death (pg 124-125)

Turbo-boost: Each time this unit Advances, do not make an Advance roll. Instead, until the end of the phase, add 6" to the Move characteristic of models in this unit.

Ravenwing: If this unit is from the Dark Angels Chapter (or one of its successor Chapters), it has the **RAVENWING** keyword.

Explodes: Each time a model in this unit is destroyed, roll one D6 before removing it from play. On a 6 it explodes, and each unit within 3" suffers 1 mortal wound.

FACTION KEYWORDS: IMPERIUM, ADEPTUS ASTARTES, <CHAPTER>
KEYWORDS: BIKER, PRIMARIS, INVADER ATV SQUAD

The Invader is a highly flexible all-terrain vehicle, perfectly adapted to an aggressive reconnaissance role. Outfitted with either a multi-melta or onslaught gatling cannon, it can rapidly deliver punishing fire against vulnerable parts of the enemy line, or swiftly engage and destroy scouting elements of opposing forces.

BIKE SQUAD

No.	NAME	M	WS	BS	S	T	W	A	Ld	Sv
2-7	Space Marine Biker	14"	3+	3+	4	5	3	1	7	3+
1	Biker Sergeant	14"	3+	3+	4	5	3	2	8	3+
0-1	Attack Bike	14"	3+	3+	4	5	4	2	7	3+

If this unit contains between 3 and 5 Space Marine Biker models, it has **Power Rating 9**. If this unit contains 6 or more Space Marine Biker models, it has **Power Rating 12**. If this unit contains an Attack Bike model, it has **Power Rating +2**.

- The Biker Sergeant and every Space Marine Biker is equipped with: bolt pistol; twin boltgun; frag grenades; krak grenades.
- An Attack Bike is equipped with: bolt pistol; heavy bolter; twin boltgun; frag grenades; krak grenades.

WEAPON	RANGE	TYPE	S	AP	D	ABILITIES
Bolt pistol	12"	Pistol 1	4	0	1	-
Boltgun	24"	Rapid Fire 1	4	0	1	-
Heavy bolter	36"	Heavy 3	5	-1	2	-
Multi-melta	24"	Heavy 2	8	-4	D6	Each time an attack made with this weapon targets a unit within half range, that attack has a Damage characteristic of D6+2.
Twin boltgun	24"	Rapid Fire 2	4	0	1	-
Astartes chainsword	Melee	Melee	User	-1	1	Each time the bearer fights, it makes 1 additional attack with this weapon.

WARGEAR OPTIONS

- The Biker Sergeant's bolt pistol can be replaced with one of the following: 1 boltgun; 1 weapon from the *Combi-weapons* list; 1 weapon from the *Melee Weapons* list; 1 weapon from the *Pistols* list.
- Any number of Space Marine Bikers can each have their bolt pistol replaced with 1 Astartes chainsword.
- Up to 2 Space Marine Bikers can each have their bolt pistol replaced with one of the following: 1 plasma pistol; 1 weapon from the *Special Weapons* list. A model can only take a plasma pistol if it is from the Space Wolves Chapter (or one of its successor Chapters).
- The Attack Bike's heavy bolter can be replaced with 1 multi-melta.

ABILITIES

Angels of Death, Combat Squads (pg 124-125)

Turbo-boost: Each time this unit Advances, do not make an Advance roll. Instead, until the end of the phase, add 6" to the Move characteristic of models in this unit.

Ravenwing: If this unit is from the Dark Angels Chapter (or one of its successor Chapters), it has the **RAVENWING** keyword.

Swiftclaw: If this unit is from the Space Wolves Chapter (or one of its successor Chapters), it has the **SWIFTCLAW** keyword and contains 1 Biker Sergeant and between 2-14 Space Marine Bikers.

If this unit contains between 3 and 5 Space Marine Biker models, it has **Power Rating 9**. If this unit contains 6-8 Space Marine Biker models, it has **Power Rating 14**. If this unit contains 9-11 Space Marine Biker models, it has **Power Rating 18**. If this unit contains 12 or more Space Marine Biker models, it has **Power Rating 23**. If this unit contains an Attack Bike, it has **Power Rating +2**.

FACTION KEYWORDS: IMPERIUM, ADEPTUS ASTARTES, <CHAPTER>
KEYWORDS: BIKER, CORE, BIKE SQUAD

Deployed in rapid-assault missions based on intelligence gathered by Scouts and Vanguard forces, Bikers can smash through enemy lines, battlefield obstacles and even ferrocrete walls due to the raw fury of their mounts' engines. Their sheer bulk belies their phenomenal power, speed and manoeuvrability.

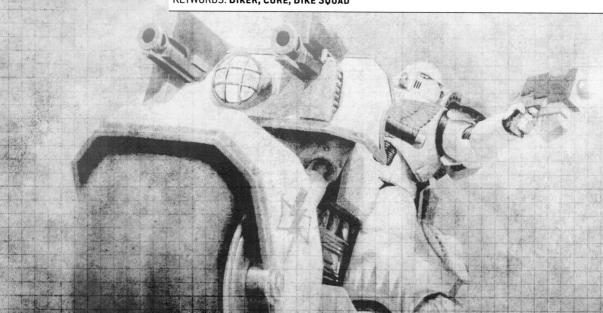

SCOUT BIKE SQUAD

5 POWER

No.	Name	M	WS	BS	S	T	W	A	Ld	Sv
2-8	Scout Biker	16"	3+	3+	4	5	2	1	7	4+
1	Scout Biker Sergeant	16"	3+	3+	4	5	2	2	8	4+

If this unit contains between 4 and 6 models, it has **Power Rating 9**. If it contains 7 or more models, it has **Power Rating 13**. Every model is equipped with: Astartes shotgun; bolt pistol; twin boltgun; combat knife; frag grenades, krak grenades.

WEAPON	RANGE	TYPE	S	AP	D	ABILITIES
Astartes grenade launcher	Before selecting targets, select one of the profiles below to make attacks with.					
- Frag grenade	30"	Assault D6	3	0	1	Blast
- Krak grenade	30"	Assault 1	6	-1	D3	-
Astartes shotgun	18"	Assault 2	4	0	1	-
Bolt pistol	12"	Pistol 1	4	0	1	-
Twin boltgun	24"	Rapid Fire 2	4	0	1	-
Combat knife	Melee	Melee	User	0	1	Each time the bearer fights, it makes 1 additional attack with this weapon.

WARGEAR OPTIONS

- The Scout Biker Sergeant's bolt pistol can be replaced with one of the following: 1 boltgun; 1 weapon from the *Combi-weapons* list; 1 weapon from the *Melee Weapons* list; 1 weapon from the *Pistols* list.
- Any number of models can each have their twin boltgun replaced with 1 Astartes grenade launcher.

ABILITIES

Angels of Death, Combat Squads, Outflank (pg 124-125)

Turbo-boost: Each time this unit Advances, do not make an Advance roll. Instead, until the end of the phase, add 6" to the Move characteristic of models in this unit.

FACTION KEYWORDS: IMPERIUM, ADEPTUS ASTARTES, <CHAPTER>
KEYWORDS: BIKER, CORE, SCOUT, SMOKESCREEN, SCOUT BIKE SQUAD

Fast-moving recon and disruption units, Scout Bike Squads operate far beyond friendly lines. They booby trap neutral ground, sever the foe's communications links, burn enemy supplies, seek out weaknesses in defences and set up locator beacons to draw down the Space Marines' fearsome orbital strikes.

ATTACK BIKE SQUAD

2 POWER

No.	Name	M	WS	BS	S	T	W	A	Ld	Sv
1-3	Attack Bike	14"	3+	3+	4	5	4	2	7	3+

If this unit contains 2 models, it has **Power Rating 4**. If this unit contains 3 models, it has **Power Rating 6**. Every model is equipped with: bolt pistol; heavy bolter; twin boltgun; frag grenades; krak grenades.

WEAPON	RANGE	TYPE	S	AP	D	ABILITIES
Bolt pistol	12"	Pistol 1	4	0	1	-
Heavy bolter	36"	Heavy 3	5	-1	2	-
Multi-melta	24"	Heavy 2	8	-4	D6	Each time an attack made with this weapon targets a unit within half range, that attack has a Damage characteristic of D6+2.
Twin boltgun	24"	Rapid Fire 2	4	0	1	-

WARGEAR OPTIONS

- Any number of models can each have their heavy bolter replaced with 1 multi-melta.

ABILITIES

Angels of Death (pg 124-125)

Turbo-boost: Each time this unit Advances, do not make an Advance roll. Instead, until the end of the phase, add 6" to the Move characteristic of models in this unit.

Ravenwing: If this unit is from the Dark Angels Chapter (or one of its successor Chapters), it has the **RAVENWING** keyword.

Swiftclaw: If this unit is from the Space Wolves Chapter (or one of its successor Chapters), it has the **SWIFTCLAW** Keyword.

FACTION KEYWORDS: IMPERIUM, ADEPTUS ASTARTES, <CHAPTER>
KEYWORDS: BIKER, CORE, ATTACK BIKE SQUAD

For those missions where a Space Marine Bike Squad is insufficient, an Attack Bike joins them. Capable of mauling infantry squads or turning tanks into raging fireballs, they render bike formations all the more deadly. They are so effective that many Chapters field squads of these rapidly moving hunters.

SUPPRESSOR SQUAD

5 POWER

No.	Name	M	WS	BS	S	T	W	A	Ld	Sv
2	Suppressor	12"	3+	3+	4	4	2	2	7	3+
1	Suppressor Sergeant	12"	3+	3+	4	4	2	3	8	3+

Every model is equipped with: accelerator autocannon; bolt pistol; frag grenades; krak grenades.

WEAPON	RANGE	TYPE	S	AP	D	ABILITIES
Accelerator autocannon	48"	Heavy 3	7	-1	2	-
Bolt pistol	12"	Pistol 1	4	0	1	-

ABILITIES

Angels of Death, Death From Above (pg 124-125)

Suppressing Fire: Each time a model in this unit makes an attack with an accelerator autocannon against an enemy **INFANTRY** unit, if a hit is scored, that enemy unit cannot fire Overwatch this turn.

FACTION KEYWORDS: IMPERIUM, ADEPTUS ASTARTES, <CHAPTER>
KEYWORDS: INFANTRY, CORE, PRIMARIS, FLY, JUMP PACK, SMOKESCREEN, SUPPRESSOR SQUAD

Girded in armour that can tolerate the vicious recoil of their weapons and the terrible stresses of grav-drops, Suppressors rapidly take up key positions on the battlefield. From there, they unleash deluges of armour-piercing rounds that decimate enemy infantry and force the survivors to dive for cover.

INCEPTOR SQUAD

6 POWER

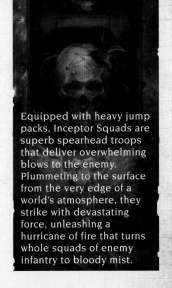

No.	Name	M	WS	BS	S	T	W	A	Ld	Sv
2-5	Inceptor	10"	3+	3+	4	5	3	2	7	3+
1	Inceptor Sergeant	10"	3+	3+	4	5	3	3	8	3+

If this unit contains 4 or more models, it has **Power Rating 12**. Every model is equipped with: 2 assault bolters.

WEAPON	RANGE	TYPE	S	AP	D	ABILITIES
Assault bolter	18"	Assault 3	5	-1	1	-
Plasma exterminator	Before selecting targets, select one of the profiles below to make attacks with.					
- Standard	18"	Assault D3	7	-3	1	Blast
- Supercharge	18"	Assault D3	8	-3	2	Blast. If any unmodified hit rolls of 1 are made for attacks with this weapon profile, the bearer is destroyed after shooting with this weapon.

WARGEAR OPTIONS

• All of the models in the unit can have their 2 assault bolters replaced with 2 plasma exterminators each.

ABILITIES

Angels of Death, Combat Squads, Death From Above (pg 124-125)

FACTION KEYWORDS: Imperium, Adeptus Astartes, <Chapter>
KEYWORDS: Infantry, Core, Primaris, Fly, Jump Pack, Mk X Gravis, Inceptor Squad

Equipped with heavy jump packs, Inceptor Squads are superb spearhead troops that deliver overwhelming blows to the enemy. Plummeting to the surface from the very edge of a world's atmosphere, they strike with devastating force, unleashing a hurricane of fire that turns whole squads of enemy infantry to bloody mist.

Ultramarines Inceptor with assault bolters

Ultramarines Inceptor Sergeant with assault bolters

Ultramarines Inceptor Sergeant with plasma exterminators

STORM SPEEDER HAILSTRIKE

8 POWER

Some of this model's characteristics change as it suffers damage, as shown below:

No.	Name	M	WS	BS	S	T	W	A	Ld	Sv
1	Storm Speeder Hailstrike (6+ wounds remaining)	16"	3+	3+	5	6	10	3	7	3+
	Storm Speeder Hailstrike (3-5 wounds remaining)	12"	3+	4+	5	6	N/A	2	7	3+
	Storm Speeder Hailstrike (1-2 wounds remaining)	8"	3+	5+	5	6	N/A	1	7	3+

A Storm Speeder Hailstrike is equipped with: 2 fragstorm grenade launchers; onslaught gatling cannon; twin ironhail heavy stubber.

WEAPON	RANGE	TYPE	S	AP	D	ABILITIES
Fragstorm grenade launcher	18"	Assault D6	4	0	1	Blast
Onslaught gatling cannon	24"	Heavy 8	5	-1	1	-
Twin ironhail heavy stubber	36"	Heavy 8	4	-1	1	-

ABILITIES

Angels of Death (pg 124-125)

Ravenwing: If this unit is from the Dark Angels Chapter (or one of its successor Chapters), it has the **Ravenwing** keyword.

Explodes: When this model is destroyed, roll one D6 before removing it from play. On a 6 it explodes, and each unit within 6" suffers D3 mortal wounds.

FACTION KEYWORDS: IMPERIUM, ADEPTUS ASTARTES, <CHAPTER>
KEYWORDS: VEHICLE, FLY, STORM SPEEDER, HAILSTRIKE

The Hailstrike is so heavily armed that it can annihilate entire swathes of infantry in fusillades of blistering projectiles. Speeding over the battlefield, its specialised loadout shatters charging formations and shreds barricades and defences.

STORM SPEEDER THUNDERSTRIKE

9 POWER

Some of this model's characteristics change as it suffers damage, as shown below:

No.	Name	M	WS	BS	S	T	W	A	Ld	Sv
1	Storm Speeder Thunderstrike (6+ wounds remaining)	16"	3+	2+	5	6	10	3	7	3+
	Storm Speeder Thunderstrike (3-5 wounds remaining)	12"	3+	3+	5	6	N/A	2	7	3+
	Storm Speeder Thunderstrike (1-2 wounds remaining)	8"	3+	4+	5	6	N/A	1	7	3+

A Storm Speeder Thunderstrike is equipped with: stormfury missiles; Thunderstrike las-talon; twin Icarus rocket pod.

WEAPON	RANGE	TYPE	S	AP	D	ABILITIES
Stormfury missiles	48"	Heavy 1	10	-3	D6	-
Thunderstrike las-talon	36"	Heavy 2	9	-3	D6	-
Twin Icarus rocket pod	24"	Heavy 2D3	7	-1	2	Blast. Each time an attack is made with this weapon against an **AIRCRAFT** unit, add 1 to that attack's hit roll.

ABILITIES

Angels of Death (pg 124-125)

Ravenwing: If this unit is from the Dark Angels Chapter (or one of its successor Chapters), it has the **Ravenwing** keyword.

Explodes: When this model is destroyed, roll one D6 before removing it from play. On a 6 it explodes, and each unit within 6" suffers D3 mortal wounds.

FACTION KEYWORDS: IMPERIUM, ADEPTUS ASTARTES, <CHAPTER>
KEYWORDS: VEHICLE, FLY, STORM SPEEDER, THUNDERSTRIKE

Thunderstrikes outmanoeuvre the foe at every turn, targeting vulnerable points in armour, fuel tanks and missile hoppers to turn tanks into raging fireballs. Just a single Thunderstrike is capable of destroying armoured breakthrough attempts, and when one is on the battlefield, few enemies are safe.

STORM SPEEDER HAMMERSTRIKE   9 POWER

Some of this model's characteristics change as it suffers damage, as shown below:

No.	Name	M	WS	BS	S	T	W	A	Ld	Sv
1	Storm Speeder Hammerstrike (6+ wounds remaining)	16"	3+	3+	5	6	10	3	7	3+
	Storm Speeder Hammerstrike (3-5 wounds remaining)	12"	3+	4+	5	6	N/A	2	7	3+
	Storm Speeder Hammerstrike (1-2 wounds remaining)	8"	3+	5+	5	6	N/A	1	7	3+

A Storm Speeder Hammerstrike is equipped with: Hammerstrike missile launcher; 2 krakstorm grenade launchers; melta destroyer.

WEAPON	RANGE	TYPE	S	AP	D	ABILITIES
Hammerstrike missile launcher	36"	Heavy 2	8	-3	3	-
Krakstorm grenade launcher	18"	Assault 1	6	-1	D3	-
Melta destroyer	24"	Heavy 3	8	-4	D6	Each time an attack made with this weapon targets a unit within half range, that attack has a Damage characteristic of D6+2.

ABILITIES

Angels of Death (pg 124-125)

Ravenwing: If this unit is from the Dark Angels Chapter (or one of its successor Chapters), it has the **Ravenwing** keyword.

Explodes: When this model is destroyed, roll one D6 before removing it from play. On a 6 it explodes, and each unit within 6" suffers D3 mortal wounds.

FACTION KEYWORDS: Imperium, Adeptus Astartes, <Chapter>
KEYWORDS: Vehicle, Fly, Storm Speeder, Hammerstrike

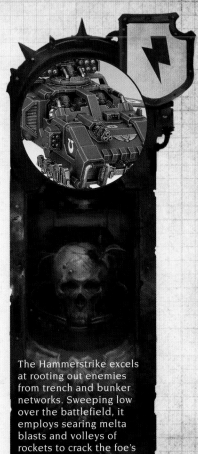

The Hammerstrike excels at rooting out enemies from trench and bunker networks. Sweeping low over the battlefield, it employs searing melta blasts and volleys of rockets to crack the foe's defence lines wide open.

LAND SPEEDERS   3 POWER

No.	Name	M	WS	BS	S	T	W	A	Ld	Sv
1-3	Land Speeder	18"	3+	3+	4	6	6	2	7	3+

If this unit contains 2 models, it has **Power Rating 6**. If this unit contains 3 models, it has **Power Rating 9**. Every model is equipped with: heavy bolter.

WEAPON	RANGE	TYPE	S	AP	D	ABILITIES
Heavy bolter	36"	Heavy 3	5	-1	2	-
Multi-melta	24"	Heavy 2	8	-4	D6	Each time an attack made with this weapon targets a unit within half range, that attack has a Damage characteristic of D6+2.

WARGEAR OPTIONS

• Any number of models can each have their heavy bolter replaced with 1 multi-melta.

ABILITIES

Angels of Death (pg 124-125)

Datalink Telemetry: At the start of your Shooting phase, select one enemy unit that is within 18" of and visible to this unit. Until the end of the phase, each time a friendly **<Chapter> Whirlwind** model makes an attack with a weapon that has the Blast ability against the selected unit, add 1 to that attack's hit roll.

Ravenwing: If this unit is from the Dark Angels Chapter (or one of its successor Chapters), it has the **Ravenwing** keyword.

Explodes: Each time a model in this unit is destroyed, roll one D6 before removing it from play. On a 6 it explodes, and each unit within 3" suffers 1 mortal wound.

FACTION KEYWORDS: Imperium, Adeptus Astartes, <Chapter>
KEYWORDS: Vehicle, Fly, Land Speeders

The remarkable grav-drives utilised by Land Speeders enables them to perform seemingly impossible feats of manoeuvrability even as they strike against the enemy. Such adaptability makes them ideal for a variety of tasks, such as scouting and counter-reconnaissance.

LAND SPEEDER TORNADOES

4 POWER

No.	Name	M	WS	BS	S	T	W	A	Ld	Sv
1-3	Land Speeder Tornado	16"	3+	3+	4	6	6	2	7	3+

If this unit contains 2 models, it has **Power Rating 8**. If this unit contains 3 models, it has **Power Rating 12**. Every model is equipped with: assault cannon; heavy bolter.

WEAPON	RANGE	TYPE	S	AP	D	ABILITIES
Assault cannon	24"	Heavy 6	6	-1	1	-
Heavy bolter	36"	Heavy 3	5	-1	2	-
Heavy flamer	12"	Heavy D6	5	-1	1	Each time an attack is made with this weapon, that attack automatically hits the target.
Multi-melta	24"	Heavy 2	8	-4	D6	Each time an attack made with this weapon targets a unit within half range, that attack has a Damage characteristic of D6+2.

WARGEAR OPTIONS

- Any number of models can each have their heavy bolter replaced with 1 multi-melta.
- Any number of models can each have their assault cannon replaced with 1 heavy flamer.

ABILITIES

Angels of Death (pg 124-125)

Ravenwing: If this unit is from the Dark Angels Chapter (or one of its successor Chapters), it has the **Ravenwing** keyword.

Explodes: Each time a model in this unit is destroyed, roll one D6 before removing it from play. On a 6 it explodes, and each unit within 3" suffers 1 mortal wound.

FACTION KEYWORDS: Imperium, Adeptus Astartes, <Chapter>
KEYWORDS: Vehicle, Fly, Land Speeder, Land Speeder Tornadoes

The Land Speeder Tornado is a highly mobile, multi-threat skimmer that can deal far more death and destruction than its relatively small profile suggests. In battle it serves as a mobile firebase, able to bring multiple heavy weapons to bear wherever the need is greatest.

LAND SPEEDER TYPHOONS

6 POWER

No.	Name	M	WS	BS	S	T	W	A	Ld	Sv
1-3	Land Speeder Typhoon	16"	3+	3+	4	6	6	2	7	3+

If this unit contains 2 models, it has **Power Rating 12**. If this unit contains 3 models, it has **Power Rating 18**. Every model is equipped with: heavy bolter; Typhoon missile launcher.

WEAPON	RANGE	TYPE	S	AP	D	ABILITIES
Heavy bolter	36"	Heavy 3	5	-1	2	-
Multi-melta	24"	Heavy 2	8	-4	D6	Each time an attack made with this weapon targets a unit within half range, that attack has a Damage characteristic of D6+2.
Typhoon missile launcher	Before selecting targets, select one of the profiles below to make attacks with.					
- Frag missile	48"	Heavy 2D6	4	0	1	Blast
- Krak missile	48"	Heavy 2	8	-2	D6	-

WARGEAR OPTIONS

- Any number of models can each have their heavy bolter replaced with 1 multi-melta.

ABILITIES

Angels of Death (pg 124-125)

Ravenwing: If this unit is from the Dark Angels Chapter (or one of its successor Chapters), it has the **Ravenwing** keyword.

Explodes: Each time a model in this unit is destroyed, roll one D6 before removing it from play. On a 6 it explodes, and each unit within 3" suffers 1 mortal wound.

FACTION KEYWORDS: Imperium, Adeptus Astartes, <Chapter>
KEYWORDS: Vehicle, Fly, Land Speeder, Land Speeder Typhoons

Mounting a formidable multi-missile launcher, the Land Speeder Typhoon launches flurries of projectiles at its targets. Such a barrage shatters order in infantry assaults as formations are broken up. Nor is enemy armour safe, for the Typhoon's armour-piercing warheads allow it to pick off battle tanks and transports.

HELLBLASTER SQUAD

8 POWER

No.	NAME	M	WS	BS	S	T	W	A	Ld	Sv
4-9	Hellblaster	6"	3+	3+	4	4	2	2	7	3+
1	Hellblaster Sergeant	6"	3+	3+	4	4	2	3	8	3+

If this unit contains 6 or more models, it has **Power Rating 16**. Every model is equipped with: bolt pistol; plasma incinerator; frag grenades; krak grenades.

WEAPON	RANGE	TYPE	S	AP	D	ABILITIES
Assault plasma incinerator	Before selecting targets, select one of the profiles below to make attacks with.					
- Standard	24"	Assault 3	6	-4	1	-
- Supercharge	24"	Assault 3	7	-4	2	Plasma Weapon (see below).
Heavy plasma incinerator	Before selecting targets, select one of the profiles below to make attacks with.					
- Standard	36"	Heavy 1	8	-4	2	-
- Supercharge	36"	Heavy 1	9	-4	3	Plasma Weapon (see below).
Plasma incinerator	Before selecting targets, select one of the profiles below to make attacks with.					
- Standard	30"	Rapid Fire 1	7	-4	1	-
- Supercharge	30"	Rapid Fire 1	8	-4	2	Plasma Weapon (see below).

WARGEAR OPTIONS

- All of the models in the unit can have their plasma incinerator replaced with 1 assault plasma incinerator each.
- All of the models in the unit can have their plasma incinerator replaced with 1 heavy plasma incinerator each.
- The Hellblaster Sergeant's bolt pistol can be replaced with 1 plasma pistol.

ABILITIES

Angels of Death, Combat Squads (pg 124-125)

Plasma Weapon: If any unmodified hit rolls of 1 are made for attacks with this weapon profile, the bearer is destroyed after shooting with this weapon.

FACTION KEYWORDS: IMPERIUM, ADEPTUS ASTARTES, <CHAPTER>
KEYWORDS: INFANTRY, CORE, PRIMARIS, HELLBLASTER SQUAD

Few foes can survive the incandescent fury of the Hellblaster Squad. Whether they be Tyranid Hive Tyrant, Ork Warboss or Heretic Astartes battle tank, all are reduced to ash and slag by searing, well-aimed plasma fire pouring from the Hellblasters' ferocious weapons.

Plasma pistol

Bolt pistol

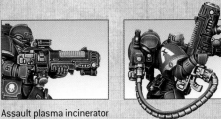

Assault plasma incinerator

Heavy plasma incinerator

Iron Hands Hellblaster Sergeant with heavy plasma incinerator and plasma pistol

Blood Angels Hellblaster with assault plasma incinerator

Ultramarines Hellblaster with heavy plasma incinerator

Imperial Fists Hellblaster with plasma incinerator

ELIMINATOR SQUAD

5 POWER

No.	Name	M	WS	BS	S	T	W	A	Ld	Sv
2	Eliminator	6"	3+	2+	4	4	2	2	7	3+
1	Eliminator Sergeant	6"	3+	2+	4	4	2	3	8	3+

Every model is equipped with: bolt pistol; bolt sniper rifle; frag grenades; krak grenades; camo cloak.

WEAPON	RANGE	TYPE	S	AP	D	ABILITIES
Bolt pistol	12"	Pistol 1	4	0	1	-
Bolt sniper rifle		Before selecting targets, select one of the profiles below to make attacks with. Each time you select a target for this weapon, you can ignore the Look Out, Sir rule.				
- Executioner round	36"	Heavy 1	5	-1	1	Each time an attack is made with this weapon profile, add 1 to that attack's hit roll. Targets do not receive the benefits of cover against attacks made with this weapon profile.
- Hyperfrag round	36"	Heavy D3	5	0	1	Blast
- Mortis round	36"	Heavy 1	5	-2	2	Each time an attack is made with this weapon profile, an unmodified wound roll of 6 inflicts 1 mortal wound on the target in addition to any normal damage.
Instigator bolt carbine	24"	Assault 1	4	-1	2	Each time you select a target for this weapon, you can ignore the Look Out, Sir rule.
Las fusil	36"	Heavy 1	8	-3	3	-

OTHER WARGEAR	ABILITIES
Camo cloak	Each time a ranged attack is allocated to the bearer while it is receiving the benefits of cover, add an additional 1 to any armour saving throw made against that attack.

WARGEAR OPTIONS

• The Eliminator Sergeant's bolt sniper rifle can be replaced with one of the following: 1 instigator bolt carbine; 1 las fusil.
• All of the Eliminators in the unit can have their bolt sniper rifle replaced with 1 las fusil each.

ABILITIES

Angels of Death, Concealed Positions (pg 124-125)

Covering Fire: In your Shooting phase, after this unit has shot, if it is not within Engagement Range of any enemy units and contains an Eliminator Sergeant equipped with an instigator bolt carbine, it can make a Normal Move as if it were your Movement phase.

FACTION KEYWORDS: IMPERIUM, ADEPTUS ASTARTES, \<CHAPTER\>
KEYWORDS: INFANTRY, CORE, PRIMARIS, PHOBOS, ELIMINATOR SQUAD

Eliminator Squads are peerless assassins, deadly marksmen who haunt the shadows of the battlefield unseen by the enemy. For hours they will lie in wait to take the perfect shot, their sophisticated scopes feeding them essential data to ensure they never fail to make the kill.

Camo cloaks

Bolt sniper rifle

Instigator bolt carbine

Raven Guard Eliminator with las fusil

Ultramarines Eliminator Sergeant

Imperial Fists Eliminator

CENTURION DEVASTATOR SQUAD 14 POWER

No.	Name	M	WS	BS	S	T	W	A	Ld	Sv
2-5	Devastator Centurion	5"	3+	3+	5	5	4	3	7	2+
1	Devastator Centurion Sergeant	5"	3+	3+	5	5	4	4	8	2+

If this unit contains 4 or more models, it has **Power Rating 28**. Every model is equipped with: grav-cannon; hurricane bolter.

WEAPON	RANGE	TYPE	S	AP	D	ABILITIES
Centurion missile launcher	36"	Assault D3	8	-2	D3	Blast
Grav-cannon	30"	Heavy 4	5	-3	1	Each time an attack made with this weapon is allocated to a model with a Save characteristic of 3+ or better, that attack has a Damage characteristic of 2.
Hurricane bolter	24"	Rapid Fire 6	4	0	1	-

WARGEAR OPTIONS

- Any number of models can each have their hurricane bolter replaced with 1 Centurion missile launcher.
- Any number of models can each have their grav-cannon replaced with one of the following: 2 heavy bolters; 2 lascannons.

ABILITIES

Angels of Death, **Combat Squads** (pg 124-125)

Omniscope: Each time a model in this unit makes a ranged attack, if this unit contains a Centurion Sergeant, then the target does not receive the benefits of cover against that attack.

Decimator Protocols: Models in this unit do not suffer the penalty to hit rolls incurred for firing Heavy weapons in the same turn that their unit has moved.

FACTION KEYWORDS: IMPERIUM, ADEPTUS ASTARTES, <CHAPTER>
KEYWORDS: INFANTRY, CENTURION, CENTURION DEVASTATOR SQUAD

Centurion Devastator Squads dominate the field of battle, the presence of but one dictating the flow of the entire action. They frequently operate closely with Stormraven Gunships, which transport the Space Marines inside their bulky warsuits to the next position, where the function as an armoured firebase.

ERADICATOR SQUAD 6 POWER

No.	Name	M	WS	BS	S	T	W	A	Ld	Sv
2-5	Eradicator	5"	3+	3+	4	5	3	2	7	3+
1	Eradicator Sergeant	5"	3+	3+	4	5	3	3	8	3+

If this unit contains 4 or more models, it has **Power Rating 12**. Every model is equipped with: bolt pistol; melta rifle; frag grenades; krak grenades.

WEAPON	RANGE	TYPE	S	AP	D	ABILITIES
Bolt pistol	12"	Pistol 1	4	0	1	-
Heavy melta rifle	24"	Heavy 1	8	-4	D6+2	Each time an attack made with this weapon targets a unit within half range, that attack has a Damage characteristic of D6+4.
Melta rifle	24"	Assault 1	8	-4	D6	Each time an attack made with this weapon targets a unit within half range, that attack has a Damage characteristic of D6+2.

WARGEAR OPTIONS

- All of the models in the unit can have their melta rifle replaced with 1 heavy melta rifle each.
- For every 3 models in this unit, 1 Eradicator's melta rifle or heavy melta rifle can be replaced with 1 multi-melta.

ABILITIES

Angels of Death, **Combat Squads** (pg 124-125)

Total Obliteration: In your Shooting phase, each time this unit is selected to shoot, if it has not Advanced this turn, it can unleash total obliteration. If it does, select one enemy unit; models in this unit can shoot twice this phase, but they can only make attacks that target that enemy unit (and only if that enemy unit is an eligible target for those attacks).

FACTION KEYWORDS: IMPERIUM, ADEPTUS ASTARTES, <CHAPTER>
KEYWORDS: INFANTRY, CORE, PRIMARIS, MK X GRAVIS, ERADICATOR SQUAD

Before the molten ire of an Eradicator Squad, heavy armour and defended positions stand little chance. Eradicators wear the heavier Gravis-pattern of Mk X power armour, allowing them to stride unharmed through waves of incoming fire before bringing their own destructive weaponry to bear at close range.

DEVASTATOR SQUAD

8 POWER

No.	Name	M	WS	BS	S	T	W	A	Ld	Sv
4-9	Devastator Marine	6"	3+	3+	4	4	2	1	7	3+
1	Devastator Marine Sergeant	6"	3+	3+	4	4	2	2	8	3+

If this unit contains 6 or more models, it has **Power Rating 12**. Every model is equipped with: bolt pistol; boltgun; frag grenades; krak grenades.

WEAPON	RANGE	TYPE	S	AP	D	ABILITIES
Bolt pistol	12"	Pistol 1	4	0	1	-
Boltgun	24"	Rapid Fire 1	4	0	1	-

OTHER WARGEAR	ABILITIES
Armorium cherub	Once per battle, in your Shooting phase, after this unit has shot, one model in this unit can immediately shoot with one of its ranged weapons again.
	We recommend placing an Armorium Cherub model next to the unit as a reminder, removing it once this ability has been used (an Armorium Cherub does not count as a model for any rules purposes).

WARGEAR OPTIONS

- The Devastator Marine Sergeant's bolt pistol can be replaced with one of the following: 1 weapon from the *Pistols* list; 1 weapon from the *Melee Weapons* list.
- The Devastator Marine Sergeant's boltgun can be replaced with one of the following: 1 weapon from the *Combi-weapons* list; 1 weapon from the *Pistols* list; 1 weapon from the *Melee Weapons* list.
- Up to 4 Devastator Marines can each have their boltgun replaced with 1 weapon from the *Heavy Weapons* list.
- The unit can be equipped with 1 Armorium Cherub.

ABILITIES

Angels of Death, Combat Squads (pg 124-125)

Signum: In your Shooting phase, each time this unit shoots, if it contains a Devastator Marine Sergeant, you can select one model in this unit. Until the end of the phase, that model has a Ballistic Skill characteristi of 2+.

FACTION KEYWORDS: **Imperium, Adeptus Astartes, <Chapter>**
KEYWORDS: **Infantry, Core, Devastator Squad**

Devastator Squads pound the enemy at long range with overwhelming heavy weapons fire, annihilating any caught in the ferocious blasts of their weapons. Once they have secured the perfect firing position, they hold it firmly, providing their battle-brothers with intense covering fire as they advance.

Missile launcher

Grav-cannon

Heavy bolter

Armorium Cherub

Ultramarines Devastator Sergeant
with combi-grav and signum

Dark Angels Devastator
with plasma cannon

Blood Angels Devastator
with multi-melta

Ultramarines Devastator
with lascannon

THUNDERFIRE CANNON

6 POWER

No.	Name	M	WS	BS	S	T	W	A	Ld	Sv
1	Thunderfire Cannon	3"	6+	2+	3	6	4	1	8	2+
1	Techmarine Gunner	6"	3+	2+	4	4	4	3	8	2+

The Thunderfire Cannon is equipped with: thunderfire cannon. The Techmarine Gunner is equipped with: bolt pistol; flamer; plasma cutter; 2 servo-arms.

WEAPON	RANGE	TYPE	S	AP	D	ABILITIES
Bolt pistol	12"	Pistol 1	4	0	1	-
Plasma cutter	Before selecting targets, select one of the profiles below to make attacks with.					
- Standard	12"	Assault 1	7	-3	1	-
- Supercharge	12"	Assault 1	8	-3	2	If any unmodified hit rolls of 1 are made for attacks with this weapon profile, the bearer is destroyed after shooting with this weapon.
Thunderfire cannon	60"	Heavy 4D3	4	0	1	Blast. This weapon can target units that are not visible to the bearer.
Servo-arm	Melee	Melee	x2	-2	3	Each time the bearer fights, no more than one attack can be made with each servo-arm.

ABILITIES

Angels of Death (pg 124-125)

Crewed Artillery: After this unit is set up on the battlefield for the first time, it is split into two units, one containing the ARTILLERY model and the other the GUNNER model. If at the end of any phase, the GUNNER unit is not within 3" of its ARTILLERY unit, that ARTILLERY unit is destroyed.

Operated Artillery: While a GUNNER unit is within 3" of its ARTILLERY unit, enemy models cannot target that GUNNER unit with ranged weapons.

Blessing of the Omnissiah: At the end of your Movement phase, a Techmarine Gunner can repair one friendly <CHAPTER> VEHICLE model within 3" of it. That VEHICLE model regains up to D3 lost wounds. Each model can only be repaired once per turn.

FACTION KEYWORDS: **IMPERIUM, ADEPTUS ASTARTES, <CHAPTER>**
KEYWORDS (THUNDERFIRE CANNON): **VEHICLE, ARTILLERY, THUNDERFIRE CANNON**
KEYWORDS (TECHMARINE GUNNER): **INFANTRY, CHARACTER, GUNNER**

A massive, multi-barrelled artillery piece mounted on heavy, grinding tracks, the Thunderfire Cannon can tear apart the enemy's assaults and blow huge holes in their strongpoints in relentless barrages of shells. Able to traverse all kinds of difficult terrain, it excels in supporting Space Marine attacks or shoring up defences.

FIRESTRIKE SERVO-TURRETS

6 POWER

No.	Name	M	WS	BS	S	T	W	A	Ld	Sv
1-3	Firestrike Servo-turret	3"	3+	2+	4	5	5	2	8	2+

If this unit contains 2 models, it has **Power Rating 12**. If this unit contains 3 models, it has **Power Rating 18**. Every model is equipped with: twin las-talon.

WEAPON	RANGE	TYPE	S	AP	D	ABILITIES
Twin accelerator autocannon	48"	Heavy 6	7	-1	2	-
Twin las-talon	24"	Heavy 4	9	-3	D6	-

WARGEAR OPTIONS

- Any number of models can each have their twin las-talon replaced with 1 twin accelerator autocannon.

ABILITIES

Angels of Death (pg 124-125)

FACTION KEYWORDS: **IMPERIUM, ADEPTUS ASTARTES, <CHAPTER>**
KEYWORDS: **VEHICLE, ARTILLERY, FIRESTRIKE SERVO-TURRETS**

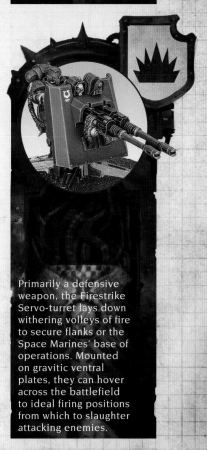

Primarily a defensive weapon, the Firestrike Servo-turret lays down withering volleys of fire to secure flanks or the Space Marines' base of operations. Mounted on gravitic ventral plates, they can hover across the battlefield to ideal firing positions from which to slaughter attacking enemies.

HUNTER

6 POWER

Some of this model's characteristics change as it suffers damage, as shown below:

No.	Name	M	WS	BS	S	T	W	A	Ld	Sv
1	Hunter (6+ wounds remaining)	10"	6+	3+	6	8	11	3	8	3+
	Hunter (3-5 wounds remaining)	5"	6+	4+	6	8	N/A	D3	8	3+
	Hunter (1-2 wounds remaining)	3"	6+	5+	6	8	N/A	1	8	3+

A Hunter is equipped with: skyspear missile launcher.

WEAPON	RANGE	TYPE	S	AP	D	ABILITIES
Skyspear missile launcher	60"	Heavy 1	9	-3	D6	Each time an attack is made with this weapon against an **Aircraft** unit, add 2 to that attack's hit roll. Each time an attack made with this weapon is allocated to an **Aircraft** model, that attack has a Damage characteristic of D6+6.

WARGEAR OPTIONS

- This model can be equipped with 1 hunter-killer missile.
- This model can be equipped with 1 storm bolter.

ABILITIES

Angels of Death (pg 124-125)

Explodes: When this model is destroyed, roll one D6 before removing it from play. On a 6 it explodes, and each unit within 6" suffers D3 mortal wounds.

FACTION KEYWORDS: **Imperium, Adeptus Astartes, <Chapter>**
KEYWORDS: **Vehicle, Smokescreen, Hunter**

The Adeptus Astartes' foremost anti-air vehicle, few foes can evade the missiles of the Hunter's skyspear missile launcher. Its deadly payload homes in on its target and can change direction with preternatural ease, guided as it is by the interred servitor-mummy of one of the Chapter's honoured ballistic serfs.

STALKER

6 POWER

Some of this model's characteristics change as it suffers damage, as shown below:

No.	Name	M	WS	BS	S	T	W	A	Ld	Sv
1	Stalker (6+ wounds remaining)	10"	6+	3+	6	8	11	3	8	3+
	Stalker (3-5 wounds remaining)	5"	6+	4+	6	8	N/A	D3	8	3+
	Stalker (1-2 wounds remaining)	3"	6+	5+	6	8	N/A	1	8	3+

A Stalker is equipped with: 2 Icarus stormcannons.

WEAPON	RANGE	TYPE	S	AP	D	ABILITIES
Icarus stormcannon	48"	Heavy 3	7	-1	2	Each time an attack is made with this weapon against an **Aircraft** unit, make 2 hit rolls instead of 1 and add 1 to both those hit rolls.

WARGEAR OPTIONS

- This model can be equipped with 1 hunter-killer missile.
- This model can be equipped with 1 storm bolter.

ABILITIES

Angels of Death (pg 124-125)

Explodes: When this model is destroyed, roll one D6 before removing it from play. On a 6 it explodes, and each unit within 6" suffers D3 mortal wounds.

FACTION KEYWORDS: **Imperium, Adeptus Astartes, <Chapter>**
KEYWORDS: **Vehicle, Smokescreen, Stalker**

The Stalker's phenomenal anti-aircraft kill rate is achieved by a pair of independently targeting repeating cannons. These are tethered to a servo-mind conclave that cogitates reams of trajectory data to ensure the Stalker's weapons fire exactly where they should, enabling it to cleanse skies darkened by enemy flyers.

WHIRLWIND

7 POWER

Some of this model's characteristics change as it suffers damage, as shown below:

No.	Name	M	WS	BS	S	T	W	A	Ld	Sv
1	Whirlwind (6+ wounds remaining)	12"	6+	3+	6	7	11	3	8	3+
	Whirlwind (3-5 wounds remaining)	6"	6+	4+	6	7	N/A	D3	8	3+
	Whirlwind (1-2 wounds remaining)	3"	6+	5+	6	7	N/A	1	8	3+

A Whirlwind is equipped with: Whirlwind vengeance launcher.

WEAPON	RANGE	TYPE	S	AP	D	ABILITIES
Whirlwind castellan launcher	72"	Heavy 2D6	6	0	1	Blast. This weapon can target units that are not visible to the bearer.
Whirlwind vengeance launcher	72"	Heavy 2D3	7	-1	2	Blast. This weapon can target units that are not visible to the bearer.

WARGEAR OPTIONS

- This model's Whirlwind vengeance launcher can be replaced with 1 Whirlwind castellan launcher.
- This model can be equipped with 1 hunter-killer missile.
- This model can be equipped with 1 storm bolter.

ABILITIES

Angels of Death (pg 124-125)

Explodes: When this model is destroyed, roll one D6 before removing it from play. On a 6 it explodes, and each unit within 6" suffers D3 mortal wounds.

FACTION KEYWORDS: **Imperium, Adeptus Astartes, <Chapter>**
KEYWORDS: **Vehicle, Smokescreen, Whirlwind**

Hails of missiles saturate the ground whenever a Whirlwind strikes, creating a carpet of explosions that launches deadly shrapnel or scorching flames in all directions. The Whirlwind fires from concealed positions in support of Space Marine attacks, utilising its speed to keep pace with the assault.

PREDATOR DESTRUCTOR

8 POWER

Some of this model's characteristics change as it suffers damage, as shown below:

No.	Name	M	WS	BS	S	T	W	A	Ld	Sv
1	Predator Destructor (6+ wounds remaining)	12"	6+	3+	6	7	11	3	8	3+
	Predator Destructor (3-5 wounds remaining)	6"	6+	4+	6	7	N/A	D3	8	3+
	Predator Destructor (1-2 wounds remaining)	3"	6+	5+	6	7	N/A	1	8	3+

A Predator Destructor is equipped with: Predator autocannon.

WEAPON	RANGE	TYPE	S	AP	D	ABILITIES
Heavy bolter	36"	Heavy 3	5	-1	2	-
Lascannon	48"	Heavy 1	9	-3	D6	-
Predator autocannon	48"	Heavy 2D3	7	-1	3	-

WARGEAR OPTIONS

- This model can be equipped with one of the following: 2 heavy bolters; 2 lascannons.
- This model can be equipped with 1 hunter-killer missile.
- This model can be equipped with 1 storm bolter.

ABILITIES

Angels of Death (pg 124-125)

Explodes: When this model is destroyed, roll one D6 before removing it from play. On a 6 it explodes, and each unit within 6" suffers D3 mortal wounds.

FACTION KEYWORDS: **Imperium, Adeptus Astartes, <Chapter>**
KEYWORDS: **Vehicle, Predator, Smokescreen, Predator Destructor**

Predator Destructors have served the Emperor for more than ten thousand years with resolute steadfastness, proving themselves by slaughtering hordes of enemy infantry, shattering assaults and laying waste to light vehicles. To the always-outnumbered Space Marines, their firepower has long been vital.

PREDATOR ANNIHILATOR

8 POWER

Some of this model's characteristics change as it suffers damage, as shown below:

No.	Name	M	WS	BS	S	T	W	A	Ld	Sv
1	Predator Annihilator (6+ wounds remaining)	12"	6+	3+	6	7	11	3	8	3+
	Predator Annihilator (3-5 wounds remaining)	6"	6+	4+	6	7	N/A	D3	8	3+
	Predator Annihilator (1-2 wounds remaining)	3"	6+	5+	6	7	N/A	1	8	3+

A Predator Annihilator is equipped with: twin lascannon.

WEAPON	RANGE	TYPE	S	AP	D	ABILITIES
Heavy bolter	36"	Heavy 3	5	-1	2	-
Lascannon	48"	Heavy 1	9	-3	D6	-
Twin lascannon	48"	Heavy 2	9	-3	D6	-

WARGEAR OPTIONS

- This model can be equipped with one of the following: 2 heavy bolters; 2 lascannons.
- This model can be equipped with 1 hunter-killer missile.
- This model can be equipped with 1 storm bolter.

ABILITIES

Angels of Death (pg 124-125)

Explodes: When this model is destroyed, roll one D6 before removing it from play. On a 6 it explodes, and each unit within 6" suffers D3 mortal wounds.

FACTION KEYWORDS: IMPERIUM, ADEPTUS ASTARTES, <CHAPTER>
KEYWORDS: VEHICLE, PREDATOR, SMOKESCREEN, PREDATOR ANNIHILATOR

Predator Annihilators excel at leading armoured spearheads, moving at high speed and firing all the while. Their crews take pride in their particularly ferocious machine spirits, and gladly thunder into the fiercest fighting to blow apart enemy armoured columns and dense bunker complexes.

GLADIATOR LANCER

11 POWER

Some of this model's characteristics change as it suffers damage, as shown below:

No.	Name	M	WS	BS	S	T	W	A	Ld	Sv
1	Gladiator Lancer (7+ wounds remaining)	10"	6+	3+	7	8	12	3	8	3+
	Gladiator Lancer (4-6 wounds remaining)	5"	6+	4+	7	8	N/A	D3	8	3+
	Gladiator Lancer (1-3 wounds remaining)	3"	6+	5+	7	8	N/A	1	8	3+

A Gladiator Lancer is equipped with: Lancer laser destroyer, 2 storm bolters.

WEAPON	RANGE	TYPE	S	AP	D	ABILITIES
Fragstorm grenade launcher	18"	Assault D6	4	0	1	Blast
Lancer laser destroyer	72"	Heavy 2	10	-3	D3+3	-
Storm bolter	24"	Rapid Fire 2	4	0	1	-

OTHER WARGEAR	ABILITIES
Auto launchers	The bearer has the **Smokescreen** keyword.

WARGEAR OPTIONS

- This model's 2 storm bolters can be replaced with 2 fragstorm grenade launchers.
- This model can be equipped with 1 ironhail heavy stubber.
- This model can be equipped with 1 Icarus rocket pod.
- This model can be equipped with 1 auto launchers.

ABILITIES

Angels of Death (pg 124-125)

Aquilon Optics: Each time this model makes an attack with a Lancer laser destroyer, add 1 to that attack's hit roll.

Hover Tank: Distances are always measured to and from this model's hull.

Explodes: When this model is destroyed, roll one D6 before removing it from play. On a 6 it explodes, and each unit within 6" suffers D3 mortal wounds.

FACTION KEYWORDS: Imperium, Adeptus Astartes, <Chapter>
KEYWORDS: Vehicle, Gladiator, Repulsor Field, Gladiator Lancer

With pinpoint accuracy, the Gladiator Lancer picks off the heaviest enemy armour, laser destroyer punching smouldering holes in their hulls. Such is the range of its heavy cannon that it can eliminate threats to the Space Marines before they encounter them, storming past burning wrecks to claim their objectives.

GLADIATOR REAPER

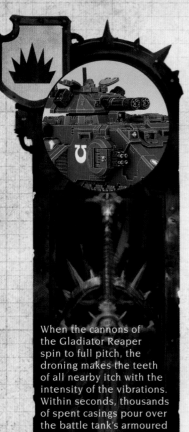

12 POWER

Some of this model's characteristics change as it suffers damage, as shown below:

No.	Name	M	WS	BS	S	T	W	A	Ld	Sv
1	Gladiator Reaper (7+ wounds remaining)	10"	6+	3+	7	8	12	3	8	3+
	Gladiator Reaper (4-6 wounds remaining)	5"	6+	4+	7	8	N/A	D3	8	3+
	Gladiator Reaper (1-3 wounds remaining)	3"	6+	5+	7	8	N/A	1	8	3+

A Gladiator Reaper is equipped with: 2 tempest bolters; twin heavy onslaught gatling cannon.

WEAPON	RANGE	TYPE	S	AP	D	ABILITIES
Tempest bolter	30"	Rapid Fire 4	4	-1	1	-
Twin heavy onslaught gatling cannon	30"	Heavy 24	6	-1	1	-

OTHER WARGEAR	ABILITIES
Auto launchers	The bearer has the SMOKESCREEN keyword.

WARGEAR OPTIONS

- This model can be equipped with 1 ironhail heavy stubber.
- This model can be equipped with 1 Icarus rocket pod.
- This model can be equipped with 1 auto launchers.

ABILITIES

Angels of Death (pg 124-125)

Hover Tank: Distances are always measured to and from this model's hull.

Explodes: When this model is destroyed, roll one D6 before removing it from play. On a 6 it explodes, and each unit within 6" suffers D3 mortal wounds.

FACTION KEYWORDS: IMPERIUM, ADEPTUS ASTARTES, <CHAPTER>
KEYWORDS: VEHICLE, GLADIATOR, REPULSOR FIELD, GLADIATOR REAPER

When the cannons of the Gladiator Reaper spin to full pitch, the droning makes the teeth of all nearby itch with the intensity of the vibrations. Within seconds, thousands of spent casings pour over the battle tank's armoured hide as enemies are erased from existence by the storm of fire.

GLADIATOR VALIANT

13 POWER

Some of this model's characteristics change as it suffers damage, as shown below:

No.	Name	M	WS	BS	S	T	W	A	Ld	Sv
1	Gladiator Valiant (7+ wounds remaining)	10"	6+	3+	7	8	12	3	8	3+
	Gladiator Valiant (4-6 wounds remaining)	5"	6+	4+	7	8	N/A	D3	8	3+
	Gladiator Valiant (1-3 wounds remaining)	3"	6+	5+	7	8	N/A	1	8	3+

A Gladiator Valiant is equipped with: 2 multi-meltas; twin las-talon.

WEAPON	RANGE	TYPE	S	AP	D	ABILITIES
Multi-melta	24"	Heavy 2	8	-4	D6	Each time an attack made with this weapon targets a unit within half range, that attack has a Damage characteristic of D6+2.
Twin las-talon	24"	Heavy 4	9	-3	D6	-

OTHER WARGEAR	ABILITIES
Auto launchers	The bearer has the SMOKESCREEN keyword.

WARGEAR OPTIONS

- This model can be equipped with 1 ironhail heavy stubber.
- This model can be equipped with 1 Icarus rocket pod.
- This model can be equipped with 1 auto launchers.

ABILITIES

Angels of Death (pg 124-125)

Hover Tank: Distances are always measured to and from this model's hull.

Explodes: When this model is destroyed, roll one D6 before removing it from play. On a 6 it explodes, and each unit within 6" suffers D3 mortal wounds.

FACTION KEYWORDS: IMPERIUM, ADEPTUS ASTARTES, <CHAPTER>
KEYWORDS: VEHICLE, GLADIATOR, REPULSOR FIELD, GLADIATOR VALIANT

The Valiant lays down blistering volleys of fire as it escorts transports or supports infantry in ferocious fighting, crossing rushing watercourses, sucking marshlands and bubbling lava lakes with equal ease. Its twin las-talons spit death at the foe, making short work of enemy armour and cracking open fortified positions.

VINDICATOR

7 POWER

Some of this model's characteristics change as it suffers damage, as shown below:

No.	Name	M	WS	BS	S	T	W	A	Ld	Sv
1	Vindicator (6+ wounds remaining)	10"	6+	3+	6	8	11	3	8	3+
	Vindicator (3-5 wounds remaining)	5"	6+	4+	6	8	N/A	D3	8	3+
	Vindicator (1-2 wounds remaining)	3"	6+	5+	6	8	N/A	1	8	3+

A Vindicator is equipped with: demolisher cannon.

WEAPON	RANGE	TYPE	S	AP	D	ABILITIES
Demolisher cannon	24"	Heavy D6	10	-3	D6	Blast

OTHER WARGEAR	ABILITIES
Vindicator siege shield	Each time a ranged attack is allocated to the bearer, add 1 to any armour saving throw made against that attack.

WARGEAR OPTIONS

- This model can be equipped with 1 Vindicator siege shield.
- This model can be equipped with 1 hunter-killer missile.
- This model can be equipped with 1 storm bolter.

ABILITIES

Angels of Death (pg 124-125)

Explodes: When this model is destroyed, roll one D6 before removing it from play. On a 6 it explodes, and each unit within 6" suffers D3 mortal wounds.

FACTION KEYWORDS: IMPERIUM, ADEPTUS ASTARTES, <CHAPTER>
KEYWORDS: VEHICLE, SMOKESCREEN, VINDICATOR

The Vindicator is a dedicated siege tank. It can smash obstacles aside with its massive shield, rumbling into the perfect firing position to unleash its demolisher cannon, a weapon so destructive it can blow apart enemy fortifications, annihilate columns of infantry and shatter armoured tanks with terrifying ease.

LAND RAIDER

15 POWER

Some of this model's characteristics change as it suffers damage, as shown below:

No.	Name	M	WS	BS	S	T	W	A	Ld	Sv
1	Land Raider (9+ wounds remaining)	10"	6+	3+	8	8	16	6	9	2+
	Land Raider (5-8 wounds remaining)	5"	6+	4+	8	8	N/A	D6	9	2+
	Land Raider (1-4 wounds remaining)	3"	6+	5+	8	8	N/A	D3	9	2+

A Land Raider is a equipped with: twin heavy bolter; 2 twin lascannons.

WEAPON	RANGE	TYPE	S	AP	D	ABILITIES
Twin heavy bolter	36"	Heavy 6	5	-1	2	-
Twin lascannon	48"	Heavy 2	9	-3	D6	-

WARGEAR OPTIONS

- This model can be equipped with 1 hunter-killer missile.
- This model can be equipped with 1 storm bolter.
- This model can be equipped with 1 multi-melta.

ABILITIES

Angels of Death (pg 124-125)

Explodes: When this transport is destroyed, roll one D6 before any embarked models disembark and before removing it from play. On a 6 it explodes, and each unit within 6" suffers D6 mortal wounds.

TRANSPORT

This model has a transport capacity of 10 <CHAPTER> INFANTRY models. Each JUMP PACK, WULFEN or TERMINATOR model takes up the space of 2 models and each CENTURION model takes up the space of 3 models. It cannot transport PRIMARIS models.

FACTION KEYWORDS: IMPERIUM, ADEPTUS ASTARTES, <CHAPTER>
KEYWORDS: VEHICLE, TRANSPORT, MACHINE SPIRIT, SMOKESCREEN, LAND RAIDER

Land Raiders are mobile fortresses that bear squads of Space Marines through the most furious firestorms without so much as a scratch. Their machine spirits are so potent that if the crew are slain they will take over, making the tank a truly formidable asset.

LAND RAIDER CRUSADER

15 POWER

Some of this model's characteristics change as it suffers damage, as shown below:

No.	Name	M	WS	BS	S	T	W	A	Ld	Sv
1	Land Raider Crusader (9+ wounds remaining)	10"	6+	3+	8	8	16	6	9	2+
	Land Raider Crusader (5-8 wounds remaining)	5"	6+	4+	8	8	N/A	D6	9	2+
	Land Raider Crusader (1-4 wounds remaining)	3"	6+	5+	8	8	N/A	D3	9	2+

A Land Raider Crusader is equipped with: 2 hurricane bolters; twin assault cannon.

WEAPON	RANGE	TYPE	S	AP	D	ABILITIES
Hurricane bolter	24"	Rapid Fire 6	4	0	1	-
Twin assault cannon	24"	Heavy 12	6	-1	1	-

WARGEAR OPTIONS

- This model can be equipped with 1 hunter-killer missile.
- This model can be equipped with 1 storm bolter.
- This model can be equipped with 1 multi-melta.

ABILITIES

Angels of Death (pg 124-125)

Explodes: When this transport is destroyed, roll one D6 before any embarked models disembark and before removing it from play. On a 6 it explodes, and each unit within 6" suffers D6 mortal wounds.

TRANSPORT

This model has a transport capacity of 16 <Chapter> Infantry models. Each Jump Pack, Wulfen or Terminator model takes up the space of 2 models and each Centurion model takes up the space of 3 models. It cannot transport Primaris models.

FACTION KEYWORDS: Imperium, Adeptus Astartes, <Chapter>
KEYWORDS: Vehicle, Land Raider, Transport, Assault Launchers, Smokescreen, Machine Spirit, Land Raider Crusader

The Land Raider Crusader is a superlative assault tank. Its bulk enables it to crush enemy defences, and its prodigious firepower cuts their defenders to ribbons. With an enhanced transport capacity, once it has stormed enemy defences, Space Marines pour from its hatches to slaughter those foes who remain.

LAND RAIDER REDEEMER

15 POWER

Some of this model's characteristics change as it suffers damage, as shown below:

No.	Name	M	WS	BS	S	T	W	A	Ld	Sv
1	Land Raider Redeemer (9+ wounds remaining)	10"	6+	3+	8	8	16	6	9	2+
	Land Raider Redeemer (5-8 wounds remaining)	5"	6+	4+	8	8	N/A	D6	9	2+
	Land Raider Redeemer (1-4 wounds remaining)	3"	6+	5+	8	8	N/A	D3	9	2+

A Land Raider Redeemer is equipped with: 2 flamestorm cannons; twin assault cannon.

WEAPON	RANGE	TYPE	S	AP	D	ABILITIES
Flamestorm cannon	12"	Heavy D6	6	-2	2	Each time an attack is made with this weapon, that attack automatically hits the target.
Twin assault cannon	24"	Heavy 12	6	-1	1	-

WARGEAR OPTIONS

- This model can be equipped with 1 hunter-killer missile.
- This model can be equipped with 1 storm bolter.
- This model can be equipped with 1 multi-melta.

ABILITIES

Angels of Death (pg 124-125)

Explodes: When this transport is destroyed, roll one D6 before any embarked models disembark and before removing it from play. On a 6 it explodes, and each unit within 6" suffers D6 mortal wounds.

TRANSPORT

This model has a transport capacity of 12 <Chapter> Infantry models. Each Jump Pack, Wulfen or Terminator model takes the space of 2 models and each Centurion model takes the space of 3 models. It cannot transport Primaris models.

FACTION KEYWORDS: Imperium, Adeptus Astartes, <Chapter>

KEYWORDS: Vehicle, Land Raider, Transport, Assault Launchers, Machine Spirit, Smokescreen, Land Raider Redeemer

In brutal urban combat, it can be impossible to root out entrenched foes. Not so for the Land Raider Redeemer. When it engages its flamestorm cannons, any caught in the raging inferno of burning promethium that follows are doomed, and bunkers, pill boxes, ruined factorums and shattered hab-blocks are cleansed of the enemy.

REPULSOR

16 POWER

Some of this model's characteristics change as it suffers damage, as shown below:

No.	Name	M	WS	BS	S	T	W	A	Ld	Sv
1	Repulsor (9+ wounds remaining)	10"	6+	3+	8	8	16	6	9	3+
	Repulsor (5-8 wounds remaining)	5"	6+	4+	8	8	N/A	D6	9	3+
	Repulsor (1-4 wounds remaining)	3"	6+	5+	8	8	N/A	D3	9	3+

A Repulsor is equipped with: heavy onslaught gatling cannon; Icarus ironhail heavy stubber; ironhail heavy stubber; 2 krakstorm grenade launchers; 2 storm bolters; twin heavy bolter; hunter-slayer missile; auto launchers.

WEAPON	RANGE	TYPE	S	AP	D	ABILITIES
Fragstorm grenade launcher	18"	Assault D6	4	0	1	Blast
Heavy onslaught gatling cannon	30"	Heavy 12	6	-1	1	-
Hunter-slayer missile	48"	Heavy 1	10	-2	D6	The bearer can only shoot with each hunter-slayer missile it is equipped with once per battle. This weapon can target units that are not visible to the bearer.
Icarus ironhail heavy stubber	36"	Heavy 4	4	-1	1	Each time an attack is made with this weapon against an AIRCRAFT unit, add 1 to that attack's hit roll.
Icarus rocket pod	24"	Heavy D3	7	-1	2	Blast. Each time an attack is made with this weapon against an AIRCRAFT unit, add 1 to that attack's hit roll.
Ironhail heavy stubber	36"	Heavy 4	4	-1	1	-
Krakstorm grenade launcher	18"	Assault 1	6	-1	D3	-
Las-talon	24"	Heavy 2	9	-3	D6	-
Onslaught gatling cannon	24"	Heavy 8	5	-1	1	-
Storm bolter	24"	Rapid Fire 2	4	0	1	-
Twin heavy bolter	36"	Heavy 6	5	-1	2	-
Twin lascannon	48"	Heavy 2	9	-3	D6	-

OTHER WARGEAR	ABILITIES
Auto launchers	The bearer has the SMOKESCREEN keyword.

WARGEAR OPTIONS

- This model can be equipped with 1 additional ironhail heavy stubber.
- This model's twin heavy bolter can be replaced with 1 twin lascannon.
- This model's heavy onslaught gatling cannon can be replaced with 1 las-talon.
- One of this model's ironhail heavy stubbers can be replaced with 1 onslaught gatling cannon.
- This model's 2 storm bolters can be replaced with 2 fragstorm grenade launchers.
- This model's auto launchers can be replaced with 2 fragstorm grenade launchers.
- This model's Icarus ironhail heavy stubber can be replaced with one of the following: 1 fragstorm grenade launcher; 1 Icarus rocket pod; 1 storm bolter.

ABILITIES

Angels of Death (pg 124-125)

Hover Tank: Distances are always measured to and from this model's hull.

Explodes: When this transport is destroyed, roll one D6 before any embarked models disembark and before removing it from play. On a 6 it explodes, and each unit within 6" suffers D6 mortal wounds.

TRANSPORT

This model has a transport capacity of 10 <CHAPTER> PRIMARIS INFANTRY models. Each MK X GRAVIS model takes up the space of 2 models. It cannot transport JUMP PACK models.

FACTION KEYWORDS: IMPERIUM, ADEPTUS ASTARTES, <CHAPTER>
KEYWORDS: VEHICLE, TRANSPORT, MACHINE SPIRIT, REPULSOR FIELD, REPULSOR

Clad in advanced armour plating and armed for any battlefield situation, the Repulsor not only transports its passengers safely, it also provides superb fire support. Dangerous terrain is little impediment to it, its ventral plates channelling gravitic energies that crush obstacles beneath the vehicle's mass.

REPULSOR EXECUTIONER

19 POWER

Some of this model's characteristics change as it suffers damage, as shown below:

No.	Name	M	WS	BS	S	T	W	A	Ld	Sv
1	Repulsor Executioner (9+ wounds remaining)	10"	6+	3+	8	8	16	6	9	3+
	Repulsor Executioner (5-8 wounds remaining)	5"	6+	4+	8	8	N/A	D6	9	3+
	Repulsor Executioner (1-4 wounds remaining)	3"	6+	5+	8	8	N/A	D3	9	3+

A Repulsor Executioner is equipped with: 2 fragstorm grenade launchers; heavy onslaught gatling cannon; macro plasma incinerator; 2 storm bolters; twin heavy bolter; twin Icarus ironhail heavy stubber; auto launchers.

WEAPON	RANGE	TYPE	S	AP	D	ABILITIES
Fragstorm grenade launcher	18"	Assault D6	4	0	1	Blast
Heavy laser destroyer	72"	Heavy 2	12	-4	D3+3	-
Heavy onslaught gatling cannon	30"	Heavy 12	6	-1	1	-
Icarus rocket pod	24"	Heavy D3	7	-1	2	Blast. Each time an attack is made with this weapon against an **AIRCRAFT** unit, add 1 to that attack's hit roll.
Ironhail heavy stubber	36"	Heavy 4	4	-1	1	-
Macro plasma incinerator	Before selecting targets, select one of the profiles below to make attacks with.					
- Standard	36"	Heavy D6	8	-4	2	Blast
- Supercharge	36"	Heavy D6	9	-4	3	Blast. Each time an unmodified hit roll of 1 is made for an attack with this weapon profile, the bearer suffers 1 mortal wound after shooting with this weapon.
Storm bolter	24"	Rapid Fire 2	4	0	1	-
Twin heavy bolter	36"	Heavy 6	5	-1	2	-
Twin Icarus ironhail heavy stubber	36"	Heavy 8	4	-1	1	Each time an attack is made with this weapon against an **AIRCRAFT** unit, add 1 to that attack's hit roll.

OTHER WARGEAR	ABILITIES
Auto launchers	The bearer has the **SMOKESCREEN** keyword.

WARGEAR OPTIONS

- This model's macro plasma incinerator can be replaced with 1 heavy laser destroyer.
- This model can be equipped with 1 ironhail heavy stubber.
- This model can be equipped with 1 Icarus rocket pod.

ABILITIES

Angels of Death (pg 124-125)

Aquilon Optics: Each time this model makes an attack with its heavy laser destroyer or macro plasma incinerator, add 1 to that attack's hit roll.

Explodes: When this transport is destroyed, roll one D6 before any embarked models disembark and before removing it from play. On a 6 it explodes, and each unit within 6" suffers D6 mortal wounds.

Hover Tank: Distances are always measured to and from this model's hull.

TRANSPORT

This model has a transport capacity of 6 <**CHAPTER**> **PRIMARIS INFANTRY** models. Each **MK X GRAVIS** model takes up the space of 2 models. It cannot transport **JUMP PACK** models.

FACTION KEYWORDS: IMPERIUM, ADEPTUS ASTARTES, <CHAPTER>
KEYWORDS: VEHICLE, TRANSPORT, MACHINE SPIRIT, REPULSOR FIELD, REPULSOR EXECUTIONER

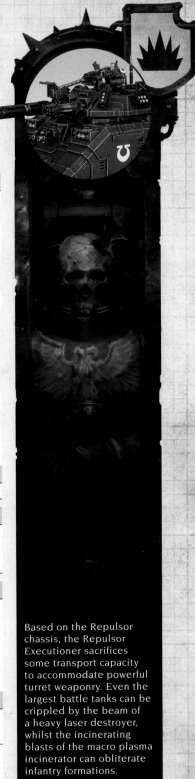

Based on the Repulsor chassis, the Repulsor Executioner sacrifices some transport capacity to accommodate powerful turret weaponry. Even the largest battle tanks can be crippled by the beam of a heavy laser destroyer, whilst the incinerating blasts of the macro plasma incinerator can obliterate infantry formations.

RHINO

4 POWER

Some of this model's characteristics change as it suffers damage, as shown below:

No.	Name	M	WS	BS	S	T	W	A	Ld	Sv
1	Rhino (6+ wounds remaining)	12"	6+	3+	6	7	10	3	8	3+
	Rhino (3-5 wounds remaining)	6"	6+	4+	6	7	N/A	D3	8	3+
	Rhino (1-2 wounds remaining)	3"	6+	5+	6	7	N/A	1	8	3+

A Rhino is a equipped with: storm bolter.

WEAPON	RANGE	TYPE	S	AP	D	ABILITIES
Storm bolter	24"	Rapid Fire 2	4	0	1	-

WARGEAR OPTIONS

- This model can be equipped with 1 hunter-killer missile.
- This model can be equipped with 1 additional storm bolter.

ABILITIES

Angels of Death (pg 124-125)

Explodes: When this transport is destroyed, roll one D6 before any embarked models disembark and before removing it from play. On a 6 it explodes, and each unit within 6" suffers D3 mortal wounds.

TRANSPORT

This model has a transport capacity of 10 **<CHAPTER> INFANTRY** models. It cannot transport **JUMP PACK**, **TERMINATOR**, **PRIMARIS**, **WULFEN** or **CENTURION** models.

FACTION KEYWORDS: IMPERIUM, ADEPTUS ASTARTES, <CHAPTER>
KEYWORDS: VEHICLE, TRANSPORT, SMOKESCREEN, RHINO

The Rhino transport has served the Space Marines for ten thousand years, and forms a part of many of their strike forces. With robust self-repair systems, the Rhino is a rugged vehicle that can swiftly navigate nightmare battlefields to deliver its deadly cargo of Space Marines into the heart of battle.

RAZORBACK

6 POWER

Some of this model's characteristics change as it suffers damage, as shown below:

No.	Name	M	WS	BS	S	T	W	A	Ld	Sv
1	Razorback (6+ wounds remaining)	12"	6+	3+	6	7	10	3	8	3+
	Razorback (3-5 wounds remaining)	6"	6+	4+	6	7	N/A	D3	8	3+
	Razorback (1-2 wounds remaining)	3"	6+	5+	6	7	N/A	1	8	3+

A Razorback is equipped with: twin heavy bolter.

WEAPON	RANGE	TYPE	S	AP	D	ABILITIES
Twin assault cannon	24"	Heavy 12	6	-1	1	-
Twin heavy bolter	36"	Heavy 6	5	-1	2	-
Twin lascannon	48"	Heavy 2	9	-3	D6	-

WARGEAR OPTIONS

- This model's twin heavy bolter can be replaced with one of the following: 1 twin lascannon; 1 twin assault cannon.
- This model can be equipped with 1 hunter-killer missile.
- This model can be equipped with 1 storm bolter.

ABILITIES

Angels of Death (pg 124-125)

Explodes: When this transport is destroyed, roll one D6 before any embarked models disembark and before removing it from play. On a 6 it explodes, and each unit within 6" suffers D3 mortal wounds.

TRANSPORT

This model has a transport capacity of 6 **<CHAPTER> INFANTRY** models. It cannot transport **JUMP PACK**, **TERMINATOR**, **PRIMARIS**, **WULFEN** or **CENTURION** models.

FACTION KEYWORDS: IMPERIUM, ADEPTUS ASTARTES, <CHAPTER>
KEYWORDS: VEHICLE, TRANSPORT, SMOKESCREEN, RAZORBACK

The Razorback replaces some of the Rhino's transport capacity for a heavy weapon turret, and provides fire support for armoured infantry assaults whilst delivering its own cargo of warriors to battle. Such is its success that for many Chapters it performs additional functions, notably as a mobile command centre.

IMPULSOR

Some of this model's characteristics change as it suffers damage, as shown below:

No.	Name	M	WS	BS	S	T	W	A	Ld	Sv
1	Impulsor (6+ wounds remaining)	14"	6+	3+	7	7	11	3	8	3+
	Impulsor (3-5 wounds remaining)	7"	6+	4+	7	7	N/A	D3	8	3+
	Impulsor (1-2 wounds remaining)	4"	6+	5+	7	7	N/A	1	8	3+

An Impulsor is a equipped with: 2 storm bolters.

WEAPON	RANGE	TYPE	S	AP	D	ABILITIES
Bellicatus missile array	Before selecting targets, select one of the profiles below to make attacks with.					
- Krak missiles	48"	Heavy 1	8	-2	D6	-
- Frag missiles	48"	Heavy D6	4	0	1	Blast
- Icarus missiles	48"	Heavy D3	7	-1	2	Blast. Each time an attack is made with this weapon profile against an AIRCRAFT unit, add 1 to that attack's hit roll.
Fragstorm grenade launcher	18"	Assault D6	4	0	1	Blast
Ironhail heavy stubber	36"	Heavy 4	4	-1	1	-
Ironhail skytalon array	36"	Heavy 8	4	-1	1	Each time an attack is made with this weapon against an AIRCRAFT unit, add 1 to that attack's hit roll.
Storm bolter	24"	Rapid Fire 2	4	0	1	-

OTHER WARGEAR	ABILITIES
Shield dome	The bearer has a 5+ invulnerable save.
Orbital comms array	In your Command phase, one model from your army with an orbital comms array that has not been used this battle can use it to call in an orbital barrage. If it does, select one point on the battlefield and roll one D6 for each unit within D6" of that point, subtracting 1 from the result if the unit being rolled for is a CHARACTER. On a 4+, that unit suffers D3 mortal wounds.

WARGEAR OPTIONS

- This model can be equipped with 1 ironhail heavy stubber.
- This model's 2 storm bolters can be replaced with 2 fragstorm grenade launchers.
- This model can be equipped with one of the following: 1 shield dome; 1 orbital comms array; 1 bellicatus missile array; 1 ironhail skytalon array.

ABILITIES

Angels of Death (pg 124-125)

Assault Vehicle: Units embarked within this transport can disembark even if it has made a Normal Move this phase. Any unit that disembarks after this transport has made a Normal Move cannot charge this turn.

Hover Tank: Distances are always measured to and from this model's hull.

Explodes: When this transport is destroyed, roll one D6 before any embarked models disembark and before removing it from play. On a 6 it explodes, and each unit within 6" suffers D3 mortal wounds.

TRANSPORT

This model has a transport capacity of 6 <CHAPTER> PRIMARIS INFANTRY models. It cannot transport JUMP PACK or MK X GRAVIS models.

FACTION KEYWORDS: IMPERIUM, ADEPTUS ASTARTES, <CHAPTER>
KEYWORDS: VEHICLE, TRANSPORT, REPULSOR FIELD, IMPULSOR

Equipped with vectored thrusters that make it faster than any other gravitic tank in the Space Marines' armouries, the Impulsor is a highly adaptable transport used by all Primaris Space Marines for rapid insertion and flanking manoeuvres. It is particularly favoured by Vanguard forces.

DROP POD

4 POWER

No.	Name	M	WS	BS	S	T	W	A	Ld	Sv
1	Drop Pod	-	-	3+	6	6	8	-	8	3+

A Drop Pod is equipped with: storm bolter.

WEAPON	RANGE	TYPE	S	AP	D	ABILITIES
Deathwind launcher	12"	Heavy D6	5	0	1	Blast
Storm bolter	24"	Rapid Fire 2	4	0	1	-

WARGEAR OPTIONS

- This model's storm bolter can be replaced with 1 deathwind launcher.

ABILITIES

Angels of Death, Death From Above (pg 124-125)

Drop Pod Assault: This transport must start the battle set up high in the skies (see Death From Above, page 125) but neither it, nor any units embarked within it, are counted towards any limits that the mission you are playing places on the maximum number of Reinforcement units you can have in your army. This transport can be set up in the Reinforcements step of your first, second or third Movement phase, regardless of any mission rules. Any units embarked within this transport must immediately disembark after it has been set up on the battlefield, and they must be set up more than 9" away from any enemy models. After this transport has been set up on the battlefield, no units can embark within it.

Explodes: When this transport is destroyed, roll one D6 before removing it from play. On a 6 it explodes, and each unit within 6" suffers 1 mortal wound.

TRANSPORT

This model has a transport capacity of 10 <Chapter> Infantry models. It cannot transport Jump Pack, Terminator, Primaris, Wulfen or Centurion models.

FACTION KEYWORDS: Imperium, Adeptus Astartes, <Chapter>
KEYWORDS: Vehicle, Transport, Drop Pod

Launched from ships in low orbit, Drop Pods full of Space Marines slam into the battlefield, their hatches blowing open upon the violent impact. Within seconds, the squad bursts out with weapons firing. Such deadly strikes send the foe into disarray as the rear of their lines are torn apart in the furious assault.

LAND SPEEDER STORM

3 POWER

No.	Name	M	WS	BS	S	T	W	A	Ld	Sv
1	Land Speeder Storm	18"	3+	3+	4	6	7	2	7	4+

A Land Speeder Storm is equipped with: cerberus launcher; heavy bolter.

WEAPON	RANGE	TYPE	S	AP	D	ABILITIES
Cerberus launcher	18"	Heavy D6	4	0	1	Blast
Heavy bolter	36"	Heavy 3	5	-1	2	-

ABILITIES

Angels of Death, Outflank (pg 124-125)

Assault Vehicle: Units embarked within this transport can disembark even if it has made a Normal Move this phase. Any unit that disembarks after this transport has made a Normal Move cannot charge this turn.

Open-topped: In your Shooting phase, units embarked within this transport can be selected to shoot with; measure distances and draw line of sight from any point on this transport when doing so. If this transport made a Normal Move, Advanced or Fell Back this turn, embarked units are considered to have done the same. While this transport is within Engagement Range of any enemy units, embarked units cannot shoot, except with Pistols.

Explodes: When this transport is destroyed, roll one D6 before any embarked models disembark and before removing it from play. On a 6 it explodes, and each unit within 3" suffers 1 mortal wound.

TRANSPORT

This model has a transport capacity of 5 <Chapter> Scout Infantry models.

FACTION KEYWORDS: Imperium, Adeptus Astartes, <Chapter>
KEYWORDS: Vehicle, Land Speeder, Scout, Fly, Transport, Land Speeder Storm

The Land Speeder Storm is equipped with additional sensor arrays and baffled engines to make it the perfect transport for Scout Squads being secretly inserted into enemy territory. Countless victories in the annals of many Chapters can be attributed to the surprise attacks carried out by this vehicle and its occupants.

STORMHAWK INTERCEPTOR

10 POWER

Some of this model's characteristics change as it suffers damage, as shown below:

No.	Name	M	WS	BS	S	T	W	A	Ld	Sv
1	Stormhawk Interceptor (6+ wounds remaining)	20-60"	6+	3+	6	7	10	3	8	3+
	Stormhawk Interceptor (3-5 wounds remaining)	20-45"	6+	4+	6	7	N/A	D3	8	3+
	Stormhawk Interceptor (1-2 wounds remaining)	20-30"	6+	5+	6	7	N/A	1	8	3+

A Stormhawk Interceptor is equipped with: 2 assault cannons; skyhammer missile launcher; las-talon.

WEAPON	RANGE	TYPE	S	AP	D	ABILITIES
Assault cannon	24"	Heavy 6	6	-1	1	-
Heavy bolter	36"	Heavy 3	5	-1	2	-
Icarus stormcannon	48"	Heavy 3	7	-1	2	Each time an attack is made with this weapon against an AIRCRAFT unit, make 2 hit rolls instead of 1 and add 1 to both those hit rolls.
Las-talon	24"	Heavy 2	9	-3	D6	-
Skyhammer missile launcher	60"	Heavy 3	7	-1	D3	Each time an attack is made with this weapon against an AIRCRAFT unit, add 1 to that attack's hit roll.
Typhoon missile launcher	Before selecting targets, select one of the profiles below to make attacks with.					
- Frag missile	48"	Heavy 2D6	4	0	1	Blast
- Krak missile	48"	Heavy 2	8	-2	D6	-

OTHER WARGEAR	ABILITIES
Infernum halo-launcher	When a ranged attack made by an AIRCRAFT model is allocated to the bearer, add 1 to any armour saving throw made against that attack.

WARGEAR OPTIONS

- This model's skyhammer missile launcher can be replaced with one of the following: 2 heavy bolters; 1 typhoon missile launcher.
- This model's las-talon can be replaced with 1 Icarus stormcannon.

ABILITIES

Angels of Death (pg 124-125)

Airborne: You cannot declare a charge with this model, and it can only be chosen as a target of a charge if the unit making the charge can FLY. You can only fight with this model if it is within Engagement Range of any enemy units that can FLY, and this model can only make melee attacks against units that can FLY. Enemy units can only make melee attacks against this model if they can FLY.

Supersonic: Each time this model makes a Normal Move, Advances or Falls Back, first pivot it on the spot up to 90° (this does not contribute to how far the model moves), then move the model straight forwards. It cannot pivot again after the initial pivot.

Hard to Hit: Each time a ranged attack is made against this model, subtract 1 from that attack's hit roll.

Explodes: When this model is destroyed, roll one D6 before removing it from play. On a 6 it explodes, and each unit within 6" suffers D3 mortal wounds.

FACTION KEYWORDS: IMPERIUM, ADEPTUS ASTARTES, <CHAPTER>

KEYWORDS: VEHICLE, AIRCRAFT, FLY, STORMHAWK INTERCEPTOR

Stormhawk Interceptors are high-altitude fighter craft designed solely for achieving aerial supremacy. Dropped from mag-cradles aboard orbiting craft, these ceramite-plated vehicles engage enemy air assets in brutal dogfights and are protected by countermeasures that launch blazing flares.

STORMTALON GUNSHIP

9 POWER

Some of this model's characteristics change as it suffers damage, as shown below:

No.	Name	M	WS	BS	S	T	W	A	Ld	Sv
1	Stormtalon Gunship (6+ wounds remaining)	20-50"	6+	3+	6	6	10	3	8	3+
	Stormtalon Gunship (3-5 wounds remaining)	20-40"	6+	4+	6	6	N/A	D3	8	3+
	Stormtalon Gunship (1-2 wounds remaining)	20-30"	6+	5+	6	6	N/A	1	8	3+

A Stormtalon Gunship is equipped with: skyhammer missile launcher; twin assault cannon.

WEAPON	RANGE	TYPE	S	AP	D	ABILITIES
Heavy bolter	36"	Heavy 3	5	-1	2	-
Lascannon	48"	Heavy 1	9	-3	D6	-
Skyhammer missile launcher	60"	Heavy 3	7	-1	D3	Each time an attack is made with this weapon against an AIRCRAFT unit, add 1 to that attack's hit roll.
Twin assault cannon	24"	Heavy 12	6	-1	1	-
Typhoon missile launcher	Before selecting targets, select one of the profiles below to make attacks with.					
- Frag missile	48"	Heavy 2D6	4	0	1	Blast
- Krak missile	48"	Heavy 2	8	-2	D6	

WARGEAR OPTIONS

- This model's skyhammer missile launcher can be replaced with one of the following: 2 heavy bolters; 2 lascannons; 1 typhoon missile launcher.

ABILITIES

Angels of Death (pg 124-125)

Airborne: You cannot declare a charge with this model, and it can only be chosen as a target of a charge if the unit making the charge can FLY. You can only fight with this model if it is within Engagement Range of any enemy units that can FLY, and this model can only make melee attacks against units that can FLY. Enemy units can only make melee attacks against this model if they can FLY.

Supersonic: Each time this model makes a Normal Move, Advances or Falls Back, first pivot it on the spot up to 90° (this does not contribute to how far the model moves), then move the model straight forwards. It cannot pivot again after the initial pivot.

Hard to Hit: Each time a ranged attack is made against this model, subtract 1 from that attack's hit roll.

Hover Jet: In your Command phase, this model can hover. If it does, then until the start of your next Command phase, its Move characteristic becomes 20" and it loses the Airborne, Hard to Hit and Supersonic abilities.

Explodes: When this model is destroyed, roll one D6 before removing it from play. On a 6 it explodes, and each unit within 6" suffers D3 mortal wounds.

FACTION KEYWORDS: **IMPERIUM, ADEPTUS ASTARTES, <CHAPTER>**
KEYWORDS: **VEHICLE, AIRCRAFT, FLY, STORMTALON GUNSHIP**

Fast and manoeuvrable, the Stormtalon is an aerial interceptor optimised for escorting Stormraven Gunships. While fast enough to engage in aerial combat, its pilot can switch on the Stormtalon's repulsor systems, making it agile enough to closely support infantry in defence or on the attack.

STORMRAVEN GUNSHIP

17 POWER

Some of this model's characteristics change as it suffers damage, as shown below:

No.	Name	M	WS	BS	S	T	W	A	Ld	Sv
1	Stormraven Gunship (8+wounds remaining)	20-45"	6+	3+	8	7	14	6	9	3+
	Stormraven Gunship (4-7 wounds remaining)	20-35"	6+	4+	8	7	N/A	D6	9	3+
	Stormraven Gunship (1-3 wounds remaining)	20-25"	6+	5+	8	7	N/A	D3	9	3+

A Stormraven Gunship is equipped with: 2 stormstrike missile launchers; twin assault cannon; typhoon missile launcher.

WEAPON	RANGE	TYPE	S	AP	D	ABILITIES
Hurricane bolter	24"	Rapid Fire 6	4	0	1	-
Stormstrike missile launcher	72"	Heavy 1	8	-3	3	-
Twin assault cannon	24"	Heavy 12	6	-1	1	-
Twin heavy bolter	36"	Heavy 6	5	-1	2	-
Twin heavy plasma cannon	Before selecting targets, select one of the profiles below to make attacks with.					
- Standard	36"	Heavy 2D3	7	-3	2	Blast
- Supercharge	36"	Heavy 2D3	8	-3	3	Blast. Each time an unmodified hit roll of 1 is made for an attack with this weapon profile, the bearer suffers 1 mortal wound after shooting with this weapon.
Twin lascannon	48"	Heavy 2	9	-3	D6	-
Twin multi-melta	24"	Heavy 4	8	-4	D6	Each time an attack made with this weapon targets a unit within half range, that attack has a Damage characteristic of D6+2.
Typhoon missile launcher	Before selecting targets, select one of the profiles below to make attacks with.					
- Frag missile	48"	Heavy 2D6	4	0	1	Blast
- Krak missile	48"	Heavy 2	8	-2	D6	-

WARGEAR OPTIONS

- This model's twin assault cannon can be replaced with one of the following: 1 twin heavy plasma cannon; 1 twin lascannon.
- This model's typhoon missile launcher can be replaced with one of the following: 1 twin heavy bolter; 1 twin multi-melta.
- This model can be equipped with 2 hurricane bolters.

ABILITIES

Angels of Death (pg 124-125)

Airborne: You cannot declare a charge with this model, and it can only be chosen as a target of a charge if the unit making the charge can **FLY**. You can only fight with this model if it is within Engagement Range of any enemy units that can **FLY**, and this model can only make melee attacks against units that can **FLY**. Enemy units can only make melee attacks against this model if they can **FLY**.

Supersonic: Each time this model makes a Normal Move, Advances or Falls Back, first pivot it on the spot up to 90° (this does not contribute to how far the model moves), then move the model straight forwards. It cannot pivot again after the initial pivot.

Hard to Hit: Each time a ranged attack is made against this model, subtract 1 from that attack's hit roll.

Hover Jet: In your Command phase, this model can hover. If it does, then until the start of your next Command phase, its Move characteristic becomes 20" and it loses the Airborne, Hard to Hit and Supersonic abilities.

Explodes: When this transport is destroyed, roll one D6 before any embarked models disembark and before removing it from play. On a 6 it explodes, and each unit within 6" suffers D6 mortal wounds.

TRANSPORT

This model has a transport capacity of 12 <Chapter> Infantry models and 1 <Chapter> Dreadnought model. Each **Jump Pack**, **Wulfen** or **Terminator** model takes the space of two **Infantry** models and each **Centurion** model takes the space of three **Infantry** models. It cannot transport **Primaris** models or **Dreadnought** models that have a Wounds characteristic of 13 or more.

FACTION KEYWORDS: Imperium, Adeptus Astartes, <Chapter>
KEYWORDS: Vehicle, Aircraft, Transport, Fly, Machine Spirit, Stormraven Gunship

The Stormraven superbly combines the role of reliable combat drop-ship and deadly aerial combatant. A capacious troop bay and thick layers of armour allow it to effectively transport squads of Space Marines – and thanks to its magna-grapples, even a Dreadnought – into the very heart of the battle.

HAMMERFALL BUNKER

9 POWER

Some of this model's characteristics change as it suffers damage, as shown below:

No.	NAME	M	WS	BS	S	T	W	A	Ld	Sv
1	Hammerfall Bunker (8+ wounds remaining)	-	-	4+	6	8	14	-	7	3+
	Hammerfall Bunker (4-7 wounds remaining)	-	-	5+	6	8	N/A	-	7	3+
	Hammerfall Bunker (1-3 wounds remaining)	-	-	6+	6	8	N/A	-	7	3+

A Hammerfall Bunker is equipped with: Hammerfall heavy bolter array; Hammerfall missile launcher.

WEAPON	RANGE	TYPE	S	AP	D	ABILITIES
Hammerfall heavy bolter array	36"	Heavy 3	5	-1	2	-
Hammerfall heavy flamer array	12"	Heavy D6	5	-1	1	Each time an attack is made with this weapon, that attack automatically hits the target.
Hammerfall missile launcher	Before selecting targets, select one of the profiles below to make attacks with.					
- Superfrag missile	72"	Heavy 2D6	6	0	1	Blast
- Superkrak missile	72"	Heavy 2	10	-2	D6	-

WARGEAR OPTIONS

• This model's Hammerfall heavy bolter array can be replaced with 1 Hammerfall heavy flamer array.

ABILITIES

Angels of Death (pg 124-125)

Defensive Array: In your Shooting phase, each time this model is selected to shoot, its Hammerfall heavy bolter array or its Hammerfall heavy flamer array can target, and resolve attacks against, every eligible enemy unit. Each time this model fires Overwatch, it only resolves attacks with its weapons against the charging unit, but when doing so the Type of its Hammerfall heavy bolter array is changed to Heavy 6, and the Type of its Hammerfall heavy flamer array is changed to Heavy 2D6.

Explodes: When this model is destroyed, roll one D6 before removing it from play. On a 6 it explodes, and each unit within 6" suffers D6 mortal wounds.

FACTION KEYWORDS: **Imperium, Adeptus Astartes, <Chapter>**
KEYWORDS: **Vehicle, Building, Hammerfall Bunker**

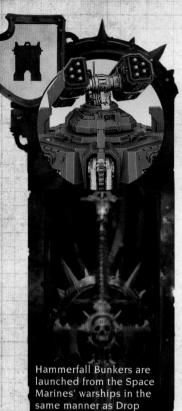

Hammerfall Bunkers are launched from the Space Marines' warships in the same manner as Drop Pods. Automated area-denial assets crewed by hard-wired servitors, they have all kinds of battlefield roles, including securing beachheads, hampering enemy assaults and wreaking havoc behind the foe's lines.

WEAPON PROFILES

On pages 196-201 you will find the profiles for all the weapons that Space Marine models can be equipped with. Note that some weapons have the Blast ability; this ability is detailed in full in the Warhammer 40,000 Core Book.

WEAPON LISTS

The wargear options section of some datasheets in this Codex refer to one of more weapon lists. These lists can be found below:

WARGEAR

COMBI-WEAPONS
- Combi-flamer
- Combi-grav
- Combi-melta
- Combi-plasma
- Storm bolter

DREADNOUGHT WEAPONS
- Heavy plasma cannon
- Helfrost cannon*
- Multi-melta
- Twin lascannon

HEAVY WEAPONS
- Grav-cannon
- Heavy bolter
- Heavy flamer**
- Lascannon
- Missile launcher
- Multi-melta
- Plasma cannon

MELEE WEAPONS
- Astartes chainsword
- Lightning claw
- Power axe
- Power fist
- Power maul
- Power sword
- Thunder hammer

PISTOLS
- Bolt pistol
- Hand flamer**
- Grav-pistol
- Inferno pistol**
- Plasma pistol

SPECIAL WEAPONS
- Flamer
- Grav-gun
- Meltagun
- Plasma gun

*   *Only models from the Space Wolves Chapter (or one of its successor Chapters) can be equipped with this weapon.*
** *Only models from the Deathwatch Chapter or the Blood Angels Chapter (or one of its successor Chapters) can be equipped with this weapon.*

WEAPON DEFINITIONS

Some rules refer to 'bolt weapons', 'flame weapons', 'melta weapons' or 'plasma weapons'. The definitions of these weapons for the purposes of such rules can be found below:

Bolt Weapons

A bolt weapon is any weapon whose profile includes the word 'bolt' (bolt rifle, boltstorm gauntlet, storm bolter etc.), and any Relic that replaces a bolt weapon (e.g. Primarch's Wrath, page 108). Rules that apply to bolt weapons only apply to the boltgun profile of combi-weapons, and the boltgun profile of Relics that replace combi-weapons. If a bolt weapon has a shooting and melee profile, rules that apply to bolt weapons only apply to the shooting profile of that weapon. Note that the following weapons found in Codex supplements are also bolt weapons:

- Blackout
- Blood Song (master-crafted boltgun profile)
- The Deliverer
- Dorn's Arrow
- Gauntlets of Ultramar
- Guardian spear
- Gorgon's Wrath
- Infernus (master-crafted boltgun profile)
- Lion's Wrath (master-crafted boltgun profile)
- Quietus

Flame Weapons

A flame weapon is any weapon whose profile includes the word 'flame' (flamer, flamestorm gauntlet, heavy flamer etc.), any Relic that replaces a flame weapon, and any incendium cannons. Rules that apply to flame weapons only apply to the flamer profile of combi-flamers, and the flamer profile of Relics that replace combi-flamers. If a flame weapon has a shooting and melee profile, rules that apply to flame weapons only apply to the shooting profile of that weapon. Note that the following weapons found in Codex supplements are also flame weapons:

- Drakkis
- Gauntlet of the Forge
- Infernus (flamer profile)

Melta Weapons

A melta weapon is any weapon whose profile includes the word 'melta' (meltagun, melta destroyer, multi-melta etc.), any Relic that replaces a melta weapon, and any inferno pistols. Rules that apply to melta weapons only apply to the meltagun profile of combi-meltas, and the meltagun profile of Relics that replace combi-meltas. Note that the following weapons found in Codex supplements are also melta weapons:

- Blood Song (meltagun profile)

Plasma Weapons

A plasma weapon is any weapon whose profile includes the word 'plasma' (plasma gun, plasma pistol, heavy plasma cannon etc.), and any Relic that replaces a plasma weapon. Rules that apply to plasma weapons only apply to the plasma gun profile of combi-plasmas, and the plasma gun profile of Relics that replace combi-plasmas. Note that the following weapons found in Codex supplements are also plasma weapons:

- Lion's Wrath (plasma gun profile)

RANGED WEAPONS	RANGE	TYPE	S	AP	D	ABILITIES
Absolvor bolt pistol	18"	Pistol 1	5	-1	2	-
Accelerator autocannon	48"	Heavy 3	7	-1	2	-
Assault bolter	18"	Assault 3	5	-1	1	-
Assault cannon	24"	Heavy 6	6	-1	1	-
Assault plasma incinerator	Before selecting targets, select one of the profiles below to make attacks with.					
- Standard	24"	Assault 3	6	-4	1	-
- Supercharge	24"	Assault 3	7	-4	2	If any unmodified hit rolls of 1 are made for attacks with this weapon profile, the bearer is destroyed after shooting with this weapon.
Astartes grenade launcher	Before selecting targets, select one of the profiles below to make attacks with.					
- Frag grenade	30"	Assault D6	3	0	1	Blast
- Krak grenade	30"	Assault 1	6	-1	D3	-
Astartes shotgun	18"	Assault 2	4	0	1	-
Auto boltstorm gauntlet (shooting)	18"	Assault 3	4	0	1	-
Auto bolt rifle	24"	Assault 3	4	0	1	-
Bellicatus missile array	Before selecting targets, select one of the profiles below to make attacks with.					
- Krak missiles	48"	Heavy 1	8	-2	D6	-
- Frag missiles	48"	Heavy D6	4	0	1	Blast
- Icarus missiles	48"	Heavy D3	7	-1	2	Blast. Each time an attack is made with this weapon profile against an AIRCRAFT unit, add 1 to that attack's hit roll.
Bolt carbine	24"	Assault 2	4	0	1	-
Bolt pistol	12"	Pistol 1	4	0	1	-
Bolt rifle	30"	Rapid Fire 1	4	-1	1	-
Bolt sniper rifle	Before selecting targets, select one of the profiles below to make attacks with. Each time you select a target for this weapon, you can ignore the Look Out, Sir rule.					
- Executioner round	36"	Heavy 1	5	-1	1	Each time an attack is made with this weapon profile, add 1 to that attack's hit roll. Targets do not receive the benefits of cover against attacks made with this weapon profile.
- Hyperfrag round	36"	Heavy D3	5	0	1	Blast
- Mortis round	36"	Heavy 1	5	-2	2	Each time an attack is made with this weapon profile, an unmodified wound roll of 6 inflicts 1 mortal wound on the target in addition to any normal damage.
Boltgun	24"	Rapid Fire 1	4	0	1	-
Boltstorm gauntlet (shooting)	12"	Pistol 3	4	-1	1	-
Centurion missile launcher	36"	Assault D3	8	-2	D3	Blast
Cerberus launcher	18"	Heavy D6	4	0	1	Blast
Combi-bolter	24"	Rapid Fire 2	4	0	1	-
Combi-flamer	Before selecting targets, select one or both of the profiles below to make attacks with. If you select both, then each time an attack is made with this weapon this phase, subtract 1 from that attack's hit roll.					
- Boltgun	24"	Rapid Fire 1	4	0	1	-
- Flamer	12"	Assault D6	4	0	1	Each time an attack is made with this weapon profile, that attack automatically hits the target.
Combi-grav	Before selecting targets, select one or both of the profiles below to make attacks with. If you select both, then each time an attack is made with this weapon this phase, subtract 1 from that attack's hit roll.					
- Boltgun	24"	Rapid Fire 1	4	0	1	-
- Grav-gun	18"	Rapid Fire 1	5	-3	1	Each time an attack made with this weapon profile is allocated to a model with a Save characteristic of 3+ or better, that attack has a Damage characteristic of 2.
Combi-melta	Before selecting targets, select one or both of the profiles below to make attacks with. If you select both, then each time an attack is made with this weapon this phase, subtract 1 from that attack's hit roll.					
- Boltgun	24"	Rapid Fire 1	4	0	1	-
- Meltagun	12"	Assault 1	8	-4	D6	Each time an attack made with this weapon profile targets a unit within half range, that attack has a Damage characteristic of D6+2.
Combi-plasma	Before selecting targets, select one or two of the profiles below to make attacks with (you can only select one of the plasma gun profiles). If you select two, then each time an attack is made with this weapon this phase, subtract 1 from that attack's hit roll.					
- Boltgun	24"	Rapid Fire 1	4	0	1	-
- Plasma gun (standard)	24"	Rapid Fire 1	7	-3	1	-
- Plasma gun (supercharge)	24"	Rapid Fire 1	8	-3	2	If any unmodified hit rolls of 1 are made for attacks with this weapon profile, the bearer is destroyed after shooting with this weapon.

RANGED WEAPONS	RANGE	TYPE	S	AP	D	ABILITIES
Cyclone missile launcher	Before selecting targets, select one of the profiles below to make attacks with.					
- Frag missile	36"	Heavy 2D6	4	0	1	Blast
- Krak missile	36"	Heavy 2	8	-2	D6	-
Deathwind launcher	12"	Heavy D6	5	0	1	Blast
Demolisher cannon	24"	Heavy D6	10	-3	D6	Blast
Executor bolt rifle	42"	Heavy 1	5	-2	2	-
Executor heavy bolter	42"	Heavy 2	5	-2	3	-
Flamer	12"	Assault D6	4	0	1	Each time an attack is made with this weapon, that attack automatically hits the target.
Flamestorm cannon	12"	Heavy D6	6	-2	2	Each time an attack is made with this weapon, that attack automatically hits the target.
Flamestorm gauntlet (shooting)	12"	Assault D6	4	0	1	Each time an attack is made with this weapon, that attack automatically hits the target.
Forge bolter	24"	Assault 3	5	-1	2	Each time the bearer shoots, it can make attacks with this weapon even if it also makes attacks with Pistols or Grenades.
Frag grenades	6"	Grenade D6	3	0	1	Blast
Fragstorm grenade launcher	18"	Assault D6	4	0	1	Blast
Grav-cannon	30"	Heavy 4	5	-3	1	Each time an attack made with this weapon is allocated to a model with a Save characteristic of 3+ or better, that attack has a Damage characteristic of 2.
Grav-gun	18"	Rapid Fire 1	5	-3	1	Each time an attack made with this weapon is allocated to a model with a Save characteristic of 3+ or better, that attack has a Damage characteristic of 2.
Grav-pistol	12"	Pistol 1	5	-3	1	Each time an attack made with this weapon is allocated to a model with a Save characteristic of 3+ or better, that attack has a Damage characteristic of 2.
Grenade harness	12"	Assault D6	4	-1	1	Blast
Hammerfall heavy bolter array	36"	Heavy 3	5	-1	2	-
Hammerfall heavy flamer array	12"	Heavy D6	5	-1	1	Each time an attack is made with this weapon, that attack automatically hits the target.
Hammerfall missile launcher	Before selecting targets, select one of the profiles below to make attacks with.					
- Superfrag missile	72"	Heavy 2D6	6	0	1	Blast
- Superkrak missile	72"	Heavy 2	10	-2	D6	-
Hammerstrike missile launcher	36"	Heavy 2	8	-3	3	-
Hand flamer	12"	Pistol D6	3	0	1	Each time an attack is made with this weapon, that attack automatically hits the target.
Heavy bolt pistol	18"	Pistol 1	4	-1	1	-
Heavy bolt rifle	36"	Rapid Fire 1	5	-1	1	-
Heavy bolter	36"	Heavy 3	5	-1	2	-
Heavy flamer	12"	Heavy D6	5	-1	1	Each time an attack is made with this weapon, that attack automatically hits the target.
Heavy laser destroyer	72"	Heavy 2	12	-4	D3+3	-
Heavy melta rifle	24"	Heavy 1	8	-4	D6+2	Each time an attack made with this weapon targets a unit within half range, that attack has a Damage characteristic of D6+4.
Heavy onslaught gatling cannon	30"	Heavy 12	6	-1	1	-
Heavy plasma cannon	Before selecting targets, select one of the profiles below to make attacks with.					
- Standard	36"	Heavy D3	7	-3	2	Blast
- Supercharge	36"	Heavy D3	8	-3	3	Blast. Each time an unmodified hit roll of 1 is made for an attack with this weapon profile, the bearer suffers 1 mortal wound after shooting with this weapon.
Heavy plasma incinerator	Before selecting targets, select one of the profiles below to make attacks with.					
- Standard	36"	Heavy 1	8	-4	2	-
- Supercharge	36"	Heavy 1	9	-4	3	If any unmodified hit rolls of 1 are made for attacks with this weapon profile, the bearer is destroyed after shooting with this weapon.
Helfrost cannon	Before selecting targets, select one of the profiles below to make attacks with.					
- Dispersed	36"	Heavy D3	6	-2	1	Blast
- Focussed	36"	Heavy 1	8	-4	D3+3	-
Helfrost pistol	Before selecting targets, select one of the profiles below to make attacks with.					
- Dispersed	12"	Pistol D3	4	-2	1	Blast
- Focussed	12"	Pistol 1	6	-4	3	-
Hellstorm bolt rifle	30"	Assault 3	5	0	1	-
Hellstorm heavy bolter	30"	Heavy 4	5	0	2	-
Hunter-killer missile	48"	Heavy 1	10	-2	D6	The bearer can only shoot with each hunter-killer missile it is equipped with once per battle.

RANGED WEAPONS	RANGE	TYPE	S	AP	D	ABILITIES
Hunter-slayer missile	48"	Heavy 1	10	-2	D6	The bearer can only shoot with each hunter-slayer missile it is equipped with once per battle. This weapon can target units that are not visible to the bearer.
Hurricane bolter	24"	Rapid Fire 6	4	0	1	-
Icarus ironhail heavy stubber	36"	Heavy 4	4	-1	1	Each time an attack is made with this weapon against an AIRCRAFT unit, add 1 to that attack's hit roll.
Icarus rocket pod	24"	Heavy D3	7	-1	2	Blast. Each time an attack is made with this weapon against an AIRCRAFT unit, add 1 to that attack's hit roll.
Icarus stormcannon	48"	Heavy 3	7	-1	2	Each time an attack is made with this weapon against an AIRCRAFT unit, make 2 hit rolls instead of 1 and add 1 to both those hit rolls.
Incendium cannon	12"	Heavy 2D6	5	-1	1	Each time an attack is made with this weapon, that attack automatically hits the target.
Inferno pistol	6"	Pistol 1	8	-4	D6	Each time an attack made with this weapon targets a unit within half range, that attack has a Damage characteristic of D6+2.
Instigator bolt carbine	24"	Assault 1	4	-1	2	Each time you select a target for this weapon, you can ignore the Look Out, Sir rule.
Ironhail heavy stubber	36"	Heavy 4	4	-1	1	-
Ironhail skytalon array	36"	Heavy 8	4	-1	1	Each time an attack is made with this weapon against an AIRCRAFT unit, add 1 to that attack's hit roll.
Kheres-pattern assault cannon	24"	Heavy 6	7	-1	1	-
Krak grenades	6"	Grenade 1	6	-1	D3	-
Krakstorm grenade launcher	18"	Assault 1	6	-1	D3	-
Las fusil	36"	Heavy 1	8	-3	3	-
Las-talon	24"	Heavy 2	9	-3	D6	-
Lascannon	48"	Heavy 1	9	-3	D6	-
Lancer laser destroyer	72"	Heavy 2	10	-3	D3+3	-
Macro plasma incinerator	Before selecting targets, select one of the profiles below to make attacks with.					
- Standard	36"	Heavy D6	8	-4	2	Blast
- Supercharge	36"	Heavy D6	9	-4	3	Blast. Each time an unmodified hit roll of 1 is made for an attack with this weapon profile, the bearer suffers 1 mortal wound after shooting with this weapon.
Marksman bolt carbine	24"	Rapid Fire 1	4	0	1	Each time an attack is made with this weapon, an unmodified hit roll of 6 automatically wounds the target.
Master-crafted auto bolt rifle	24"	Assault 3	4	0	2	-
Master-crafted boltgun	24"	Rapid Fire 1	4	-1	2	-
Master-crafted heavy bolt rifle	36"	Rapid Fire 1	5	-1	2	-
Master-crafted instigator bolt carbine	30"	Assault 1	4	-2	3	Each time you select a target for this weapon, you can ignore the Look Out, Sir rule.
Master-crafted occulus bolt carbine	24"	Rapid Fire 1	4	0	2	Each time an attack is made with this weapon, the target does not receive the benefits of cover against that attack.
Master-crafted special issue bolt pistol	12"	Pistol 1	4	-2	2	-
Master-crafted stalker bolt rifle	36"	Heavy 1	4	-2	3	-
Melta destroyer	24"	Heavy 3	8	-4	D6	Each time an attack made with this weapon targets a unit within half range, that attack has a Damage characteristic of D6+2.
Melta rifle	24"	Assault 1	8	-4	D6	Each time an attack made with this weapon targets a unit within half range, that attack has a Damage characteristic of D6+2.
Meltagun	12"	Assault 1	8	-4	D6	Each time an attack made with this weapon targets a unit within half range, that attack has a Damage characteristic of D6+2.
Missile launcher	Before selecting targets, select one of the profiles below to make attacks with.					
- Frag missile	48"	Heavy D6	4	0	1	Blast
- Krak missile	48"	Heavy 1	8	-2	D6	-
Multi-melta	24"	Heavy 2	8	-4	D6	Each time an attack made with this weapon targets a unit within half range, that attack has a Damage characteristic of D6+2.
Neo-volkite pistol	15"	Pistol 2	5	0	2	Each time an attack is made with this weapon, an unmodified wound roll of 6 inflicts 1 mortal wound on the target in addition to any normal damage.
Occulus bolt carbine	24"	Rapid Fire 1	4	0	1	Each time an attack is made with this weapon, the target does not receive the benefits of cover against that attack.
Onslaught gatling cannon	24"	Heavy 8	5	-1	1	-

RANGED WEAPONS	RANGE	TYPE	S	AP	D	ABILITIES
Plasma blaster	Before selecting targets, select one of the profiles below to make attacks with.					
- Standard	18"	Assault 2	7	-3	1	-
- Supercharge	18"	Assault 2	8	-3	2	If any unmodified hit rolls of 1 are made for attacks with this weapon profile, the bearer is destroyed after shooting with this weapon.
Plasma cannon	Before selecting targets, select one of the profiles below to make attacks with.					
- Standard	36"	Heavy D3	7	-3	1	Blast
- Supercharge	36"	Heavy D3	8	-3	2	Blast. If any unmodified hit rolls of 1 are made for attacks with this weapon profile, the bearer is destroyed after shooting with this weapon.
Plasma cutter	Before selecting targets, select one of the profiles below to make attacks with.					
- Standard	12"	Assault 1	7	-3	1	-
- Supercharge	12"	Assault 1	8	-3	2	If any unmodified hit rolls of 1 are made for attacks with this weapon profile, the bearer is destroyed after shooting with this weapon.
Plasma exterminator	Before selecting targets, select one of the profiles below to make attacks with.					
- Standard	18"	Assault D3	7	-3	1	Blast
- Supercharge	18"	Assault D3	8	-3	2	Blast. If any unmodified hit rolls of 1 are made for attacks with this weapon profile, the bearer is destroyed after shooting with this weapon.
Plasma gun	Before selecting targets, select one of the profiles below to make attacks with.					
- Standard	24"	Rapid Fire 1	7	-3	1	-
- Supercharge	24"	Rapid Fire 1	8	-3	2	If any unmodified hit rolls of 1 are made for attacks with this weapon profile, the bearer is destroyed after shooting with this weapon.
Plasma incinerator	Before selecting targets, select one of the profiles below to make attacks with.					
- Standard	30"	Rapid Fire 1	7	-4	1	-
- Supercharge	30"	Rapid Fire 1	8	-4	2	If any unmodified hit rolls of 1 are made for attacks with this weapon profile, the bearer is destroyed after shooting with this weapon.
Plasma pistol	Before selecting targets, select one of the profiles below to make attacks with.					
- Standard	12"	Pistol 1	7	-3	1	-
- Supercharge	12"	Pistol 1	8	-3	2	If any unmodified hit rolls of 1 are made for attacks with this weapon profile, the bearer is destroyed after shooting with this weapon.
Predator autocannon	48"	Heavy 2D3	7	-1	3	-
Reaper autocannon	36"	Heavy 4	7	-2	1	-
Reductor pistol	3"	Pistol 1	4	-4	2	-
Scout sniper rifle	36"	Heavy 1	4	-1	1	Each time you select a target for this weapon, you can ignore the Look Out, Sir rule. Each time an attack is made with this weapon, an unmodified wound roll of 6 inflicts 1 mortal wound on the target in addition to any normal damage.
Skyhammer missile launcher	60"	Heavy 3	7	-1	D3	Each time an attack is made with this weapon against an AIRCRAFT unit, add 1 to that attack's hit roll.
Skyspear missile launcher	60"	Heavy 1	9	-3	D6	Each time an attack is made with this weapon against an AIRCRAFT unit, add 2 to that attack's hit roll. Each time an attack made with this weapon is allocated to an AIRCRAFT model, that attack has a Damage characteristic of D6+6.
Special issue bolt carbine	24"	Assault 2	4	-2	2	-
Special issue bolt pistol	12"	Pistol 1	4	-2	1	-
Special issue boltgun	30"	Rapid Fire 1	4	-2	1	-
Stalker bolt rifle	36"	Heavy 1	4	-2	2	-
Storm bolter	24"	Rapid Fire 2	4	0	1	-
Stormfury missile	48"	Heavy 1	10	-3	D6	-
Stormstrike missile launcher	72"	Heavy 1	8	-3	3	-
Tempest bolter	30"	Rapid Fire 4	4	-1	1	-
Thunderfire cannon	60"	Heavy 4D3	4	0	1	Blast. This weapon can target units that are not visible to the bearer.
Thunderstrike las-talon	36"	Heavy 2	9	-3	D6	-
Twin accelerator autocannon	48"	Heavy 6	7	-1	2	-
Twin assault cannon	24"	Heavy 12	6	-1	1	-
Twin auto bolt rifle	24"	Assault 6	4	0	1	-

RANGED WEAPONS	RANGE	TYPE	S	AP	D	ABILITIES
Twin bolt rifle	30"	Rapid Fire 2	4	-1	1	-
Twin boltgun	24"	Rapid Fire 2	4	0	1	-
Twin heavy bolter	36"	Heavy 6	5	-1	2	-
Twin heavy onslaught gatling cannon	30"	Heavy 24	6	-1	1	-
Twin heavy plasma cannon	Before selecting targets, select one of the profiles below to make attacks with.					
- Standard	36"	Heavy 2D3	7	-3	2	Blast
- Supercharge	36"	Heavy 2D3	8	-3	3	Blast. Each time an unmodified hit roll of 1 is made for an attack with this weapon profile, the bearer suffers 1 mortal wound after shooting with this weapon.
Twin Icarus ironhail heavy stubber	36"	Heavy 8	4	-1	1	Each time an attack is made with this weapon against an AIRCRAFT unit, add 1 to that attack's hit roll.
Twin ironhail autocannon	48"	Heavy 6	7	-1	2	-
Twin ironhail heavy stubber	36"	Heavy 8	4	-1	1	-
Twin las-talon	24"	Heavy 4	9	-3	D6	-
Twin lascannon	48"	Heavy 2	9	-3	D6	-
Twin multi-melta	24"	Heavy 4	8	-4	D6	Each time an attack made with this weapon targets a unit within half range, that attack has a Damage characteristic of D6+2.
Typhoon missile launcher	Before selecting targets, select one of the profiles below to make attacks with.					
- Frag missile	48"	Heavy 2D6	4	0	1	Blast
- Krak missile	48"	Heavy 2	8	-2	D6	-
Volkite charger	20"	Heavy 2	5	0	2	Each time an attack is made with this weapon, an unmodified wound roll of 6 inflicts 1 mortal wound on the target in addition to any normal damage.
Whirlwind castellan launcher	72"	Heavy 2D6	6	0	1	Blast. This weapon can target units that are not visible to the bearer.
Whirlwind vengeance launcher	72"	Heavy 2D3	7	-1	2	Blast. This weapon can target units that are not visible to the bearer.
Wrist-mounted grenade launcher	12"	Assault D3	4	-1	1	Blast

MELEE WEAPONS	RANGE	TYPE	S	AP	D	ABILITIES
Astartes chainsword	Melee	Melee	User	-1	1	Each time the bearer fights, it makes 1 additional attack with this weapon.
Auto boltstorm gauntlet (melee)	Melee	Melee	x2	-3	2	Each time an attack is made with this weapon, subtract 1 from that attack's hit roll.
Boltstorm gauntlet (melee)	Melee	Melee	x2	-3	2	Each time an attack is made with this weapon, subtract 1 from that attack's hit roll.
Chainfist	Melee	Melee	x2	-4	D3	Each time an attack is made with this weapon, subtract 1 from that attack's hit roll, and if that attack is allocated to a VEHICLE model, that attack has a Damage characteristic of 3.
Combat knife	Melee	Melee	User	0	1	Each time the bearer fights, it makes 1 additional attack with this weapon.
Crozius arcanum	Melee	Melee	+2	-1	2	-
Dreadnought chainfist	Melee	Melee	x2	-4	2D3	Each time an attack made with this weapon is allocated to a VEHICLE model, that attack has a Damage characteristic of 6.
Dreadnought combat weapon	Melee	Melee	x2	-3	3	-
Eviscerator	Melee	Melee	+3	-4	2	Each time an attack is made with this weapon, subtract 1 from that attack's hit roll.
Executioner relic blade	Melee	Melee	+3	-3	2	Each time an attack is made with this weapon, an unmodified wound roll of 6 inflicts 1 mortal wound on the target in addition to any normal damage.
Fenrisian great axe	Each time an attack is made with this weapon, select one of the profiles below to make that attack with.					
- Cleave	Melee	Melee	+4	-3	D3+3	Each time an attack is made with this weapon profile, subtract 1 from that attack's hit roll.
- Scythe	Melee	Melee	User	-3	1	Each time an attack is made with this weapon profile, make 2 hit rolls instead of 1.
Flamestorm gauntlet (melee)	Melee	Melee	x2	-3	2	Each time an attack is made with this weapon, subtract 1 from that attack's hit roll.
Force axe	Melee	Melee	+2	-2	D3	-
Force stave	Melee	Melee	+3	-1	D3	-
Force sword	Melee	Melee	+1	-3	D3	-
Great wolf claw	Melee	Melee	+4	-2	3	Each time an attack is made with this weapon, you can re-roll the wound roll.

MELEE WEAPONS	RANGE	TYPE	S	AP	D	ABILITIES
Heavy thunder hammer	Melee	Melee	x2	-3	4	Each time an attack is made with this weapon, subtract 1 from that attack's hit roll.
Invictor fist	Melee	Melee	x2	-3	3	-
Ironclad combat weapon	Melee	Melee	x2	-3	3	-
Lightning claw	Melee	Melee	User	-2	1	Each time the bearer fights, it makes 1 additional attack with this weapon. Each time an attack is made with this weapon, you can re-roll the wound roll.
Master-crafted power axe	Melee	Melee	+2	-2	2	-
Master-crafted power sword	Melee	Melee	+1	-3	2	-
Mechadendrite	Melee	Melee	+1	0	1	Each time the bearer fights, it makes 2 additional attacks with this weapon.
Omnissian power axe	Melee	Melee	+2	-2	2	-
Paired combat blades	Melee	Melee	User	-1	1	-
Power axe	Melee	Melee	+2	-2	1	-
Power fist	Melee	Melee	x2	-3	2	Each time an attack is made with this weapon, subtract 1 from that attack's hit roll.
Power maul	Melee	Melee	+3	-1	1	-
Power sword	Melee	Melee	+1	-3	1	-
Redemptor fist	Melee	Melee	x2	-3	D3+3	-
Relic blade	Melee	Melee	+3	-3	2	-
Seismic hammer	Melee	Melee	x2	-4	5	Each time an attack is made with this weapon, subtract 1 from that attack's hit roll.
Servo-arm	Melee	Melee	x2	-2	3	Each time the bearer fights, no more than one attack can be made with each servo-arm.
Siege drills	Melee	Melee	x2	-4	3	-
Tempest hammer	Melee	Melee	x2	-3	3	Each time an attack is made with this weapon, subtract 1 from that attack's hit roll.
Thunder hammer	Melee	Melee	x2	-2	3	Each time an attack is made with this weapon, subtract 1 from that attack's hit roll.
Xenophase blade	Melee	Melee	+1	-4	1	Each time an attack is made with this weapon, invulnerable saving throws cannot be made against that attack.

POINTS VALUES

You can use this section to determine the points (pts) value of each unit in your army. Each entry lists the unit's size (i.e. how many models the unit can contain) and how many points the unit costs. If an entry has a unit cost of '*x* pts/model', then the unit costs *x* points for every model in that unit. You must then add points for each weapon, or other item of wargear, that is included in that unit if it is listed in that unit's entry (weapons and other wargear not listed in a unit's entry cost no additional points to include in that unit).

 HQ

Captain (pg 129)
Unit size .... 1 model
Unit cost .... 85 pts
- Combi-flamer .... +5 pts
- Combi-grav .... +5 pts
- Combi-melta .... +5 pts
- Combi-plasma .... +5 pts
- Jump pack .... +25 pts
- Lightning claw (single/pair)* .... +5 pts
- Power axe .... +5 pts
- Power fist .... +10 pts
- Power maul .... +5 pts
- Power sword .... +5 pts
- Relic blade .... +10 pts
- Storm shield .... +10 pts
- Thunder hammer .... +20 pts
- Xenophase blade .... +10 pts

* It is the same points cost to take a single
lightning claw or a pair of lightning claws on
this model.

Captain in Gravis Armour (pg 128)
Unit size .... 1 model
Unit cost .... 115 pts

Captain in Phobos Armour (pg 127)
Unit size .... 1 model
Unit cost .... 95 pts

Captain in Terminator Armour (pg 128)
Unit size .... 1 model
Unit cost .... 100 pts
- Chainfist .... +5 pts
- Combi-flamer .... +5 pts
- Combi-grav .... +5 pts
- Combi-melta .... +5 pts
- Combi-plasma .... +5 pts
- Power fist .... +5 pts
- Relic blade .... +5 pts
- Storm shield .... +5 pts
- Thunder hammer .... +15 pts
- Wrist-mounted grenade launcher .... +5 pts

Captain on Bike (pg 130)
Unit size .... 1 model
Unit cost .... 100 pts
- Combi-flamer .... +10 pts
- Combi-grav .... +10 pts
- Combi-melta .... +10 pts
- Combi-plasma .... +10 pts
- Grav-pistol .... +5 pts
- Hand flamer .... +5 pts
- Inferno pistol .... +5 pts
- Lightning claw .... +5 pts
- Master-crafted boltgun .... +5 pts
- Plasma pistol .... +5 pts
- Power axe .... +5 pts
- Power fist .... +10 pts
- Power maul .... +5 pts
- Power sword .... + 5 pts
- Storm bolter .... +5 pts
- Storm shield .... +10 pts
- Thunder hammer .... +20 pts

Captain with Master-crafted Heavy Bolt Rifle (pg 127)
Unit size .... 1 model
Unit cost .... 105 pts

Chaplain (pg 137)
Unit size .... 1 model
Unit cost .... 80 pts
- Combi-flamer .... +10 pts
- Combi-grav .... +10 pts
- Combi-melta .... +10 pts
- Combi-plasma .... +10 pts
- Grav-pistol .... +5 pts
- Hand flamer .... +5 pts
- Inferno pistol .... +5 pts
- Jump pack .... +25 pts
- Plasma pistol .... +5 pts
- Power fist .... +10 pts
- Storm bolter .... +5 pts

Chaplain in Terminator Armour (pg 137)
Unit size .... 1 model
Unit cost .... 95 pts
- Combi-flamer .... +5 pts
- Combi-grav .... +5 pts
- Combi-melta .... +5 pts
- Combi-plasma .... +5 pts

Chapter Command (pg 98-101)
Chapter Ancient .... +30 pts
Chapter Champion .... +25 pts
Chapter Master .... +40 pts
Chief Apothecary .... +25 pts
Chief Librarian .... +35 pts
Master of Sanctity .... +35 pts
Master of the Forge .... +30 pts

Librarian (pg 134)
Unit size .... 1 model
Unit cost .... 90 pts
- Combi-flamer .... +10 pts
- Combi-grav .... +10 pts
- Combi-melta .... +10 pts
- Combi-plasma .... +10 pts
- Grav-pistol .... +5 pts
- Hand flamer .... +5 pts
- Inferno pistol .... +5 pts
- Jump pack .... +25 pts
- Plasma pistol .... +5 pts
- Storm bolter .... +5 pts

Librarian in Phobos Armour (pg 135)
Unit size .... 1 model
Unit cost .... 100 pts

Librarian in Terminator Armour (pg 135)
Unit size .... 1 model
Unit cost .... 105 pts
- Combi-flamer .... +10 pts
- Combi-grav .... +10 pts
- Combi-melta .... +10 pts
- Combi-plasma .... +10 pts
- Storm bolter .... +5 pts

Lieutenant (pg 132)
Unit size .... 1 model
Unit cost .... 70 pts
- Combi-flamer .... +5 pts
- Combi-grav .... +5 pts
- Combi-melta .... +5 pts
- Combi-plasma .... +5 pts
- Jump pack .... +25 pts
- Lightning claw (single/pair)* .... +5 pts
- Power axe .... +5 pts
- Power fist .... +10 pts
- Power maul .... +5 pts
- Power sword .... +5 pts
- Thunder hammer .... +20 pts

* It is the same points cost to take a single
lightning claw or a pair of lightning claws on
this model.

Lieutenant in Phobos Armour (pg 133)
Unit size .... 1 model
Unit cost .... 80 pts

Lieutenant in Reiver Armour (pg 132)
Unit size .... 1 model
Unit cost .... 75 pts

Primaris Captain (pg 126)

Unit size..1 model
Unit cost...90 pts
- Master-crafted power sword...................+5 pts
- Power fist...+10 pts
- Relic shield...+10 pts

Primaris Chaplain (pg 136)

Unit size..1 model
Unit cost...85 pts

Primaris Chaplain on Bike (pg 136)

Unit size..1 model
Unit cost...115 pts

Primaris Librarian (pg 133)

Unit size..1 model
Unit cost...95 pts

Primaris Lieutenant (pg 131)

Unit size..1 model
Unit cost...75 pts
- Master-crafted power axe......................+5 pts
- Neo-volkite pistol.................................+15 pts
- Plasma pistol...+5 pts

Primaris Techmarine (pg 138)

Unit size..1 model
Unit cost...80 pts

Techmarine (pg 139)

Unit size..1 model
Unit cost...70 pts
- Combi-flamer...+10 pts
- Combi-grav...+10 pts
- Combi-melta...+10 pts
- Combi-plasma...+10 pts
- Grav-pistol...+5 pts
- Hand flamer...+5 pts
- Inferno pistol...+5 pts
- Plasma cutter...+15 pts
- Plasma pistol...+5 pts
- Power fist...+5 pts
- Storm bolter..+5 pts
- Tempest hammer...................................+20 pts
- Thunder hammer...................................+15 pts

▶ TROOPS

Assault Intercessor Squad (pg 141)

Unit size..5-10 models
Unit cost...19 pts/model
- Hand flamer...+5 pts
- Plasma pistol...+5 pts
- Power fist...+10 pts
- Power sword..+5 pts
- Thunder hammer...................................+20 pts

Heavy Intercessor Squad (pg 141)

Unit size..5-10 models
Unit cost...28 pts/model
- Executor heavy bolter..........................+10 pts
- Heavy bolter...+10 pts
- Hellstorm heavy bolter.........................+10 pts

Incursor Squad (pg 142)

Unit size..5-10 models
Unit cost...21 pts/model
- Haywire mine.......................................+10 pts

Infiltrator Squad (pg 142)

Unit size..5-10 models
Unit cost...24 pts/model
- Helix gauntlet.......................................+10 pts
- Infiltrator comms array..........................+5 pts

Intercessor Squad (pg 140)

Unit size..5-10 models
Unit cost...20 pts/model
- Astartes grenade launcher....................+5 pts
- Hand flamer...+5 pts
- Plasma pistol...+5 pts
- Power fist...+10 pts
- Power sword..+5 pts
- Thunder hammer...................................+20 pts

Tactical Squad (pg 143)

Unit size..5-10 models
Unit cost...18 pts/model
- Combi-flamer...+10 pts
- Combi-grav...+10 pts
- Combi-melta...+10 pts
- Combi-plasma...+10 pts
- Flamer..+5 pts
- Grav-cannon..+10 pts
- Grav-gun..+10 pts
- Grav-pistol...+5 pts
- Hand flamer...+5 pts
- Heavy bolter...+10 pts
- Heavy flamer...+10 pts
- Inferno pistol...+5 pts
- Lascannon...+15 pts
- Lightning claw..+5 pts
- Meltagun...+10 pts
- Missile launcher....................................+15 pts
- Multi-melta..+20 pts
- Plasma cannon......................................+15 pts
- Plasma gun..+10 pts
- Plasma pistol...+5 pts
- Power axe...+5 pts
- Power fist...+10 pts
- Power maul..+5 pts
- Power sword..+5 pts
- Storm bolter..+5 pts
- Thunder hammer...................................+15 pts

✠ ELITES

Aggressor Squad (pg 155)

Unit size...3-6 models
Unit cost...40 pts/model
- Fragstorm grenade launcher................+5 pts

Ancient in Terminator Armour (pg 148)

Unit size..1 model
Unit cost...100 pts
- Storm shield...+10 pts
- Thunder hammer...................................+10 pts

Apothecary (pg 145)

Unit size..1 model
Unit cost...75 pts

Bladeguard Ancient (pg 147)

Unit size..1 model
Unit cost...85 pts

Bladeguard Veteran Squad (pg 150)

Unit size...3-6
Unit cost...35 pts/model
- Neo-volkite pistol....................................+5 pts
- Plasma pistol...+5 pts

Centurion Assault Squad (pg 159)

Unit size...3-6 models
Unit cost...55 pts/model
- Hurricane bolter.....................................+10 pts
- Meltagun...+5 pts

Company Ancient (pg 146)

Unit size..1 model
Unit cost...75 pts
- Combi-flamer...+10 pts
- Combi-grav...+10 pts
- Combi-melta...+10 pts
- Combi-plasma...+10 pts
- Grav-pistol...+5 pts
- Hand flamer...+5 pts
- Inferno pistol...+5 pts
- Lightning claw..+5 pts
- Plasma pistol...+5 pts
- Power axe...+5 pts
- Power fist...+10 pts
- Power maul..+5 pts
- Power sword..+5 pts
- Storm bolter..+5 pts
- Thunder hammer...................................+20 pts

Company Champion (pg 143)

Unit size..1 model
Unit cost...55 pts

Company Veterans (pg 151)

Unit size...2-5 models
Unit cost...20 pts/model
- Combat shield...+3 pts
- Combi-flamer...+10 pts
- Combi-grav...+10 pts
- Combi-melta...+10 pts
- Combi-plasma...+10 pts
- Flamer..+5 pts
- Grav-cannon..+10 pts
- Grav-gun..+10 pts
- Grav-pistol...+5 pts
- Hand flamer...+5 pts
- Heavy bolter...+10 pts
- Heavy flamer...+10 pts
- Inferno pistol...+5 pts
- Lascannon...+15 pts
- Lightning claw..+3 pts
- Meltagun...+10 pts
- Missile launcher....................................+15 pts
- Multi-melta..+20 pts
- Plasma cannon......................................+15 pts
- Plasma gun..+10 pts
- Plasma pistol...+5 pts
- Power axe...+3 pts
- Power fist...+8 pts
- Power maul..+3 pts
- Power sword..+3 pts
- Storm bolter..+5 pts
- Storm shield...+4 pts
- Thunder hammer...................................+12 pts

Contemptor Dreadnought (pg 160)

Unit size .... 1 model
Unit cost .... 150 pts

Dreadnought (pg 160)

Unit size .... 1 model
Unit cost .... 120 pts
- Heavy flamer .... +5 pts
- Helfrost cannon .... +5 pts
- Multi-melta .... +5 pts
- Twin lascannon .... +20 pts

Invictor Tactical Warsuit (pg 159)

Unit size .... 1 model
Unit cost .... 160 pts

Ironclad Dreadnought (pg 162)

Unit size .... 1 model
Unit cost .... 135 pts
- Heavy flamer .... +5 pts
- Hunter-killer missile .... +5 pts
- Hurricane bolter .... +5 pts
- Ironclad assault launchers .... +5 pts

Judiciar (pg 153)

Unit size .... 1 model
Unit cost .... 85 pts

Primaris Apothecary (pg 145)

Unit size .... 1 model
Unit cost .... 80 pts

Primaris Ancient (pg 146)

Unit size .... 1 model
Unit cost .... 80 pts

Redemptor Dreadnought (pg 163)

Unit size .... 1 model
Unit cost .... 175 pts
- Icarus rocket pod .... +5 pts
- Onslaught gatling cannon .... +5 pts

Reiver Squad (pg 154)

Unit size .... 5-10 models
Unit cost .... 18 pts/model
- Grapnel launcher .... +2 pts
- Reiver grav-chute .... +2 pts

Relic Terminator Squad (pg 158)

Unit size .... 5-10 models
Unit cost .... 34 pts/model
- Chainfist .... +5 pts
- Grenade harness .... +5 pts
- Heavy flamer .... +5 pts
- Plasma blaster .... +5 pts
- Power fist .... +5 pts
- Reaper autocannon .... +5 pts
- Volkite charger .... +5 pts

Scout Squad (pg 144)

Unit size .... 5-10 models
Unit cost .... 14 pts/model
- Camo cloak .... +2 pts
- Combi-flamer .... +10 pts
- Combi-grav .... +10 pts
- Combi-melta .... +10 pts
- Combi-plasma .... +10 pts
- Flamer .... +5 pts
- Grav-gun .... +5 pts
- Grav-pistol .... +5 pts
- Hand flamer .... +5 pts
- Heavy bolter .... +10 pts
- Inferno pistol .... +5 pts
- Lightning claw .... +5 pts
- Meltagun .... +10 pts
- Missile launcher .... +15 pts
- Plasma gun .... +10 pts
- Plasma pistol .... +5 pts
- Power axe .... +5 pts
- Power fist .... +10 pts
- Power maul .... +5 pts
- Power sword .... +5 pts
- Scout sniper rifle .... +2 pts
- Storm bolter .... +5 pts
- Thunder hammer .... +15 pts

Servitors (pg 138)

Unit size .... 4 models
Unit cost .... 30 pts
- Heavy bolter .... +5 pts
- Multi-melta .... +15 pts
- Plasma cannon .... +10 pts

Sternguard Veteran Squad (pg 153)

Unit size .... 5-10 models
Unit cost .... 20 pts/model
- Combi-flamer .... +5 pts
- Combi-grav .... +5 pts
- Combi-melta .... +5 pts
- Combi-plasma .... +5 pts
- Flamer .... +5 pts
- Grav-cannon .... +10 pts
- Grav-gun .... +10 pts
- Grav-pistol .... +5 pts
- Hand flamer .... +5 pts
- Heavy bolter .... +10 pts
- Heavy flamer .... +10 pts
- Inferno pistol .... +5 pts
- Lascannon .... +15 pts
- Lightning claw .... +5 pts
- Meltagun .... +10 pts
- Missile launcher .... +15 pts
- Multi-melta .... +20 pts
- Plasma cannon .... +15 pts
- Plasma gun .... +10 pts
- Plasma pistol .... +5 pts
- Power axe .... +5 pts
- Power fist .... +10 pts
- Power maul .... +5 pts
- Power sword .... +5 pts
- Storm bolter .... +3 pts

Terminator Assault Squad (pg 156)

Unit size .... 5-10 models
Unit cost .... 33 pts/model
- Teleport homer .... +5 pts
- Thunder hammer .... +10 pts

Terminator Squad (pg 157)

Unit size .... 5-10 models
Unit cost .... 38 pts/model
- Assault cannon .... +10 pts
- Cyclone missile launcher .... +25 pts
- Heavy flamer .... +5 pts
- Teleport homer .... +5 pts

Vanguard Veteran Squad (pg 152)

Unit size .... 5-10 models
Unit cost .... 19 pts/model
- Grav-pistol .... +5 pts
- Hand flamer .... +5 pts
- Heavy thunder hammer .... +15 pts
- Inferno pistol .... +5 pts
- Jump pack .... +2 pts
- Lightning claw .... +3 pts
- Plasma pistol .... +5 pts
- Power axe .... +3 pts
- Power fist .... +8 pts
- Power maul .... +3 pts
- Power sword .... +3 pts
- Relic blade .... +10 pts
- Storm shield .... +4 pts
- Thunder hammer .... +12 pts

Venerable Dreadnought (pg 161)

Unit size .... 1 model
Unit cost .... 135 pts
- Blizzard shield .... +15 pts
- Fenrisian great axe .... +10 pts
- Heavy flamer .... +5 pts
- Helfrost cannon .... +5 pts
- Multi-melta .... +5 pts
- Twin lascannon .... +20 pts

Veteran Intercessor Squad (pg 149)

Unit size .... 5-10 models
Unit cost .... 22 pts/model
- Astartes grenade launcher .... +5 pts
- Hand flamer .... +5 pts
- Plasma pistol .... +5 pts
- Power fist .... +10 pts
- Power sword .... +5 pts
- Thunder hammer .... +20 pts

⚡ FAST ATTACK

Assault Squad (pg 164)

Unit size .... 5-10 models
Unit cost .... 18 pts/model
- Combat shield .... +5 pts
- Eviscerator .... +10 pts
- Flamer .... +5 pts
- Grav-pistol .... +5 pts
- Hand flamer .... +5 pts
- Inferno pistol .... +5 pts
- Jump pack .... +2 pts
- Lightning claw .... +5 pts
- Plasma pistol .... +5 pts
- Power axe .... +5 pts
- Power fist .... +10 pts
- Power maul .... +5 pts
- Power sword .... +5 pts
- Thunder hammer .... +15 pts

Attack Bike Squad (pg 168)

Unit size .... 1-3 models
Unit cost .... 45 pts/model
- Multi-melta .... +10 pts

Bike Squad (pg 168)

Unit size .... 3-9 models*
Unit cost .... 30 pts/model
- Combi-flamer .... +10 pts
- Combi-grav .... +10 pts
- Combi-melta .... +10 pts
- Combi-plasma .... +10 pts
- Flamer .... +5 pts
- Grav-gun .... +10 pts
- Grav-pistol .... +5 pts
- Hand flamer .... +5 pts
- Heavy bolter .... +15 pts
- Inferno pistol .... +5 pts
- Lightning claw .... +5 pts
- Meltagun .... +10 pts
- Multi-melta .... +25 pts
- Plasma gun .... +10 pts
- Plasma pistol .... +5 pts
- Power axe .... +5 pts
- Power fist .... +10 pts
- Power maul .... +5 pts
- Power sword .... +5 pts
- Storm bolter .... +5 pts
- Thunder hammer .... +15 pts

* If Space Wolves (or one of its successor Chapters), unit size is 3-16.

Inceptor Squad (pg 169)

Unit size .... 3-6 models
Unit cost .... 40 pts/model
- Plasma exterminator .... +5 pts

Invader ATV Squad (pg 165)

Unit size .... 1-3 models
Unit cost .... 80 pts/model
- Multi-melta .... +5 pts

Land Speeders (pg 171)

Unit size .... 1-3 models
Unit cost .... 60 pts/model
- Multi-melta .... +10 pts

Land Speeder Tornadoes (pg 172)

Unit size .... 1-3 models
Unit cost .... 75 pts/model
- Assault cannon .... +5 pts
- Multi-melta .... +10 pts

Land Speeder Typhoons (pg 172)

Unit size .... 1-3 models
Unit cost .... 110 pts/model
- Multi-melta .... +10 pts

Outrider Squad (pg 165)

Unit size .... 3 models
Unit cost .... 45 pts/model

Scout Bike Squad (pg 167)

Unit size .... 3-9 models
Unit cost .... 30 pts/model
- Combi-flamer .... +10 pts
- Combi-grav .... +10 pts
- Combi-melta .... +10 pts
- Combi-plasma .... +10 pts
- Grav-pistol .... +5 pts
- Hand flamer .... +5 pts
- Inferno pistol .... +5 pts
- Lightning claw .... +5 pts
- Plasma pistol .... +5 pts
- Power axe .... +5 pts
- Power fist .... +10 pts
- Power maul .... +5 pts
- Power sword .... +5 pts
- Storm bolter .... +5 pts
- Thunder hammer .... +15 pts

Storm Speeder Hailstrike (pg 170)

Unit size .... 1 model
Unit cost .... 150 pts/model

Storm Speeder Hammerstrike (pg 171)

Unit size .... 1 model
Unit cost .... 170 pts/model

Storm Speeder Thunderstrike (pg 170)

Unit size .... 1 model
Unit cost .... 175 pts/model

Suppressor Squad (pg 168)

Unit size .... 3 models
Unit cost .... 100 pts

★ HEAVY SUPPORT

Centurion Devastator Squad (pg 175)

Unit size .... 3-6 models
Unit cost .... 70 pts/model
- Grav-cannon .... +15 pts
- Heavy bolter .... +15 pts
- Lascannon .... +20 pts

Devastator Squad (pg 176)

Unit size .... 5-10 models
Unit cost .... 18 pts/model
- Armorium cherub .... +5 pts
- Combi-flamer .... +10 pts
- Combi-grav .... +10 pts
- Combi-melta .... +10 pts
- Combi-plasma .... +10 pts
- Grav-cannon .... +10 pts
- Grav-pistol .... +5 pts
- Hand flamer .... +5 pts
- Heavy bolter .... +10 pts
- Heavy flamer .... +10 pts
- Inferno pistol .... +5 pts
- Lascannon .... +15 pts
- Lightning claw .... +5 pts
- Missile launcher .... +15 pts
- Multi-melta .... +20 pts
- Plasma cannon .... +15 pts
- Plasma pistol .... +5 pts
- Power axe .... +5 pts
- Power fist .... +10 pts
- Power maul .... +5 pts
- Power sword .... +5 pts
- Storm bolter .... +5 pts
- Thunder hammer .... +15 pts

Eliminator Squad (pg 174)

Unit size .... 3 models
Unit cost .... 30 pts/model
- Las fusil .... +10 pts

Eradicator Squad (pg 175)

Unit size .... 3-6 models
Unit cost .... 40 pts/model
- Heavy melta rifle .... +5 pts
- Multi-melta .... +10 pts

Firestrike Servo-turrets (pg 177)

Unit size .... 1-3 models
Unit cost .... 90 pts/model
- Twin las-talon .... +40 pts

Gladiator Lancer (pg 181)

Unit size .... 1 model
Unit cost .... 200 pts
- Auto launchers .... +5 pts
- Icarus rocket pod .... +5 pts
- Ironhail heavy stubber .... +5 pts

Gladiator Reaper (pg 182)

Unit size .... 1 model
Unit cost .... 230 pts
- Auto launchers .... +5 pts
- Icarus rocket pod .... +5 pts
- Ironhail heavy stubber .... +5 pts

Gladiator Valiant (pg 182)

Unit size .... 1 model
Unit cost .... 250 pts
- Auto launchers .... +5 pts
- Icarus rocket pod .... +5 pts
- Ironhail heavy stubber .... +5 pts

Hellblaster Squad (pg 173)

Unit size .... 5-10 models
Unit cost .... 33 pts/model
- Plasma pistol .... +5 pts

Hunter (pg 178)

Unit size .... 1 model
Unit cost .... 110 pts
- Hunter-killer missile .... +5 pts
- Storm bolter .... +5 pts

Land Raider (pg 183)

Unit size .... 1 model
Unit cost .... 285 pts
- Hunter-killer missile .... +5 pts
- Multi-melta .... +25 pts
- Storm bolter .... +5 pts

Land Raider Crusader (pg 184)

Unit size .... 1 model
Unit cost .... 285 pts
- Hunter-killer missile .... +5 pts
- Multi-melta .... +25 pts
- Storm bolter .... +5 pts

Land Raider Redeemer (pg 185)

Unit size .... 1 model
Unit cost .... 285 pts
- Hunter-killer missile .... +5 pts
- Multi-melta .... +25 pts
- Storm bolter .... +5 pts

Predator Annihilator (pg 181)

Unit size...1 model
Unit cost.. 130 pts
- Heavy bolter...................................+15 pts
- Hunter-killer missile ....+5 pts
- Lascannon.....................................+20 pts
- Storm bolter...................................+5 pts

Predator Destructor (pg 179)

Unit size...1 model
Unit cost.. 140 pts
- Heavy bolter...................................+15 pts
- Hunter-killer missile ....+5 pts
- Lascannon.....................................+20 pts
- Storm bolter...................................+5 pts

Repulsor (pg 186)

Unit size...1 model
Unit cost .... 315 pts
- Las-talon..+5 pts
- Onslaught gatling cannon ....+15 pts
- Twin lascannon.............................+10 pts

Repulsor Executioner (pg 187)

Unit size...1 model
Unit cost.. 355 pts
- Heavy laser destroyer....................+10 pts
- Icarus rocket pod...........................+5 pts
- Ironhail heavy stubber....................+5 pts

Stalker (pg 178)

Unit size...1 model
Unit cost.. 115 pts
- Hunter-killer missile ....+5 pts
- Storm bolter...................................+5 pts

Thunderfire Cannon (pg 177)

Unit size.............. 2 models (1 Gunner, 1 Artillery)
Unit cost.. 120 pts

Vindicator (pg 183)

Unit size...1 model
Unit cost.. 130 pts
- Hunter-killer missile ....+5 pts
- Storm bolter...................................+5 pts
- Vindicator siege shield..................+10 pts

Whirlwind (pg 179)

Unit size...1 model
Unit cost.. 125 pts
- Hunter-killer missile ....+5 pts
- Storm bolter...................................+5 pts
- Whirlwind vengeance launcher..........+10 pts

DEDICATED TRANSPORTS

Drop Pod (pg 190)

Unit size...1 model
Unit cost...70 pts

Impulsor (pg 189)

Unit size...1 model
Unit cost.. 110 pts
- Bellicatus missile array ....+20 pts
- Ironhail heavy stubber....................+5 pts
- Ironhail skytalon array ....+10 pts
- Orbital comms array ....+15 pts
- Shield dome ....+15 pts

Land Speeder Storm (pg 190)

Unit size...1 model
Unit cost...55 pts

Razorback (pg 188)

Unit size...1 model
Unit cost.. 110 pts
- Hunter-killer missile ....+5 pts
- Storm bolter...................................+5 pts
- Twin assault cannon ....+15 pts
- Twin lascannon......................................+10 pts

Rhino (pg 188)

Unit size...1 model
Unit cost...80 pts
- Additional storm bolter.............................+5 pts
- Hunter-killer missile ....+5 pts

FLYERS

Stormhawk Interceptor (pg 191)

Unit size...1 model
Unit cost.. 185 pts
- Heavy bolter...................................+5 pts
- Las-talon..+25 pts
- Typhoon missile launcher..................+20 pts

Stormraven Gunship (pg 193)

Unit size...1 model
Unit cost.. 310 pts
- Hurricane bolter ....+15 pts
- Twin lascannon.............................+10 pts
- Twin multi-melta............................+20 pts
- Typhoon missile launcher..................+10 pts

Stormtalon Gunship (pg 192)

Unit size...1 model
Unit cost.. 165 pts
- Heavy bolter...................................+5 pts
- Lascannon.....................................+10 pts
- Typhoon missile launcher..................+20 pts

FORTIFICATIONS

Hammerfall Bunker (pg 194)

Unit size...1 model
Unit cost .... 175 pts

GLOSSARY

On this page you will find a glossary that contains a number of terms used in this Codex. These are intended to provide precise definitions to help resolve some of the more complex rules interactions that may arise, and players should feel under no obligation to memorise this list. This section also includes a bullet-pointed summary of several Space Marine rules. In most games, you may find referencing this summary is all you need to resolve a rule, but if not, follow the page reference to read the entirety of the rule.

Active combat doctrine (pg 125): The combat doctrine that is currently active for your army.

Adeptus Astartes Detachment (pg 93): A Detachment in a Battle-forged army where every model has the **ADEPTUS ASTARTES** keyword (excluding models with the **AGENT OF THE IMPERIUM** or **UNALIGNED** keywords).

Adeptus Astartes secondary objectives (pg 113): Additional secondary objectives that can be used in certain matched play mission packs if every Detachment in your army is an **ADEPTUS ASTARTES** Detachment.

All of the models in the unit can have their *Weapon A* replaced with 1 *Weapon B* each: When this wargear option is selected for a unit, every single model in that unit that is equipped with Weapon A must have its weapon replaced with Weapon B. It is not possible for only some of the models in that unit to have their weapon replaced and for others not to.

Any number of models can each have their *Weapon A* replaced with 1 *Weapon B*: When this wargear option is selected for a unit, any number of models in that unit that are equipped with Weapon A can each have its weapon replaced Weapon B. It is possible for only some of the models in that unit to have their weapon replaced and for others not to.

Bolt weapon (pg 195): A ranged weapon whose profile includes the word 'bolt', or a Relic that replaces a bolt weapon. The boltgun profile of a combi-weapon is also a bolt weapon, as are the weapons listed under Bolt Weapons on page 195.

Chapter Command (pg 98): An upgrade that can be applied to **ADEPTUS ASTARTES CHARACTER** models (excluding named characters).

Chapter Relic: A type of Relic that can be given to **ADEPTUS ASTARTES CHARACTER** models.

Chapter Tactic (pg 93): Detachment ability for **ADEPTUS ASTARTES** Detachments. An ability gained by **ADEPTUS ASTARTES** models (excluding **SERVITOR** and **BEAST** models) based on the Chapter they are drawn from, if all models in that Detachment are drawn from the same Chapter.

Combat doctrine (pg 125): There are three combat doctrines: Devastator Doctrine; Tactical Doctrine; Assault Doctrine.

Drawn from (pg 124): The Chapter that a unit belongs to is the Chapter they are drawn from. A unit is drawn from a certain Chapter if they have that Chapter's name listed on its Faction keyword line.

First Founding Chapter (pg 124): The following Chapters are First Founding Chapters: Dark Angels; White Scars; Space Wolves; Imperial Fists; Blood Angels; Iron Hands; Salamanders; Ultramarines; Raven Guard.

Flame weapon (pg 195): A ranged weapon whose profile includes the word 'flame', or a Relic that replaces a flame weapon. An incendium cannon and the flamer profile of a combi-flamer is also a flame weapon, as are the weapons listed under Flame Weapons on page 195.

Honorifics (pg 118): A Crusade Battle Honour category that can only be taken by **CAPTAINS**.

Litany: A Litany of Battle. **ADEPTUS ASTARTES CHAPLAINS** can attempt to recite litanies that they know.

Maximum number of models: A unit contains the maximum number of models if it includes every model it possibly can, as described on its datasheet.

Melta weapon (pg 195): A ranged weapon whose profile includes the word 'melta', or a Relic that replaces a melta weapon. An inferno pistol and the meltagun profile of a combi-melta are also melta weapons, as are the weapons listed under Melta Weapons on page 195.

Plasma weapon (pg 195): A ranged weapon whose profile includes the word 'plasma', or a Relic that replaces a plasma weapon. The plasma gun profile of a combi-plasma is also a plasma weapon, as are the weapons listed under Plasma Weapons on pg 195.

Psychic power type: A psychic power's type is written in **bold** at the start of its rules. There are three types of psychic power described in this Codex: Blessing, Malediction and Witchfire.

Stratagem label: A Stratagem's labels are written beneath its title and can include: Adeptus Astartes; Battle Tactic; Epic Deed, Strategic Ploy; Requisition; Wargear. A Stratagem can have more than one label; for example, a Stratagem with 'Adeptus Astartes – Wargear Stratagem' has both the Adeptus Astartes and Wargear labels.

Successor Chapter (pg 124): Any Chapter, other than the Deathwatch, that is not a First Founding Chapter is a successor Chapter.

Successor Chapter Tactic (pg 96): Detachment ability for **ADEPTUS ASTARTES** Detachments whose units are all drawn from the same successor Chapter. A successor Chapter Tactic typically consists of two different Successor Tactics.

Successor of: Successor Chapters are successors of one of the First Founding Chapters. For example, the Angels of Absolution Chapter is a successor of the Dark Angels Chapter.

REFERENCE

AND THEY SHALL KNOW NO FEAR (PG 124)

- Ignore modifiers when taking Combat Attrition tests.

ANGELS OF DEATH (PG 124-125)

- Unit has the following abilities: And They Shall Know No Fear, Bolter Discipline, Shock Assault, Combat Doctrines.

BOLTER DISCIPLINE (PG 124)

- Make double the number of attacks when shooting a Rapid Fire bolt weapon if the target is within half range, or if the shooting model is an **INFANTRY** model whose unit Remained Stationary in its previous Movement phase, or if the shooting model is a **TERMINATOR** or **BIKER** model.

<CHAPTER> KEYWORD (PG 124)

- When you include a unit with the **<CHAPTER>** keyword, nominate which Chapter it is drawn from.
- Replace every instance of the **<CHAPTER>** keyword on that unit's datasheet with the name of your chosen Chapter.

CHAPTER COMMAND (PG 98)

- If Battle-forged, can upgrade **CAPTAIN, CHAPLAIN, LIBRARIAN, TECHMARINE, APOTHECARY, ANCIENT** or **COMPANY CHAMPION**.
- Doing so increases model's Power Rating and points value.
- Upgraded character will gain a new Chapter Command keyword, and additional abilities.
- Army cannot contain more than one model from same Chapter with the same Chapter Command keyword.
- Crusade armies must use Chapter Command Requisition to upgrade characters.
- Cannot upgrade named characters, **BLOOD ANGELS ANCIENTS, DEATHWATCH CAPTAINS** or **BLACK TEMPLARS COMPANY CHAMPIONS**.

CHAPTER TACTICS (PG 94-95)

- If every unit in a Detachment is drawn from the same Chapter, all **ADEPTUS ASTARTES** units (except **SERVITORS** and **BEASTS**) in that Detachment gain a Chapter Tactic.
- Chapter Tactic gained depends on what Chapter they are from.
- If Chapter does not have an associated Chapter Tactic, you must create a Successor Chapter Tactic for them. To do so, select two Successor Tactics from page 96-97 (Inheritors of the Primarch counts as two selections).

COMBAT DOCTRINES (PG 125)

- Combat doctrines only applies if every model in your army has the **ADEPTUS ASTARTES** keyword (excluding **AGENT OF THE IMPERIUM** and **UNALIGNED** models).
- During the first battle round, Devastator Doctrine is active for your army.
- During the second battle round, Tactical Doctrine is active for your army.
- At start of third battle round, select either Tactical Doctrine or Assault Doctrine: until the end of that battle round the selected doctrine is active for your army.
- During the fourth and subsequent battle rounds, Assault Doctrine is active for your army.
- **Devastator Doctrine is active:** Improve AP of all Heavy and Grenade weapons by 1.
- **Tactical Doctrine is active:** Improve AP of all Rapid Fire and Assault weapons by 1.
- **Assault Doctrine is active:** Improve AP of all Melee and Pistol weapons by 1.

COMBAT SQUADS (PG 125)

- If unit contains maximum number of models, it can be split into two units at the start of deployment, containing as equal a number of models as possible.

COMPANY COMMAND (PG 93)

- Can include a maximum of one **CAPTAIN** and two **LIEUTENANT** models in each Detachment.

CONCEALED POSITIONS (PG 125)

- During deployment, can set unit up anywhere on battlefield more than 9" from enemy deployment zone and more than 9" from any enemy models.

DEATH FROM ABOVE (PG 125)

- During deployment, can set unit up high in the skies instead of setting them up on the battlefield.
- Unit can then arrive during Reinforcements step of one of your Movement phases.
- When unit arrives, set it up on battlefield more than 9" from any enemy models.

DETACHMENT ABILITIES (PG 93)

- **ADEPTUS ASTARTES** Detachments gain Company Command ability.
- **ADEPTUS ASTARTES** units in **ADEPTUS ASTARTES** Detachments gain Chapter Tactics ability.
- Troops units in **ADEPTUS ASTARTES** Detachments gain Objective Secured ability (see Warhammer 40,000 Core Book).

HONORIFICS (PG 118)

- **CAPTAINS** can have a single Honorific instead of gaining a Battle Trait.
- Increases model's Crusade points by 1.
- Cannot have two **CAPTAINS** in your Order of Battle drawn from the same Chapter with the same Honorific.

OUTFLANK (PG 125)

- During deployment, can set unit up behind enemy lines instead of setting them up on the battlefield.
- Unit can then arrive during Reinforcements step of one of your Movement phases.
- When unit arrives, set it up on battlefield wholly within 6" of a battlefield edge, more than 9" from any enemy models.

SHOCK ASSAULT (PG 125)

- Each model in this unit makes 1 additional melee attack if its unit made a charge move, was charged or performed a Heroic Intervention this turn.

SUCCESSOR CHAPTERS (PG 124)

- If a Chapter is not the Deathwatch or a First Founding Chapter, it is a successor Chapter.
- All successor Chapters are successors of a First Founding Chapter. If a successor Chapter's First Founding Chapter is not known, select one of the First Founding Chapters for it to be a successor of.

TELEPORT STRIKE (PG 125)

- During deployment, can set unit up in a teleportarium chamber instead of setting them up on the battlefield.
- Unit can then arrive during Reinforcements step of one of your Movement phases.
- When unit arrives, set it up on battlefield more than 9" from any enemy models.